TEACHING INFORMATION LITERACY AND WRITING STUDIES

Volume 2

Upper-Level and Graduate Courses

Purdue Information Literacy Handbooks

Clarence Maybee, Series Editor
Sharon Weiner, Founding Series Editor

TEACHING INFORMATION LITERACY AND WRITING STUDIES

Volume 2

Upper-Level and Graduate Courses

edited by **Grace Veach**

Purdue University Press, West Lafayette, Indiana

Printed in the United States of America.

Library of Congress Cataloging-in-Publication Data

Names: Veach, Grace, 1963– editor.
Title: Teaching information literacy and writing studies / edited by Grace Veach.
Description: West Lafayette : Purdue University Press, [2018–2019] | Series: Purdue information literacy handbooks | Includes bibliographical references and index. Contents: Volume 1. First-year composition courses — Volume 2. Upper-level and graduate courses.
Identifiers: LCCN 2018031597| ISBN 9781557538284 (v. 1 : pbk. : alk. paper) | ISBN 9781612495477 (v. 1 : epub) | ISBN 9781612495484 (v. 1 : epdf) | ISBN 9781557538314 (v. 2 : pbk. : alk. paper) | ISBN 9781612495569 (v. 2 : epub) | ISBN 9781612495552 (v. 2 : epdf)
Subjects: LCSH: Information literacy—Study and teaching (Higher)—United States. | English language—Rhetoric—Study and teaching (Higher)—United States. | Academic libraries—Relations with faculty and curriculum—United States.
Classification: LCC ZA3075 .T425 2018 | DDC 028.7071/173—dc23 LC record available at https://lccn.loc.gov/2018031597

Cover images
Top: Jacob Ammentorp Lund/iStock/Thinkstock
Bottom left: Jacob Ammentorp Lund/iStock/Thinkstock
Bottom center: Wavebreakmedia/iStock/Thinkstock
Bottom right: Dekdoyjaidee/iStock/Thinkstock

CONTENTS

FOREWORD

This fourth volume in the Purdue Information Literacy Handbooks series explores some relevant theories and frameworks, and proposes practical strategies for integrating information literacy in the teaching of first-year college composition. In these pages, readers can observe how academic librarians and writing instructors effectively collaborate to meld concepts in information literacy with the teaching of composition studies. The authors enlighten readers about successes and some of the challenges in contextualizing information literacy instruction in the writing disciplines. The book elucidates the synergies that can result from collaborations that value mutual expertise. Inherent in these collaborations is mutual learning—librarians learning about composition and composition instructors learning about information literacy.

Together with Veach's previous volume, which covered information literacy and writing courses for first-year students, these works provide a wealth of material that can be incorporated into writing programs in all colleges and universities. Students will benefit greatly from learning information literacy in this applied setting.

Sharon Weiner, EdD, MLS
Founding Series Editor
Professor of Library Science Emerita and W. Wayne Booker Chair Emerita in Information Literacy, Purdue University Libraries
August 2018

INTRODUCTION

In the companion volume to this one, *Information Literacy and Writing Studies: First-Year Composition*, librarians and writing scholars presented suggestions for equipping first-year composition students with information literacy skills using a variety of approaches. First-Year Composition is the most common way that librarians and writing instructors present information literacy to college students, but it is by no means the only way, just the first. This second volume asks the same questions: how can faculty, especially librarians and writing instructors, promote student learning of information literacy within the context of writing studies? A visit to the library, known in librarian parlance as a "one-shot," was for many years the standard, but faculty in both disciplines realized that the one-shot was only a brief beginning to a much more complex task.

One-shots bifurcated the writing classroom, reinforcing the idea that librarians taught students how to search for sources and writing instructors taught everything else. When Google made it easy to search, librarians shifted their focus to teaching students how to find high-quality resources, a message that was all too easily reduced to either "don't use Google," or to "use only peer-reviewed journal articles." Both of these approaches are obviously too simple, but when a librarian has only an hour to convey a message, it is easy to see why and how the message became simplified. The contributors to this volume are creatively imagining new approaches to teaching students at all levels to be information literate in their writing.

Part One, Theorizing Information Literacy and Writing Studies, offers alternative frames from which to view these two related disciplines. Traditionally, the relationship has been a hierarchical binary, in which information literacy is one topic that is taught in a writing class. It was taught by a librarian, not the course instructor, therefore reinforcing the binary. Even elements of the course such as the course title, the assignments, and the location of the course (i.e., not in the library) privilege writing over information literacy. While I am not arguing for the reverse (privileging information literacy over writing), bringing the two into a more equal relationship can alter the way that students value information literacy. The authors in this section challenge the binary, whether by trying to reverse it or by bringing the two disciplines into relationship with yet a third (or even more).

In "Writing as a Way of Knowing: Teaching Epistemic Research Across the University," Phyllis Mentzell Ryder, Dolsy Smith, and Randi Kristensen point to Writing in the Disciplines as the site for teaching disciplinary epistemologies using information literacy. Students can be guided to examine disciplinary ways of knowing as demonstrated in various disciplinary genres. The actions taken by researchers and practitioners in the discipline are then modeled by first the professor, and then the students as they do their own research and writing. Teresa Quezada pictures the boundary area between information literacy and writing studies as a beach; there is no clearly drawn demarcation, and students may become confused about which "territory" they are trying to navigate, not to mention what they need to be doing there. Quezada posits that this disciplinary blend can be more successfully handled by students when professors take the students' initial confusion into account and develop assignments and classwork that helps them to gain confidence.

Christine McClure and Randall McClure offer Information Behavior Theory as a component of the research/writing classroom. Many of the classroom pedagogical behaviors that are still commonly seen are relics of the time before the Information Age. The shift of the information landscape necessitates that Writing Studies professionals take the proliferation of information into account as we teach research and writing. McClure and McClure focus on Wilson's "Universe of Knowledge" model (1981) to suggest that instructors need to be assisting students with the research process, which can be every bit as overwhelming as the writing process.

Joshua Hill also concerns himself with the information environment in scrutinizing the impact of technology on learning. He recognizes both its positives and its negatives, borrowing the term "media ecology" from Neil Postman (1992) and seeking the successor to print literacy. Hill argues for the preservation of linear thought in the midst of the recursive firehose of information that our students receive. He envisions how this will look in the composition classroom as writing instructors seek to both guide students in navigating the landscape of information and also to alert them to subtleties in what might be found there.

James Purdy concludes this section by advancing the conversation between the ACRL *Framework* (2015) and the WPA *Framework* (2011), which has been started in the first volume of this collection and elsewhere. Purdy compares "dispositions" and "habits of mind" and how they connect the two *Frameworks*; students who truly have a change in dispositions and habits of mind feel the effects long after a memorized fact has buried itself in memory. Although the *Frameworks* are not perfect, Purdy finds value in the way they model interdisciplinarity and transfer.

Part Two, Information Literacy as a Rhetorical Skill, recognizes that in the past, "library searching" was seen as a skill that librarians taught. As the library world shifted from "bibliographic instruction" to teaching information literacy around the turn of the century, and especially as the ACRL

Information Literacy Standards gave way to the Information Literacy Framework (Association of College and Research Libraries, 2015), librarians have been recognizing that although library orientation is important to students' use of a local campus library (or online library), librarians also bear a responsibility to help teach students about the world of information in general.

The difference in terminology from "standards" to "framework" also signaled a shift from skills to ways of thinking. And while it is much easier to teach skills, the acquisition of skills produces little actual learning unless the skills are accompanied by the understanding of why and how the skills should be utilized. As librarians and writing professionals began to have more conversation, they began to recognize that source use can and should be taught rhetorically. Joseph Bizup's BEAM (2008) was a landmark approach to teaching students why and how sources are used in the writing task, and others are both continuing to fill out this framework and suggesting new rhetorical lenses from which to focus on information literacy and source use.

Bizup and his co-authors open Part Two with an article that reviews how BEAM has been used in information literacy and Writing Studies since its introduction. Rhetoric has long been the domain of the Composition classroom; librarians traditionally taught students how to find sources and then their job was done. With more interdisciplinary conversation in the past ten years or so, and with more intentional collaborative partnering taking place between Writing Studies and librarians, librarians have become aware that rhetoric is not the sole property of the writing faculty, and that sources are rhetorical tools that skillful writers can manipulate to serve their purposes.

Mark Dibble also incorporates BEAM and theory from problem-based learning into his chapter. His conjecture is that by changing the language that students use to speak and think about research, instructors can advance students' learning toward a more sophisticated view of source use. Because instructors in the disciplines use the language of their own discourse community (often without even realizing it), Dibble invites librarians to be "translators," helping students to begin to understand some of this varied language, or at least to be aware that some terms may be used by professors in meanings and contexts with which students might not be familiar. Dibble extends his suggestions to using problem-solving language rather than topic-centered language when determining what to write about, and to using BEAM-centered language as students consider working with sources.

Caroline Fuchs and Patricia Medved examine the rhetorical canon of invention as it relates to information literacy. Information literacy has traditionally been taught "outside" of the canons of rhetoric and students are left to integrate it into the canons, if they even conceive of such a project. Fuchs and Medved explore how information literacy can make a space for invention to occur, as it should, since students should be using sources to learn about their research, to answer questions, and to prompt new questions. They suggest allowing space for creative thinking in addition to critical thinking, so that students can gain agency during the research process to respond to new ideas generatively.

The rhetorical appeal of *ethos* is key to Melanie Lee and Lia Vella's chapter in which they posit source use as a tool for strengthening *ethos* (which can be difficult to prove, especially as an undergraduate). They highlight qualities from the two *Frameworks* that can be drawn upon to begin to build this *ethos* as the process is modeled by instructors. Lee and Vella remind us that both information literacy and composition reside in largely feminized disciplines, and that the disciplines themselves can benefit from increased *ethos*.

In Part Three, Pedagogies and Practices, the focus shifts from broad (theory and rhetoric) to narrower: the writing classroom itself. Here we have librarians and writing professionals inviting us into their classrooms to examine new approaches to student learning about information literacy and writing. Other authors in this section envision moving away from the traditional composition or writing studies classroom to other sites for this information literacy/writing instruction, some out of frustration with a model that has not been remarkable in its results, and others as a response to environmental prompts such as the media ecology referenced by Joshua Hill.

Opening the section, Crystal Bickford and Megan Palmer survey the field of information literacy from its inception through the introduction of the *Framework* and beyond. They give a taxonomy of types of information literacy instruction and note best practices identified from successful programs of all types. William Badke's chapter addresses initiating students into their disciplines. Badke argues that teaching disciplinary conventions is a start, but that to truly understand writing within a given discipline, students need to be doing critical reading in the discipline. He offers a model assignment for students receiving information literacy instruction, which involves librarians guiding them through the examination of disciplinary writing, including inviting disciplinary faculty into the conversation to explain their discipline's values and conventions in published works.

Matthew Kaeiser, April Mann, and Ava Brillat take us to a bridge program for international students at the University of Miami. Although both librarians and the writing center provide support, international students still frequently struggle to flourish in higher education. This chapter focuses on attempts to couple research instruction with writing instruction for incoming international students in order to give them more academic tools and to maximize their chances for success at the university.

Information literacy in the Technical Communication classroom is addressed by Kelly Diamond, who describes working with a writing professor to redesign an online Technical Communication class to better accommodate both information literacy and problem-based learning. To mimic a workplace environment, topics were assigned and few guidelines were given; students were asked to analyze the audience, information need, appropriateness of sources, and so on. Scaffolding was provided throughout the course to help the students gain facility with each of these tasks. Diamond found that the ACRL *Framework* supports problem-based learning well, as it also encourages students to think critically about such elements as audience and authority.

Linda Macri and Kelsey Corlett-Rivera explore the graduate writing environment, specifically the literature review, as their site for information literacy integration. As a standard element of the scholarly article, the literature review is a familiar genre to graduate students, but many of them do not receive instruction on how to construct an effective literature review. Macri and Corlett-Rivera describe a "Literature Review Boot Camp" workshop that they conduct, which uses the ACRL *Framework* to guide students in writing effective literature reviews.

Kathy Kempa makes the case for librarians interacting in upper-division classrooms by focusing on the ACRL *Framework* as it might relate to students becoming more conversant in their disciplinary discourse communities. She gives suggestions for classroom techniques for each frame as they could be used with students learning disciplinary habits of mind. In spite of librarians' generalist status, the *Framework* gives them language to contribute even to advanced students' writing and research.

Law Bohannon and Janice R. Walker close the section with an update on their LILAC Project research in which they find that the traditional information literacy instruction in the composition classroom does not seem to have much of an effect on actual student behavior as students are doing research. Their LILAC Project involves students doing a survey and then conducting research for an actual assignment while they narrate their thinking process (research aloud protocol). Their marked preference for Google-initiated searching despite librarians' emphasis on database searching suggests that their own habits and comfort override classroom instruction when they actually initiate research sessions.

Part Four, Writing and Information Literacy in Multiple Contexts, focuses most narrowly on either specific aspects of information literacy/writing, or specific settings: the graduate classroom, the writing center, and so on. Matthew Bodie opens this section with his research on librarians' attitudes toward teaching writing in the course of performing their roles. Bodie centers this research around the rhetorical canons, querying librarians about helping students with specific tasks that he categorizes around the canons.

Copyright is the topic that concerns Laura Giovanelli and Molly Keener. Internet and popular culture have made sampling a part of today's creative process, and writing professionals know that intertextuality has always been an element of writing. How do we best engage undergraduates in conversation about intellectual property in the information age? Especially with more professors assigning multimodal compositions, this dialogue needs to be updated. Giovanelli and Keener suggest using popular culture (especially music) to give examples of attribution (or nonattribution) and giving special care to assignment design. They offer a workshop on intellectual property as a part of the multimodal composition assignment to introduce students to concepts such as Creative Commons, fair use, and citation of nonprint materials.

Nathan Schwartz looks at the status of citation instruction within information literacy and writing studies. Plagiarism is problematic on a widespread scale, and knowledge of correct citation conventions will surely help with this problem, but exactly how and where is citation taught? In recent years, citation generators and citation managers have proliferated, and many college students are aware of them to the extent that they will use a generator or manager and assume that their citations are therefore correct. Without basic knowledge of citation styles, students cannot find errors in their own citations.

Katie McWain considers writing centers as spaces for information literacy instruction in her chapter entitled "Learning in the Middle: Writing Centers as Sponsors of Information Literacy Across the University." Although many faculty and students see the writing center as having a limited role, it can actually be a place where much information literacy instruction happens, especially when librarians and writing center staff are cross-trained and when writing center staff are seeking opportunities to discuss information literacy and research writing.

Concluding the volume, Barry Maid and Barbara J. D'Angelo remind us that learning is recursive, complicated, and sometimes messy. Focusing on threshold concept learning as they prepare students for the workplace, Maid and D'Angelo realize that even more advanced students often lack the vocabulary to reflect on their own composing practices. The fact that we have become better at identifying threshold concepts in our disciplines does not necessarily mean that they have suddenly become easier for students to navigate, and often students' acquisition of these concepts will be partial in any given class.

This certainly seems to be a time of synchrony in information literacy and writing studies. The multiple librarian/WS faculty partnerships that have been formed, the production of frameworks documents, and the introduction of threshold concepts all occurring within several years of each other in these disciplines have given us in the fields many opportunities to cross-pollinate ideas and move information literacy instruction from the library orientation/one-shot into many new sectors.

REFERENCES

Association of College and Research Libraries. (2015, February 9). *Framework for information literacy for higher education* [Text]. Retrieved January 27, 2017, from http://www.ala.org/acrl/standards/ilframework

Bizup, J. (2008). BEAM: A rhetorical vocabulary for teaching research-based writing. *Rhetoric Review, 27*(1), 72–86.

Framework for success in postsecondary writing. (2011). Retrieved July 12, 2017, from http://wpacouncil.org/framework

Postman, N. (1992). *Technopoly: The surrender of culture to technology*. New York: Vintage.

Wilson, T. D. (1981). On user studies and information needs. *Journal of Documentation, 37*(1), 3–15.

PART I

Theorizing Information Literacy and Writing Studies

CHAPTER 1

WRITING AS A WAY OF KNOWING

Teaching Epistemic Research Across the University

Phyllis Mentzell Ryder
Dolsy Smith
Randi Gray Kristensen

INTRODUCTION

Faculty teaching upper-division courses across the disciplines are often frustrated by the quality of writing and research in papers they receive from their students, yet they are unsure how to improve the outcomes, or, indeed, whether this task is their responsibility. Writing studies research has led to promising results through university initiatives such as Writing in the Disciplines. When faculty can identify how their writing and research processes are integral to their disciplines' ways of knowing, and how those processes differ from the practices in other fields, they realize that they already have the disciplinary expertise to help students write and research within their fields. Librarians are excellent partners in such endeavors.

To give faculty and librarians tools for such collaboration, we parse the layers of disciplinary writing and research knowledge and provide examples of activities for teaching these knowledge-making processes—specifically information literacy processes. This explicit focus on processes is an integral step for students' development as writers and researchers in upper-division courses.

AN EVOLUTION IN WRITING AND RESEARCH PROCESSES

The latest recommendations from professional organizations in both academic librarianship and writing studies focus on the recursive and rhetorical nature of research and writing. Both the Association of College and Research Libraries (ACRL) and the Council of Writing Program Administrators (WPA) have revised their public guiding documents to reflect research in these fields. Instead of a focus on competencies and standards, these updated pedagogies emphasize knowledge practices, processes, and dispositions.

The new ACRL and WPA documents no longer prescribe standard levels of achievement, and they no longer depict researchers as people who look for discrete pieces of information. ACRL's 2000 document, the *Information Literacy Competency Standards,* emphasized assessment and served to "pinpoint specific indicators that identify a student as information literate" (p. 5). The most recent (2016) ACRL document, the *Framework for Information Literacy for Higher Education*, describes research as a set of processes and dispositions, a model where researchers are understood as being in conversation with other researchers. This model emphasizes the values of discovery, collaboration, and sensitivity to context, because the rhetorical context of a given scholarly conversation proves crucial to how scholars evaluate the relevance and appropriateness of potential sources. Similarly, the 2016 WPA committee responsible for the *Outcomes for First-Year Composition (3.0)* explains that "where the former versions approached writing as more a stable act—even among emerging technologies—the new version embraces emerging forms of composing in a world of fluid forms of communication" (Dryer et al., 2014, p. 138).

The pedagogical implications of this shift point to an evolution in the role of librarians. The ACRL *Competency Standards* presented information literacy as a set of skills that could be inserted into any curricula across the disciplines. That approach positioned librarians as the experts in, and the parties primarily responsible for, teaching information literacy: either through the provision of "one-shot" instruction in disciplinary courses or, more rarely, the design and execution of stand-alone, credit-bearing courses (Johnston & Webber, 2003). While collaboration between faculty and librarians has been a core tenet of the information literacy platform since its inception, programmatic integration of the *Competency Standards* into the curriculum remained a challenge at many institutions (Lindstrom & Shonrock, 2006; Rapchak & Cipri, 2015).

The *Framework for Information Literacy*, on the other hand, acknowledges that librarians can often work most effectively not as experts but as what Simmons (2005) called "disciplinary discourse mediators." This formulation highlights the unique perspective that librarians bring to collaborations with faculty, in virtue of their position as "simultaneously insiders and outsiders" vis-à-vis the practices of a given discipline (p. 298). In other words, instead of depicting these collaborations as the marriage of two distinct kinds of expertise—disciplinary knowledge and information literacy knowledge—the *Framework* suggests that librarians should help faculty articulate their own practices and dispositions as researchers within the context of the goals of the course (or course sequence or major). This mediated articulation may generate specific assignments and/or specific moments requiring a librarian's presence in the classroom. More to the point, it may produce new approaches to structuring a course or course sequence.

This evolution in the role of librarians aligns with an evolution within writing studies. First-year courses in writing have also been thought of as "one-shot" instruction, courses that could inoculate students against seemingly universal writing problems such as unwieldy structure or inadequate citation. More recently, however, writing program scholars and administrators recognize that those seemingly universal conventions differ within scholarly fields. Many universities have developed Writing in the Disciplines programs to support faculty and departments as they consider how to articulate and incorporate this new approach to teaching writing (Colorado State University, 2017).

While Writing in the Disciplines programs are an important step forward, few of these programs include explicit analysis of information literacy processes. We contend that faculty from across the university will benefit greatly from collaborating with both Writing in the Disciplines programs and research librarians to make visible and to teach disciplinary ways of writing and conducting research in their fields.

DISCIPLINARY KNOWLEDGES

Given the historical development of research universities, rooted in the German tradition of highly specialized scholarship among researchers siloed in their fields, the defining identity within most departments is subject-matter knowledge. Departments sequence their courses to introduce increasingly more sophisticated content in the field, including careful practice of disciplinary research methods (lab work, ethnography, big data, and so on). A focus on content lends itself to one-shot approaches to writing and information literacy instruction.

Research in writing studies challenges that model. As Riedner, O Sullivan, and Farrell (2015) explain, "teaching the distinctive writing and communicative practices of a disciplinary community are inseparable from teaching disciplinary knowledge. Because writing embodies ways of knowing and values of a discipline, disciplinary knowledge

TABLE 1.1 *Disciplinary Knowledges*

Subject Matter Knowledge	What content do you need to know? History, theories, methods, ethics.
Genre Knowledge	What types of documents do you create?
Disciplinary Discourse Knowledge	How do you speak as an insider?
Rhetorical Knowledge	How can you adjust the structure, tone, and content based on your readers and content? What are some of the rhetorical features or hallmarks of writing in your field? How have these expectations changed?
Writing Process Knowledge	What are the usual stages of writing and research?
Information Literacy Knowledge	What materials are required for meeting the various rhetorical needs in the genres?

Data from Riedner (2015).

and writing are inextricable from each other" (p. 10). Riedner (2015) parses out multiple kinds of knowledge that inform how scholars in different fields build knowledge and write about that knowledge. (See Table 1.1.)

If faculty members have been tasked with teaching subject knowledge, they may have had little opportunity to reflect on the other areas of their expertise. But they are experts in all the areas. From their initial forays into disciplinary writing in graduate school, professors internalize through practice their understanding of genre, disciplinary discourses, writing processes, research methods, and source use. As they are "disciplined," the knowledges common in their field become naturalized as simply "good writing" and "good research" habits. However, a comparison across disciplines shows that "good writing" and "good research" vary by field. Consider how these knowledges might be manifest in a field like anthropology, for example (see Table 1.2).

Because most professors learn how to research and write in their field through their initiation-by-doing in graduate school, it's not surprising that recent research "shows that faculty believe disciplinary information skills are acquired by a kind of 'learning by doing' (p. 580)—that is to say, through the situated information practices of the disciplines themselves" (McGuiness, as cited in Farrell & Badke, 2015, p. 324). We agree that sustained practice is essential to learning, and we propose that undergraduate students will benefit when professors can name the ways of knowing and doing that are practiced in their field and when they design activities that help students gain experience with them. Writing in the Disciplines initiatives offer faculty strategies for developing courses and department-wide curricula along these lines, but—as we will explain later—they could go farther in preparing faculty to introduce information literacy knowledges and practices.

Ways of Knowing, Doing, and Writing in the Disciplines

An article we find particularly helpful for introducing this way of thinking about disciplinary knowledge is Michael Carter's (2007) "Ways of Knowing, Doing, and Writing in the Disciplines." Carter argues that disciplinary writing is not just a set of techniques whereby

TABLE 1.2 *Disciplinary Knowledges in Anthropology*

Kind of Knowledge	Examples
Subject Matter Knowledge What content do you need to know? History, theories, methods, ethics.	History of anthropology; key theories in the field; specific information about different cultures; ethical guidelines; best practices
Genre Knowledge What types of documents do you create?	Field notes; thick descriptions; journal articles; grant applications; IRB applications
Disciplinary Discourse Knowledge How do you speak as an insider?	What is the common terminology about cultures and rituals? What are the expected attributions for certain historical shifts in the discipline?
Rhetorical Knowledge What are some of the rhetorical features or hallmarks of writing in your field? How have these expectations changed?	How much self-reflection should the researcher include within a journal article or book about his or her relationships and interactions with the groups being studied? What is the appropriate balance between reviewing past literature and introducing the new study?
Writing Process Knowledge What are the usual stages of writing and research?	When and how to keep notes; where and with whom to share drafts; when to borrow across genres, such as expanding literature reviews from grant proposals within later drafts of a book chapter
Information Literacy Knowledge What materials are required for meeting the various rhetorical needs in the genres?	What counts as data in anthropology, and how is this gathered? How should the anthropologist think about and analyze her data so it serves as credible evidence for new arguments? How does he identify gaps in the literature and design studies to address those gaps? How does she find appropriate theories to deploy in analyzing field research?

a field communicates its knowledge, but also a way that knowledge is constituted, a mode through which disciplinary faculty can see the connection between the content of their disciplines (subject knowledge), the practices of their disciplines (quantitative or qualitative or textual research methods), and writing in their disciplines (the genre, discourse, and rhetorical knowledges). We extend Carter's analysis to include ways of thinking about the "ways of doing" in information literacy.

Carter asserts,

> The disciplinary ways of doing that faculty identify provide a direct link between ways of knowing and ways of writing in the disciplines. Doing enacts the knowing through students' writing and the writing gives shape to the ways of knowing and doing in the discipline. So instead of focusing only on the conceptual knowledge that has traditionally defined the disciplines, faculty are encouraged to focus also on what their students should be able to do, represented largely in their writing. (p. 391)

For example, the lab experiment in a science class represents a way of doing that leads to a way of knowing, which is materialized in the writing of the lab report, whose genre reflects the disciplinary values of knowledge-creation in the sciences (p. 388).

Carter identifies four "metagenres" that reflect "certain ways of doing . . . repeated in general terms across a variety of disciplines: responses to academic learning situations that call for problem solving, for empirical inquiry, for research from sources, and for performance" (p. 394). We will explore three of these metagenres.

Empirical Inquiry, as Carter (2007) notes, "is a way of doing that consists of answering questions by drawing conclusions from systematic investigation based on empirical data" (p. 396); the genres include lab reports, scientific articles, poster presentations, and the like. In *Problem-Solving* activities, writers tackle problems similar to those they might encounter in their professions (p. 396); they produce business plans, marketing plans, project proposals, and similar, practical pieces. For *Research from Sources,* the main sources are drawn from other published work (p. 398), and the general process will sound familiar to most professors and librarians: identify a question, look for secondary sources, use the sources to develop an argument in response to the question. Carter warns that "the similarity in ways of doing tends to mask the different ways of knowing in the various disciplines" (p. 399). Which sources to find and how to use them signal distinct disciplinary identities: for example, a historian and a religious scholar would use passages of the Bible in very different ways.

We want to take Carter's argument farther and argue that faculty not only should identify "ways of doing," they also should make explicit how accomplished procedural knowledge is composed of discrete subroutines. For someone who has mastered a particular activity, these subroutines may flow together smoothly, without requiring conscious attention to manage them, and allowing the practitioner to give attention to the holistic effect (in the way that an accomplished musician focuses on the nuances of dynamics, rhythm, and tone). But the apprentice needs to focus on the subroutines themselves, learning how their complex interaction *produces* holistic effects (in the way that a novice must systematically perfect her scales, her embouchure, etc.). This granular learning—what we later discuss as "scaffolding"—is necessary not only to give a convincing performance, but also to understand the possibilities of the activity itself.

Metagenres and Information Literacy Processes

Metagenres are cross-disciplinary ways of doing: faculty from any discipline may choose to assign empirical, problem-solving, performance, or research from sources genres. Therefore, it can be useful for faculty to distinguish the general research moves in each metagenre and then to consider how those might manifest uniquely in a specific field. We have identified one layer of information literacy moves of the various metagenres in Table 1.3. For each, faculty and librarians might drill down to identify the subroutines that they use. For example, one way to trace a scholarly conversation in a literature review is to practice "citation-chaining"—following the in-text citations from one article to its predecessor and then that article's predecessor, and paying close attention to how each author is drawing on, extending, or countering key concepts.

How might faculty develop a stronger sense of the information literacy and other knowledges in their fields, and how might they design class activities and assignments around those knowledges? We offer some examples from the Writing in the Disciplines (WID) program at George Washington University (GWU).

TABLE 1.3 *Information Literacy Processes by Metagenre*

Metagenre	Information Literacy Processes
Empirical Inquiry	• "review literature to identify the scope and nature of the problem to study • [research] appropriate methods for the study • compar[e] findings to the secondary literature • [reconsider] the theoretical frame because of anomalies in the research findings" (Ryder & Nutefall, 2016, p. 35)
Problem Solving	• "identify, define, and analyze a problem: what it is that generates the problem, what is given, what is unknown, and what are the criteria for viable solutions to the problem • determine what information is appropriate to solving the problem and then find it, assess its authority and validity, and use it effectively" (Carter, 2007, p. 395)
Research from Sources	• review literature to identify a significant scholarly conversation to enter and a way into the conversation—what is missing, what is misunderstood, how can the conversation be extended? • locate relevant sources that can serve a range of purposes (background, framework, argument, etc. See Bizup [2008] and Harris [2006]) • evaluate and analyze sources; explore multiple perspectives • use sources to compose an argument that answers the research question

WRITING IN THE DISCIPLINES AT GWU

History of WID at GWU

In 2003, George Washington University reconfigured its literacy requirement in response both to internal pressure for more opportunities for student research and writing, and to external research indicating that student learning was enhanced by sustained writing throughout their undergraduate careers. Students are required to take First-Year Writing, a four-credit themed writing seminar, and two Writing in the Disciplines courses, preferably one in the sophomore year and the second in the junior year. Ideally, and typically, at least one of those courses is in a student's major. Additionally, each major is expected to offer a capstone course that engages students in the discipline's common communication.

While the First-Year Writing division was able to hire a multidisciplinary faculty trained in writing pedagogies, the WID program relied on the voluntarism of faculty and departments across the university. Just as the First-Year Writing courses share a template of learning outcomes (University Writing Program, n.d.a), courses receiving the WID designation must meet certain expectations. WID courses must:

- require students to write throughout the course rather than only at the end of the course;
- provide opportunities to revise writing assignments in collaboration with peers and faculty;
- require students to complete multiple writing projects designed to communicate for different purposes and with a variety of audiences; and

- teach the conventions of writing and thinking in a particular discipline or in a particular interdisciplinary context. (University Writing Program, n.d.b)

Some disciplinary faculty had already adopted many of these recommended practices, such as peer review and opportunities for revision. To support and encourage more faculty to consider teaching WID courses, the WID program offered workshops open to all faculty interested in WID classes. Topics included assignment design, conducting effective peer reviews, strategies for efficient and effective commenting on student writing, and so on. Faculty were also asked to read Carter's (2007) "Ways of Knowing, Doing, and Writing in the Disciplines."

These workshops, attended by faculty from different schools and departments from across the university, were effective at quickly providing tools and practices that faculty could use to meet the first three expectations of a WID course. Moreover, they were especially effective at revealing that each discipline, or interdiscipline, had its own "conventions of writing and thinking," and at destabilizing the idea that there is a single gold standard of "good writing." In the workshops, faculty from Business, for example, could hear that English faculty valued close reading, peer-reviewed sources, and complex arguments. English faculty learned that Business students were expected to write with pointed immediacy, and that sources like company annual reports could serve as evidence. The multidisciplinary WID workshops helped to shift the expectation that the First-Year Writing seminar instructed students in all genres of writing (Kristensen & Claycomb, 2009), and reinforced the importance for disciplinary writing faculty to make explicit to student writers the writing expectations specific to their disciplines.

Scaffolding Knowing, Writing, and Doing at GWU

The most effective WID courses provide scaffolding for students' learning by constructing a sequence of writing (and/or research) assignments that build one on the other in such a way that allows students to focus on particular subroutines while also working toward the larger course project. Such courses also make explicit for students the rationale for each assignment, highlighting its relationship with other assignments in the sequence, and how the genre of each assignment is also a way of knowing and doing relevant to the discipline.

Below we provide examples from assignments in three WID courses, covering three of Carter's four metagenres. These examples show how faculty can scaffold research practices by identifying the specific information-literacy processes involved.

Scaffolding for Problem Solving in the Social Sciences: International Affairs

In her course on science and technology policy, Catherine Woytowicz leads students in International Affairs through the process of creating a "briefing book" on an issue of their choice. The briefing book is designed to convey a policy argument to a nonacademic audience. In her "handbook" for the course, Woytowicz notes that "[b]uilding a briefing book may seem like a daunting task but it is really an iterative process. Each step expands on the previous step and adds more detail." She provides a detailed flowchart that decomposes the briefing book into a series of interlocked pieces of writing. These micro-genres—like the "talking point," the "backgrounder," and the "graphic"—represent discrete exercises undertaken throughout the semester. Moreover, her scaffolding helps students understand that research is not one stage in a linear process from research question to written product, in which each new stage would exhaust the output from the previous stage. Rather, information literacy, like disciplinary knowledge itself, involves gathering, sifting, sorting, discarding, rearranging, synthesizing, and gathering again—activities that persist from assignment to assignment and from course to course. As she writes, "Things that may not fit in one assignment should not be discarded; they may have a place in the briefing book or they may belong in your morgue." This statement makes explicit what accomplished writers working in their genres know: that knowing happens around the edges, in the friction between moments of research and writing that crystallize facts, arguments, and ideas.

Scaffolding for Research for Problem Solving/Empirical Inquiry in Science and Engineering: Engineering Management and Systems Engineering

Royce Francis's engineering course requires students to write a white paper and a policy analysis on a "critical infrastructure system." While these larger assignments perhaps better exemplify Carter's problem-solving metagenre, we focus below on a smaller assignment preliminary to the white paper that might prove equally useful in the context of empirical inquiry: the annotated bibliography. (See Box 1.1.)

What distinguishes Francis's approach to this assignment is his attention to specifying (a) the particular objectives of this assignment and (b) the relation of these objectives to the academic and professional contexts of research

BOX 1.1
ANNOTATED BIBLIOGRAPHY ASSIGNMENT (FRANCIS)

- Students will articulate the difference between peer-reviewed archival literature and gray literature. Both of these types of literature are important sources of data and arguments for infrastructure systems work. Due to the industrial nature of infrastructure systems, it is crucial that students learn to identify the most important peer-reviewed academic and gray literature sources from which they may draw data to support their arguments.
- Students will use Compendex to initiate a literature search, and manage their search results using a bibliographic manager such as Mendeley Desktop.
- Students will use Google Scholar and well-known government agencies, reputable non-governmental organizations (NGOs), or independent industry trade associations to obtain gray literature. Students will manage their search results using a bibliographic manager such as Mendeley Desktop.
- Students will discuss the tension that exists among government agencies, NGOs, and trade associations. Students will discuss the role of understanding this tension when evaluating primary or secondary sources for use in engineering practice and research.
- Students will write an annotated bibliography of 3–5 sources obtained through their literature search. The annotated bibliography will use IEEE citation referencing style. This assignment will be collected and graded as a low-stakes, formative assessment.

Excerpt from EMSE 3855W: Critical Infrastructure Systems.

in engineering. For instance, he notes that the assignment "points to a more important skill that engineers must possess—the ability to synthesize arguments using the data collected or generated by another engineer or scientist." He further explains that the synthesis of prior relevant research is necessary *both* to "establish [. . .] authority" before an audience of professionals *and* to "persuade diverse audiences." This attention to the rhetorical nature of information-literacy processes frames the annotated bibliography as more than just an exercise in finding and summarizing sources.

Furthermore, Francis's assignment decomposes the assignment into concrete steps, explaining how the activity of each step relates to the overall goals of the course (i.e., being able to make a persuasive and well-informed argument about a critical infrastructure system). Note that while the assignment gives explicit instruction about specific library resources (Compendex, Google Scholar) and research tools (Mendeley Desktop), it also emphasizes concepts (e.g., "the difference between peer-reviewed archival literature and gray literature," "the tension [. . .] among government agencies, NGOs, and trade associations") that are necessary to understand in order to be able to evaluate and present research persuasively.

Scaffolding for Research from Sources in the Humanities: French Literature

In her upper-division course on French literature, Kathryn Kleppinger provides short, scaffolded assignments that help her students identify and practice the discursive moves specific to literary criticism, in preparation for two longer essays. As she writes in her syllabus, "These assignments are meant to model the type of close reading you should do with all of your work, to help you develop your instincts and reading strategies."

Most of these focus on reading literary texts, but one assignment steps through a close reading of a scholarly work of literary analysis (an article by Frank Bowman analyzing a text by Victor Hugo; see Box 1.2.) The assignment demonstrates one way in which humanities faculty can prepare their students to bridge the gap between working with primary and with secondary sources: by making explicit how the "instincts" for critical engagement that students hone on individual works of literature are fundamentally the same as scholars use when developing an argument in the context of a broader scholarly conversation. We note in particular that Kleppinger's assignment (a) calls attention to the rhetorical moves that the author makes (e.g., "Bowman changes his sources on page 30 (bottom). What type of source does he

BOX 1.2
QUESTIONS FOR ANALYZING SOURCE USE (KLEPPINGER)

- Analyze the first paragraph (which is too long!). Determine the progression of ideas (make a list). What is the primary argument of this essay?
- What difficulties in analysis does he raise immediately following his introduction?
- Bowman changes his sources on page 30 (bottom). What type of source does he consult here, and why?
- What is the last source Bowman analyzes (page 34)? What reason does he give for using it?
- How does Bowman justify and explain Hugo's approach (page 37, bottom)?

Excerpt from assignment: French 3100W: Introduction to French Literature.

consult here, and why?"), and (b) that these moves are also often instances of information literacy processes. By paying attention to the multiple ways in which other scholars use secondary sources in their writing, students can better appreciate the work such sources can do in their own.

Additional Resources for Research from Sources

Three additional resources are helpful for teaching students to recognize the different rhetorical purposes for sources within an academic argument: Joseph Bizup's (2008) "BEAM: A Rhetorical Vocabulary for Teaching Research-Based Writing," a 2015 response to Bizup by Phillip Troutman and Mark Mullen's "I-BEAM: Instance Source Use and Research Writing Pedagogy," and Joseph Harris's (2006) *Rewriting: How to Do Things with Texts*. (See Box 1.3.)

Using different schema, these texts provide productive vocabularies to name the often-invisible functions that sources play. The vocabulary in Bizup (2008) maps more closely onto the usual formats for academic research essays: Background, Exhibit, Argument, Method. Troutman and Mullen (2015) extend those categories by including Instancing. Harris (2006), on the other hand, delves more deeply into the ways authors draw on sources to arrive at new ideas; he identifies a series of moves for forwarding and countering texts that get beyond seeing sources as "pro" or "con." Being able to identify these moves in an article helps students recognize that their task in gathering sources is not only about finding information, but also about staging conversations, and evaluating whether a source might be productive as background, illustration, framework, method, or any of several layers of argument.

Additional GWU Initiatives to Support Writing and Research in the Disciplines

Developing a strong Writing in the Disciplines program happens not only through close work with individual faculty, but also by facilitating conversations within departments, across campus, and with the library.

At GWU, the WID program supports departments in conducting reviews of the writing conventions and processes specific to their disciplines. The writing review team usually consists of a faculty member and a graduate student from the department, and a writing faculty member in a consultative role. Through meeting with department faculty and analyzing teaching materials using rubrics provided by the WID program, the team elicits the desired writing abilities for students at each level of the curriculum, and maps where and how writing instruction currently is located in that curriculum. This process creates a useful articulation of writing goals for the department and offers the department the opportunity to consider whether the curriculum is fulfilling those goals, and what additional resources—faculty workshops, shared assignments, and so on—could help bring goals and curriculum into alignment. The process instigates a conversation about disciplinary writing that continues long after the review is completed.

GWU affirms its commitment to the WID program through university-wide awards. The annual WID awards for Best Teaching, Best Assignment Design, and Best Graduate Student Teaching recognize and celebrate exceptional contributions to teaching writing in the disciplines. These awards are presented at the annual university-wide Faculty Honors Awards ceremonies, which reflects the commitment and participation of the entire

BOX 1.3
VOCABULARY FOR SOURCE USE—HARRIS AND BIZUP

Notes from Harris's *Rewriting: How to Do Things With Texts*

Coming to Terms: "Defining the projects of other writers in a fair and generous way, so that you can make use of the source" (p. 19)

Forwarding: "In forwarding a text, you extend its uses" (p. 38; see list p. 39)

- *Illustrating:* Examples of a point you want to make; material to think about
- *Authorizing:* Invoking the expertise of person to support your thinking
- *Borrowing:* Drawing on terms or ideas to think through your subject
- *Extending:* Putting your own spin on the terms or concepts that you take from other texts

Countering: "Using problems in a text as a springboard to get at something [you] wouldn't otherwise say" (p. 55)

- *Arguing the other side:* Showing the usefulness of a term/idea that a writer has criticized or noting problems with one that she or he has argued for
- *Uncovering values:* Surfacing a word or concept for analysis that a text has left undefined or unexamined
- *Dissenting:* Identifying a shared line of thought on an issue to note its limits

Taking an Approach: "When you take on the approach of another writer both your thinking and theirs needs to change" (p. 74)

- *Acknowledging influences:* Noting those writers whose work has in some way provided a model of your own (p. 79)
- *Turning an approach on itself:* Asking the same question of a writer that he or she asks of others (p. 79)
- *Reflexivity:* Noting and reflecting on the key choices you have made (concerning method, values, language) when constructing your text (p. 79)

Note: Authors rarely make these moves in isolation (p. 49)

Notes from Bizup's "BEAM: A Rhetorical Vocabulary for Teaching Research-Based Writing"

B = Background: Using sources for uncontested facts and information

- You *rely* on these
- You expect readers to accept these as factually credible

E = Exhibit: Using sources as occasions for exploration and evidence for claims

- You *describe*, *analyze*, and *interpret* these
- You assume your readers may see things differently than you do

A = Argument: Using sources for discrete claims and arguments

- You *engage* these, *extending*, *countering*, and *qualifying* their claims
- You want your readers to distinguish between those claims and your own claims

M = Method: Using sources for concepts, frameworks, approaches, methods

- You *follow* these, *apply* them, *modify* them to suit your purposes
- You want your readers to distinguish between the original use and your own application/modification

university in creating a learning environment for student research writing.

We plan to build on our current WID program by extending our relationship with GW librarians. The First-Year Writing program at GW has laid the groundwork for such a collaboration. It features an extraordinarily successful partnership between writing faculty and instructional librarians, who are paired to develop and integrate instruction on information literacy into the course. As these partnerships develop over the course of multiple semesters, faculty and librarians refine their approaches and experiment with new methods, while also sharing best practices.

At the WID level, partnerships between librarians and faculty have developed organically, though not programmatically. Moving forward, the WID program and the GWU librarians wish to make the potential for productive collaborations more visible. We recommend initiating WID faculty workshops, run jointly with librarians, that focus on making disciplinary information literacy knowledges visible, and (as capacity allows) facilitating one-on-one discussions between faculty and librarians as they design, stage, and sequence assignments that involve research. Such relationships benefit both faculty and librarians. Faculty are able to communicate their disciplinary knowledge more effectively when librarians provide context about how disciplinary knowledges are instantiated in the organization of library resources. And librarians, who generally have rich knowledge not only about library resources but also about students' research habits, can improve their understanding of the goals and expectations for student research across the disciplines.

CONCLUSION

Learning to see, name, and teach the multiple knowledges of a discipline is hard work. We want to emphasize that the process, while difficult, is very rewarding. We find it exciting to see the many approaches our colleagues take to introduce students to the ways of knowing and doing in their fields, and we learn a great deal from meeting with faculty across the disciplines and librarians who have a wide range of expertise about student research habits, disciplinary information networks, and collections.

We are, of course, proud of the Writing in the Disciplines program and faculty at George Washington University, but we would emphasize that there is not *one* right way to build an "Information Literacy in the Disciplines" program, nor *one* right way to teach writing and information literacy within a course. The best teaching and program designs happen organically, mindful of the local context and goals. What we offer here are introductory steps: resources to help faculty reflect on disciplinary writing and information literacy practices; examples of how to make them explicit to students; opportunities to open department-wide conversation; and the overarching wisdom that librarian colleagues are excellent partners in such adventures.

REFERENCES

Association of College and Research Libraries. (2000). *Information literacy competency standards for higher education.* Retrieved from http://www.ala.org/acrl/standards/informationliteracycompetency

Association of College and Research Libraries. (2016). *Framework for information literacy for higher education.* Retrieved from http://www.ala.org/acrl/standards/ilframework

Bizup, J. (2008). BEAM: A rhetorical vocabulary for teaching research-based writing. *Rhetoric Review, 27*(1), 72–86.

Carter, M. (2007). Ways of knowing, doing, and writing in the disciplines. *College Composition and Communication, 58*(3), 385–418.

Colorado State University. (2017). *WAC Programs.* Retrieved from https://wac.colostate.edu/programs/

Council of Writing Program Administrators. (2014). WPA outcomes statement for first-year composition (3.0). *WPA: Writing Program Administration, 38*(1), 144–148. Retrieved from http://wpacouncil.org/positions/outcomes.html

Dryer, D., Bowden, D., Brunk-Chavez, B., Harrington, S., Halbritter, B., & Yancey, K. (2014). Revising FYC outcomes for a multimodal, digitally composed word: The WPA outcomes statement for first-year composition (version 3.0). *WPA: Writing Program Administration, 38*(1), 129–143.

Farrell, R., & Badke, W. (2015). Situating information literacy in the disciplines: A practical and systematic approach for academic librarians. *Reference Services Review, 43*(2), 319–340.

Harris, J. (2006). *Rewriting: How to do things with texts.* Boulder, CO: University Press of Colorado.

Johnston, B., & Webber, S. (2003). Information literacy in higher education: A review and case study. *Studies in Higher Education, 28*(3), 335–352.

Kristensen, R., & Claycomb, R. (2009). Introduction: Writing against the curriculum. In R. Kristensen & R. Claycomb (Eds)., *Writing against the curriculum: Anti-disciplinarity in the writing and cultural studies classroom* (pp. 1–20). Lexington, KY: Lexington Books.

Lindstrom, J., & Shonrock, D. D. (2006). Faculty-librarian collaboration to achieve integration of information literacy. *Reference & User Services Quarterly, 46*(1), 18–23.

Rapchak, M., & Cipri, A. (2015). Standing alone no more: Linking research to a writing course in a learning community. *portal: Libraries and the Academy, 15*(4), 661–675.

Riedner, R. (2015). "Designing and communicating a WID curriculum." Unpublished manuscript. George Washington University.

Riedner, R., O Sullivan, I., & Farrell, A. (2015). *An introduction to writing in the disciplines* (Report No. 5). All Ireland Society for Higher Education. Retrieved from http://www.aishe.org/wp-content/uploads/2016/01/5-Writing-in-the-Disciplines.pdf

Ryder, P. M., & Nutefall, J. (2016). Teaching serendipity. In T. M. Race & S. Makri (Eds.), *Accidental information discovery: Cultivating serendipity in the digital age* (pp. 27–52). Cambridge, MA: Chandos Publishing.

Simmons, M. H. (2005). *Librarians as disciplinary discourse mediators: Using genre theory to move toward critical information literacy. portal: Libraries and the Academy, 5*(3), 297–311. Retrieved from http://scholarworks.sjsu.edu/cgi/viewcontent.cgi?article=1065&context=slis_pub

Troutman, P., & Mullen, M. (2015). I-BEAM: Instance source use and research writing pedagogy. *Rhetoric Review, 34*(2), 181–199.

University Writing Program. (n.d.a). *First-year writing (UW 1020) template.* George Washington University. Retrieved from https://writingprogram.gwu.edu/first-year-writing-uw1020-template

University Writing Program. (n.d.b). *WID course guidelines.* George Washington University. Retrieved from https://writingprogram.gwu.edu/program-resources

CHAPTER 2

INFORMATION LITERACY AND WRITING STUDIES

The Beachfront Instructors and Students Navigate

Teresa Quezada

INFORMATION LITERACY AND WRITING STUDIES

The link between information literacy and writing studies has long been acknowledged. Both compositionists and librarians have developed and presented models where information literacy is integrated into writing courses (Margolin & Hayden, 2015; Sonntag & Ohr, 1996), and continue discussing the ensuing collaborations between librarians and instructors (McClure, 2016). Librarians and compositionists have also developed guidelines to foster student experiences and habits of mind that will serve them throughout their college career and beyond. The Association of College and Research Libraries' (ACRL) *Framework for Information Literacy for Higher Education* (2016) and the *Framework for Success in Postsecondary Writing* developed by the Council of Writing Program Administrators, the National Council of Teachers of English, and the National Writing Project (CWPA, NCTE, & NWP, 2011) share commonalities designed to foster metaliteracies and metacognition (ACRL, 2016, p. 2; CWPA, NCTE, & NWP, 2011, p. 5) so students become critical information consumers, readers, and writers. Both *Framework* documents can help writing instructors and librarians design writing courses where the information ocean meets the composing landscape. Such a metaphor may help instructors, instructional librarians, and especially students recognize that the relationship between information literacy and writing ebbs and flows based on a composition's purpose, audience, and genre. Further, since the beachfront created by information literacy and writing studies varies depending on the students' educational experience, using the two *Framework* documents in tandem may help course designers identify the beach students will experience in a given course.

First-year writing students, for example, may feel overwhelmed by pounding information surf if they have little experience in researching for academic purposes; they may feel the undertow of too much information and may not know strategies to help them find appropriate resources to respond to their instructors' requirements. Students in upper-division courses may feel that information is a mere ripple when their topic is more narrowly defined; their needs are different since they have learned to narrow their topics yet must also provide adequate support for their research and analysis to meet their instructors' expectations. In this chapter, I propose that the two *Framework* documents can and should be used to help instructors and instructional librarians design writing courses where students learn strategies that strengthen their skills in navigating the research and writing shore. To illustrate potential navigation strategies using the two *Framework* documents, I analyze two courses I have taught: a first-semester rhetoric and writing studies class and an upper-division technical writing class designated for health science majors. Both courses incorporated information literacy modules and included an instructional librarian embedded into the learning management system. I conclude by proposing how these courses can be further strengthened using both *Framework* documents to develop learning objectives and pedagogical practices that foster habits of mind critical to students and emerging professionals of the 21st century.

INCORPORATING THE *FRAMEWORKS*

The *Framework for Success in Postsecondary Writing* (*Success in Writing*) and the *Frame-*

work for Information Literacy for Higher Education (*Information Literacy*) share commonalities that, used in tandem, have previously influenced course design (Quezada, 2016a). *Success in Writing* describes habits of mind instructors should foster and writing, reading, and critical analysis experiences faculty and staff should afford students so they can succeed in college. The habits of mind include curiosity, openness, engagement, creativity, persistence, responsibility, flexibility, and metacognition (CWPA, NCTE, & NWP, 1). The writing, reading and critical analysis experiences should develop students' rhetorical knowledge, critical thinking, and knowledge of conventions, among other skills (CWPA, NCTE, & NWP, p. 1). These habits of mind and experiences align with the six concepts and corresponding dispositions of *Information Literacy* and can be incorporated into writing courses (ACRL, 2016, p. 2). Four concepts in particular, "authority is constructed and contextual, information creation as a process, research as inquiry, and searching as strategic exploration" (ACRL, p. 2) complement the habits of mind and can be utilized to design undergraduate writing courses that afford students rich opportunities to become discerning information consumers and informed, rhetorically adept writers. Analyzing the course design and assignments for two undergraduate writing courses provides a starting point for instructors and librarians to consider how to develop courses and collaborations that advance the habits of mind and core concepts in the *Framework* documents. The first step in using the *Framework* documents is to develop course goals and learning objectives that echo *Framework* documents and alert students to the types of activities they will be expected to complete.

COURSES: RHETORIC AND WRITING STUDIES I AND TECHNICAL WRITING IN THE HEALTH SCIENCES

The two courses where I have incorporated the *Framework* documents are Rhetoric and Writing Studies I (RWS 1301), the first course in the two-semester first-year rhetoric and writing studies program, and Technical Writing in the Health Sciences (RWS 3359) a junior-level technical writing course. Both courses are taught by faculty in the Rhetoric and Writing Studies program at a large Hispanic-serving institution in the southwestern United States. Program faculty follow uniform course learning objectives for the first-year course designed to introduce students to rhetorical concepts so they can develop effective writing practices. As stated in the course syllabus,

> [t]he goal of RWS 1301 is to develop students' critical thinking skills in order to facilitate effective communication in all educational, professional, and social contexts. This effective communication is based on an awareness of and appreciation for discourse communities as well as knowledge specific to subject matter, genre, rhetorical strategy, and writing process. . . . Through [the course] assignments, [students] will learn how to write to explore, to inform, to analyze, and to convince/problem solve. (RWS Program Syllabus, spring semester 2016)

The course objectives echo the habits of mind and core concepts more directly. By the end of the semester, students are expected to, among other objectives,

- Draw on existing knowledge bases to create "new" or "transformed" knowledge.
- Develop a knowledge of genres as they are defined and stabilized within discourse communities.
- Address the specific, immediate rhetorical situations of individual communicative acts.
- Develop procedural knowledge of the writing task in its various phases.
- Engage reflection about their own learning. (RWS program syllabus, spring 2016)

The technical writing course addresses effective communication within professional health care contexts and is designed to build upon the concepts introduced in the first-year courses. The course learning objectives incorporate the Society of Technical Communication's (STC) core competencies while retaining the RWS perspective. In addition to reminding students about discourse communities, genres, and rhetorical strategy and process, "[t]he class presents an approach to communication that helps students determine the most effective strategies, arrangements, and media. [Students] will produce a variety of documents and presentations to gain more confidence and fluency in visual, oral, and written communication" (Quezada, 2016b). Recognizing that students enrolled in technical writing are more experienced than the first-year students, the syllabus explicitly states that students are expected to strengthen their self-learning skills.

Course objectives for the technical writing course also incorporate the *Framework* documents' concepts while making multimodal composition more explicit throughout the course. Specifically, a few course objectives that advance habits of mind and dispositions include asking students to

- Analyze the rhetorical situation and define the users and/or audience as well as the tasks that the information must support.
- Apply rhetorical principles to plan and design effective technical documents for diverse media.
- Research appropriate sources that inform [students'] writing.
- Apply technological and visual rhetorical skills (e.g., document design, graphics, computer documentation, electronic editing, and content management applications) in the composing process. Publish, deliver and archive the composed documents as required.
- Recognize and respect various cultural attitudes toward and conventions for health care communications.
- Understand what health literacy is and how it will influence writing. (Quezada, 2016b)

As indicated in the course objectives, students are expected to practice the habits of mind articulated in the *Success in Writing* document and recognize the concepts presented in the *Information Literacy* framework throughout the course.

OPERATIONALIZING THE *FRAMEWORK* DOCUMENT CONCEPTS: INQUIRY-BASED RESEARCH

While the course goals and learning objectives introduce students to the guiding principles for the course, the assignments and associated activities provide students with the recommended experiences. Both writing courses include research projects that then inform additional assignments where students can practice visual rhetoric, adapt information to different media and audiences, and allow students to collaborate with a multidisciplinary team of colleagues. Both courses ask students to engage in *inquiry-based research* as described by Justice, Rice, Roy, Hudspith, and Jenkins (2009). That is, students are asked to generate their questions for research and then focus on answering them or obtaining an informed understanding of the questions they have raised. In their pursuit for answers, students are guided by supportive instructors and other resource people (Justice et al., 2009, p. 843). Their investigations and research demands that they practice curiosity, be open to consideration of new information they encounter, and think critically about that information—habits of mind and experiences recommended by the *Success in Writing* document.

Recognizing that research can be a daunting requirement for undergraduates as Bodi (2002) explains, research projects in the first-year course are introduced after students have worked in groups and been introduced to rhetorical and writing process theories. Further, scaffolding assignments designed to emphasize the reiterative nature of research and writing are incorporated into low-stakes exercises and the overall research project deliverables. To instill curiosity, students are asked to explore unanswered or underanswered issues within their intended major or field of study. Asking students to address an issue that has multiple perspectives allows students to review at times conflicting information without believing they have done something wrong because they are finding differing perspectives. As Bodi contrasts the research process of scholars and undergraduate students, she identifies that one of the frustrations undergraduates experience is navigating the "ambiguity and self-doubt inherent in research" (Bodi, 2002, p. 110). Helping students understand that ambiguity and dissonance in the literature is to be expected and explicitly indicating that it will be inherent in their topic choice begins fostering persistence, another habit of mind important for students.

To begin their inquiry-based research, first-year students submit a research proposal that identifies three to five questions of inquiry the students plan to research, the specific audience to whom they will be addressing their research, the exigency for their research, and the dissonance they have identified. The questions usually involve a question of policy—what should be done about an issue? Students learn that to fully answer that question, they will have to explain or answer other questions such as questions of definition or fact, questions of interpretation, questions of value, and questions of consequence. To effectively answer these questions, students must synthesize information to arrive at this analysis. Thus, the first assignment introduces students to the analysis, synthesis, and evaluation processes they will be expected to follow throughout their inquiry. The proposal memo also allows the instructor to ask guiding questions about the topic so students can further refine their questions and resulting topic. This first assignment in the research effort sequence incorporates the recommendations Bodi proposes (2002, p. 111).

To support the initial investigation students must conduct to submit their research proposal, students participate in a research workshop led by an instructional librarian at the university library. Many first-year students have limited academic research experience, so the purpose of the initial workshop is to introduce students to databases available to them and to specific research strategies. The ACRL *Framework* document heavily influences this initial session because students learn information's value, authority, and relevance. As the librarian explains how information is created and refined over time, students are introduced to the different modes of reporting they can expect to find depending on their topic's timeline. During this workshop, students also practice identifying different terms to research their topic. Students' inexperience within their field of study means they may not know the conventions or terms used to discuss their topic. Asking students to consider different terms for their searches and to refine those searches based on the terms they may encounter in their initial sources fosters their persistence and emphasizes that research is strategic exploration.

Although the subsequent deliverable in the research effort is a fairly consistent academic genre, the annotated bibliography, it serves two important purposes. First, it encourages students to begin searching for relevant, current, and credible sources and begin evaluating those sources earlier than they would if they did not have a deadline. Second, and perhaps most importantly, the assigned bibliography requires students to present their research questions again and to indicate, for each source, how that source will help them answer at least one of their research questions. Students are encouraged to refine and focus their questions of inquiry. As their instructor and research resource, I emphasize that changes to their questions, and perhaps to their topic are acceptable—that this is a result of their research and that they should not discard information that does not fit with a question they may have initially posed. While the assignment focuses on the annotated bibliography as an academic genre and convention, it also presents an opportunity for students to understand the reiterative quality of research and to wade in its ambiguity.

The students' research paper, as a major course deliverable, is expected to follow academic conventions, but the paper is also expected to demonstrate the various arguments students located for their topic and the relative value of each. Rather than merely informing, the researched argument, designed for a specific audience, consolidates many of the habits of mind and experiences recommended by the *Success in Writing* framework. To meet assignment requirements, students must have also practiced the *Information Literacy* concepts since they must provide an argument that is current, relevant, and credible based on their field of study and intended audience.

The final deliverable in the research project sequence for first-year students is a group project where one student's topic is translated into a visual argument, a 30–60 second video, infographic, or brochure, presented to their peers, and potentially presented at the end-of-semester showcase sponsored by the RWS program. This assignment asks students to "analyze and act on understandings of audience, purposes and contexts" and "compose in multiple environments" (CWPA, NCTE, & NWP, p. 1). As a group project, it also fosters creativity, persistence, and responsibility since each group member is expected to contribute to the final deliverable as determined by each student group through a group contract.

The research project assignment sequence for the technical writing course is similar to that for first-year students, but demands greater sophistication from the students since they have had more exposure to their field of study and may possess a better understanding of alternate views within their selected topic. Students in this course submit a research proposal, annotated bibliography, informative research paper, and educational brochure or illustrated instructions based on their research topic.

Technical writing students submit a research proposal that identifies a health issue pertinent to the university community or the broader regional community. While the topics are thus narrowed given the student population in the course, students can select topics that interest them rather than having topics assigned to them. Currency and relevance is discussed both by the instructor and the librarian in the first-year course; however, these concepts become increasingly important in the health sciences where information is continually evolving. Thus, the librarian-led workshop that precedes the students' research proposal focuses on medical databases rather than general searching strategies. Less time is dedicated to identifying research terms than in the first-year workshop, and more time is dedicated to identifying the methodologies utilized by researchers.

As in the first-year course, students are encouraged to develop questions of inquiry that will help them identify conflicting information and the value, credibility, and relevance of the information they are locating. The annotated bibliography serves a similar purpose for technical writing students as it did for first-year students, and the research paper presents a literature review appropriate for health sciences including integrative reviews, systematic reviews, or meta-analysis. As Garrard explains in the first chapter of *Health Sciences Literature Review Made Easy: The Matrix Method*, these reviews evaluate publications based on research methods, summarize findings from multiple studies, and draw conclusions based on scientific evidence (Garrard, 2014, pp. 4–5). Although discipline specific, introducing students to these research papers fosters the knowledge of conventions the *Success in Writing* framework encourages. At this stage in their research, students are again encouraged to revise their research questions to reflect the information they are locating rather than excluding relevant research that does not match their initial line of inquiry. The resulting informative research paper summarizes the current literature about a health topic. Students practice adapting scientific research information for lay audiences and users—their typical clients or patients—by developing a visual assignment. Students must design the educational brochure or set of instructions assignment for patients/clients and their families. The brochure or instructions are meant to outline important information users would need and is based on the research topic the students have been exploring throughout the semester. Like first-year students, through the brochure and illustrated instruction assignment, students practice analyzing and designing for audiences whose information needs and health literacy will vary from their own as designers. Through this assignment, students also learn to compose in a multimedia environment. Thus the assignment provides students with the experiences recommended by compositionists and writing program administrators.

Students in both courses proceed from identifying a topic that is of interest to them and refine their research to answer questions that would be relevant to a particular audience. Throughout their exploration, students receive guidance and instruction from their instructor and course librarian who collaborate to provide students with *Framework*-recommended learning experiences. Inquiry-based research introduces students to the reiterative nature of investigation and exploration. Although the students' frustration may not be completely eliminated, the course design aims to ameliorate that frustration. The instructional team emphasize that it is usual to find oceans of information and the student must then refine his/her research scope. Alternatively, if the research questions are too narrowly drafted, the instructional team encourages students to consider broader contexts or audiences to locate credible resources.

RECOGNIZING SOCIAL MEDIA IN THE RESEARCH PROCESS

Most recently, I have scheduled a second library workshop to help students assess the credibility and reliability of social media and newsfeed information they, or in the case of health science professionals, their clients or patients may encounter. Understanding that a single library workshop is the oft-criticized single-shot attempt to introduce students to information literacy (Artman, Frisicaro-Pawlowski, & Monge, 2010), realizing that despite my best efforts to foster discussions with the instructional librarian through learning management system discussion boards I did not successfully engage students, and recognizing that all students are bombarded with newsfeeds and comments that can be construed as information through social media channels, the second library workshop is designed to help students critically assess social media feeds.

Addressing social media used by news sources and multiplatform journalism, Bowd indicates that "[s]ocial media provide opportunities to create and expand audiences, increase geographical reach, respond more quickly than ever before to news events and issues and interact with news consumers in more immediate and direct ways" (2016, p. 129). Thus, helping students recognize the reach, currency, and audience impacts of social media becomes a learning objective for writing instructors and librarians seeking to implement the *Framework* documents. Not only will students continue to be audiences for social media, they may be asked to contribute to or even produce social media in their college and professional careers. The key when addressing critical analysis in social media is determining how to develop experiences and assignments within these writing courses that remain relevant to students and are not merely another exercise.

The positive aspects of social media have been discussed in multiple studies; however, scholars also recognize the uncertainty associated with "the credibility of both the information shared and that of the information source" (Osatuyi, 2013, p. 2622). Credibility is further complicated when concerns about users' gratification, as discussed by Lee and Ma, are considered (2011). Lee and Ma suggest that social media users, or the audience, may share news stories to achieve gratification and a perceived sense of status. Some outlets may encourage users' sharing and further distributing news stories, all while adding the user/sharer's personal commentary (Lee & Ma, 2011). Thus students, as social media users, may find social media posts that they may consider credible to inform their research, particularly when they are trying to meet a deadline or a source count requirement.

The second librarian-led workshop then asks students to find a newsfeed or social media post about their research topic and investigate its credibility. The specific assignment requirements and prompts are identified in Box 2.1. It is important to note that students are encouraged to find credible, current sources that *either* confirm or call into question the points they initially encountered in the social media post. Once students have critically assessed the social media post, they are asked to consider either the post or the resulting research for inclusion in their research efforts—either the annotated

BOX 2.1
SOCIAL MEDIA NEWSFEED—CRITICAL ASSESSMENT RESEARCH EXERCISE

You have now become quite familiar with your topic, and since your topics are current and relevant, they appear on the news and may even appear in social media. For this assignment, you will find your topic in an electronic news source or social media (Facebook, Twitter, Pinterest) and then try to locate a credible source that either supports or contradicts (debunks) the initial newsfeed.

For example, I saw the video below in a Facebook feed. I don't know if it is accurate, but by researching it and corroborating it—meaning finding credible sources that support it—your classmate who is researching college costs could certainly use the information in her research project. https://www.facebook.com/DavidAvocadoWolfe/videos/10154628150831512/

This assignment will allow you to critically analyze information you may find casually. That information may help you identify areas and issues that interest you and that you want to pursue, change, or prove wrong.

To complete this assignment, answer the following questions:

1. Identify the original source. That is, did you find a Facebook post, something on Pinterest, something on a news feed? Let me know what that source was and the argument it indicated. In my example above, I would state: Facebook video indicating that several developed countries provide free college education and comparing the cost of a U.S. college education of over $77,000.
2. Identify at least one credible source you found that either confirmed or denied the initial source.
3. Cite this source in APA format.
4. In 3–5 sentences, indicate whether your second source corroborates or debunks your initial source and whether you are planning to use this second source in your research assignment.

bibliography or the final research manuscript. My goal in this assignment is not to discredit social media in total, but to foster a healthy skepticism in students. Doing so encourages students to recognize how information is created, who is creating the information, and the credibility these disseminators possess. In summary, this exercise also implements the *Framework*-recommended experiences.

CONCLUSION AND RECOMMENDATIONS: SCENIC BEACH OR ROCKY SHORE

The resulting student research projects in both courses suggest that incorporating the *Frameworks* as guiding principles in writing course design is helpful to students' writing success and information literacy acquisition; the *Frameworks* seem to help students navigate the information literacy and writing studies beachfront. Critical to *Framework* integration is forming an instructional team between the writing instructor and an instructional librarian. Although specific strategies must be adapted depending on the students' trajectory in their undergraduate studies, the instructor and librarian can and should collaborate and discuss how the pedagogical practices they enact will foster the habits of mind and dispositions identified. For example, the team should strive to foster inquiry and curiosity in first-year students. Instructors and librarians can serve as life guards.

Having first-year students explore areas and topics that interest them while accepting and encouraging dead ends or changed perspectives is critical. It is equally important to help students at all levels of their undergraduate career learn to consistently and critically evaluate information points for timeliness and credibility. Perhaps the most important concept for the instructional team to remember is to help students realize they are very likely facing an ocean of information, but they need not explore every aspect of it nor let it drown them. Strategic exploration can lead students to formulate effective research, and the instructional team is charged with providing students with the guiding questions that can reduce their haphazard approach to inquiry. For juniors and seniors who have greater content-specific knowledge, the team helps them realize that although their specific area has been researched, the key to effective investigation is locating sources that apply to their research questions directly. Rather than having to wade through miles of beach without finding a suitable research entry point, discussing research questions and terms with the instructional team can help more experienced undergraduate students navigate the research process. Guiding students to dedicated databases becomes an important distinction in the strategies deployed in the two courses.

Once course goals and objectives reflect the *Framework* documents, the following strategies can provide students with ample learning experiences:

- Introduce inquiry-based research; such research fosters curiosity.
- Guide students through their selected topic by allowing multiple iterations of their questions of inquiry as students proceed through the research process; allowing students to stumble with questions prior to finalizing their draft emphasizes that research is reiterative and circular rather than linear.
- Provide multiple opportunities for students to refine their questions and submit them to the instructor and potentially the librarian; multiple feedback opportunities allow for support and comment from the instructional team.
- Provide information literacy workshops at multiple points in the course; aside from providing continuity and scaffolding, more than one workshop reiterates that research requires perseverance and strategic searches.
- Afford opportunities for ongoing dialogue with a collaborating instructional librarian; embedding a librarian in the course introduces students to additional resources and fosters discussions with multidisciplinary experts.

The greatest difficulty I have encountered is objectively assessing the application of the two *Framework* documents. From an anecdotal, instructor perspective, students' research papers topics have varied from preventing soldier suicide to the proliferation of autonomous vehicles. Student presentations are animated and, in some instances, have engaged their classmates with further questions. Students demonstrate a reiterative process where the questions of inquiry become more focused and refined; topics engage students. From first-year student reflections, we learn that their academic research has been a new endeavor, but rather than feeling overwhelmed, they found that the scaffolding, including library visits, helped first-year students navigate the beachfront.

REFERENCES

Artman, M., Frisicaro-Pawlowski, E., & Monge, R. (2010). Not just one shot: Extending the dialogue about information literacy in composition classes. *Composition Studies, 38*(2), 93–109.

Association of College and Research Libraries. (2016). *Framework for information literacy for higher education.*

Bodi, S. (2002). How do we bridge the gap between what we teach and what they do? Some thoughts on the place of questions in the process of research. *Journal of Academic Librarianship, 28*(3), 109–114.

Bowd, K. (2016). Social media and news media: Building new publics or fragmenting audiences? In M. Griffiths & K. Barbour (Eds.), *Making publics, making places* (pp. 129–144). South Australia: University of Adelaide Press.

Council of Writing Program Administrators, National Council of Teachers of English, National Writing Project. (2011). *Framework for success in postsecondary writing.*

Garrard, J. (2014). *Health sciences literature review made easy: The matrix method.* Burlington, MA: Jones & Bartlett Learning.

Justice, C., Rice, J., Roy, D., Hudspith, B., & Jenkins, H. (2009). Inquiry-based learning in higher education: Administrators' perspectives on integrating inquiry pedagogy into the curriculum. *Higher Education, 59*(6), 841–855.

Lee, C. S., & Ma, L. (2011). News sharing in social media: The effect of gratifications and prior experience. *Computers in Human Behavior, 28,* 331–329.

Margolin, S., & Hayden, W. (2015). Beyond mechanics: Reframing the pedagogy and development of information literacy teaching tools. *Journal of Academic Librarianship, 41,* 602–612.

McClure, R. (2016). *Rewired: Research-writing partnerships within the Frameworks.* ACRL.

Osatuyi, G. (2013). Information sharing on social media sites. *Computers in Human Behavior, 29,* 2622–2631.

Quezada, T. (2016a). Teaching the frameworks for writing and information literacy: A case study from the health sciences. In R. McClure (Ed.), *Rewired: Research-writing partnerships within the Frameworks* (pp. 189–207). ACRL.

Quezada, T. (2016b). RWS 3359–Technical Writing fall 2016 syllabus.

Sonntag, G., & Ohr, D. M. (1996). The development of a lower-division, general education, course-integrated information literacy program. *College & Research Libraries, 57*(4), 331–338.

University of Texas at El Paso. Rhetoric and Writing Studies—Undergraduate Program. (2016). Program syllabus for RWS 1301 course.

CHAPTER 3

INFORMATION IN THE MAKING

Information Behavior Theory and the Teaching of Research-Writing in the Digital Age

Christine I. McClure
Randall McClure

REWARDING BEHAVIOR

Feminist rhetoric. Process theory. Critical rhetoric. Basic writing theory. Expressive rhetoric. Writing center theory. Digital rhetoric. And the list goes on.

The field of Writing Studies has matured quite a bit over the past half-century. From origins in its break from Literary Studies and the paradigm shift from product to process to a field now full of rhetorics of all kinds, Writing Studies is a lively discipline in today's academy, one that we should certainly look to in teaching students to become better researchers and writers, particularly in the digital age. For example, Writing Studies professionals routinely consider the processes students use to author texts and participate in digital spaces, and they have blown the lid off the types of products that students compose in the college writing classroom, including multimodal and new media compositions of all kinds, social bibliographies, infographs, word clouds, and much more. The college writing classroom of today is clearly not what it was in the 20th century, and digital rhetoric is one reason why. Another reason, albeit one much less discussed in the literature of this burgeoning field, is the information revolution.

In this chapter, we offer readers—including writing teachers, librarians, and writing center professionals—another lens through which to view the information explosion and its corresponding influence on how students research and how they write. While the field of Writing Studies is largely focused on acts of composing, most notably in the expanding realm of digital rhetoric, it appears to theorize the teaching of writing in many ways that are blind to the rich landscape of information in which it now resides. To widen this lens to where we can capture the information landscape in its rich, vibrant detail, we suggest a turn to information behavior theory. In fact, we believe information behavior theory offers writing across the curriculum in general and the teaching of research-writing in particular a new and exciting arena in which to explore. To this end, we first introduce the four tenets of information behavior theory to readers. Second, we offer several suggestions for librarians, teachers, and writing center professionals when working with students on research-writing projects. Taken together, these suggestions offer readers a roadmap for helping students identify the research need, sources to meet that need, methods for mining those sources, and strategies for producing digital, information-savvy work.

GROWING UP TOGETHER

As we offer in our opening, the place, or space, of Writing Studies within the academy is well defined. Writing teachers and writing center professionals are able to theorize their practice in a whole host of ways, to view the teaching and learning of writing through a wide array of theoretical perspectives on teaching and learning. The development of a strong theoretical base has, to some degree, coincided with the development of the Web. In short, as writing professionals were considering the processes as well as the products of composing over the past few decades, the Web was maturing from its read-only origins to the dynamic interactive composing and publishing platform it is today.

In many respects, the rise of digital rhetoric, of the study of composing in digital spaces, was a natural one for those in Writing Studies. As students started to read and write in digital spaces, Writing Studies professionals were there to investigate. Despite more than three decades of research on digital rhetoric, however, we contend that the theoretical base remains incomplete if we desire to truly capture and understand how students compose with and are composed by the information that constantly swirls around them, particularly in online spaces. Standing rhetorics and other theories of composing have been applied and adapted to account for the developments related to writing in electronic environments and now online spaces, and these moves have made digital rhetoric and the teaching of writing all the richer. Still, though, we believe that ample consideration has not been given to the impact of the information explosion on the writing behaviors and habits of students, particularly those that directly (and often indirectly) involve information culled from the Web.

ENTERING THE CONVERSATION

Despite its absence from the theoretical discussions in Writing Studies, we believe that information behavior theory offers those teaching or supporting the teaching of research-writing across the curriculum a robust theoretical vantage point from which to view their work.

In his 2000 work "Human Information Behavior," University of Sheffield researcher T. D. Wilson defines information behavior as he distinguishes four areas of it:

- Information Behavior [the grand term] is the totality of human behavior in relation to sources and channels of information, including both active and passive information seeking, and information use. Thus, it includes face-to-face communication with others, as well as the passive reception of information as in, for example, watching TV advertisements, without any intention to act on the information given.
- Information **Seeking** Behavior is the purpose[ful] seeking for information as a consequence of a need to satisfy some goal. [For example, a student user, in responding to a homework assignment in a History class, conducts a search online to identify sources that discuss the historical factors that led to the start of World War II.]
- Information **Searching** Behavior is the "micro-level" of behavior employed by the searcher in interacting with information systems of all kinds. It consists of all the interactions with the system, whether at the level of human computer interaction (for example, using a mouse and clicking on links) or at the intellectual level (for example, adopting a Boolean search strategy or determining the criteria for deciding which [search result] is most useful), which itself involves mental acts, such as judging the relevance of data or information retrieved.
- Information **Use** Behavior consists of the physical and mental acts involved in incorporating the information found into the person's existing knowledge base. It may involve, therefore, physical acts such as marking sections in a text to note their importance or significance, as well as mental acts that involve, for example, comparison of new information with existing knowledge. (Wilson, 2000, pp. 49–50)

We maintain that the concepts common to all four areas of information behavior are likely foreign to most Writing Studies and writing center professionals as theoretical constructs, though many of them routinely explore these concepts in their work with students in the writing classroom or writing center environment. Writing teachers and writing center professionals do have their students search for and use information in their compositions, though the information is not often the focus of either their instruction or their investigations into such instruction.

Given the sheer amount of information along with the diversity in information pathways and sources available to and commonly used by students today, we contend that the "research" half of the research-writing assignment can no longer just be along for the ride, that it should no longer be an afterthought or omission in the instructional process within the writing classroom and writing center environment. For these reasons, we believe the umbrella of information behavior theory presents a host of opportunities for research and pedagogy, particularly that surrounding the teaching of the research paper, or really any assignment in which students do or could engage with information sources.

PRESENTING AN EXAMPLE

Take, for example, one illustration (Figure 3.1) drawn from information behavior theory, Wilson's (2018) "Universe of Knowledge" where he depicts the organization and flow of information (personal communication, September 24, 2018). In this illustration, one with roots dating back to the early 1970s, Wilson (2007) attempts to "map the processes involved in what was known at the time as the 'user needs research.'" Wilson shows us a universe of knowledge or information, one ripe with information systems, embodiments of knowledge, life experiences, and technologies, among others. Wilson (1981) defines this universe of knowledge as "an abstract concept which embraces all knowledge related objects, events, and phenomena and as such, clearly interacts with the physical universe" (p. 6). In our opinion, the teaching and study of research-writing stand to gain much by projecting or imagining such work through the many facets of the research-writing relationship suggested by this illustration.

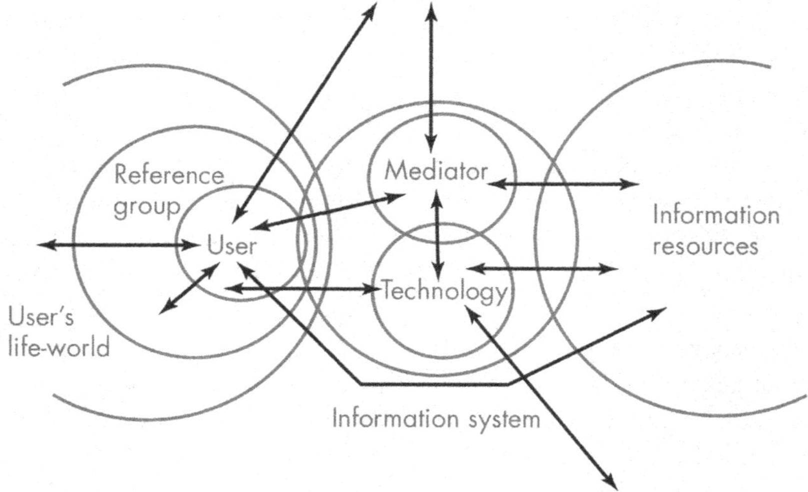

Figure 3.1 T. D. Wilson's "Universe of Knowledge." (Courtesy of T. D. Wilson.)

Wilson's illustration (Figure 3.1), for example, takes into consideration the "barriers that may prevent the [researcher] from taking action to seek information" (2007). The study of barriers, anxieties, or areas of resistance to and in writing has often been of interest to Writing Studies and writing center professionals, so looking at similar concepts in the research-writing process, to us, seems not just natural, but necessary. In fact, Wilson's "Universe of Knowledge" is just one of three illustrations that he has offered over the years "aimed at linking theories to action [or inaction]" (Wilson, 2007). In short, we believe that there is much to explore in linking information behavior theory to current research-writing scholarship and pedagogy.

The three sets of circles in the "Universe of Knowledge" illustration (Figure 3.1) represent to Wilson, as he notes in his 2007 article "Evolution in Information Behavior Modeling: Wilson's Model," a "three-fold view of information seeking," which includes the researcher's domains or context (left circles), the available research systems (center circles), and the possible information sources (right circle). Clearly, the concept of "technology," which Wilson "interpret[s] widely" as "anything that aids action," along with the volume of information sources as Wilson illustrates them in 1981 could be interpreted much differently today. In fact, we suggest that writing teachers, writing center tutors, and reference librarians consider activities that have students redraw Wilson's illustration to reflect information seeking today. Such activities should ask student to discuss not only their changes to the illustration, but also the implications of these changes for their research-writing tasks.

To this point, we also wonder how Writing Studies and writing center professionals would alter Wilson's diagram to account for the rise of information production in general and the production and consumption of information in digital spaces. In other words, if we brought this image 37 years forward to the present day, what would it look like? Would it or could it change our collective work with students as research-writers? We think so.

For example, in roughly the one minute that it took you to read the proceeding two paragraphs, the following bits (or should we say bytes) of information have found their way to and have been viewed on the Web:

- 463,140 tweets
- 47,820 photos uploaded to Instagram
- 76,440 Tumblr posts
- 4,223,160 YouTube videos viewed
- 156,896,460 e-mails sent ("In 1 second," n.d.)
- 510,000 posted comments, 293,000 status updates, and 136,000 uploaded photos to Facebook (Pring, 2012)
- 300 hours of new video uploaded to YouTube ("YouTube Company Statistics," 2017)

Yes, these bits all occurred in the past 60 seconds. Combining these with the countless other information sources littering the information landscape each minute and add the almost 4 million Google searches and 2,847,600 GB of Internet traffic ("In 1 second," n.d.) that also occur worldwide every minute, it is not difficult to see from just this one small example how our information behaviors have changed, and changed in ways that are nothing short of incredible.

Moreover, we offer that current writing pedagogy, a field of "action" in its own right, with its work cemented in a global and digital information economy, is not just incomplete, but also insufficient without larger contemplations of information needs, methods of retrieval and use (and reuse), production avenues, and documentation systems, nearly all of which have connections with information behavior theory. Instead, the focus of Writing Studies remains, in our opinion, squarely on the writer, what he or she composes, and how he or she is personally composed by it, whereas information retrieval and use, often typically cast aside as "library research," remain part of a formulaic, ancillary process, a second-class citizen to the products and processes of composing. How else could we explain the continuing prevalence of the inoculation tactic of the one-shot library research workshop or the passive acceptance of basic search results as acceptable sources?

OFFERING SOME ADVICE

By this time, we hope to have made a sufficient case for the potential of information behavior theory to affect the teaching of and research on research-writing. Therefore, we offer several applications derived from Wilson's definition of information behavior theory along with his "Universe of Knowledge" illustration in order to assist librarians, writing teachers, and Writing Studies professionals engaged with students on research-writing assignments in a world of digital information sources. Before doing so, however, we pause a moment to agree with Wilson that information behavior theory in general and his models and illustrations in particular are unable to explain or account for every information encounter students have as research-writers. Instead, we, like Wilson, see such models and illustrations as ways to better understand information needs and solve information problems (2007).

The first of four areas that Wilson discusses in his definition of information behavior theory includes both passive and active information seeking along with the channels through which information flows. Given the amount of information that students encounter, it seems necessary to include knowledge inventories and information pathways in our work with students on research-writing projects. For example, one activity might ask students to discuss not just what they know about topics that interest them, but also how they get their information. Do they watch a lot of TV news? Are they always on Twitter? Do they run to Wikipedia when they don't know something? Have they had personal or educational experiences that are relevant to what they are writing and researching? Answers to questions like these would help to understand how information flows around the student and could lead to research-writing strategies that are tailored to the student's present information behaviors.

Another activity might include discussion or active learning projects in which students engage a variety of sources and discuss their usefulness and trustworthiness, similar to the oft-used CRAAP test, but working instead with sources students are using currently. We cannot stress this point enough; any investigation into or work with student researchers on "information channels," as Wilson calls them, must begin with the channels students are using and are comfortable with before being expanded to others; otherwise, students will be unlikely to change their current information behaviors for the better. This is one reason why we believe the one-shot library session doesn't, from our experience, impact students' research behaviors. Students enter such sessions with researching habits with which they are comfortable and which they believe work well enough; therefore, they are rarely enticed to see searching differently. These behaviors, as Project Information Literacy and Citation Project researchers among others have pointed out, are unfortunately laced with habits leading to quick research "wins" and shallow, often commercial information sources. For a more extended discussion of activities aimed at uncovering and working with students' information-seeking channels, consider McClure's (2011) "Googlepedia: Turning Information Behaviors Into Research Skills."

The second area turns to information need, reaching an information goal or solving an information problem. In Writing Studies circles, information need is somewhat akin to the traditional research question or hypothesis found in the early stages of the typical research-writing assignment. After the formation of the question or hypothesis, though, information need often gets turned awkwardly into a simple quantitative measure (read as the number of sources required to complete the assignment) instead of the deeper implications of satisfying an information goal or offering a solution to an information problem. When it is twisted as such, information becomes the means to an end when it should be, in most research-writing situations, the end in itself.

Since research is still often and only included as a separate, isolated activity within larger research-writing assignments, we recommend that writing teachers, writing center professionals, and research librarians work to intertwine, or braid, the research process and the writing process from beginning to end. For example, much like writing teachers emphasize prewriting, an assortment of techniques for idea generation, we suggest that teachers use pre-researching or "presearching" in unison with other prewriting strategies. We suggest having students work with research at the earliest stages of the research-writing process. For example, students could work back and forth from search results to their own writing. Students could analyze the initial search results, then freewrite on or make a list of ideas drawn from the results that are returned on a search subject. We believe activities like this one that have students moving between researching and writing from the beginning of a research-writing project reflect the ways in which students work naturally when they encounter an information need. Further, such activities suggest to students the importance and value that information and research have in such projects, that research is a full partner, not a single, isolated activity. Doing such could lead to both more effective and more sustained research and writing.

The third area is Wilson's "micro-level of behavior," including both the mental and physical interactions with information systems. Janice Walker (2016), Writing Studies scholar and co-founder of the LILAC Project (http://lilac-group.blogspot.com/), is one researcher already engaged in the study of information behavior. The LILAC Project, which stands for Learning Information Literacy Across the Curriculum, is a multi-institutional study of student information-seeking behaviors that aims to uncover the research habits common among students today. At the center of Walker's work is the research-aloud protocol (RAP), in which Walker and her co-researchers capture video of students conducting and talking out their online research for actual research-writing tasks, in other words where there exists a real and defined information need. Walker and her group then code the behaviors that students demonstrate during the RAPs in order to identify habits or trends that may help teachers and librarians across the curriculum better understand what students do and don't do when they are researching (Walker, 2016). We suggest that readers of this article look to the LILAC Project as well as the RAP methodology as ways to help themselves and their student writers make better sense of how students today are interacting with and within the information universe.

The fourth and final area of Wilson's definition of information behavior is the large umbrella of information use. Similar to Walker's work with the LILAC Project and the group's examinations of information-seeking behavior, Writing Studies researchers Sandra Jamieson and Rebecca Moore Howard have started to shed light on information use in the research essays of college students. In their Citation Project (http://citationproject.net/), Jamieson and Howard have led a group of researchers who are intent on better understanding "how first-year student writers incorporate ideas from the sources they cite in their papers, and what the selected sources reveal about their information literacy skills." While the group's stated goal is the prevention of plagiarism, the researchers in the group have noted that students struggle using sources, particularly longer and more complex sources, in their writing. They comment, "If instructors [knew] how shallowly students are engaging with their research source[s]—and that is what the Citation Project research reveals—then they [would] know what responsible pedagogy needs to address." Much like our suggestion in the preceding paragraph, we propose that writing teachers make a sincere investment in understanding how their students are using (and not using) source information. Having students write about the information they use and choose to leave out in their essays seems a logical first step.

Much like the activity suggested above for understanding what students know and how they get their information, asking students to write about their source information could help writing teachers, writing center professionals, and research librarians better understand how students use it. Asking students to write about how they identified the information that they decided to use in their compositions along with the information that they chose to leave out could suggest to teachers and librarians ideas for helping students better mine their sources. Like the Citation Project results offer, asking students to identify the page (first page, second page, etc.) or paragraph number where their information is found in their original source could increase instructors' as well as their students' understanding of the depth of interaction between students' researching and writing behaviors. In other words, could we find ways to better understand how well students themselves understand the sources that they use? We think so. In fact, such investigations stand to improve not just the quality of source use within our students' research-writing projects, but also the critical thinking and synthesis skills that such projects are intended to cultivate.

Taken a step further, having students write about their research use, such as when in the research-writing process they tend to actually read and work with their sources as well as the reasons behind why they chose to paraphrase, quote, or summarize a source could also suggest the level of skill or flexibility that students have in "reading" their sources in order to use them most effectively. Further, understanding these habits could help teachers to identify students more likely to plagiarize, either intentionally or unintentionally, and lead to instruction on source documentation and fair use, topics that themselves have only become more complex in the digital age.

PROJECTING AHEAD

In closing, we wish to raise some questions that emerge from an activity we suggest earlier in this chapter. We wonder about the implications of a revised version of Wilson's 1981 model, one that takes into consideration advancements in technology and both availability and production of information. If we believe, for example, that the sheer volume of what Wilson labels as "information resources" from 1981 to 2018 is no longer adequately represented by the size and shape Wilson affords, then what implications does that have for our, and our students', universe of knowledge? To what they read (or don't read), research (or fail to find), and write (or rewrite)?

More specific to the teaching of research-writing in the digital age, do differences or changes in the shape and influence of, using Wilson's terms, potential "mediators" and technologies, students' very compositions themselves, many of them often made public through social and other media, alter the information system in some profound way? And please note that Wilson has these in the center of the knowledge universe. If so, then what does that mean for our own research and our teaching of research? Stretching it out even further, should we be doing more, perhaps much more, with information and information behavior than what we typically label today "research"?

While perhaps just a start to the conversation, we hope questions such as these will lead to answers that bring the teaching of research-writing in sync with the global information economy that our students navigate every day.

REFERENCES

In 1 second each, each and every second, there are. (n.d.). Retrieved from http://www.internetlivestats.com/one-second/#traffic-band

Jamieson, S. (2017). What the Citation Project tells us about information literacy in college composition. In B. D'Angelo, S. Jamieson, B. Maid, & J. R. Walker (Eds.), *Research and collaboration across disciplines* (pp. 119–143). Fort Collins, CO: WAC Clearinghouse and University Press of Colorado.

McClure, R. (2011). Googlepedia: Turning information behaviors into research skills. In C. Lowe & P. Zemliansky (Eds.), *Writing spaces: Readings on writing* (vol. 1, pp. 221–241).

Pring, C. (2012). 100 social media statistics for 2012. Retrieved from http://thesocialskinny.com/100-social-media-statistics-for-2012/

Walker, J. (2016). LILAC Project workshop. Retrieved from http://lilac-group.blogspot.com/

What is the citation project? (n.d.). Retrieved from http://citationproject.net/

Wilson, T. D. (1981). On user studies and information needs. *Journal of Documentation, 37*(1), 3–15.

Wilson, T. D. (2000). Human information behavior. *Informing Science, 3*(2), 49–55.

Wilson, T. D. (2007). Evolution in information behavior modeling: Wilson's model. In K. Fisher, S. Erdelez, & L. McKechnie (Eds.), *Theories of information behavior* (pp. 31–36). Medford, NJ: Information Today.

YouTube company statistics. (2017). Retrieved from http://www.statisticbrain.com/youtube-statistics/

CHAPTER 4

TEACHING "DIGITAL NATIVES" TO THINK

A Media Ecology Approach

Joshua D. Hill

Our students learn in response to their learning environment, including their technological media, not just in response to a curriculum (Kop, 2012, p. 2). But students' learning environments are no longer bounded by the space of the classroom or the direction of the instructor. Rather, because of mobile technologies, educational environments are now "edgeless," and students create personal learning environments (PLEs) that are largely outside the purview and control of their professors (Jones & Sclater, 2010, p. 6). This cultural sea change, engendered by the overlapping technological revolutions of the Internet, social media, and mobile technology, has been applied to education in various ways, but the earliest and loudest voices have enthusiastically recommended that our classrooms and institutions be continually remodeled to fit the learning preferences of incoming "digital natives" (Prensky, 2001). In this gestalt, the technological environment of our students becomes unassailable *ground* while educational practices and institutions become problematic *figures*.

I want to bring into focus a counternarrative, a reversal of the figure and ground, in which the problematic figure in the foreground becomes our students' technological learning environment. This counternarrative is pertinent to the collaborative partnership between librarians, composition programs, and university administrators because they share the burden of introducing students to a different information ethos, one that involves a more linear and critical form of thinking. This burden is, of course, information literacy (IL), a discipline whose short history has been one of searching for its disciplinary and thematic home (Jackson, 2009), shifting from an emphasis on technological training in search tools to an emphasis on critical thinking—and expanding from its corner in the library to a cross-campus concern (Coonan, 2011). The 2015 ACRL *Framework*, specifically, revised its approach to embed critical thinking and deep literacy into all six of its frames (ACRL, 2015), meeting the renewed call in higher education to address critical literacy[1] (Liu, Frankel, & Roohr, 2014). But IL is still missing a key aspect of this literacy question. I argue that a media ecology approach to IL can provide it the perspective on technology necessary to negotiate between the dominant narrative (i.e., "technology advances humanity") and the counternarrative (i.e., "technology erodes humanity") and preserve some of the advantages of both.

In this, I am rearticulating and modifying for IL Neil Postman's original call to supplement standard English curricula with the critical perspective and informed practice that Postman named "media ecology" (Postman, 1992, pp. 184–189; Strate, 2004, p. 4). Media ecology calls attention to the impact of the technological media environment on our messages and social practices, including our current shift away from a culture rooted in print literacy. Though the effects of print literacy do not make it an unmitigated good (see Branch, 2017), print literacy is still the coin of the realm, undergirding the systems and history on which Western civilization is built.

INTERROGATING INFORMATION: IL GROWS UP

Fortunately, we can start with the lens of IL's new and improved approach to *information*. The 2015 ACRL *Framework* was "substantially revised" from the 2000 version to reframe itself "through a richer, more complex set of core ideas," including more complex core ideas about information. IL could no longer be limited to efficient search processes for authoritative sources of reified information, a narrow "technological literacy" that meets half of IL's objectives while undercutting the other half. Now, rather, while still teaching the tools of information search, IL targets metaliterate frameworks of scholarly "inquiry," information as embedded in scholarly "conversation," authority as "contextual," and search as "exploration" (ACRL, 2015). Thus, IL now emphasizes the critical literacy skills needed to actually engage with academic sources, however they are accessed.

In IL's past, librarians were seen as the taskmasters of "process," teaching a universal method of search tool use, while disciplinary instructors were purveyors of "content," teaching disciplinary ideas and critical disciplinary literacy (Badke, 2010). This problematic dichotomy was exploded in the revised ACRL *Framework*, which acknowledges that disciplinary knowledge paradigms (or "threshold concepts") determine what constitutes a good research question and an apt answer. Disciplinary content constitutes what information *is* in a particular situation. This move toward a rhetorical paradigm is fitting for IL's partnership with rhetoric and composition.

In the rhetorical paradigm, what constitutes information cannot be divorced from the community/audience, the purpose, and the structure of a disciplinary threshold concept. Therefore, to search for information is, at the same time, to learn a particular set of paradigms, purposes, and people. These searches are partly done through the *vocabulary* of particular disciplinary communities—a vocabulary that is *partly* database-searchable. However, because such words are always in flux—sites of contested meanings in the discipline—this searchable vocabulary cannot deliver to students any comprehensive or uncontested units of information. Coonan (2011) argued that what is needed, therefore, is a "reflective or metacognitive structure which allows the learner to recognise that each has its own validity *within a given context*" (p. 17)—that is, a metaliteracy.

The ACRL's metaliteracy "see[s] inquiry as a process that focuses on problems or questions in a discipline or between disciplines that are open or unresolved," one that eschews "discrete answers to complex problems" and is not only "nonlinear and iterative" but also "serendipit[ous]" (2015, p. 9). Serendipity is a key concept here. The best or "right" answers cannot always be found through *method* and thus cannot be married to method-driven media. The ACRL says that IL learners should therefore "recognize the value of browsing and other serendipitous methods of information gathering" (p. 9). Kop (2012) seconds this idea of serendipity, adding to it the importance of human media who not only bring in unexpected connections and sources but also actualize the trust and community that are a significant part of human knowledge creation. Shifting information-seeking from an *individual action with technological tools* to a *social endeavor* also fits the rhetorical paradigm.

So far, so good. As Badke (2010) summarizes, this human-centered and nonlinear research process is one that disciplinary experts themselves normally use. We who are already familiar with the strange and sometimes excruciating research journey should be honest guides for our students. However, to do this, we need to become more articulate and intentional about the information media and research habits that best enable critical literacy and "metaliterate" thought. This metaliteracy,

I argue, should make visible the impact of different technological media on research contexts. We who grew up with physical books and journals, handwritten notes, and long periods of audio and video silence in the library—we need to pass on our knowledge of these IL tools to the next generation.

KEY QUESTIONS FOR THE FUTURE OF IL

The goals of this broadened IL are generally at cross-purposes with our students' technological habits. This conflict leads to a couple of soul-searching questions for instructors and administrators. The curricular beachhead of these questions is the IL environment of the composition classroom, but the discussion here has broader implications for university administration. Our responses (implicit or explicit) to the questions below influence a wide range of academic and amenities decisions, from the distribution of campus Internet access, to the campus investment in new technological toys, to the curricular approach to IL itself. The following are the two basic questions:

1. Do we want to preserve attention-intensive linear thought—that is, the traditional literacy of the last four hundred years of Western civilization?
2. What can composition classes actually *do* toward guiding students in a different information ethos based in a different information environment?

I answer "yes" to the first question. To the second, I argue that composition classes can teach a critical metaliteracy of research media instead of joining, uncritically, the digital information revolution. This would provide students with real options in their educational media environment, enabling real, rational choices in their future education and careers.

DO WE WANT TO PRESERVE LOGICAL, LINEAR THOUGHT?

Both scholars who argue for the further integration of digital technology in the classroom (Biddix, Chung, & Park, 2015; Kolikant, 2010; Kop, 2012; Prensky, 2001) and those who urge caution (Alliance for Childhood, 2004; Bennett, Maton, & Kervin, 2008; Carr, 2010; Jackson, 2009; Postman, 1992; Turkle, 2011, 2015) agree that digital and Internet-based learning environments change students' habits of and capacities for linear, logical thought. The boosters argue that students are evolving to work efficiently with new technology, creating new search strategies and thought patterns that fit the tools and the needs of the information age. Because they adapt to an app-supported utilitarian rationality, they are said to be more fit to thrive in an "app culture" (Turkle, 2015). "Literacy, as we've traditionally understood it," says Mark Federman of the University of Toronto, "is now nothing but a quaint notion, an aesthetic form that is as irrelevant to the real questions and issues of pedagogy today as is recited poetry," and he calls for educational institutions to "abandon the 'linear, hierarchical' world of the book" in favor of the different intellectual ethic of the Internet (Carr, 2010, p. 111).

Detractors argue that the constant "interruption" and "distraction" of the new media and corresponding social habits keep students focused on the *surfaces* of ideas rather than their critical *depths*, undercutting the time and attention needed for sustained interactions with ideas (Jackson, 2009, p. 65; Turkle, 2015). That is, the linearity and hierarchy of the "world of the book" are inextricably part of training students in what we know as critical thinking, which most of us still uphold as an important learning objective. New media help students find sources but erode their ability to critically understand them. "Students could find and cite sources better than they were able to judge their relevance and authority," one representative study summarized, "and were even less able to use information they gathered to support their arguments" (Carr, 2010, p. 165). Surrounded by terabytes of both substance and offal, students can neither discern one from the other nor incorporate either into their own thought. They starve in the midst of a fruitful land. Trained to think and act however their technology suggests they should, students are cut off from their historical heritage of complex Western ideas, distracted from their individual exploration of ideas, and unaware that their tools are using them more than they are using their tools (Postman, 1992).

But how can a technological environment affect our students' levels of literacy? Let us consider the information-seeking technologies that inundate both the culture and the academy: Google, social media outlets, blogs, e-books, academic databases, and vetted websites—which overlay and replace books, library stacks, interviews, and other longform methods of engagement. These are the "intellectual technologies" that, when incorporated into a learning environment, can become extensions of our brains in the same way that a hammer becomes an extension of our hand (Carr, 2010, p. 44). These technologies, these media, are not neutral. "Every intellectual technology . . . embodies an intellectual ethic" (Carr, 2010, p. 45), an implicit value of its creator, often a value subservient to hidden commercial interests (Kop, 2012; Jackson, 2009, pp. 163–164).

What is the intellectual ethic behind search engines, which promise a multitude of quick and targeted results in response to a few reified subject terms/keywords? Such technologies promote the value of speed, bypassing the human need for time and reflection in complex problem solving (Carr, 2010, p. 119). Along with speed, these technologies *devalue* "the degree of attention we devote to [a piece of writing] and the depth of our immersion in it" (Carr, 2010, p. 90).

Such technologies also value the "part" over the "whole," fragmenting books through different search and summary apps (Carr, 2010, p. 91). Because search engines offer us an impossible multitude of sources that are, themselves, keyword searchable, there is felt to be little need to actually read the sources, but rather to skim, search, snip, and find summaries. "Skimming" and "interruption" become virtues, a technologically sanctioned way of life (Turkle, 2015). Moreover, since our Internet habits tend "to turn all media into social media" (Carr, 2010, p. 106), most larger works, news stories, and complex problems are distilled for (and by) our students into memes: palatable, fragmented oversimplifications that tend toward "the short, the sweet, and the bitty" (quoted in Carr, 2010, p. 94), highlighting the embedded values of simplification and entertainment.

Such search technologies also promote troubling values concerning language. Subject terms and keywords become reified tools to be plugged into algorithms. Here, the surface of the word constitutes its value (see Jackson, 2009, pp. 160–161). The older rhetorical understanding of language starts with the foundation of committed social relationships, within which meaning is *approximated* by language but never fully mapped by language. Thus, meaning and its context of human relationship is the primary value, while language is a shifting set of often imprecise tools used on the journey.

How this shallowing out of language affects IL can often be exemplified in composition student conferences. When students' keywords (and "thesaurus synonyms") tag no helpful sources, they are completely stymied, unable to explore the meaning or history of the question or otherwise find indirect paths to relevant sources. They seek information from no living sources, walk no library stacks, ask no exploratory questions. Not only do students come back from database searches with the conclusion that "there is no information on this topic" but research librarians also (I have eavesdropped) often quickly reach the same conclusion—all because the technological apparatus of database keywords could not return a quick and direct result. What do we teach students about information, about language, about thought, when we rely so much on the one-trick pony of a searchable database?

IL that can be connected to critical literacy, as sought by the ACRL, has to promote an "intellectual ethic" of the patient pursuit of meaning *through language* but not *corresponding exactly to language*. In contrast, a technologically centered IL "promotes cursory reading, hurried and distracted thinking, and superficial learning" (Carr, 2010, p. 116), partly because language is removed from its human context and atomized to fit the requirements of the machine. But our students have to learn, as one of the key aspects of IL metaliteracy, that "meaning" is not reducible to searchable linguistic "data" (Jackson, 2009, p. 161). Otherwise, how are students going to understand or engage with the language surrounding any of today's complex or socially contested issues? When different sides approach the same problem with different vocabularies, it is only with significant patience, persistence, and trust that they can get to a shared understanding of the problem. They can't even begin to search for thoughtful solutions until they have "clearly and consciously defined the problem" (Carr, 2010, p. 119).

There is no hiding the fact that training students in critical literacy is (and has always been) difficult. As Jackson points out, "We are not born to read" (2009, p. 166). With the memory aid of the printed word, the complexities of problems, ideas, and self-consciousness have all been able to proliferate, leading to an explosion of complex thought in grammatical gymnastics of long, compound-complex sentences (Carr, 2010, p. 107). Critical literacy is not "efficient," it is resource-intensive, and by definition it involves conflicting perspectives, which means it flourishes best in relational and institutional contexts characterized by security and commitment (Jackson, 2009, pp. 149–150). Institutions committed to their students' free speech can encourage disagreement and discovery, not just ideological camps technologically gerrymandered around their vetted search terms.

Jones and Sclater (2010) correctly point out that technology is not destiny, but a particular technological environment does present a restricted range of choices. The technology of multiple-choice questions, for example, presents a restricted and simplified set of choices (4 or 5) while hiding the complexity of the question behind a delineated "right" answer. Such restrictive technological environments make critical literacy difficult by hiding most aspects of an issue and most of the messy approaches to it. No vendor-driven educational product should make necessary complexity *simple* for our students, or make IL pedagogy *easy* for us. We have to stay skeptical of such technological solutions because fighting for a curriculum and a learning environment that moves students toward logical, linear thought—toward metaliteracy—is essential for both Western culture and healthy selfhood.

Literacy for the Sake of Culture

First, without a technological learning environment that enables critical literacy, students will necessarily lose the connections between our culture's past, present, and future. As Postman argues, to learn any academic discipline is really to learn the history of that discipline, how its ideas unfolded as a conversation over time. This also teaches students the rules of engagement and the socially centered use of language in that conversation (1992, p. 190). "There is no definitive history of anything," Postman reminds us, "there are only *histories*, human inventions which do not give us the answer, but give us only those answers called forth by the questions that have been asked" (1992, p. 191). The technocrats may say, with their icon Henry Ford, that "history is bunk," but historical content is the substance of critical thought and is essential for even business and technological innovation.

The business case for critical literacy is compelling. Though universities have been pressured to make students more "career ready," it has been largely overlooked that many business leaders are looking for this broader and deeper humanities education in their hiring (Adler-Kassner, 2014). Even pioneering advertising executives such as Jon Steel (1998) explicitly urge young recruits to read widely and deeply *outside* their fields if they want to develop the acumen to do well *in* their fields (p. 119). Also, as Turkle reports, cutting-edge businesses have been moving away from the supposed "cost savings" of many technologies and moving back to human-centered knowledge (2015, pp. 283–289). In this, business leaders have been more pedagogically savvy than education-reform politicians.

Promoting a literacy-friendly technological environment to foster history-conscious critical thought is also essential for the flourishing of democratic citizenship. As in any age, we face complex problems that are further complicated by their interactions with other complex problems and systems resistant to change—what are now called "wicked problems" (Roberts, 2000). While these problems have often been dealt with in different societies through authoritarian action, the principle of democratic governance requires shared decisions based in shared understandings developed through significant critical thinking in dialogue. This involves understanding the histories *of* and stakeholders *in* the different aspects of the complex problem, the ability to discern and prioritize goals, and the persistence to follow linear chains of reasoning to their ends. And it involves finding and sifting the most relevant and authoritative information for the multiple stakeholders involved. How can we approach the wicked problem of national energy policy and climate change, for example, when all sides approach the problem politically as a zero-sum game instead of a complex policy question that requires cooperation and trade-offs, working through slippery language to shared understanding? It is possible that our current balkanized political climate is a result of our current technological environment, which discourages depth of thought and encourages tribalism. Don't we owe it to our past and future citizens to pursue a technological environment that can support a better critical literacy?

Literacy for a Healthy Self

Second, we should promote the technological media and literacy habits that preserve humans' ethical and emotional well-being. While humans have always been able to see the world through multiple perspectives—enabling ethics—the proliferation of perspectives made possible by the layers of sensibility (of oneself and others) represented in printed text has sharpened that sense of self and other, manifesting in the late modern idea of human rights (Hunt, 2007; Postman, 1992, 1994, pp. 20–36). As Turkle (2015), among others, points out, the practice of literacy teaches us how to be alone with layers of thought, which gives us the resources for empathetic interaction with others. In our current digital culture, though, we are never alone with our thoughts and never allowed to follow a series of thoughts, alone or together, without being interrupted by some completely unrelated media ping. This swimming in the shallows of ideas—with no depth of perspective—has been shown to make us perpetually anxious and to short-circuit the development of empathy for people around us (Carr, 2010; Turkle, 2011, 2015). "Free" to choose between the products and search results marketed to us, we are kept from the deeper freedom of choice that comes with a more literate understanding of the complex questions facing our society.

META(TECH)LITERACY IN THE COMP CLASS

It is in the composition classroom that college students get their first, and sometimes only, unit on IL in the context of critical literacy. There, students are guided not only in how to find sources but also in how to read and engage them critically in their own persuasive writing. While this introductory, general education class does not normally introduce students to the specialized vocabulary and threshold concepts of a particular discipline, it does, ideally, introduce students to the dialogic and exploratory nature of academic inquiry, including the linguistic labor required to interpret sources. The composition class is also set, itself, within the discipline of rhetoric, which has as one of its chief themes how the message is affected by context, including the context of its medium. Thus, in both content and context, the composition class is set up to introduce students to metaliteracy—the awareness and ability to take a step back and choose the best meaning, expression, argument, audience, and medium.

What would teaching a metaliteracy about technological media look like in this composition class IL? First, it would invest *more* time in training students in the use of library databases, not less. Second, it would include a unit of content on the impact of different technological environments on critical literacy, behavior, and our physical bodies. Third, it would model a balanced use of technology by weaving electronics-free requirements and attention exercises into the instructional design of classroom time and assignments.

Databases and Beyond

Investing more time in using database tools means that we need to take the existing frameworks of database training and add at least two things: metaliteracy training and human resources. When all the keywords seem to fail and the search turns up nothing helpful or relevant, IL guides have a golden opportunity to teach IL metaliteracy. Instead of agreeing with students that there is "nothing on the topic," we should point out what is more accurate—that the media of searchable databases are narrowly conceived and prone to failure. We should also take this opportunity to explain *why*, including the problems of reified language, varied approaches to indexing, and contested disciplinary language. We should guide them also in the next, positive, steps toward metaliteracy: the pursuit of serendipitous information through a return to exploratory questioning, browsing in library stacks and other generally disciplinary venues, and, especially, accessing human resources.

Even expert humans are biased and limited in their knowledge of a subject, but *only humans have access to meaning* and *only humans can make leaps of intuition* to make connections between apparently disparate realms of knowledge. Though many of us now are losing our skill at accessing our knowledge networks (Google is so tempting!), networks of humans who know things is still the gold standard for tracking down information and making sense of specific disciplinary problems. Most of our students are unaware of this resource, and most of them are unpracticed in the social skills needed to tap human knowledge networks (Turkle, 2015), except maybe Wikipedia. We have to teach them how to find and approach knowledgeable people in order to get both primary information and the vocabulary that they can plug back into their library and database searches. Incorporating a structured "expert interview" assignment into research assignments would be a practical step toward teaching human resources as one of the broader IL options.

Teach Media's Messages

Second, the composition class should make students aware of the impact of technological media on our bodies, our critical literacy, and our ability to concentrate on long-term projects. I do not have the space to rehearse this data, which has been emphasized by the media ecology tradition, but I have had success in classes using as supplementary texts the material in Turkle's *Alone Together* (2011) and Jackson's *Distracted* (2009). Texts such as these help give depth to the "why" behind what students sometimes feel are Luddite teaching methods.

Practice Better IL Habits

Third, students need help in developing better technological habits. We are deeply habitual and social creatures who tend to follow the path of least resistance despite our knowledge of the more rational and beneficial paths. Composition classes, like weight training classes, should be both painful and habit-forming. What kinds of habits should be taught and practiced in the composition class?

- Required periods of reading and note-taking on sources *without multitasking*, in class and out of class.
- Required interpersonal interviews, marked by synchronic note-taking and postinterview summary.
- Note-taking and drafting using the older technologies of pen/pencil and composition book. This would involve doing some full first drafts by hand, including writing out quotations from sources.
- Library days in which students learn how to browse the general areas of the stacks and how to physically survey the broader context of a discipline or issue. This would include significant time browsing the (normally) untapped resources of the reference section.

- Finding, with the help of an instructor or librarian, a key (physical) book early in the research process, reading it in linear fashion, and taking notes on it.

These, of course, are only a few suggestions, ones that pursue the print literacy values of concentrated attention, serendipity, physical and social engagement, deeper interaction with fewer wholes (instead of many fragmented parts), and "unitasking" (Turkle, 2015, p. 216). A broader approach to IL implementation across the curriculum would invite many more suggestions.

CONCLUSION

Students habituated to a digital media environment of multitasking and interruption are undermined in their ability to achieve critical literacy, especially when IL technologies of the classroom follow the lead of digital industries whose objectives are radically different (Kop, 2012, p. 3). These students need to be told and shown that there are research choices beyond searchable databases, choices both more difficult and more rewarding. The composition class is an ideal starting place to enact the newly robust ACRL focus on critical literacy, but inculcating this metaliteracy must include teaching a broader, messier concept of information, teaching a critical perspective on the messages of search media, and making those understandings real through the practice of different, broader media habits. Media ecology provides a wealth of critical perspectives on information technologies and should thus be used as a resource for IL reform in college composition and cross-disciplinary IL administration.

NOTE

1. Because critical thinking and deep literacy are intimately linked (Ong, 1982), I focus more on the *overlap* between this deep literacy, critical thinking, and the resourced exploration of thought than on any analytical lines of separation between them. In most of this chapter, I refer to this overlap as "critical literacy."

REFERENCES

Adler-Kassner, L. (2014). Liberal learning, professional training, and disciplinarity in the age of educational "reform": Remodeling general education. *College English, 76*(4), 436–457.

Alliance for Childhood. (2004). *Tech tonic: Towards a new literacy of technology*. College Park, MD: Alliance for Childhood.

Association of College and Research Libraries. (2015). *Framework for information literacy for higher education*. Retrieved from http://www.ala.org/acrl/standards/ilframework

Badke, W. (2010). Why information literacy is invisible. *Communications in Information Literacy, 4*(2), 129–141.

Bennett, S., Maton, K. A., & Kervin, L. (2008). The "digital natives" debate: A critical review of the evidence. *British Journal of Educational Technology, 39*(5), 775–786.

Biddix, J. P., Chung, C. J., & Park, H. W. (2015). The hybrid shift: Evidencing a student-driven restructuring of the college classroom. *Computers & Education, 80*, 162–175. https://doi.org/10.1016/j.compedu.2014.08.016

Branch, K. (2017). Review: Literacy hope and the violence of literacy: A bind that ties us. *College English, 79*(4), 407–420.

Carr, N. (2010). *The shallows: What the internet is doing to our brains*. New York: W. W. Norton.

Coonan, E. (2011). A new curriculum for information literacy: Theoretical background: Teaching learning: Perceptions of information literacy. Arcadia Project, Cambridge University Library. Retrieved from https://www.academia.edu/3866681/Teaching_learning_perceptions_of_information_literacy

Hunt, L. (2007). *Inventing human rights: A history.* New York: W. W. Norton.

Jackson, M. (2009). *Distracted: The erosion of attention and the coming dark age.* Amherst, NY: Prometheus Books.

Jones, C., & Sclater, N. (2010). Learning in the age of digital networks. *International Preservation News, 51*, 6–10.

Kolikant, Y. B-D. (2010). Digital natives, better learners? Students' beliefs about how the Internet influenced their ability to learn. *Computers in Human Behavior, 26*, 1384–1391. https://doi.org//10.1016/j.chb.2010.04.012

Kop, R. (2012). The unexpected connection: Serendipity and human mediation in networked learning. *Educational Technology & Society, 15*(2), 2–11.

Liu, O. L., Frankel, L., & Roohr, K. C. (2014). Assessing critical thinking in higher education: Current state and directions for next-generation assessment. ETS Research Report No. RR-14-10, J. Carlson (ed.). https://doi.org/10.1002/ets2.12009

Ong, W. (1982). *Orality and literacy: The technologizing of the word.* London: Routledge.

Postman, N. (1992). *Technopoloy: The surrender of culture to technology.* New York: Vintage Books.

Postman, N. (1994). *The disappearance of childhood.* New York: Vintage Books.

Prensky, M. (2001). Digital natives, digital immigrants, part I. *On the Horizon, 9*(5). Retrieved from http://www.marcprensky.com/writing/Prensky%20-%20Digital%20Natives,%20Digital%20Immigrants%20-%20Part1.pdf

Roberts, N. (2000). Wicked problems and network approaches to resolution. *International Public Management Review, 1*(1), 1–19.

Steel, J. (1998). *Truth, lies, and advertising: The art of account planning.* New York: John Wiley & Sons.

Strate, L. (2004). A media ecology review. *Communication Research Trends, 23*(2), 3–48.

Turkle, S. (2011). *Alone together: Why we expect more from technology and less from each other.* New York: Basic Books.

Turkle, S. (2015). *Reclaiming conversation: The power of talk in a digital age.* New York: Penguin Books.

CHAPTER 5

COMMON DISPOSITIONS AND HABITS OF MIND

The ACRL and WPA Frameworks in Conversation for Tomorrow's Researcher-Writer

James P. Purdy

INTRODUCTION

The work of the writing teacher-scholar and the library and information scientist has become increasingly connected and overlapping in a networked, digital age. Writing teachers and librarians have arguably always been closely connected, especially through the first-year writing course required at most colleges and universities in which students traditionally complete a research project that asks them to use the library's resources. Yet digital technologies like JSTOR, Wikipedia, and Zotero that connect research and writing spaces, as well as a more explicit focus on information literacy practices in approaches to research-writing processes and instruction, have both strengthened and broadened this connection. As contributors to this and the prior volume of *Teaching Information Literacy and Writing Studies* explain, models of first-year writing increasingly seek to link formally instruction in information and verbal/rhetorical literacies in order to give students a more robust approach to information seeking and delivery. Similarly, attention to information literacy has moved beyond the first-year writing course to become a more integral component of students' coursework during their entire postsecondary education.

This chapter argues for writing studies to cultivate connections with library and information science and vice versa by putting the *Framework for Success in Postsecondary Writing* (hereafter WPA *Framework*) into conversation with the *Framework for Information Literacy for Higher Education* (hereafter ACRL *Framework*). That is, the ACRL *Framework* can and should be adopted by writing studies professionals, and the WPA *Framework* can and should be adopted by library and information science professionals.

As Randall McClure and I affirm in the Conclusion to our edited volume *The Future Scholar: Researching and Teaching the Frameworks for Writing and Information Literacy*, both *Frameworks* show considerable agreement about what it will take for college students to be successful researcher-writers (Purdy & McClure, 2016, pp. 308–310). The *Frameworks* thereby provide a view into the attributes and ways of thinking that universities seek to cultivate in students across the curriculum. The WPA *Framework* calls these "habits of mind" (Council of Writing Program Administrators, National Council of Teachers of English, & National Writing Project, 2011, p. 1), and the ACRL *Framework* labels these "dispositions" (Association of College and Research Libraries, 2015, "Introduction"). These habits of mind and dispositions from the *Frameworks* will be the focus of this chapter.

Some brief background on the *Frameworks* can help to situate and substantiate why recognizing linkages among the habits of mind and dispositions is important. As readers may know, the ACRL *Framework*, published in 2015 by the Association of College and Research Libraries (ACRL), advances a revised approach to information literacy, offering six "frames" or central threshold concepts, for this updated definition.[1] Each frame includes a set of knowledge practices, or "demonstrations of ways in which learners can increase their understanding of these information literacy concepts," and a set of dispositions, which the ACRL *Framework* offers as "ways in which to address the affective, attitudinal, or valuing dimension of learning" (ACRL, 2015, "Introduction"). It defines a disposition as "a tendency to act or think in a particular way [. . .] a cluster of preferences, attitudes, and intentions, as well as a set of capabilities that allow the preferences to become realized" (ACRL, 2015, "Introduction," note 6). In the WPA *Framework*, published several years earlier in 2011, the Council of Writing Program Administrators, National Council of Teachers of English, and the National Writing Project (CWPA, NCTE, & NWP) advance and describe the rhetorical skills and habits of mind that they contend are critical for 21st-century students to succeed in college. They define habits of mind as "ways of approaching learning that are both intellectual and practical that will support students' success in a variety of fields and disciplines" (CWPA, NCTE, & NWP, 2011, p. 4). In other words, these habits of mind are applicable not just to first-year writing courses but also to courses across the curriculum. Similarly, the ACRL *Framework* (2015) precedes each list of dispositions with the introduction "Learners who are developing their information literate abilities do the following." Through using such language, both documents suggest that students cultivate dispositions and habits of mind over time rather than learn them once and for all. Considering the ways in which these habits of mind and dispositions speak to each other, then, can help us teach students to approach their learning, writing, and researching activities in ways that prepare them for their future college, career, and civic work.

This chapter begins by highlighting commonalities among the habits of mind and dispositions as they appear in the *Frameworks*. The chapter then considers critiques of the *Frameworks*, offering ways of understanding and using the *Frameworks* that address these concerns. The chapter closes by affirming that writing studies and library and information science professionals can accomplish three important goals for tomorrow's researcher-writer by joining the *Frameworks*.

TWO SIDES OF THE SAME COIN: DISPOSITIONS AND HABITS OF MIND

As shown in Table 5.1, McClure and I (2016b) identified what we see as correspondences among the ACRL *Framework*'s threshold

TABLE 5.1 *Comparing ACRL Framework Threshold Concepts and WPA Framework Habits of Mind*

Threshold Concepts in the ACRL Framework	Habits of Mind in the WPA Framework
Authority Is Constructed and Contextual	Openness, flexibility
Information Creation as a Process	Creativity, metacognition, flexibility
Information Has Value	Responsibility
Research as Inquiry	Curiosity
Scholarship as Conversation	Engagement
Searching as Strategic Exploration	Persistence, creativity, flexibility

Source: McClure & Purdy, 2016b (p. xviii). *The Future Scholar: Researching and Teaching the Frameworks for Writing and Information Literacy*; Copyright © 2016 by the Association for Information Science and Technology (ASIS&T) for Information Today, Inc. Used with permission.

concepts and the WPA *Framework*'s habits of mind. For instance, we stipulated that a student coming to believe Authority Is Constructed and Contextual would cultivate the habits of mind of Openness and Flexibility, a student coming to see Research as Inquiry would cultivate the habit of mind of Curiosity, a student coming to view Scholarship as Conversation would cultivate the habit of mind of Engagement, and so forth.

For my purposes in this chapter, I drill down deeper into the ACRL *Framework*'s threshold concepts to discuss their dispositions. Recognizing the ways in which the habits of mind and dispositions reinforce each other matters for two related reasons. First, these connections shift our focus from what students learn to who they learn to be. This is not to say that the *Frameworks* advance that content is unimportant; it is to say that the *Frameworks* remind us that long after students have forgotten the particular content of our courses, they (can) retain the ways of being in the world that our courses cultivate in them through their writing and information literacy behaviors. Second, that organizations from two distinct disciplines frame in such similar ways the qualities students need for success in postsecondary education reinforces the kind of students our coursework should work to develop, including students who are open, persistent, flexible, and reflective. In a political climate of increased scrutiny on the value of higher education, these connections are a helpful reminder of what are, can, or should be fundamental goals of higher education.

Table 5.2 shows which ACRL *Framework* dispositions resonate with each WPA *Framework* habit of mind.[2] It reveals that the WPA habits of mind of Openness, Persistence, Flexibility, and Metacognition are particularly emphasized in the ACRL dispositions, with five of the six frames invoking them. Though all habits of mind are heartily represented, these four stand out as particularly important for students, especially with respect to their information literacy development. This resonance suggests that writing and library instructors might particularly emphasize the development of these habits of mind for research-writing projects.

Table 5.2 also sheds light on which habits of mind correlate with each frame. For example, the dispositions for ACRL's threshold concept Authority Is Constructed and Contextual echo the WPA habits of mind of Curiosity, Openness, Persistence, Flexibility, and Metacognition. In other words, students are more likely to understand that Authority Is Constructed and Contextual if they are curious, open, persistent, flexible, and metacognitive. Thus, helping students develop these attributes can likewise help them take a more productive approach to source authority.

The table can also be read to identify which WPA habits of mind appear across ACRL frames. For instance, the habit of mind of Engagement resonates across several frames, including Information Creation as a Process, Information Has Value, and Scholarship as Conversation, suggesting that helping students be engaged learners benefits not only their writing and rhetorical skills, but also their ways of finding and evaluating information. That is, when we help students learn to engage, they are more likely not only to write and research more effectively, but also to learn the ways of thinking about writing and information that will benefit them in higher education and beyond.

TABLE 5.2 *WPA Framework Habits of Mind and Corresponding ACRL Framework Dispositions*

	ACRL Frames and Dispositions*					
WPA Habits of Mind†	Authority Is Constructed and Contextual	Information Creation as a Process	Information Has Value	Research as Inquiry	Scholarship as Conversation	Searching as Strategic Exploration
Curiosity	**Question traditional notions** of granting authority	—	—	**Value intellectual curiosity in developing questions**	—	—
Openness	**Develop and maintain an open mind...**	**Understand that different methods** of information dissemination with different purposes **are available**	—	**Consider research as open-ended exploration and engagement** with information **Maintain an open mind...**	**Suspend judgment** on the value of a particular piece of scholarship until the larger context for the scholarly conversation is understood	**Understand that first attempts at searching do not always produce adequate results**
Engagement	—	**Value the process** of matching an information need with an appropriate product	**Value the skills, time, and effort** needed to produce knowledge **See themselves as contributors** to their information marketplace...	—	**See themselves as contributors** to scholarship...	—
Creativity	—	**Resist the tendency** to equate format with the underlying creation process	—	**Value ... learning new investigative methods**	—	**Exhibit ... creativity**
Persistence	**Motivate themselves** to find authoritative sources...	Are **inclined to seek out** characteristics of information products...	—	**Value persistence...**	**Seek out conversations** taking place in their research area	**Persist in the face of challenges...**

(Continued)

TABLE 5.2 *(Continued)*

WPA Habits of Mind†	ACRL Frames and Dispositions*					
	Authority Is Constructed and Contextual	Information Creation as a Process	Information Has Value	Research as Inquiry	Scholarship as Conversation	Searching as Strategic Exploration
Responsibility	—	—	**Respect** the original ideas of others	**Follow ethical and legal guidelines …**	**Understand the responsibility** that comes with entering the conversation …	—
Flexibility	**Recognize** the value of **diverse ideas and worldviews**	**Accept** that the creation of information may begin initially through communicating in **a range of formats or modes** **Accept the ambiguity** surrounding the potential value of information creation expressed in emerging formats or modes	—	**Value … adaptability, and flexibility …** **Seek multiple perspectives** during information gathering and assessment	**Recognize** that scholarly conversations take place in **various venues**	**Exhibit mental flexibility…**
Metacognition	**Develop awareness** of the importance of assessing content with a skeptical stance and **with a self-awareness …** Are conscious that maintaining these attitudes and actions **requires frequent self-evaluation**	—	**Are inclined to examine** their own information privilege	**Recognize their own** intellectual or experiential **limitations**	**Recognize that systems privilege authorities** and that not having fluency in the language and processes of a discipline disempowers their ability to participate and engage	**Realize that information sources vary greatly** in content and format and have varying relevant and value … **Know when** enough information completes the information task

* Text in these columns of Table 5.2 is quoted directly from the ACRL *Framework* (2015).

† Text in this column of Table 5.2 is from the WPA *Framework* (2011).

THE CHALLENGES OF CAPTURING LITERATE PERFORMANCE: CRITIQUES OF THE *FRAMEWORKS*

While both the ACRL and WPA *Frameworks* have been widely taken up, they have not been without criticism. This section considers some of these concerns and responds to them in light of viewing the *Frameworks* together. The goal is not to dismiss these concerns or prove them wrong but to offer dialogue among the *Frameworks* as one lens for addressing them. In 2012 *College English* published "Symposium: On the *Framework for Success in Postsecondary Writing*," which included the text of the WPA *Framework* itself as well as responses from six writing studies teacher-scholars; these comprise the critiques I review here as they represent the prevailing concerns. In 2014 several New Jersey librarians (Berg et al.) published online an open letter to the ACRL board expressing concerns that they hoped would be addressed in the final draft of the ACRL *Framework*. These, together with critiques discussed by historian and librarian Ian Beilin (2015), comprise the ACRL concerns I address here as they also represent the prevailing critical responses. Critiques of each *Framework* are remarkably similar; therefore, to enact the chapter's call to pair the *Frameworks*, I address the critiques together. These critiques focus on each *Framework*'s premise, its form and language, its lack of specific implementation and assessment guidelines, and its omissions.

Each *Framework* was critiqued for its premises. For the WPA *Framework*, one such premise is that habits of mind and rhetorical practices can be identified and correlated with higher education readiness and success. For instance, rhetorical scholar and writing program administrator Kristine Hansen (2012) argues against the idea of universal "college readiness" and instead argues for the importance of local context (p. 542). That is, she challenges the notion that universal statements can be made about what students need to be successful in college. Moreover, Hansen contends that the habits of mind outlined in the WPA *Framework* do not necessarily correlate with improved writing. In other words, she professes that students can possess the habits of mind without being good writers (pp. 541–542). For her, then, to claim that these habits of mind prepare students for college-level writing is disingenuous.

Professional writing and rhetorical theory scholar Bruce McComiskey (2012) challenges another premise of the WPA *Framework*: its presentation as an antidote to the Common Core State Standards (CCSS). In their introduction to the *College English* Symposium, members of the WPA *Framework* task force, Peggy O'Neill, Linda Adler-Kassner, Cathy Fleischer, and Anne-Marie Hall (2012), assert that though the CCSS claim to prepare students to be college ready, they failed to include "the voices of college writing teachers and researchers" when drafted (p. 522). McComiskey, however, affirms that the WPA *Framework* and CCSS agree significantly regarding "what kinds of students will succeed after high school" and calls for viewing the WPA *Framework* as supporting the CCSS rather than rivaling it (pp. 537–538).

In their "Open Letter Regarding the *Framework for Information Literacy for Higher Education*," Cara Berg et al. (2014) challenge the premise of the ACRL *Framework* as a document that replaces the Information Literacy Competency Standards for Higher Education (IL Standards). They reject the notion that the IL Standards should be replaced, arguing instead that the IL Standards are not outdated, that they already work well in New Jersey libraries, and that standards documents are necessary for information literacy in particular and in higher education more broadly (pp. 1–3). In his analysis of the ACRL *Framework* from a critical information literacy perspective, Beilin (2015) takes issue less with the absence of standards in the ACRL *Framework* and more with its basis in threshold concepts. For him, threshold concepts "may end up functioning as the means to merely reinforce disciplinary boundaries and institutional hierarchies. [. . .] If threshold concepts are cultural constructs, then a critical information literacy must move beyond them somehow." He worries that the ACRL *Framework* asks students, as individuals, to "master" the "world of information" rather than to question, challenge, or change it ("Critical"). Beilin (2015) contends that scholarly research is not, in fact, a conversation, as the ACRL *Framework* professes in the frame Scholarship as Conversation ("Critical").

From a rhetorical perspective, these objections indicate that the *Frameworks* are not exigent for their critics: The *Frameworks* do not meet the needs they purport to meet. This first set of objections points to a desire for *Frameworks* that are both more particular (e.g., more specific to writing proficiency) and more universal (e.g., more applicable to challenges to hegemonic systems). Such is a particularly difficult critique to redress. Librarian Barbara Fister (2015), after expressing initial concerns about the ACRL *Framework*, offers one response:

> If we focus too much on how to get stuff done, we run the risk of encouraging a linear process, a smash-and-grab collection of sources that will subsequently be mashed into a paper full of patchwriting. If we focus too much on concepts, we run the risk of losing students who are understandably concerned about getting stuff done. The sweet spot is somewhere in the middle, where students aren't defeated by practical tasks but where they see the bigger picture.

She reminds us that neither extreme is helpful, and the *Frameworks* seek to exist in this "sweet spot."

Interpreting the *Frameworks* within local, situated contexts can also help answer this first set of concerns. For example, the ACRL *Framework* might be used with the IL Standards in a particular library, and the WPA *Framework* might be used with the CCSS in a particular preservice teacher training program. Moreover, putting the *Frameworks* themselves into dialogue can respond to Beilin's (2015) concern that scholarly research is not a conversation ("Critical") by enacting that very frame.

A second critique centers on the form and language of each *Framework*. Berg et al. (2014), for instance, contend that the ACRL *Framework* is accessible only to faculty in a few disciplines (namely, "education, psychology, and writing") because it relies heavily on "educational jargon that does not resonate with librarians" (p. 3).[3] Berg et al. (2014) do not specify what language they find inaccessible, though their attention to threshold concepts suggests that this vocabulary may be the culprit (see Beilin, 2015, "Variety"). Berg et al. (2014) also critique the ACRL *Framework* for a lack of grammatically parallel structure in the frames themselves, charging that such a document should reflect the best of academic writing (p. 3). Writing center scholar and director Carol Severino (2012) points to similar structural and language problems in the WPA *Framework*. For example, she objects that the WPA *Framework* defines conventions in terms of "disciplinary variation" rather than "general language abilities," or, for her preferably, a "minimal 'threshold' of English language proficiency" (pp. 535, 536). She also asserts that the WPA *Framework*'s "Experiences with Writing, Reading, and Critical Analysis" are incorrectly ordered, the *Framework* overuses lists, and it lacks clear connections between its two primary sections: the "Habits of Mind" and the "Experiences with Writing, Reading, and Critical Analysis" (pp. 535, 544–545).

A third critique is that the *Frameworks* lack precise guidelines for how to use them. Urban education and English professor Judith Summerfield and urban education and secondary education professor Philip M. Anderson (2012), for instance, charge that the WPA *Framework* fails to offer guidance for how to implement it; thus, they label it "A Framework Adrift" (p. 544), riffing off the title of Richard Arum and Josipa Roksa's (2011) anti–higher education polemic *Academically Adrift*. In their "Open Letter," Berg et al. (2014) similarly claim that the ACRL *Framework*, written as a "theoretical document," cannot be implemented and, therefore, cannot be assessed (pp. 2–3). To them, this lack of concrete assessment risks "making information literacy irrelevant to the learning outcomes emphasis in higher education" (p. 3).

These second and third sets of critiques reflect criticism of the "*Framework* document" genre as much as the documents' content. That is, they illustrate a desire for the *Frameworks* to do work that, generically, they do not do. A desire for more direct and precise implementation suggestions is understandable. Indeed, this wish for the *Frameworks* to offer more explicit applications led McClure and me to edit *The Future Scholar* (2016a), which seeks to offer examples of concrete strategies for implementing and assessing the *Frameworks*. The *Frameworks*, however, do not purport to provide such examples; in fact, they resist doing so (though "Appendix 1" of the ACRL *Framework* [2015] and the final paragraph of the introduction to the WPA *Framework* [2011] each offer some broad suggestions; see Purdy & McClure, 2016b, pp. 312–313). As McClure and I put it, the *Frameworks* "are intentionally written to move beyond outcomes and to offer guidance rather than checklists" (p. 308). For instance, the Introduction to the ACRL *Framework* (ACRL, 2015) clarifies, "Neither the knowledge practices nor the dispositions that support each concept are intended to prescribe what local institutions should do in using the *Framework*; each library and its partners on campus will need to deploy these frames to best fit their own situation, including designing learning outcomes." The WPA *Framework* (CWPA, NCTE, & NWP, 2011) similarly clarifies its goal by distinguishing itself from the CWPA Outcomes Statement, which it notes offers concrete outcomes for first-year writing instruction (p. 3). Both *Frameworks* present themselves as certain kinds of texts that do certain kinds of work. Accepting the *Frameworks* on their own terms, then, asks us to look past the desire for out-of-the-box curricula, assignments, or activities. It asks us to do the work of creating them for our own local contexts.

A final critique is that, beyond direct guidelines for implementation and assessment, other important elements are missing from the *Frameworks*. For instance, Berg et al. (2014) indicate that they still want standards to be part of the ACRL *Framework*. They claim standards "have practical applications that are universally understood" and are necessary because " '[s]tandards' are now part of the vernacular" of the educational climate at the time of their writing (pp. 1–2). Likewise, Severino (2012) identifies what she sees as four troubling omissions from the WPA *Framework*:

1. Acknowledgement of students' differential access to resources that can cultivate the habits of mind and experiences it champions
2. Habits of "a good classroom citizen," particularly with regard to how to conduct peer reviews
3. Emotional skills (e.g., empathy)
4. "[M]ulticultural and global literacy," including awareness and knowledge of how to research "the plight of populations involved in controversies examined in class" (pp. 535–536)

For her, a document claiming to identify what students need to be successful in higher education should also include the emotional and civic habits needed, as well as acknowledge the uneven access students have to resources to develop these habits. In their separate responses, McComiskey and English instructor and scholar Patrick Sullivan similarly suggest additional habits of mind be included in the WPA *Framework*: independence (McComiskey, 2012, p. 537) and humility and character/grit (Sullivan, 2012, pp. 550–551). This criticism about missing habits of mind is especially pointed in Summerfield and Anderson's (2012) response. They contend that the WPA *Framework* lacks rationale for why it attends to habits of mind in the first place and fails to include the eight additional habits of mind identified by education professor emeritus Arthur Costa and education consultant Bene Kallick as necessary for workplace and school success (p. 545). This critique resonates with Severino's concern, particularly as one of the habits of mind that Summerfield and Anderson lament that the WPA *Framework* omits from Costa and Kallick's list is "listening to others—with understanding and empathy" (p. 545).

Affirming the WPA habits of mind and ACRL dispositions as necessary but not sufficient for higher education success would be a helpful clarification to address these concerns. Another might be noting that the habits of mind and dispositions identified reflect those most relevant for writing and information-seeking activities. That is, while they apply to writing and information literacy behaviors throughout college, they do not seek to represent an exhaustive list of all students will need to be and do to be successful in college.

Taken together, these four sets of critiques reveal several important aspects of information literacy and writing that support pairing the *Frameworks*. Both disciplines encompass content knowledge, skills, and ways of being in the world. Students, in other words, must know, do, and be in certain ways to be effective researcher-writers. However, both writing and research are (too) often limited either to knowing the right templates or databases or to following a particular linear step-by-step sequence. The *Frameworks* can remind us of (the necessity of) that "be" component. Moreover, both fields are "owned" by disciplinary specialists but also fall within the purview of the entire higher education community—arguably more so than many (or even most) other disciplines. In other words, information literacy and writing are unique components of higher education. Students must call upon them throughout their higher education experience—indeed, arguably in every course. It is this unique widespread reach that makes information literacy and writing both fraught and exciting—and that make them need each other.

CULTIVATING CONNECTIONS FOR TOMORROW'S RESEARCHER-WRITER

In providing instruction based on joining the two *Frameworks*, writing studies professionals and librarians can accomplish three important goals for tomorrow's researcher-writer. The first goal is to shift the assessment landscape to attend to who as well as what, that is, to how students think and be in the world rather than only or primarily what they produce. Certainly products and artifacts of learning are important. But the *Frameworks* remind us that we educate people—people whom we want to train to gather, evaluate, and use information to think, write, and create in ways that prepare them for the complexities, challenges, and opportunities that come with being informed and responsible global citizens in an interconnected digital world.

The second goal is to model interdisciplinary/cross-disciplinary collaboration, to move beyond a siloed approach to educating students that helps them see connections among their coursework. Noting the commonalities across the *Frameworks* can help reinforce to students that they can and should carry particular approaches to learning across individual classes, courses, and disciplines. A compartmentalized approach to learning is inadequate for today's students. For instance, in much university coursework, research is addressed in a separate unit, positioned at the end of a course or sequence of courses, particularly the first-year writing course. Even for specific assignments, students are instructed to march through a linear process that separates research and writing: formulate a thesis, find scholarly sources to support that thesis, and then write a paper. This model disconnects research from writing, artificially separates the academic from the nonacademic, and misrepresents how knowledge is created. This compartmentalization incorrectly leads students to believe that research and writing are wholly separate and separable, that they are uninformed by each other. However, effective writing and research respond to each other, and we need to prepare students to see these activities as cyclical and recursive in knowledge production. Pairing the *Frameworks* does so explicitly.

The third goal is to facilitate transfer. Because the *Frameworks* do not focus on one particular course, instruction based in them is limited less by the strictures of one semester. The key terms and ideas reflected in the habits of mind and dispositions can help students connect old and new knowledge because recognition of learning as ongoing, situated, and contextual is built in to the *Frameworks*. Such instruction can help equip students to carry what they learn throughout their college career (and ideally beyond) because it becomes part of who they are as meaning makers.

Some practical suggestions for pairing the *Frameworks* include:

- Acquaint students with the *Frameworks*. Ask them to read what has been written about them.
- Introduce faculty to the *Framework* documents in workshops or other professional development activities. Discuss the *Frameworks* as ways to help students achieve the goals for research-writing courses, particularly in writing across the curriculum or writing in the disciplines programs.

- Include on an assignment prompt which habit(s) of mind and disposition(s) that assignment seeks to cultivate in students.
- Use Table 5.2 to help design research-writing assignments and activities that cultivate particular habits of mind and dispositions. See Emily A. Wierszewski's (2016) "Finding Their Voices: Comics and Synthesis in First-Year Research-Writing" for an example from a first-year writing course.
- Do the same for program curricula. Map out which habit(s) of mind and disposition(s) a program's courses help students develop. See Angela Messenger, Hillary Fuhrman, Joseph Palardy, and Tod Porter's (2016) "Adapting the VALUE Rubrics to Build a ROAD to Curriculum Mapping" for an example of using the *Frameworks*, together with the VALUE (Valid Assessment of Learning in Undergraduate Education) rubrics, to accomplish this work.
- Ask students to explain, through a reflective essay, introductory memo, or other assignment, the ways in which they developed and/or applied particular habits of mind and dispositions when completing a project.

This ending gesture to the practical is not incidental. Liberal arts subjects like writing and information literacy are often criticized for lacking practical value and application (e.g., Crane, 2011; Flaherty, 2014; Neem, 2012). The *Frameworks* remind us, however, that such disciplines have practical benefits precisely because they prepare students not just for one particular disciplinary competence or career. Rather, they prepare students to be people in the world who use and produce information and create and communicate in ways that demonstrate audience awareness, reasoned analysis, and ethical judgment. In the words of authors of the Association of American College and Universities report *Greater Expectations: A New Vision for Learning as a Nation Goes to College* (2002), this work develops "just those capacities needed by every thinking adult" (Ramaley et al., 2002, p. 26). Instruction grounded in the *Frameworks* helps make this development more visible.

NOTES

1. Given the ACRL *Framework*'s attention to threshold concepts, writing studies professionals might ask why this chapter juxtaposes the ACRL *Framework* with the WPA *Framework* rather than Linda Adler-Kassner and Elizabeth Wardle's edited collection *Naming What We Know: Threshold Concepts of Writing Studies* (2015), as it explicitly addresses threshold concepts. That collection, however, explains the ways of thinking privileged in the discipline of writing studies—that is, is directed at writing studies professionals and novice academics rather than undergraduate students more broadly. The WPA *Framework*, like the ACRL *Framework*, applies to postsecondary students across disciplines.
2. Others, of course, might identify different connections or link each disposition with multiple habits of mind; however, for my purposes in this chapter, I match each disposition with the single habit of mind it most echoes. Language in the disposition that reinforces the habit of mind I selected is boldfaced. For space, some dispositions are excerpted. Table 5.2 is organized by WPA habits of mind not to privilege those over the ACRL dispositions but because some dispositions do not correspond with any habits of mind (so not all dispositions are included in the table).

3. Berg et al.'s (2014) explicit mention of writing specialists (p. 3) perhaps reinforces why writing studies professionals would do well to take up the ACRL *Framework* alongside the WPA *Framework*.

REFERENCES

Adler-Kassner, L., & Wardle, E. (2015). *Naming what we know: Threshold concepts of writing studies*. Boulder, CO: Utah State University Press.

Arum, R., & Roksa, J. (2011). *Academically adrift: Limited learning on college campuses*. Chicago: University of Chicago Press.

Association of College and Research Libraries. (2015). *Framework for information literacy for higher education*. Retrieved from www.ala.org/acrl/standards/ilframework

Beilin, I. (2015, February 25). Beyond the threshold: Conformity, resistance, and the ACRL information literacy framework for higher education. *In the library with the lead pipe*. Retrieved from www.inthelibrarywiththeleadpipe.org/2015/beyond-the-threshold-conformity-resistance-and-the-aclr-information-literacy-framework-for-higher-education/

Berg, C., et al. (2014). An open letter regarding the *Framework for information literacy for higher education*. Retrieved from https://docs.google.com/document/d/1Q3PCZU2c39tmT8fGYPLOCOZFxqLwgCBtRkYCsVpfGSc/edit?pli=1

Council of Writing Program Administrators, National Council of Teachers of English, & National Writing Project. (2011). *Framework for success in postsecondary writing*. Retrieved from wpacouncil.org/framework

Crane, M. (2011, January 17). Stop defending the liberal arts. *Inside Higher Ed*. Retrieved from https://www.insidehighered.com/views/2011/01/17/mary_crane_on_a_different_way_to_help_the_liberal_arts

Fister, B. (2015, January 22). The information literacy standards/framework debate. Library babel fish. *Inside Higher Ed*. Retrieved from https://www.insidehighered.com/blogs/library-babel-fish/information-literacy-standardsframework-debate

Flaherty, C. (2014, October 20). Doing themselves in? *Inside Higher Ed*. Retrieved from https://www.insidehighered.com/news/2014/10/20/conference-speakers-say-liberal-arts-must-return-purer-form-survive

Hansen, K. (2012). The *Framework for success in postsecondary writing*: Better than the competition, still not all we need. *College English, 74*(6), 540–543.

McClure, R., & Purdy, J. P. (Eds.). (2016a). *The future scholar: Researching and teaching the frameworks for writing and information literacy*. Medford, NJ: Information Today.

McClure, R., & Purdy, J. P. (2016b). Introduction: The frameworks and the future scholar. In R. McClure & J. P. Purdy (Eds.), *The future scholar: Researching and teaching the frameworks for writing and information literacy* (pp. xv–xxvii). Medford, NJ: Information Today.

McComiskey, B. (2012). Bridging the divide: The (puzzling) *Framework* and the transition from K–12 to college writing instruction. *College English, 74*(6), 537–540.

Messenger, A., Fuhrman, H., Palardy, J., & Porter, T. (2016). Adapting the VALUE rubrics to build a ROAD to curriculum mapping. In R. McClure & J. P. Purdy (Eds.), *The future scholar: Researching and teaching the frameworks for writing and information literacy* (pp. 273–306). Medford, NJ: Information Today.

Neem, J. (2012, October 23). The liberal arts, economic value, and leisure. *Inside Higher Ed*. Retrieved from https://www.insidehighered

.com/views/2012/10/23/dont-make-economic-case-liberal-arts-essay

O'Neill, P., Adler-Kassner, L., Fleischer, C., & Hall, A. (2012). Creating the *Framework for success in postsecondary writing*. *College English*, *74*(6), 520–524.

Purdy, J. P., & McClure, R. (2016). Conclusion: Moving forward with the frameworks and the future scholar. In R. McClure & J. P. Purdy (Eds.), *The future scholar: Researching and teaching the frameworks for writing and information literacy* (pp. 307–316). Medford, NJ: Information Today.

Ramaley, J. A., et al. (2002). *Greater expectations: A new vision for learning as a nation goes to college*. Association of American Colleges and Universities. Retrieved from https://www.aacu.org/sites/default/files/files/publications/GreaterExpectations.pdf

Severino, C. (2012). The problems of articulation: Uncovering more of the composition curriculum. *College English*, *74*(6), 533–536.

Sullivan, P. (2012). Essential habits of mind for college readiness. *College English*, *74*(6), 547–551.

Summerfield, J., & Anderson, P. M. (2012). A framework adrift. *College English*, *74*(6), 544–547.

Wierszewski, E. A. (2016). Finding their voices: Comics and synthesis in first-year research-writing. In R. McClure & J. P. Purdy (Eds.), *The future scholar: Researching and teaching the frameworks for writing and information literacy* (pp. 155–175). Medford, NJ: Information Today.

PART II

Information Literacy as a Rhetorical Skill

CHAPTER 6

USING BEAM TO INTEGRATE INFORMATION LITERACY AND WRITING

A Framework With Cases

Joseph Bizup
Melissa Cherry
Kundai Chirindo
Rhonda V. Gray
Autumn Haag
Kay Halasek
Ken Liss
Kate Rubick

In 2008, Joseph Bizup proposed a new vocabulary, BEAM, to describe the different ways in which writers use sources and data in academic writing: *background* for information a writer accepts as fact and expects readers to accept as fact as well (at least provisionally); *exhibit* for materials a writer offers for interpretation or analysis; *argument* for sources whose claims a writer engages or responds to; *method* for materials that provide a writer with procedures, modes of analysis, or framing terminologies (Bizup, 2008). Students and teachers in writing classes, he suggests, are not well served by the conventional terms for sources—primary, secondary, tertiary—because these terms characterize sources according to their proximity to the topic or object of research rather than according to the rhetorical purposes of the researcher and writer: "reality" is represented by primary sources, which are interpreted in secondary sources, which in turn are summarized and synthesized in tertiary sources. These conventional terms likewise suit some disciplines—history and literary studies especially—better than others and contribute to a bias in writing curricula toward treating source-based research as the paradigm for research generally. BEAM, in contrast, identifies sources and data according to how writers *use* them: writers *rely* on their background sources, in the sense that they (at least provisionally) accept them as true and implicitly ask their readers to do the same; they *interpret*, *analyze*, or *evaluate* exhibits, which includes deploying various sorts of data as evidence; they *engage* or *respond to* arguments, thus orchestrating and participating in intellectual "conversations"; they *follow*, *invoke*, or *draw on* methods.

Because BEAM names rhetorical actions performed in all sorts of researched writing, it provides a discipline-neutral model of the "ecology" of sources and data in academic arguments. Across fields of study, writers respond to past arguments either by reinterpreting exhibits presented by other scholars and researchers or by introducing new exhibits into the conversation, using background to establish common ground and drawing on methods of analysis and interpretation sanctioned by the discourse communities to which their arguments are addressed. Moreover, the four components of BEAM align with four defining dimensions of intellectual disciplines: the common knowledge practitioners, scholars, and researchers share (*background*); the subjects they study (*exhibits*); the debates in which they engage (*arguments*); the techniques, theories, and perspectives they employ (*methods*).[1] Because of this generality, BEAM is an attractive framework not only for teaching researched writing and argumentation but also for facilitating transfer of rhetorical knowledge and capacities from the writing classroom to other contexts.

In its original conception, however, BEAM "black-boxes" the activity of research to concentrate exclusively on the moves of research-based writing, and while this narrowing of focus may have heuristic value, it also led at least one librarian to cite Bizup's article as an example of the unfortunate tendency of writing studies scholars to ignore the large literature on information literacy in the field of library science (Veach, 2012b). Since the article's publication, however, scholars and practitioners in both fields have become increasingly aware of one another's work and have championed a more comprehensive approach to fostering information literacy predicated on the genuine integration of research and writing as both activities and areas of instruction, and several have specifically noted BEAM's utility for furthering this project (Jones, 2012; Nutefall & Ryder, 2010; Shields, 2014; Thomas & Hodges, 2015; Veach, 2012a).

This chapter contributes to this conversation by documenting ongoing efforts to develop such integrated approaches to information literacy at four very different institutions. At Boston University, BEAM is used to facilitate collaboration between the library and the College of Arts & Sciences Writing Program. The vocabulary is introduced in Writing Program classes and is used in the program's professional development seminars to facilitate course design. Writing Program and library faculty have also collaborated to integrate information literacy more fully into writing classes and to develop such resources as course-specific research guides organized around BEAM. At Lewis & Clark College, an instructional librarian has partnered with a Rhetoric and Media Studies professor to implement a BEAM-based approach to research and writing in a methods class for majors. At Roxbury Community College, the Honors Program and library are using BEAM to connect students' classroom work to their library experiences and also to frame both course outcomes and assessment rubrics. At Ohio State University, BEAM serves as a common conceptual frame across three units foundational to undergraduate student success in writing and information literacy: University Libraries, the University Writing Center, and the Second-Year Writing Program. Library resources, Writing Center tutor training, and Writing Program assignments and activities are all informed by BEAM, creating a cohesive approach to teaching and learning.

BOSTON UNIVERSITY

The College of Arts & Sciences Writing Program at Boston University (BU), which Bizup directed from 2008 to 2016, offers a two-semester sequence of theme-based writing seminars through which most BU students have traditionally satisfied their general-education writing requirements. The first course in this sequence (WR 100 through the spring of 2018, now WR 120) introduces students to responsible academic argumentation; the second course (WR 150/151/152 in different versions) builds on the first and emphasizes college-level research. Since 2018, these two seminars have fulfilled (and, in fact, were the model for) the First-Year Writing Seminar and Writing, Research, and Inquiry requirements in BU's new general education curriculum, the BU Hub.

The Writing Program and Boston University Libraries have long worked together, especially in the context of this second course, but historically this collaboration was largely between individuals: writing instructors were simply paired with librarians, and these pairs were left to determine for themselves how to approach the teaching of research. While some of these pairings blossomed into sustained partnerships, most were more limited, with instructors consulting only sporadically with their librarians and librarians delivering "one-shot" library sessions for writing enduring.

What was missing was a common intellectual framework that could inform the institutional partnership between the Writing Program and library and allow it to reach its potential. While many but not all writing instructors had been using BEAM in their classes, librarians remained largely unaware of it. The way BEAM was positioned within the institution, in other words, paralleled the focus on writing and the "black-boxing" of research that characterizes Bizup's 2008 article.

Since 2014, however, BEAM has increasingly served to support stronger collaboration between the library and the Writing Program in integrating the teaching of writing and research. This development was driven in part by the library's early embrace of the Association of College and Research Libraries' *Framework for Information Literacy in Higher Education,* which the library was using even before its final adoption by the ACRL board in January 2016. BEAM and the ACRL *Framework* share an emphasis on context and rhetorical purpose in their treatment of information sources, and this common ground has improved communication and collaboration on both individual and institutional levels. Discussions among and between individual librarians and writing instructors have produced a richer understanding of the possibilities for integrating information literacy into the writing classroom, and both the Writing Program and library have created structured opportunities and resources to encourage and capitalize on this development. For example, in the spring of 2015, some 25 librarians and Writing Program faculty came together in a three-session seminar on writing and information literacy. Participants read and discussed selected scholarship from both writing studies and library science, including the *Framework*, and also shared their own approaches. A number of writing faculty are using BEAM to pursue learning outcomes based on the language of the *Framework* in their individual sections, and the library has developed a course guide template for WR 150/151/152 classes that uses the BEAM model to present library resources.

Within this context, librarians and writing faculty have worked together to develop structured library sessions, activities, and exercises organized in terms of BEAM. For example, instructors teaching sections of a WR 150 seminar titled "BU and the Culture of College" collaborated with a librarian to develop an exhibit-focused exercise they called the Library Challenge, which asks students to use a range of library resources—including newspaper databases, a public opinion archive, online collections of documentary films and TV news broadcasts, and an image database—to identify potential exhibits beyond what they would ordinarily come across on the Web or in the stacks.[2] The exercise introduces students to the range of resources available to them at BU, but it also does more than that by leading students to see how an exhibit, in the words of the assignment, "fits into a larger *history* or *system*, or how it compares to or contrasts with other things like it." It demonstrates how exhibits can raise questions, leading to potential arguments and helping students "to discover potentially interesting avenues for further research."

Likewise, custom BEAM-based library guides have been produced for a number of Writing Program courses.[3] The library guide for the course "The American Family: 1950 to Today," one of many that organized resources according to BEAM, exemplifies the strengths of the approach. The instructional librarian who developed the guide met twice with the class, once to provide an overview of library resources such as the university's Primo-based discovery system and subject databases and a second time to work with students as they used these resources to investigate particular topics. The instructor's directions to students used BEAM to emphasize the interaction of different types of sources and data and the iterative and integrated nature of the research and writing processes. Rather than beginning with a topic, students were encouraged to start with an exhibit, or with multiple exhibits in conversation with each other, and then work their way toward questions and topics that would be fresh and surprising. "Research," the instructor wrote to her students, "is a creative process: be open-minded, creative, and free at first! If you go in thinking you know what you're going to argue, you'll miss the whole point. . . . You may begin with research questions to guide you, but your research will lead you in unexpected directions, and the resources available to you will guide you to unexpected places." This approach to inquiry—open-ended yet purposeful—is what the *Framework* and BEAM both aim to inspire.

Some librarians nevertheless remain ambivalent about BEAM's efficacy as a general framework for cultivating information literacy, noting that students rarely encounter it outside of the Writing Program. As one writes, "I can see the value of it in terms of helping students understand the process of scholarly inquiry, but I sometimes wonder whether this terminology, so different than what is used in other classes and scholarly venues (exhibit rather than primary source, etc.), might be confusing rather than helpful in some cases." A response to such objections is that BEAM, while novel, need not supplant a more traditional terminology. Rather, it can complement this terminology by foregrounding rhetorical purpose in a way that the traditional terminology does not. "I have used this approach [BEAM] in teaching information literacy and in student research consultations outside of the WR classes because it is so clear and practical," comments a librarian in the Music Library: "The BEAM approach makes explicit both how to look for different types of materials and, more importantly, why to look for different types. When I work with students individually, it helps in narrowing down not just the topic to research but what kinds of information sources are most useful for different stages of research and writing."

ROXBURY COMMUNITY COLLEGE

At Roxbury Community College (RCC), a small, urban community college in Boston with a majority of nontraditional students, BEAM has similarly been used to structure collaboration between the library and the Honors Program. The program is governed by the Honors Committee comprising faculty and staff from a range of disciplines responsible for vetting proposals for Honors projects and for fostering a community of practice characterized by strong relationships between students and their faculty sponsors. For example, committee members meet with Honors students and their faculty sponsors to provide feedback on students' annotated bibliographies and initial research questions. These meetings with a third party dramatize the public nature of research and often lead to revisions and refinements that make for better projects.

Despite this structure, the Honors Committee was troubled by the diversity of approaches to teaching research and writing that often compromised the effective use of sources and data in students' writing. While it was clear that both students and faculty sponsors were diligent in their work, with students conducting thorough literature reviews with guidance from their sponsors, students nevertheless persisted in presenting sources as "add-ons" to their arguments rather than entering into genuine conversation with them. In other words, the rhetorical value of the sources was mostly neglected. Given this emphasis on claims over conversation, too many Honors students failed to translate their sophisticated research materials into strong academic writing.

To address this challenge, the program in August 2015 adopted BEAM as a common framework for teaching research and

The sources:	The sources:	The sources:
• demonstrate awareness of their functions (BEAM) based on writer's posture toward the sources • accurately support the argument • are followed by accurate parenthetical citations in either MLA or APA format	• show some awareness of their functions (BEAM) • mildly support the argument • are followed by some errors in citations	• lack awareness of their functions (BEAM) • do not support the argument • are followed by either incorrect or no citations

Figure 6.1 Research paper rubric.

academic writing. The BEAM vocabulary was added to the Honors faculty handbook and is embedded in the program's rubrics for facilitating and assessing students' work at all stages of the research and writing process (see Figure 6.1). Since both students and faculty use these rubrics to assess student work as part of the requirements for the Honors program, the rubrics had to be flexible and widely applicable. The program has therefore allowed faculty to customize them to meet the needs of their particular courses and disciplines. Ideally, these revised rubrics would be reviewed by the committee to ensure that BEAM is being accurately applied across a variety of projects and disciplines.

After the fall 2015 semester, the first in which BEAM was used, the Honors faculty met to discuss and assess student work, including how well students made use of BEAM. This assessment revealed that students were using too many sources in their papers in an attempt to fit as much of BEAM as possible into their bibliographies. In response, the faculty adjusted their practices, making a concerted effort to emphasize the function of each source in supporting the student's argument instead of mere quantity.

The use of BEAM in the Honors Program is supported through a collaboration with the library. A librarian dedicated specifically to the Honors Program sits on the Honors Committee and provides input on resources for students and faculty. At the start of the semester, the librarian has an individual meeting with each faculty member to discuss his or her syllabus and course goals. The librarian and faculty member then collaborate to create a course-specific library guide with links to books, articles, videos, and Web resources on the class's topic.

Some Honors LibGuides have a BEAM & Bibliography tab that includes a brief explanation of the BEAM taxonomy and an annotated bibliography (see Figure 6.2). The annotations use BEAM to suggest different ways students could use the sources in their own work. By using BEAM to display the various functions of each source, the LibGuides give students permission to use sources from the course bibliography in ways that reflect their own purposes as thinkers and researchers, ways that may differ from how their peers would use the same source.

Once the LibGuide has been completed, the librarian presents it to students at an hour-long library instruction session, typically scheduled in the second half of the semester, after students have formulated their research questions and a week or two before their annotated bibliographies are due. The session has at least three goals: to give students a sense of the breadth and depth of resources available to them; to enrich their understanding of the research

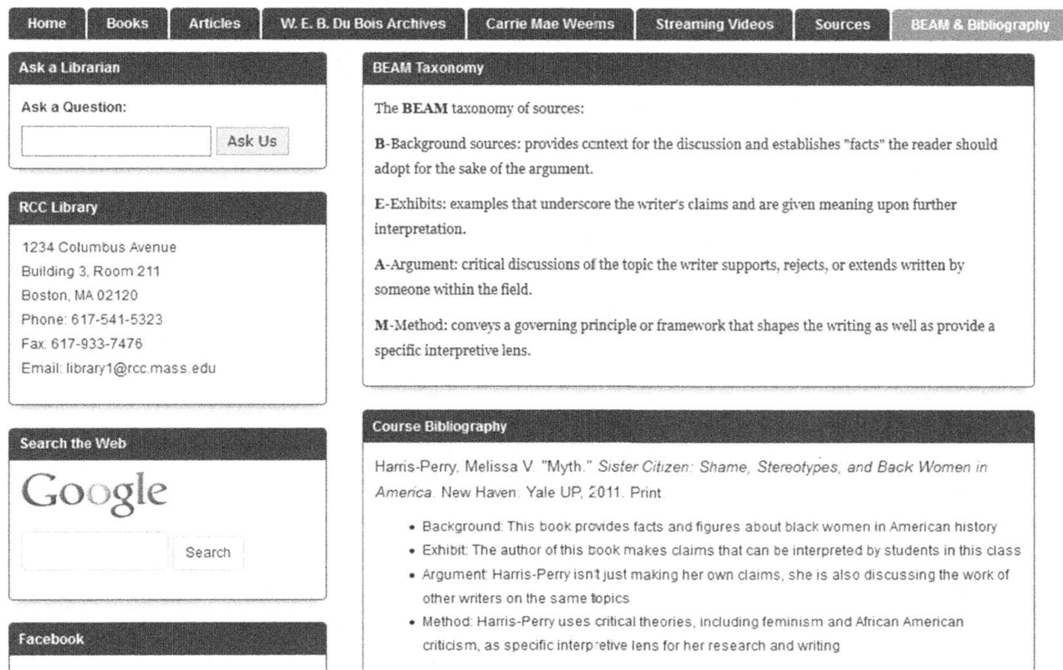

Figure 6.2 EN 102 LibGuide.

process; and to help them develop their specific research projects. Ideally, the faculty member shares students' research questions with the librarian in advance, and students are encouraged to discuss their work with the rest of the class, making use of the BEAM framework. The librarian offers practical suggestions about how students might locate sources to use for their various purposes: for example, for background, a student might turn to an encyclopedia article; for an argument to engage, she might search a database such as JSTOR. As a result of these exchanges, students come to view BEAM as a practical research tool rather than as an abstract framework.

BEAM has been a good fit for the RCC Honors Program. Armed with BEAM and other resources that are part of an Honors toolkit, students are able to meet the academic expectations established by the program. BEAM has also had a positive effect on Honors students' sense of identity as researchers and writers. Like many other students, students entering the Honors Program can be accustomed to seeing research as a chore. The BEAM model, however, leads them to develop a sense of agency as researchers and writers, as it presupposes that their work is motivated by a sense of purpose. This in itself leads students to think more deeply about their work and empowers them to take "a seat at the table" of academic conversation where their ideas warrant the same weight and recognition as those of established critics and scholars. BEAM helps students move away from viewing themselves as passive vessels for information delivered to them by others and toward a conception of themselves as active participants in a lively intellectual exchange. For community college students, this is a major and profoundly significant shift.

LEWIS & CLARK COLLEGE

Like many small liberal arts colleges, Lewis & Clark College has no centrally coordinated writing curriculum. BEAM, consequently, has entered the institution's curriculum through its adoption in individual courses. Perhaps most prominently, it has been used for several years in a rhetorical criticism course for majors taught by a Rhetoric and Media Studies professor. BEAM is part of the content of this course, with students reading and discussing Bizup's 2008 article, and also important to its pedagogy: the course requires students to follow a seven-step sequence, called the "Rhetorical Criticism Process Sequence" (RCPS), to produce a critical essay on a rhetorical artifact of their choice. Over the course of this sequence, students identify critical problems, write historical and descriptive analyses, write annotated bibliographies, do critical analysis, compose complete essays, and prepare conference-style presentations. This sequence is facilitated through a collaboration with an instructional librarian, and all of this work is framed in terms of BEAM.

The use of BEAM in the course has evolved over time. In the past, students attended one librarian-led Information Literacy (IL) workshop in which they discussed Bizup's article and used BEAM to identify the functions of sources in a peer-reviewed journal article. The workshop widened the scope of information literacy instruction by moving beyond traditional bibliographic instruction and incorporating more aspects of critical inquiry (Rubick, 2015). This workshop was recently overhauled, and a second one was added to give students the opportunity to use BEAM with their own sources. The workshops have shifted from treating BEAM as a tool for reading and analysis to emphasizing its utility in writing as well. Throughout the iterations of the course and workshops, two constants have remained: (1) students are introduced to BEAM by reading Bizup's original article proposing it as an alternative research framework, and (2) BEAM serves almost exclusively as a common vocabulary in discussions and assignments for the RCPS. Bizup's article works well in this class because the class itself concerns rhetorical theory and criticism. When introducing BEAM to other disciplines, however, the library relies on other mediations, such as handouts and infographics, to present the BEAM taxonomy (see, for example, Figure 6.3).

In a recent iteration of the course, students were asked to prepare for the IL workshop by reading Bizup's article together with an interview of a Portland Black Panther Party (BPP) leader published in a 1970 issue of the campus newspaper, *Pioneer Log*. Students were also asked to independently locate one additional source on the BPP. The workshop included an overview of BEAM and an activity in which small groups of students discussed the BPP sources and identified how they might be used in a rhetorical criticism essay that took the *Pioneer Log* interview as its exhibit. This exercise required students to move beyond simply seeing their sources as being "about" the BPP to consider potential uses of these sources in their essays. Each group summarized its discussion for the whole class, which allowed the librarian and

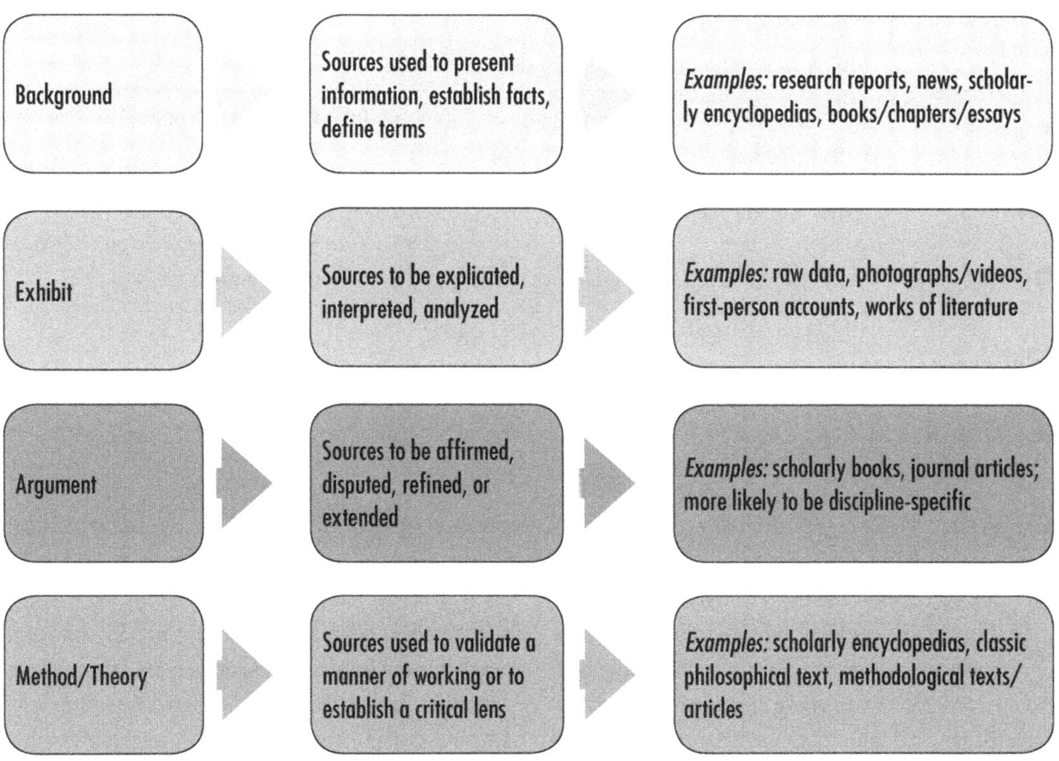

Figure 6.3 Bizup's BEAM: Using sources rhetorically. (Adapted from Doherty [2014] and Ganski & Woodward [2013].)

instructor to assess students' level of comfort with the BEAM vocabulary.

Most of the groups initially struggled to assign a potential BEAM function to the BPP source—not entirely surprisingly, since BEAM was a new vocabulary and the students had been asked to imagine a hypothetical research project—but their uncertainty generated a productive brainstorming discussion about the potential uses of the BPP sources. This episode illuminated a particular pitfall for those new to BEAM: whether students or teachers, they may be prone to mistaking the BEAM vocabulary for a rigid system of classification in which each source can serve one and only one function. To the contrary, a given source might potentially serve two or more functions, depending on the purpose of the writer. The experience of the workshop suggested that an introductory exercise and discussion can help students identify the different purposes for which writers deploy their sources, leading students to emulate these moves in their own work in turn.

Throughout the course, students' grasp of BEAM is continually evaluated via the assignments submitted at each stage of RCPS. The second IL workshop was scheduled ahead of the due date for the annotated bibliography assignment. By this point in the semester, students had identified the specific critical problems and single exhibits on which they would focus in their projects, and they were actively engaged in their research. They each brought a working list of sources to the second workshop. Once again, they were split into small

What	What is your critical problem? What sources have you found so far?
How	How do you intend to use your sources—specifically referring to the functions of BEAM? (Use your handout.)
Strengths	What are the strengths of your current sources according to the functions of BEAM?
Weaknesses	What sources are you currently lack in terms of the functions of BEAM?
Next Steps	What sorts of sources might suit your needs? Where can you find these sorts of sources?

Figure 6.4 BEAM workshop prompt.

groups and asked to work through some discussion prompts (see Figure 6.4) with the librarian and professor circulating as guides.

In this activity, BEAM was used not just as a framework for reading and writing but as a means of prompting students to strategize about and plan their research. Students scored their need for sources for each BEAM function (have sufficient sources, need more sources, and no sources yet), and they helped one another strategize about the next steps in research. Background and exhibit were most often scored as "have sufficient sources." Argument and method were most often scored as "no sources yet." All left the workshop with written summaries of the kinds of sources they most needed as well as some strategies for proceeding with research. The success of our two-workshop format is evinced in the productivity of the second workshop: students were demonstrably prepared to use BEAM to discuss their own sources, which allowed them to direct their efforts effectively toward successful completion of the annotated bibliography.

This collaboration around BEAM signals a shift in information literacy pedagogy at Lewis & Clark. The recently adopted *Framework for Information Literacy in Higher Education* describes a nuanced information landscape, requiring librarians to take "a greater responsibility in identifying core ideas within their own knowledge domain that can extend learning for students, in creating a new cohesive curriculum for information literacy, and in collaborating more extensively with faculty" (Association of College and Research Libraries, 2015). The rhetorical vocabulary of BEAM typifies a core idea, with traction for both librarians and disciplinary faculty. BEAM provides a common vocabulary and bridges the work we do teaching students to find sources and synthesize them into writing.

OHIO STATE UNIVERSITY

At Ohio State (OSU), BEAM began circulating among writing instructors almost from the date of its initial publication in 2008. It was quickly embraced by the English department's Second-Year Writing Program (SYWP), which is responsible for offering the required across-the-curriculum second-year writing course taken by most OSU undergraduates, and it has become central to that program's approach to teaching researched writing. By

2010, BEAM had become a signature feature of the SYWP's professional development programming for the English department's graduate teaching associates, and in 2013, it was incorporated into the SYWP's massive open online course (MOOC) "Rhetorical Composing," funded jointly by the university and the Bill & Melinda Gates Foundation. This MOOC has been revised annually and has now reached over 60,000 participants. The SYWP has likewise reimagined its on-campus hybrid and online courses for OSU students to use BEAM as a primary framework for teaching research-based writing. However, as a large state university with a highly decentralized curricular landscape, OSU has no cohesive approach to writing across the curriculum, and both structurally and culturally, it tends to resists strategic, systematic, and sustainable initiatives. Consequently, despite the SYWP's successes with BEAM, the model's impact to date has been limited largely to that program.

The SYWP is now collaborating with University Libraries (UL) in an effort to reach beyond the 1,500 students enrolled in English-department versions of the second-year course (English 2367) to impact the way research-based writing across the curriculum is taught to all undergraduates. UL is an ideal partner in this effort because of both its broad co-curricular engagement with students and its affinity for the BEAM approach. Indeed, before the beginning of any formal collaboration, UL staff had already created and launched a net.TUTOR online instructional tutorial, "BEAM—A Solution That Might Shine," which introduced the framework to those who opted to access it through the University Libraries website.[4] This resource was available to any student but was not linked directly to or integrated within any university writing course. In an effort to bring together the disconnected but well-aligned work of UL and the SWYP, staff from both units met to strategize about how they could best coordinate their efforts. These conversations led to the creation of new online library resources tied more closely to the writing curriculum as well as to the introduction of BEAM into the university's Writing Center.

In 2015, an English subject librarian created a new English 2367 LibGuide (see Figure 6.5) that uses BEAM to frame its discussion of using and integrating sources.[5] More recently, UL has expanded the resources it originally provided through net.TUTOR into a Unizin-supported open online textbook, *Choosing and Using Sources: A Guide to Academic Research*.[6] BEAM figures prominently in each of the three informational or instructional modules that make up the book's chapter on "Roles of Research Sources": a summary of BEAM that explains the terms and their relationship, an example of a published scholarly essay for which students are to identify and analyze the author's use of sources using BEAM, and a set of reading and writing exercises and inventories that engage students in identifying the various roles of sources in their own writing and the writing of others. *Choosing and Using Sources* now provides instructors and students a robust resource to support rhetorically based engagement with research sources.

In 2016, the SYWP staff collaborated with a reference librarian at nearby Denison University to pilot a BEAM workshop for a writing center context. This librarian was familiar with the SYWP and OSU Libraries and had also been a writing center consultant herself when an undergraduate, so she was well positioned to create and pilot a BEAM training workshop for Denison writing center

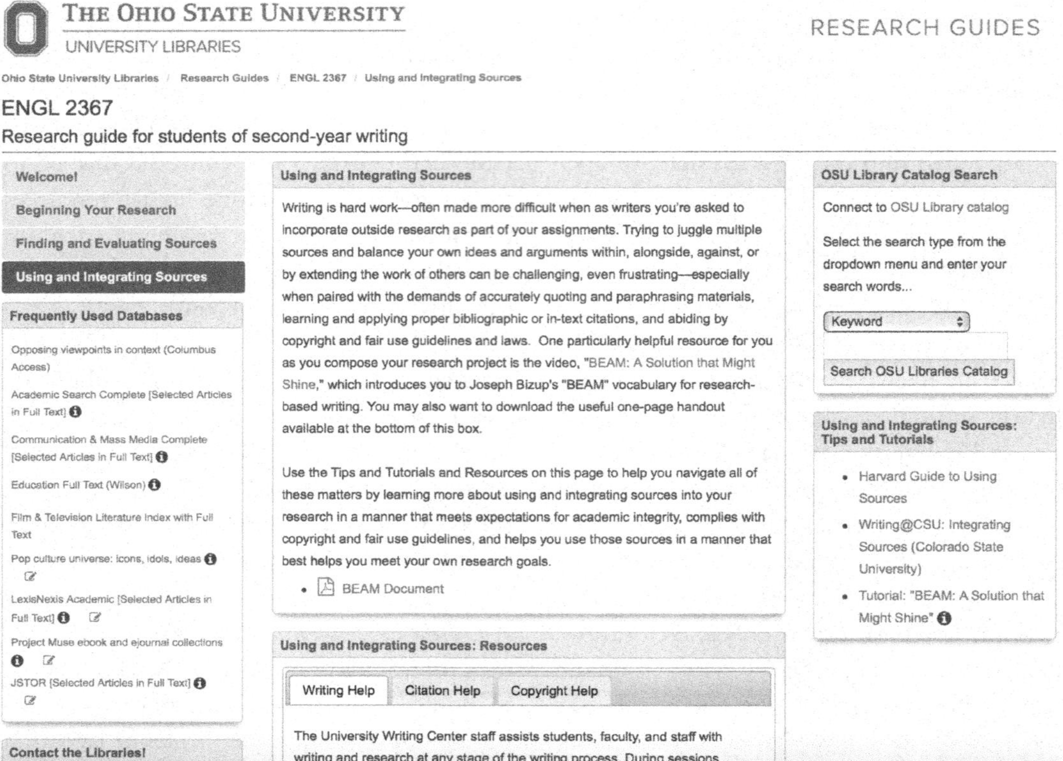

Figure 6.5 English 2367 LibGuide.

consultants. Seeking to introduce BEAM as a critical means of reshaping how the writing center could support researched writing and mentor undergraduate students through the research process, she focused at the training pilot on introducing the consultants (all undergraduate students) to BEAM and collaborated with them on approaches to integrating BEAM into their writing and research tutorials. Drawing on OSU's net.TUTOR resource, which the consultants had been asked to review prior to the workshop, the librarian invited consultants to consider their own assumptions and faculty expectations about research, as well as the constraints of traditional approaches to research requirements in writing assignments. The consultants also discussed strategies for introducing the concepts behind BEAM without invoking the full vocabulary, instead seeking means of introducing the concepts of background, exhibit, argument, and method without overburdening students, who often come to the writing center already overwhelmed by their assignments, expectations, and deadlines. This pilot workshop serves as a model for future implementation of a similar partnership with the OSU writing center.

OSU continues to work toward a sustainable, systematic, and enterprise-wide approach to using BEAM as a common conceptual frame for research-based writing and research. Its vision includes bringing the Denison workshop to OSU and using BEAM as a common conceptual framework for coordinating approaches to research and writing across three units foundational to undergraduate student success in writing and information literacy: University Libraries, the University Writing Center, and the Second-Year Writing Program.

CONCLUSION

The experiences of these four institutions with BEAM differ in many ways, but they also have several important elements in common. First, at all of these institutions, BEAM proved useful in facilitating the development of research guides and other online resources that put the student at the center of the research and writing process and that directly connect specific courses to the library. The model is flexible and can be instantiated in a variety of contexts, and it provides a concrete way of operationalizing the perspectival turn in information literacy pedagogy, exemplified by the new ACRL *Framework*, toward the cultivation of purpose and habits of mind rather than mere technical skills. As shown by the various library guides and other resources developed at these institutions, BEAM offers a concrete way to explain the ways in which the library can support students' classroom work, allowing students to recognize and treat reading, research, and writing as aspects of a larger process. Second, the BEAM vocabulary resonates with many classroom teachers and librarians alike and thus encourages and facilitates their collaboration. Third, those faculty and students who remain ambivalent about BEAM's usefulness express similar reservations and challenges: in particular, they do not see the need for a new terminology, and they can struggle to grasp that BEAM names different ways in which writers might *use* their sources and data, rather than different and mutually exclusive *types*. This is a misunderstanding that must be guarded against, as BEAM's efficacy follows directly from its explicit focus on researchers' and writers' rhetorical purposes. It is entirely possible, even likely, that a writer could use the same source in multiple ways. Finally, the successful implementations of BEAM at all four institutions evolved over a period of years in the context of wider changes in curriculum and pedagogical approach. BEAM is not a silver bullet but a model that can contribute to the cultivation of a rhetorically informed approach to writing and information literacy.

NOTES

1. See for example Toulmin, 1972.
2. http://library.bu.edu/cultureofcollege
3. http://library.bu.edu/beamguides
4. http://liblearn.osu.edu/tutor/les7/index.html
5. http://guides.osu.edu/ENGL2367
6. https://osu.pb.unizin.org/choosingsources/

REFERENCES

Association of College and Research Libraries. (2015). *Framework for information literacy for higher education.* Retrieved from http://www.ala.org/acrl/sites/ala.org.acrl/files/content/issues/infolit/Framework_ILHE.pdf

Bizup, J. (2008). BEAM: A rhetorical vocabulary for teaching research-based writing. *Rhetoric Review, 27*(1), 72–86.

Doherty, B. (2014). What could you do with this type of source? [image]. Retrieved from http://libguides.brookdalecc.edu/ld.php?content_id=12372387

Ganski, K., & Woodward, K. (2013). What could a writer do with this source? [image]. Retrieved from https://ganski.files.wordpress.com/2013/03/beam.png

Jones, M. (2012). Teaching research across disciplines: Interdisciplinarity and information literacy. Interdisciplinarity and research libraries. Ed. Daniel C. Mack & Craig Gibson. ACRL Publications in Librarianships, No. 66. Chicago: Association of College Research Libraries, 2012, pp. 167–181. Retrieved from https://escholarship.org/uc/item/9cz653xd

Nutefall, J. E., & Ryder, P. M. (2010). The timing of the research question: First-year writing faculty and instruction librarians' differing perspectives. Portal: Libraries and the Academy, 10(4), 437–449.

Rubick, K. (2015). Flashlight: Using Bizup's BEAM to illuminate the rhetoric of research. *Reference Services Review, 43*(1), 98–111.

Shields, K. (2014). Research partners, teaching partners: A collaboration between FYC faculty and librarians to study students' research and writing habits. *Internet Reference Services Quarterly, 19*(3–4), 207–218.

Thomas, A. B., & Hodges, A. R. (2015). Build sustainable collaboration: Developing and assessing metaliteracy across information ecosystems. Proceedings from ACLR 2015: Creating Sustainable Community (March 25–28). Ed. Dawn Mueller. Chicago, IL: Association of College and Research Libraries, pp. 79–94.

Toulmin, S. (1972). *Human understanding: The collective use and evolution of concepts*. Princeton, NJ: Princeton University Press.

Veach, G. (2012a). At the intersection: Librarianship, writing studies, and sources as topoi. Journal of Literacy and Technology, 13(1), 102–129.

Veach, G. (2012b). Tracing boundaries, effacing boundaries: Information literacy as an academic discipline. (Doctoral dissertation.) Retrieved from ProQuest.

CHAPTER 7

MOLDING OF IDEAS

How to Shift Language and Create Better Researchers

Mark Dibble

The goal of information literacy is to encourage our students to think widely about information and research. Students need to not only understand where information comes from, but what that information represents, and how to best use and find information for their own research and knowledge. One of the best ways instructors can help their students understand the nature of information and research is to shift the language instructors use to discuss information and research with their students through the use of the Association of College and Research Libraries' (ACRL) *Framework for Information Literacy for Higher Education*, problem-based learning (PBL), and BEAM.

The new ACRL *Framework for Information Literacy* is designed to aid librarians and instructors in helping to shift how students think about research. Behind the new *Framework* is the concept of expressing the principles of information literacy as a set of core ideas. These core ideas are threshold concepts. When students understand the new information literacy core ideas, the students will have adjusted their thinking about research and information. Two other pedagogical tools that can aid this change in thinking are problem-based learning and BEAM. Problem-based learning can not only help students develop the skills of research, but can also help shift students' understanding of the purpose of research. By adjusting the focus and the language of talking about research, instructors can help students understand that research is not just about finding information on a topic, but instead is about answering questions or solving problems. This shift can play a fundamental role in helping students truly understand why they are conducting research and how understanding the nature of research will aid them in their future endeavors. Like problem-based learning, BEAM also offers a way to shift how research and sources are discussed with students. Instead of focusing on what type of source something is, that is, primary, secondary, and so on, BEAM directs students to think about how they will use the source in their research.

This chapter will look at how these ideas can be used by librarians and writing instructors to help students better understand the nature of research. Instead of just focusing on the mechanics of research, instructors can use these tools to help their students grasp why the students are looking for sources, and how they can best use these sources in their own writing. The chapter will outline how librarians and writing instructors can work together to make students better researchers, providing both a theoretical grounding in how to combine these ideas and practical examples of how to use these tools.

NEW *FRAMEWORK FOR INFORMATION LITERACY*

The new *Framework for Information Literacy* represents a shift in thinking from the old *Information Literacy Standards*. The ACRL committee members who wrote the *Framework* (2016) think "information literacy as an educational reform movement will realize its potential only through a richer, more complex set of core ideas" (Introduction, para. 1). Without a shift in focus, the idea of information literacy cannot grow and adapt. The new *Framework* is a movement away from the teaching of a static set of skills about conducting research, to an idea that what students should learn are a set of core principles or ideals about how information is used in research and the in world. As the *Framework* (2016) states, "the rapidly changing higher education environment, along with the dynamic and often uncertain information ecosystem in which all of us work and live, require new attention to be focused on foundational ideas about that ecosystem" (Introduction, para. 1).

Our rapidly changing environment places a greater responsibility on student, teachers, and librarians on how we think about and talk about research and information:

> Students have a greater role and responsibility in creating new knowledge, in understanding the contours and the changing dynamics of the world of information, and in using information, data, and scholarship ethically. Teaching faculty have a greater responsibility in designing curricula and assignments that foster enhanced engagement with the core ideas about information and scholarship within their disciplines. Librarians have a greater responsibility in identifying core ideas within their own knowledge domain that can extend learning for students in creating a new cohesive curriculum for information literacy, and in collaborating more extensively with faculty. (ACRL, 2016, Introduction, para. 1)

Librarians' greater role in helping students understand research requires new thinking. The new *Framework* has embraced the idea that information literacy is not just a skill to be taught. With this *Framework*, the goal is for students to change their understanding of research. Research can now be seen not solely as a skill, but as fundamental knowledge of how information works and functions. The *Framework* moves away from such standard base ideas as accessing "needed information effectively and efficiently" (ACRL, 2000) to more conceptual ideas such as Research as Inquiry. The *Framework* allows for a greater range of understanding about how expert researchers think about the research process. Librarians and instructors can then use these ideas to teach novice researchers. The information literacy ideals expressed in the *Framework* call for librarians and writing instructors to shift their language to bring about a change in thinking about research for students. Instead of thinking of research as finding information about a particular topic or piece of information with the *Standards*, the *Framework* stresses how research is about exploring questions or problems and how new information can bring new or refined questions. This change in understanding affects not only how students view the process of research, but how librarians and writing instructors teach the research process. We should now not just teach skills, but fundamental concepts, so students not only understand the skills of research but also understand the fundamental nature of information and research. This involves understanding how information fits into the larger structure of knowledge and knowledge creation. Shifting our teaching about research itself will help students better develop the skills of research. If students have a better understanding of research, they will be better prepared for using information in the digital and information age in which we now live.

New thinking does not mean completely throwing out what we previously used, taught, and learned, but it does mean changing our understanding of how students should be taught. Research is not just a set of skills, although there are skills involved. Good research needs an understanding of certain core ideas, as expressed in the *Framework*. The fact that students need to understand not just the skills of research, but the core ideas of research is why the new *Framework* embraces the notion of threshold concepts, and the ideals of information literacy are threshold concepts.

THRESHOLD CONCEPTS AND LANGUAGE

Jan Meyer and Ray Land (2003) describe a threshold concept as "akin to a portal, opening up a new and previously inaccessible way of thinking about something" (p. 1). In addition, they write that a threshold concept "represents a transformed way of understanding, or interpreting, or viewing something without which the learner cannot progress" (p. 1). This transformation is the goal of library instruction, and especially information literacy instruction. The *Framework* states it this way: "At the heart of this *Framework* are conceptual understandings that organize many other concepts and ideas about information, research, and scholarship into a coherent whole" (Introduction, para. 2). Librarians want to change the way students view research. If librarians cannot help students make a change in the way the students view the role and purpose of research, then students will not be able to successfully join the research community.

In discussing threshold concepts, Meyer and Land write about "troublesome knowledge." Items of troublesome knowledge are the impediments to learning. One specific impediment is troublesome language. As librarians teach research they are confronted with this impediment regularly. As Meyer and Land acknowledge, different disciplines each have their own language (2003, p. 9). Students who are taking courses across the curriculum have to learn how to "speak" in all these different languages. Their instructors generally do not have to pay attention to the language of other disciplines. Instructors are only focused on the language of their own subject matter. Students are the ones traveling between the disciplines and must understand when to shift their understanding of the meaning of the words for each discipline. Librarians are able to help students bridge this language divide. Instructors need to be aware of this language problem and work with librarians to make sure that they use clear language and that assignments they give to students also are clear to someone working in various disciplines.

The language impediment also is prevalent when students do research. Different databases have different points of view and use language in different ways. Words that mean something in one place have a different meaning somewhere else. This language impediment can be compounded with cross-subject databases. Students have to ascertain if the database uses a specific subject-based term or if there is a more general term that is used. A good example is the term "cancer." In a general database such as Academic Search Complete, the term "cancer" is a subject term. If a student uses a more specialized database such as Medline, she would find that "cancer" is no longer a subject term; instead the term is "neoplasms." When conducting research, students are often butting up against this language issue, and they generally do not have the depth of knowledge of a discipline or of research to always successfully make it through this problem. Librarians play an important role in helping students and instructors navigate through these cross-disciplinary language issues.

A related issue with students, especially younger students, is how concrete their thinking is. Students are not often adept at moving from a concrete example to an abstract idea, or vice versa, and as a librarian, I have often confronted the problems of concrete thinking for students and instructors. A couple of times when I was confronted with students' concrete thinking really stand out. Both examples involve presenting students with a research problem to help guide students through the research process. In the first example, students were given a research problem about medical ethics, which cited, without listing the doctor's name, an example of faulty research. From my perspective, I did not think that the name of the doctor was relevant to the larger question of medical ethics that was presented in the research problem. Just about all of the students who received this research problem thought otherwise. One of the first steps the students took was to figure out the name of the doctor in question before they proceeded to any other angles to answer the research question. The second example was focused on global warming and cited record temperatures for a particular city. Students had a hard time getting past looking for sources about the weather in that city. When the students thought about which search terms to use in a database, invariably the name of the city was one of the search terms they used. In both of these examples when I asked the students if that concrete example was needed to answer the search term, many of the students said that it was. I was then able to use the students' current experiences and practices to show them how they needed to expand how they looked at a research problem as they develop a strategy for finding the sources to answer their research problem. The discussion was not just about how to use a particular database, but instead was about the nature of research itself and how you take a specific example and build out to more general ideas as you develop an argument and conduct research.

These language problems are why it is important that librarians and writing instructors be mindful of the language they use. Students are bombarded with new language and new information in new and sometimes confusing environments. Two tools that can aid librarians and writing instructors in being mindful of the language they use to teach students, and that allow for new ways of thinking, are problem-based learning and BEAM.

PROBLEM-BASED LEARNING

Problem-based learning (PBL) was first developed at McMaster University Medical School in the mid-1960s. Instructors at the medical school developed PBL to "enhance acquisition, retention, and use of knowledge" (Norman & Schmidt, 1992, p. 558). The idea was to place students into real-world problems that they would face as practicing doctors. The goal was to move the learning process away from straight memorization, with no connection to clinical situations, to a process where students would have to apply their prior knowledge to answer a new problem (Norman & Schmidt, 1992, p. 558). Instructors wanted to teach the students to think like doctors, so the students were placed in situations similar to those they would face as doctors. Now instead of learning in a vacuum, students were researching and thinking like doctors. Students were not sent off to learn about a topic, but instead were faced with a problem that they had to solve. In PBL, the instructor is not the source of knowledge who lectures the students telling them what they need to know; instead the instructor is a guide who provides pointers and a basic map to help the students find their own ways to the proper solutions.

By moving away from a demonstration model of instruction to a PBL model, librarians and instructors can change the focus from just showing their knowledge to allowing students to start conducting research themselves. Understanding all the ins and outs of proper research is a complicated process; generally no one learns it just by seeing it demonstrated or reading about conducting research. Students need to get their hands dirty and actually practice conducting research.

PBL is a natural fit for information literacy and library instruction. The ALA Presidential Committee on Information Literacy stated: "to be information literate, a person must be able to recognize when information is needed and have the ability to locate, evaluate, and use effectively the needed information" (ACRL, 2000). PBL is an instructional pedagogy that puts a student directly into a situation where he or she must accomplish each part of this definition. Applied to library instruction, PBL puts students into a real-world research situation and the librarian guides the students through the process so they can learn good research practices.

Because PBL puts students directly into the research process, librarians and instructors can easily change the way they talk about research. Librarians and instructors can make sure that the language they use directly models the true research process. Too often research is talked about in terms of finding a topic to research. Unfortunately, talking about research in terms of topics is confusing for students. When students are told that they need to research a topic, invariably they think big and whole, for example capital punishment, germs, and so on. Students have a difficult time making the next step to a smaller, more manageable research problem. Part of the problem is because librarians and instructors are using the wrong language to describe the research process.

Students often do not understand that their research topic needs to be broken down. As Michael Pelikan (2004) states, "By far the toughest challenge my students face is that of having some idea of what they are looking for and why" (p. 511). Barbara Fister (1992, p. 164), in her study of undergraduate research habits, found that "getting a focus for research was the most challenging and the most time-consuming" task for students. This difficulty is because the student is only thinking about research in terms of a topic, not as a research problem or question. This part of the research process is the point where there is confusion and immediately creates problems for students.

Generally researchers are not researching topics. Instead, researchers are trying to solve a problem or answer a question. Solving a research question is a much smaller and a more directed task than researching a topic. By shifting the language of the purpose of research, by telling students they need to answer a question, librarians and instructors can set up students closer to what true researchers do. Students still do need guidance on learning how to develop a good research question, because developing good research questions does not always come naturally, but what is most important is that librarians and instructors make sure that their language closely matches the research process. Also, by using the idea of a research question or problem, we are closer to the type of research students already do. Students go to the Internet or to their phones to answer a question that they have. Students understand the idea of answering a question about something they do not understand. Students also understand how to search for the answers for these simple questions. Their questions shape the words they use to find information. Topics are generally too big for students to break down into good search terms that will lead them to appropriate sources. Although answering a simple, fact-based question is not all that is involved in academic research, it is closer to the idea of academic research than expressing research in terms of researching a topic, because it is focused on a directed outcome instead of being fully open ended like researching a topic.

BEAM

PBL is a tool to help teach students how to think about the research process. BEAM is a writing teaching tool developed by Joseph Bizup (2008) that can be used to help students understand what type of information the students need to find and then how to use that information in their writing. With BEAM, Bizup has developed a tool for helping students shift the language of sources used in research. Bizup focuses on the confusion of the language of primary, secondary, and tertiary sources.

The letters in BEAM stand for background, exhibits, arguments, and methods. Background sources are "materials whose claims a writer accepts as fact, whether these 'facts' are taken as general information or deployed as evidence to support the writer's own assertions" (Bizup, 2008, p. 75). Exhibits are "materials a writer offers for explication, analysis, or interpretation" (Bizup, 2008, p. 75). Arguments are "materials whose claims a writer affirms, disputes, refines, or extends in some way" (Bizup, 2008, p. 75). Methods are "materials from which a writer derives a governing concept or a manner of working" (Bizup, 2008, p. 76).

The distinction between primary, secondary, and tertiary sources often confuses students. Bizup claims that some of this confusion comes from the fact that by classifying sources as primary, secondary, or tertiary "we attend not to their rhetorical functions or effects but to their relationship to some external point of reference" (Bizup, 2008, p. 73). Students are not sure how to distinguish between a primary source versus a secondary source. To add to the confusion, different disciplines define these types of sources differently. While the distinction can be fairly straightforward in history, it is often unclear or not even seen as necessary in many of the sciences. To tie into the *Framework*, the distinction between the classification of sources is context-dependent.

Bizup avoids this confusion by shifting the focus of how instructors should talk about sources. Instead of focusing on what the sources are, he claims that instructors and students should focus on how sources are used. Bizup (2008) states,

> If we want students to adopt a rhetorical perspective towards research-based writing, then we should use language that focuses their attention not on what their sources and other materials are (either by virtue of their genres or relative to some extratextual point of reference) but on what they as writers might do with them. (p. 75)

BEAM is both a shift of language and a change of meaning about how students should think about sources and how sources relate to their own research and writing.

Combined, the four elements of BEAM allow an instructor to shift how she talks about the sources a writer uses in a text. This is helpful not only for a student's own writing, but also for looking at other texts as well. As Bizup (2008) claims,

> BEAM's main advantage over the standard nomenclature, again, is that is allows us to describe writer's materials straightforwardly in terms of what writers do with them: Writers *rely on* background sources, *interpret* or *analyze* exhibits, *engage* arguments, and *follow* methods. (p. 76)

As problem-based learning presents an opportunity to shift the language of research away from a focus on the issues of research topics, BEAM provides a way to change the language of how instructors talk about sources. In this respect, BEAM can be seen as a threshold concept. By introducing students to a different way of understanding and thinking about sources, we as librarians and instructors are able to shift students' thinking about how they think about research and using sources as a whole.

Although Bizup does not cite the *Information Literacy Standards*, BEAM relates to information literacy and especially to the *Framework* in a number of ways. He acknowledges how writers and researchers are members of specific disciplines and how those disciplines often have their own way of classifying source material (Bizup, 2008, p. 74). He also acknowledges how students "become perplexed when classifications (i.e., primary, secondary, etc.) they have taken as absolute turn out to be context-dependent" (Bizup, 2008, p. 74).

The most significant connection between BEAM and the *Framework* is in the idea of helping students understand how information works. By focusing on how a writer uses sources, BEAM helps students see that sources are not just something extra that is added to a text to fulfill a requirement. Students need to understand how sources are used by authors to bolster and support their arguments. By looking at what the sources do in a new piece of text, in a new piece of information, students can have a better understanding of how different types of information fit together.

Often when librarians and instructors talk about primary and secondary sources, the type of source is the most important feature, not the information itself. By focusing on how the information is used, there is a shift to making the information itself the most important as opposed to the type of source. This focus is a much more dynamic understanding of information itself. Pair this focus with exploring the idea of authority and you can further expand students' understanding of the dynamic nature of information and help them understand that the way they use information is important. They are not just putting words on a page. They are part of a scholarly dialogue that is building knowledge.

PRACTICAL EXERCISES

How does this language shift work in practice? One of the most basic ways is to make sure that the language we use when we talk to students mirrors the actual method of research. In instruction sessions, I always start by asking students: "What are you doing when you are doing research?" Generally, I get silence, and then someone will answer along the lines that you are looking for information. "What information?" I ask. "All information or just some information?" They reply, "Information about your topic." Again, I ask, "All information or just some information?"

"The relevant information," they say. "Are you looking for the information you already know or information you do not know?" In answering this question some do say that you might need to back up what you already do know, which shows that they do understand how we use information to back up what we are going to say. Generally the students do say that you need to look for information you do not know. This is the point where I talk about research being about answering a question or solving a problem, not just about a topic. Talking about research being about answering a question makes research much more directed and goal oriented than just saying one is researching a topic.

In other instruction sessions I use more directed language in PBL exercises. For these sessions, students are presented with a specific research question. This exercise usually happens over two instruction sessions. In the first class session, I visit the class in its normal classroom and introduce the class to a research problem. The research problem is developed by me in consultation with the instructor and is relevant to the issues being addressed in the class. I introduce the idea that research is about answering questions as opposed to focusing on a topic. Students are then divided into groups and given a worksheet. The worksheet presents the research problem, asks the students to think about what information they will need to solve the research problem, asks them where the students think they will find that information, and asks them to develop some keywords and phrases to search for the information they will need.

The second session takes place in the library's computer lab. During this session, the students again work in the same groups from the first day. We give the students another worksheet to guide the work they are doing. This worksheet directs the students to a few preselected resources (each group has slightly different resources) to work with to find sources to assist them in answering the research problem that was presented on the first day. The students try out the keywords and phrases they developed in the first session and then are asked to evaluate the results as to what type of source they are finding (newspapers, books, scholarly articles, etc.), and if the information they are finding will help them answer the research problem. I visit each group to see how they are doing and to offer suggestions as needed. After the groups search individually, I bring the whole class together to discuss what worked and what did not work for each of the groups.

Another sticking point for students when they look for sources is that they often look for the one source that completely answers their research question. Instructors can help students understand that if they do find such a source, then they have not asked the right question. One of the concepts from the *Framework* is for students to understand Research as Inquiry, and part of this idea is that researchers are in dialogue with other researchers. The purpose of research is not to say the same thing over and over again, but to move the discussion forward. Students often think that the purpose of their research assignments is to report on what others say about a topic. As this reporting is how they understand research, they are looking for that one source that completely answers their research question and are often frustrated when they cannot find that one source. Once again, librarians and instructors need to be mindful of our language. Often instructors assume that students know how to do research, instead of clearly explaining to students the purpose of research. Instructors will often just assign students a research paper, telling students to pick a topic and turn in a paper of a certain length. Instructors need to explain that research is a dialogue, and that a good research question will have several ways to come at the answer, and, maybe hardest for students, the research question might not be answerable, but could still be worth exploring. PBL can help students move past this problem. Librarians and instructors can use PBL to model what a good research question look like. Besides modeling good research questions, librarians and instructors can use PBL to show students how the whole research process works, that is, how some sources can address part of a good research question, other sources additional parts of the question. Instructors can then focus on how students combine these separate ideas to move the students' own arguments forward as they explore their research question.

BEAM is easily incorporated into the PBL approach to instruction. As students explore how they would search for information to answer a research question, they can also think about how they will use information as they make the arguments they will put forth in their writing. What background information will they need? As Bizup claims, having students think about how they will use information often makes more sense than thinking about what type of source contains the information. Typically, one thinks of background material coming from tertiary sources, but some background information could easily come from primary sources. As students look at their research problem, they can be thinking about what type of information will help them make and prove their claims as they make their arguments. Instead of just tasking students with doing research, instructors can break down the research process and have students think about how the research process fits into the writing that they will do.

BEAM can also be used to illustrate and teach the concepts of the *Framework*. As students look for sources that will assist them in making their own claims, instructors can talk about concepts from the *Framework*, such as "Authority Is Constructed and Contextual." Authority does not come just from the type of source, but from the expertise of the author of the source. What might be an authority in one place might not be an authority on different subject matter. Instructors can explore with their students why some sources are better suited for their purpose than others. This idea fits in with the exhibits and materials that the students are going to need in their writing.

To illustrate this idea of the notion of authority, I want to share an example from an instruction session. I was using a problem-based exercise in the database Academic Search Complete. Students were using their own search terms, and one student found an article in a journal I did not recognize. I had the student use the feature to explore the information about the journal, and the student and I discovered that the journal was published by the John Birch Society. Now I had the opportunity to talk about point of view and authority. I could talk to the students about understanding the point of view of their sources. Here was a journal published by an organization with a strong point of view, and we could talk about how this author uses information and the notions of authority, and that students might need to balance one point of view with contrasting views. In explaining ideas of authority, part of the lesson was that here was a journal indexed in a well-respected academic database. Librarians want students to find articles through databases such as Academic Search Complete. The database itself provides some level of authority to the articles, which are indexed, especially when contrasted with searching in a general search engine. Part of being a good user of information is understanding how all of these ideas fit together, from the point of view of the author and journal, to which journals get indexed in a database, to how they use the information themselves. Using tools such as problem-based learning and BEAM can help instructors explain to students how these pieces fit together.

CONCLUSION

How librarians and instructors talk about research with our students matters. We need to work together to make sure we are clear in our language about the purpose of research and how research fits in with the writing and arguments that students are going to do. The *Framework* fits very well with understanding about how librarians and instructors should talk about research and information. Problem-based learning and BEAM provide a great framework to help students understand the nature of research and information, so that students can have a change in understanding about how to conduct research. This change in understanding of the nature of research is the type of transformation that Meyer and Land discuss in the idea of threshold concepts. When students have a change in their understanding of what research is, they will have a transformation in their thinking, which will stick with them throughout their lives.

REFERENCES

Association of College and Research Libraries (ACRL). (2000). *Information Literacy Standards for Higher Education*. Retrieved from http://www.ala.org/acrl/standards/informationliteracycompetency

Association of College and Research Libraries (ACRL). (2016). *Framework for Information Literacy for Higher Education*. Retrieved from http://www.ala.org/acrl/standards/ilframework

Bizup, J. (2008). BEAM: A rhetorical vocabulary for teaching research-based writing. *Rhetoric Review, 27*(1), 72–86.

Fister, B. (1992). The research process of undergraduate students. *Journal of Academic Librarianship, 18*(3), 163–169.

Meyer, J., & Land, R. (2003). *Threshold concepts and troublesome knowledge: Linkages to ways of thinking and practicing within the disciplines* (Occasional Report 4). ETL Project: Edinburgh.

Norman, G. R., & Schmidt, H. G. (1992). The psychological basis of problem-based learning: Review of the evidence. *Academic Medicine, 67*(9), 556–565.

Pelikan, M, (2004). Problem-based learning in the library: Evolving a realistic approach. *portal: Libraries and the Academy, 4*(4), 496–508.

CHAPTER 8

CREATIVE INVENTION

The Art of Research and Writing

Caroline Fuchs
Patricia Medved

INTRODUCTION: WHAT BRINGS US TOGETHER

Somewhere along the way, we got lost. Or perhaps we became so focused on the final destination that we neglected to think about the journey itself. We began to teach research and writing as related skills, as paths to an end product. We forgot that research and writing are not simply concrete and discrete actions, but rather more fluid interwoven processes. We forgot about creativity. But we can change that.

Librarians and writing instructors can embrace the inherent creative potential of research and writing, and as a result of doing so, elevate the quality and value of such work. We can encourage our students and our colleagues to consider both research and writing as an integrated process of creative invention. At the same time, we need to recognize that technology in the digital age allows both research and writing to be iterative and recursive and simultaneous, not separate activities. But how do we forge a new path? A first step might be to move away from teaching information literacy in composition as a correction to unethical or sloppy research and citation practices, and instead move toward an approach of teaching both research and writing as inherently connected artful processes. We need to teach information literacy not for students to avoid plagiarism or to signal writerly authority and ethos but as a means of developing and documenting new ideas. But before we do that, we must recognize the changing and disruptive dynamics of the 21st-century information ecosystem.

To be frank, we are tired of hearing students complain about having to do (and learn) researched-based writing, without realizing how much research they already do each day and how their skills can be useful to their student goals (a.k.a. "transliteracy"). And as instructors, we are partially to blame. They don't recognize and we don't promote the notion to our students that asking questions, finding answers, and connecting that information to what they already know is at the very core of learning. What they are doing is directly related to the constructivist theory of learning. Based on Vygotsky's social development theory, and building on the later work of Piaget, Dewey, and Bruner, Constructivism posits that we create knowledge and meaning from our own experiences. New information is linked to our prior knowledge, enabling us, as learners, to construct new information. When that moment occurs while researching and writing, creativity happens. As Anderson (2011) notes: "The metaphor of the eureka moment helps illustrate the instrumental role that information and more specifically the contexts of our engagements with information play in research, innovation and other markers of our creativity" (p. 3). If we allow ourselves to view our students as already immersed in a world of information and writing, answer-seeking and communicating, we enable the potential of their connecting that experience to their academic work. Likewise, we must allow them the opportunity to recognize this in themselves. When that happens, we enable a safe space for creativity.

RESEARCH AND WRITING IN CONVERSATION

Research and writing are sometimes viewed as interdependent academic activities. Good writing (and thinking) can't happen without the influence of information, and good information (and thinking) cannot be represented in the absence of some type of writing. But a close look at some of the language shows a continual de-linking and an emphasis on research as responding to "information need." We'd like to suggest that even when a need has not been defined, students regularly engage information that potentially inspires critical and creative thinking, and that in the act of engaging information, whether by reading, listening, or viewing, students generate new and exciting ideas and links between ideas that can be explored, expanded, or abandoned as they write to substantiate the primary material and the thinking stimulated by it.

Historically, knowledge making has been perceived as a conversation, or a democratic, socially situated, collaborative enterprise (Bruffee, 1984). We can look back to the idealized image of Socrates engaging his students in dialogues that were meant to stimulate their own thinking. Though this image and approach has been adopted by progressive educators most readily since the early 19th century, its pedagogical link to antiquity is superficial, albeit imbued with authority and credibility (Schneider, 2013). The "Socratic method," understood as teaching through questions, gained traction in liberal arts curriculums as it differentiated intellectual pursuits from vocational learning and from authoritarian, lecture-based pedagogies. It confirms a "social constructivist" approach to learning. This understanding is codified in the ACRL frame titled Scholarship as Conversation. As it is used here, the metaphor of conversation would denote that multiple perspectives come together in published academic work. Citation protocols allow scholars to indicate and acknowledge the influences on their thinking, and in turn be acknowledged for what they contribute to a discipline's knowledge base.

Such a reliance on the conversation metaphor seemingly invites all voices to engage in ongoing intellectual discovery. However, as the frame points out: "While novice learners and experts at all levels can take part in the conversation, established power and authority structures may influence their ability to participate and can privilege certain voices and information." It goes on to warn: "not having a fluency in the language and process of a discipline disempowers their ability to participate and engage" (ACRL, 2015). This view is especially problematic in our work with students as novices, prompting a closer examination of "conversation" as a metaphor for knowledge work.

We suspect that the academy's long-abiding reliance on this idea of conversation reflects a familiar and comfortable dynamic for an experienced academic, while a student may be struggling to find agency in confronting new and complex topics and may be resistant to fully engage. If we break down the metaphor, the research and reading part of scholarly work would be listening to what others have to say, while writing in response becomes the talking or contributing part. Indeed, significant attention must be directed toward the reading or "listening to others" component of "conversation" so we may better understand how students read and engage their source material. Terrific work by Alice Horning (2013) and Ellen Carillo (2016) investigates students' often underdeveloped reading skills, especially when it comes to sophisticated academic source material. While this is important work to better understand and address general information literacy, the ultimate, understated value in promoting more sophisticated reading attainment is that student reading can and should yield stronger creative thinking and writing. While much information literacy scholarship remains focused on electronic information-seeking behaviors and "responsible" engagement, it risks losing sight of the creative impetus and potential that drive authentic research journeys. If we can adopt a theoretical shift from emphasizing "critical thinking" with its focus on reading, processing, and analyzing already available information, to "creative thinking" with its focus on new applications and fresh representations that build on what is available, we might better realize the conceptual movement from "student as consumer" to "student as producer." By reasserting the importance of creative thinking as a construct that focuses on the contribution of the learner, we support a contemporary approach to student learning in the digital 21st century. If we are truly to hear them in "conversation," we must stop seeing students as pretenders to knowledge who need to be policed and indoctrinated into some idealized academic discourse community. Instead, we must be ready to welcome and learn from the resources students know and bring to the classroom, and be ready to transform the landscape of academic knowledge making.

In bringing research and writing into closer proximity, we see the potential for more creative, original, and personally meaningful academic journeys for our students, allowing them to forge a path more similar to the kind that expert academics regularly wander down. We acknowledge just how deeply these two recursive processes can be co-generative, as do scholars such as Anderson (2011, 2014), Nutefall and Ryder (2010), and Liestman (1992), who use the words "eureka" and "serendipity" to characterize academic work with especially rewarding and unanticipated coincidences. Important to acknowledge is that students' inexperience with scholarly output doesn't imply an inability to think deeply and to offer ideas and opinions in their everyday interactions with peers around familiar topics. However, in academic settings and in some formal research writing, their participation has been limited.

RESEARCH AND WRITING AS CREATIVE THINKING

"Invention," as adopted from classical rhetoric, is part of the writing process that refers to idea generation. Just as writing is an iterative process, so too is research. By this logic, "invention" should be integrated into the reading and research process, making room for the unplanned, unexpected, and personally satisfying discoveries within the sources we engage. It is in the creative space of engaging ideas that research is made meaningful, and the products of such research gain value.

A few notions of how "creativity" is understood in academia prove especially useful in opening new spaces for student invention. Those are:

- "adjacent possible" (Johnson, 2010)
- "receptivity" or an open stance
- balancing divergent and convergent thinking
- "domain-generality"

"ADJACENT POSSIBLE"

The adjacent possible refers to encountering the boundaries of what is known, by an individual and within disciplines. Johnson (2010) describes the discovery process as similar to exploring a house. You can't see what is in the next room without passing through the room you are in. Each new space requires passing through some familiar space to get there. Similarly, new ideas don't come from cognitive leaps as we generally think of them, but are very tied into what we are exposed to. We can only move one step at a time—which relates back to the importance of disciplinary threshold concepts. The "adjacent possible" is especially relevant to discussing how research stimulates ideas. As instructors, we might consider more actively working from the metaphorical "rooms" our students already occupy to point them in the direction of new rooms or new, more complex understandings of the subjects they already show interest in and involvement with. These "rooms" or articles, websites, blog posts, documentaries, conversations, and so on are engaged naturally as an integral part of every individual's literate life. The trick for instructors lies in helping students to recognize their own unique direction for where they want to move and why. *Which rooms will they explore next?* The concept of "the adjacent possible" demands pedagogies that bridge student learning from novice perspectives toward unique and meaningful, more nuanced, expert perspectives. The approach doesn't shy away from sophisticated academic material but rather links that material to something already accessible to the student while recognizing the individual path each learner can choose to take as he or she encounters additional information. Those choices reflect students' innate creativity.

"RECEPTIVITY"

In academic environments where so much authoritative information is readily available, novices (and even experts) may feel that they aren't entitled to question or challenge ideas that seem well established. The ACRL *Framework* defines one effective student disposition as: "develop and maintain an open mind when encountering varied and sometimes conflicting perspectives" (ACRL, 2015). A "receptive" stance promotes curiosity and a tolerance for uncertainty. Rather than seeking direct and neat answers, receptive thinkers seek information that will substantiate, but more importantly, complicate and challenge their understanding of a topic. Such a stance encourages student behaviors that look for underexplored or unrecognized (from their novice perspective, at least) connections in information as they engage it. Kompridis (2012) recognizes an inherent contradiction in looking for the "new." He asks: "How does one work toward that which cannot be known, seen, heard in advance of the work one does to know, see, and hear 'it.' What kind of work is this? In which direction does one go, looking for, expecting what, exactly? Toward 'what' does one work?"

Cultivating a receptive or open stance must be deliberate. For students who have been conditioned to expect "right" answers or to produce correct responses, this stance may feel uncomfortable or unnatural. Several studies have shown that students find research most satisfying when they "find what they were looking for." They engage in research as a "search and gather" mission and tend to engage only at the sentence level (Head & Eisenberg, 2010; Jamieson & Howard, 2013). Yet, poets, artists, writers, and even academics find joy in their work because of the new discoveries they make along the way, and they approach their research and writing in pursuit of those unknowns.

Adapting the often-applied metaphor for creative people, "thinking outside the box," creativity researcher Frederick Ullen characterizes the most productive thinkers as those who have a "less intact box" (Kaufman &

Gregoire, 2015). A "less intact box" describes a receptive way of looking at new ideas. These thinkers don't readily filter and compartmentalize seemingly irrelevant information. Their minds are sometimes described as "messy." They appreciate established disciplinary foundations but also make unexpected connections and modify their thinking to allow for innovation and change.

BALANCING DIVERGENT AND CONVERGENT THINKING

Divergent thinking or "thinking outside the box" is often thought of as the basis of creative thinking. However, more accurately, the most productive creative thinkers have a strong sense of how to balance divergent thinking with convergent thinking or thinking that more closely aligns with disciplinary knowledge. In other words, in order to recognize the breakthrough potential of an idea, they must understand the work that has already been done. Various researchers have tried to identify breakthrough moments and have kept detailed records, which show that small insights closely tied to the work being done lead to a final product that may be considered innovative. Though applying a different conceptual framework to a problem might lead to fresh solutions, deep knowledge and expertise are essential in recognizing useful insights (Sawyer, 2012).

DOMAIN GENERALITY

Researchers conclude that when students are freed from looking for the most correct or "right" answer, they exhibit greater creativity. And studies into whether individual creativity is typically tied to specific domains conclude that it is not. Rather, it is a general cognitive capacity strengthened by exercising it. Developing a stronger appreciation for their own everyday creative capacity boosts a student's self-esteem and leads to a more positive approach to problem solving (Cropley, 2001). The other good news coming from creativity research is that students are more creative when simply directed to be more creative (Chen, Himsel, Kasof, Greenberger, & Dmitrieva, 2006). Such conclusions point to the value of a culture shift, so that in all disciplines students are encouraged to seek new, individual perspectives to contribute, and fresh applications and presentations of information encountered along the way.

THE POWER OF THE ACRL FRAMES FOR CREATIVITY AND A FREE-FLOWING APPROACH

With the ACRL *Framework for Information Literacy for Higher Education* (a.k.a. the frames) as a guide, we can take a new approach to information literacy with our students. The frames are:

- Authority Is Constructed and Contextual
- Information Creation as a Process
- Information Has Value
- Research as Inquiry
- Scholarship as Conversation
- Searching as Strategic Exploration

Adopted in 2016 by the Association of College and Research Libraries (ACRL), the frames, which are "based on an interconnected cluster of interconnected core concepts," replaced the ACRL *Standards of Information Literacy* with its focus on skills-based learning, representing a distributive shift in the way we approach student learning. The frames are foundational or core concepts that are necessary for students to master in order to participate in the discourse of the discipline. As such, information literacy is recognized as a process, rather than a skill. Fundamental to this new approach is the acknowledgment that students are both consumers and producers of information in the digital age, thus creating an overlap between use (research) and the creation of information (writing) in a variety of media. Adopting this course of action, "[b]oth writing teachers and librarians want to position students as knowledge producers across various media, and they want students to ask genuinely perplexing questions for which they do not have ready answers" (Johnson & Kolk, 2016, p. 7). Mills and Levido (2011) take this a step further: "The model begins with learners making connections between their experiences and the world, while scaffolding the production of digital media-based texts through a process of coproduction between experts, novices, and the built-in features of the technologies" (p. 81).

For us, one of the key components of the frames that has bearing upon student research and writing includes the contrast in the practice of thinking (and creating) between the novice learner and the expert in any given field. Librarians and instructors have the opportunity here to help them move along that continuum. Additionally, the frames provide a lens under which to consider the similarities and differences between the information students work with and the resulting information they produce. The adoption of the frames offers a new focus on student research to include:

- Metaliteracy
- Metacognition/critical self-reflection
- Self-directed scholarship
- Collaborative research
- Creative engagement

Within the constructivist model, the frames enable us to focus on student research that builds on our students' prior knowledge, helping them to recognize, identify, and/or create pathways to the appropriate resources for their needs. These pathways will change depending on their information needs, as well as on their prior knowledge and experience. Then, by engendering a safe, honest space for recursive research and writing, we might provide our students the "room" in which to engage creatively with information and be creative in producing new information. In a digital, global, multidisciplinary world, the old skills-based approach to literacy no longer makes sense. Students do not research or write in an analog environment. So we need to shed our "print-based" ideas of the ways in which they acquire and generate knowledge. This brings us to Reynolds's (2016) notion that "[t]he proposed conceptualization of 'social constructivist digital literacy' builds upon theoretical perspectives that view the human as an autonomous agent who holds a productive purpose driving technology use, for instance the design and creation of a concrete artifact or product" (p. 737). To promote creativity, we need to understand and incorporate multimodal, multimedia, multiliteracy research and writing practices. Within the environment of digital scholarship, research and writing—indeed learning—are no longer isolated linear practices. This must compel us to remove our own "linear" or "analog" approaches to teaching and learning. In order to have our students creatively engage with research and writing as they aim to produce new information in the digital age, we must first be willing to accept that it is often the case that our students have research and writing skills that we, and they, do not readily acknowledge.

Librarians and instructors must also allow students "room" for the *reflective* discovery and creation of information. This might mean that we "reinvigorate [the] discussion about the productivity of engagements with ambiguous and imperfect information and the potential contribution this offers in relation to creativity and innovation" (Anderson, 2011, p. 5).

In theory, an interdisciplinary positioning should bring the teaching of research and writing into closer proximity and better align it with the general goals of higher education. Therefore, cultivating an approach to information-seeking that is less academically restrictive, using methods that are already familiar to students, encourages a stance without disengaging students from the important recursive cycle of asking questions, seeking answers, discovering information, and representing thinking through writing.

Students engage different voices and positions but putting them together into "conversation" is their work as writers. If we accept that premise, embracing the inherent creativity enabled through research and research-based writing becomes inevitable. Yet, as Anderson (2011) notes about student research: "The challenge now before us is how to support creativity and innovation in these contexts; to engage with information and not to necessarily just be able to find it" (p. 2). The same holds true for student writing.

The *Framework for Success in Postsecondary Writing* are the "Eight Habits of Mind," which likewise are consistent with the ACRL frames and reinforce our premise that if we want our students to do good research and writing, we need to create a space that encourages openness, engagement, creativity, and flexibility. As presented by Maid and D'Angelo (2016), these are:

- *Curiosity*—the desire to know more about the world
- *Openness*—the willingness to consider new ways of being and thinking in the world
- *Engagement*—a sense of investment and involvement in learning
- *Creativity*—the ability to use novel approaches for generating, investigating, and representing ideas
- *Persistence*—the ability to sustain interest in and attention to short and long-term projects
- *Responsibility*—the ability to take ownership of one's actions and understand the consequences of those actions for oneself and others
- *Flexibility*—the ability to adapt to situations, expectations, or demands
- *Metacognition*—the ability to reflect on one's own thinking as well as on the individual and cultural processes used to structure knowledge (pp. 44–45)

An additional point to note here is how the ACRL *Framework* acknowledges the broad spectrum of research material available and encourages skepticism in evaluating sources. Its language is very democratic in its insistence that "various communities may recognize different kinds of authority" and "unlikely voices can be authoritative." Further, in the Practices list, it is noted that "content may be packaged formally or informally," and in "Dispositions" learners are encouraged to "recognize the value of diverse ideas." This stance effectively shifts away from a traditional notion of valid academic research and, more obliquely, the accepted products or forms of intellectual work. In relation to the frames, creating, revising, and disseminating are also associated to the understanding of writing as a process. Research and writing are inextricably linked.

The frame of Research as Inquiry underscores the iterative process that empowers students to asks new and increasingly more complex questions, which prompts further research from which new questions may emerge. But students must be given time to work through the process. This consideration must be taken into account in how we assign research to students as novice academic research writers, and also calls us to evaluate our expectations of finished products. This frame acknowledges an open-endedness that is unexpected and not always encouraged. Further, as in the case of Scholarship as Conversation, students can recognize this positioning but may not fully participate in such conversations, depending on their purposes and products. How can we encourage them or direct them to participate in the conversation? Is that too much to ask? In the novice stage, are they just learning to listen? How do we encourage them to get their voices heard?

The same is true for the Searching as Strategic Exploration frame, which calls for students to see the research process as nonlinear and iterative. This frame likewise calls for a recognition of a gap in practice between experts and novices, and encourages a developing sophistication. It also implies that research requires trial and error, and the willingness to fail, which makes it imperative that we make a safe space for that creative process. Again, to do this successfully we need to focus more on our students' strategies for searching, rather than their results/end products. The importance here is to help them discover new strategies, to help them identify the good results from the bad in the context of the task at hand, to help them see how research results can be raw material for "invention" work and new ways of thinking. We need to remind them, and ourselves, that sometimes to move forward, they may need to take a step back; sometimes they need to stray off the path before they return to it. The strategy that worked for one question may not work for another. This brings us back to our position of researching and writing as art, a creative practice.

RELATED THEMES IN COMPOSITION SCHOLARSHIP

There are themes in composition scholarship that are in sync with the ACRL frames, allowing librarians and instructors to work with common ground. These include:

- **Researched writing as conversation**
  An often-used metaphor for asking students to engage in research and researched writing is to imagine themselves in conversation. This is formalized in the *They Say, I Say* approach. How readily can a novice jump into conversation with expert discourse? And if experts aren't responding to them, is it really conversation?
- **Invention as defined in rhetoric**
  Composition teaches writing as a process with one of the earliest stages being "invention," drawn from Aristotle's Rhetoric. It points to idea generation as separate from drafting. Often in the classroom, this will include free writing or brainstorming with

an expectation that much of what is generated won't be used in a particular project. But shouldn't the same happen within the research process? Can we position invention as something that can happen along with reading and research, allowing students to use outside voices and materials to get ideas and shape thinking?

- **Authority and voice of a novice writer**
  Research points to the problems that early writers have in seeing themselves beyond their student or novice status.
- **Adopting multimodal approaches**
  Where possible many composition instructors are incorporating multimodal composition in the classroom, having students create podcasts, movies, websites, Prezi presentations, even collages. They recognize that composing meaning is no longer restricted to words on a page. Librarians need to follow suit and recognize that student researching must entail more than locating and evaluating scholarly peer-reviewed articles.

According to Fullard (2016), "[Students] will also be aware that scholarly conversations take place in a number of unlikely places. Assessing the strengths and shortcomings of genres, forms and modes of textual and multimodal information may be tied to their reception in different contexts. Once these dimensions are well understood, discernment may be an easier task" (p. 52). Can we not say the same for librarians and composition instructors?

To be clear, the iterative process of student research and writing rises above the simplistic notion of these two disciplines as skills that support academic success to become something akin to a creative art form.

So, the question for us is: How do we create a pedagogical space in the classroom that fosters meaningful, creative novice engagement with expert and nonexpert ideas?

WHAT MAKES THIS AN ART?

As educators, we can help students navigate their unique intellectual journeys as they build their capacity for increasingly complex questions and representations. Despite more access to and immersion in information than ever before, a narrative of their reluctance and inadequacy for academic research assignments persists. Thus, previous inquiries into student research practices focus primarily on anxieties about information literacy and citation. By repositioning research as a creative knowledge-building endeavor, driven by students' already realized resourcefulness and intellectual curiosity, we enable much broader possibilities for students' researched work.

But how is this an "art"?

In our title, we use the word "art" to imply the creativity involved in research and writing, no matter what the experience of the learner has been. Art, in its essence, is the exploration, expression, and application of creativity. It implies a unique conception of the world, tied to one's individual experience and perspective. It is an end product, but it is also a process. And that process can be messy. Art can take on many forms: painting, sculpture, dance, music, literature, theater. But art can also be seen as a craft, as in "the art of conversation." As such, we would like to expand the definition of art to include student research and writing.

To be sure, we are not saying that just because many students aren't ready to read professional, academic journal articles with deep appreciation, doesn't mean they shouldn't. But we must find ways to bridge the gaps so that they don't have to wait until senior year or graduate school to do work that they will find intellectually satisfying and that we will find acceptable and appropriate. Before we get there, we need to allow them to build upon the research skills they already possess. Our students have been living in a digital information–seeking world their whole lives. Their immersion should prompt us to reconsider what "research" means and what "academic work" might include. We should consider how their research and writing can cultivate a spirit of inquiry, curiosity, and self-worth.

REFERENCES

Anderson, T. D. (2011). Beyond eureka moments: Supporting the invisible work of creativity and innovation. *Information Research: An International Electronic Journal, 16*(1).

Anderson, T. D. (2014). Making the 4Ps as important as the 4Rs. *Knowledge Quest, 42*(5), 42–47.

Association of College and Research Libraries (ACRL). (2015, February 9). *Framework for information literacy for higher education* [Text]. Retrieved November 17, 2017, from http://www.ala.org/acrl/standards/ilframework

Bruffee, K. (1984). Collaborative learning and the "conversation of mankind." *College English, 46*, 635–652.

Carillo, E. C. (2016). Engaging sources through reading-writing connections across the disciplines. *Across the Disciplines, 13*(1).

Chen, C., Himsel, A., Kasof, J., Greenberger, E., & Dmitrieva, J. (2006). Boundless creativity: Evidence for the domain generality of individual differences in creativity. *Journal of Creative Behavior, 40*(3), 179–199.

Cropley, A. J. (2001). *Creativity in education & learning: A guide for teachers and educators*. Psychology Press.

Fullard, A. (2016). Using the ACRL Framework for Information Literacy to foster teaching and learning partnerships. *South African Journal of Libraries and Information Science, 82*(2), 46–56.

Graff, G., Birkenstein, C., & Durst, R. (2015). *"They say / I say": The moves that matter in academic writing, with readings* (3rd ed.). New York: W. W. Norton.

Head, A. J., & Eisenberg, M. B. (2010, November 1). Project Information Literacy progress report: "Truth be told."

Horning, A. (2013). *Reading, writing, and digitizing: Understanding literacy in the electronic age.* Cambridge Scholars Publishing.

Jamieson, S., & Howard, R. M. (2013). Sentence-mining: Uncovering the amount of reading and reading comprehension in college writers' researched writing. *The new digital scholar: Exploring and enriching the research and writing practices of nextgen students*, 111–133.

Johnson, B., & McCracken, I. M. (2016). Reading for integration, identifying complementary threshold concepts: The ACRL Framework in conversation with Naming What We Know: Threshold Concepts of Writing Studies. *Communications in Information Literacy, 10*(2), 178–198.

Johnson, K., & Kolk, S. (2016). Frameworks in conversation: Habits of mind, curriculum, and assessment. In R. McClure & J. P. Purdy (Eds.), *The future scholar: Researching and teaching the frameworks for writing and information literacy* (pp. 3–18). Medford, NJ: Information Today.

Johnson, S. (2010). *Where good ideas come from: The natural history of innovation*. New York: Riverhead Books.

Kaufman, S. B., & Gregoire, C. (2015). *Wired to create: Unraveling the mysteries of the creative mind.* New York: Perigee Books.

Kompridis, N. (2012). The priority of receptivity to creativity (Or: I trusted you with the idea of me and you lost it). *Critical Horizons, 13*(3), 337–350. https://doi.org/10.1558/crit.v13i3.337

Liestman, D. (1992). Chance in the midst of design: Approaches to library research serendipity. *RQ*, 524–532.

Maid, B., & D'Angelo, B. (2016). Threshold concepts: Integrating and applying information literacy and writing instruction. *Information literacy: Research and collaboration across disciplines.* Fort Collins, CO: WAC Clearinghouse and University Press of Colorado.

Mills, K. A., & Levido, A. (2011). iPed: Pedagogy for digital text production. *Reading Teacher, 65*(1), 80–91.

Nutefall, J. E., & Ryder, P. M. (2010). The serendipitous research process. *Journal of Academic Librarianship, 36*(3), 228–234.

Reynolds, R. (2016). Defining, designing for, and measuring "social constructivist digital literacy" development in learners: A proposed framework. *Educational Technology Research and Development, 64*(4), 735–762. https://doi.org/10.1007/s11423-015-9423-4

Sawyer, R. K. (2012). *Explaining creativity: The science of human innovation* (2nd ed.). New York: Oxford University Press.

Schneider, J. (2013). Remembrance of things past: A history of the Socratic method in the United States. *Curriculum Inquiry, 43*(5), 613–640.

Shepherd, R. P. (2014). *Composing Facebook digital literacy and incoming writing transfer in first-year composition* (Doctoral dissertation). Retrieved from ASU Electronic Theses and Dissertations. http://hdl.handle.net/2286/R.I.26807

CHAPTER 9

TOWARD A *RESEARCHERLY ETHOS*

Building Authority With Inquiry in Information Literacy and Writing

Melanie Lee
Lia Vella

INTRODUCTION

The process of building credible authority, of making new knowledge through inquiry and writing, is an arduous task. Learning outcomes for not only composition, but also writing-intensive courses across the curriculum, often require written research: typically, a long paper that synthesizes and cites multiple primary and secondary sources. Evidence suggests that learning outcomes are improved by process-based pedagogy: dialogic instruction, frequent student-faculty interaction, and open-ended, inquiry-driven, information seeking and composing that converge through a kind of invention nexus (Berlin, 1987, 2003a, 2003b; Booth, 2015; Murray, 2003). Yet outdated, product-focused "banking concepts" (Freire, 2000) of information literacy and composition instruction dominate many academic landscapes. Students are expected to engage complex information literacy techniques while conducting research, to master specific academic citation styles that vary according to discipline, to blend borrowed ideas and their own fresh prose with rhetorical conventions in correct Standard Written English, to craft and support theses and sustain researched "arguments." They are often expected to do so without adequate dialogue, instruction, or practice. Consequently, many students graduate lacking the ability to locate, evaluate, and organize information; to think analytically, critically; and to synthesize and write well.

We theorize that the study and practice of information literacy, like the study and practice of composition, is feminized (Connors, 1997; Enos, 1996; Miller, 1991a; Schell, 1992, 1998). That is to say, postsecondary structure and curricula marginalize library faculty and writing faculty (Enos, 2009)—the majority of whom are women—and their work, relegating their work to ancillary positions rather than recognizing both as foundational for making new knowledge. As a result, the gendered "performativity" (Butler, 1993) expected of library and writing faculty works against their teaching and achievement of learning outcomes. Feminization negates our authority, intellectual recognition, and institutional support; negation of our authority, in turn, impacts our students' efforts toward acquiring the ethos they must hone to know their subjects and excel in their majors. Further, library and writing faculty struggle with identity and status, respect from students and colleagues, pedagogical autonomy, funding, and adequate time in and out of classrooms for teaching and learning.

For instance, librarians are expected to instill complex information literacy concepts in students to sustain a semester's worth of research in a single 50-minute session (Oakleaf et al., 2012). On the other hand, composition faculty, those "sad women in the basement," are expected to improve students' compositions through countless, unremunerated hours responding to students' writing, a task that nonexperts may misconstrue as correcting and editing students' writing (Miller, 1991b). Both approaches—the 50-minute library one-shot and the 24/7 editor/grammarian—are expected to produce students who are competent researchers and writers, whose skills will smoothly transfer and transcend their courses (Hartwell, 2003). However, neither approach, the patterns of which structurally conform to current traditional models, allows adequate time, interactivity, or practice, the kind of guided dialogue needed to achieve their social epistemic outcomes. Students, therefore, are unable to engage in the kinds of context-specific, generative conversations, composing, and feedback that encourage learning and mastery of these important heuristics.

To address the mismatch between outcome expectations and practice, James Elmborg (2003) proposes that librarians develop theoretical underpinnings to challenge the status quo; the Association of College and Research Libraries' (ACRL, 2016) *Framework for Information Literacy for Higher Education* moves toward this effort. Likewise, Douglas Downs and Elizabeth Wardle (2007) suggest that compositionists develop inquiry-based curricula focused on writing scholarship to contest misconceptions of what writing courses should be and do; the *Framework for Success in Postsecondary Writing* authored by the Council of Writing Program Administrators (CWPA), National Council of Teachers of English (NCTE), and National Writing Project (NWP) (2011) supports their endeavor. In a more process-oriented approach, Marshall Gregory (2001) suggests that faculty develop a friendly "teacherly ethos" with ten "ethical qualities" to engage learners. While Gregory's emphasis on process-based pedagogy is certainly useful, he neglects to recognize the already imperiled authority and disempowerment that feminized composition and library faculty face. Moreover, stressing the faculty role reduces the importance of *student* dialogue, inquiry, and responsibility essential for productive teaching-learning relationships. We propose that faculty instead work with students toward what we call a *researcherly ethos.*

UNDERSTANDING *RESEARCHERLY ETHOS*

A pedagogical attitude applicable to learners and teachers, researcherly ethos relies upon inquiry as the basis of discovery that propels research. In seeking and synthesizing information, a researcherly ethos approach emphasizes dialogue, energeia,[1] invention, and rhetoric. Our model (see Table 9.1) incorporates Gregory's "ethical qualities" of honesty and curiosity, the latter of which appears in the *Framework for Success in Postsecondary Writing*; however, a researcherly ethos includes additional characteristics from the writing framework as well as those identified

TABLE 9.1 *Researcherly Ethos: Informed by ACRL Framework and CWPA/NCTE/NWP Habits of Mind*

Researcherly Ethos Qualities	ACRL Framework	CWPA/NCTE/NWP Habits of Mind
Curiosity	Research as Inquiry	Curiosity
Honesty	Authority Is Constructed and Contextual, Information Has Value	Openness, Responsibility
Dialogic	Scholarship as Conversation	Engagement, Responsibility
Energeiatic	Information Creation as a Process	Persistence
Inventive	Searching as Strategic Exploration	Creativity
Rhetorical	All of the above	Engagement, Flexibility, Metacognition, Persistence

by the *Framework for Information Literacy for Higher Education*. We believe these characteristics are crucial for effective information literacy and writing pedagogy.

Through a sequence of lessons designed to experientially underscore students' participation in knowledge-creating conversation, a researcherly ethos encourages them to develop authority in their fields rather than remain passive information consumers and composer/writers. We believe that students, as potential researchers, writers, and disciplinary initiates, bear responsibility for joining the Kenneth Burke-ian parlor conversation called learning that is equal to faculty responsibility for teaching. Students should be responsible for their own research, composing, citation, documentation, and revision. For if postsecondary policies on plagiarism expect students to demonstrate high levels of responsibility for written products that result from these researcherly processes, it follows that the academy should also expect students to demonstrate high levels of agency in the process of acquiring information literacy and composition proficiency.

However, the structures commonly employed to achieve these goals—the 50-minute one-shot and the 3-hour composition course—vex students' efforts toward attaining learning outcomes. Indeed, any course that requires students to conduct, integrate, and synthesize research from multiple primary and secondary courses with their own ideas in specific documentation styles without providing adequate time for this learning within the structure of the course fails its students. Working toward a researcherly ethos contests feminization of library and composition faculty work by moving from an ancillary, static position to a pivotal, active position the dialogic negotiation between students and faculty that is needed to achieve research and writing intensive learning outcomes. In this way, cultivating a researcherly ethos also contests the feminization of library and composition faculty, enhancing their authority through formal recognition of their expertise. To this end, the following lesson sequence alternates composing / drafting / writing / revising with information literacy and research lesson questions to engage students in a progression of dialogic, inquiry-based tasks that build over an eight-week period to hone their researcherly ethos. Successful implementation of these lessons, we suggest, demands close collaboration between composition and library faculty as well as the addition of one weekly lab hour, a structure common in inquiry-based science courses, to three-hour writing and research-intensive courses.

Toward a Researcherly Ethos Lesson Sequence[2]

1. Growing Curiosity

This lesson challenges students to reflect on the nature of inquiry-based research by considering many angles of a research question and articulating what type of information they will seek *before* they search.

Part 1 (25 mins): Pair students in teams of two and introduce the following activity:

> Please read this scenario, discuss questions A–C, and then write your own, individual responses to all three. Do not search for information; respond to these questions with only what you know:
>
> Imagine that you are a professional analyst team consulting with a congressional committee on higher education. You are studying how earning a bachelor's degree affects women's and men's salaries 20 years after they graduate.
>
> A. What questions do you have about this issue?
> B. What do you need to know to start exploring your questions?
> C. How can you locate the information you need? Where do you look?

Part 2 (35 mins): Ask students to read aloud their responses to A–C in whole-class discussion. Record students' responses in three columns (A, B, C) on the board. When finished, invite students to photograph the board with smartphones, to review this work, and note a few reasons why studying this issue is important—encourage several responses to this question, about one handwritten page—before the next lab session.

2. Examining Authority

This lesson encourages students to consider authority's contextual nature. Authors gain authority in their subjects in many ways, and while some types of authority and information are relevant in some situations, in other situations, they are not. Critically distinguishing between context-appropriate and inappropriate authority builds reader-researcher credibility.

Part 1 (30 mins): Ask students to review pictures of the board and writing from Lesson 1. Place students in teams of four and distribute copies of one of two or three different, short (1–3 pages) seed articles from different sources that address how earning a bachelor's degree affects women's and men's salaries to each team. Students should read articles individually and note their main points in writing—one list of main points per team.

Next, ask each team to elect a scribe, and divide the board equally into spaces that correspond with the number of teams. Scribes note their team's article's main points on the board (two or three scribes write at once to save time), including source titles, authors, publication venues, and dates.

Part 2 (30 mins): Faculty discuss what the students' lists reveal about the nature of information. Discussion questions include the following:

A. Were there factual differences between the sources the groups looked at? If so, which source seems more correct or convincing, and why?

B. How do these sources address questions you have and/or what you wrote about in Lesson 1? Would these sources be okay to cite in a research paper? Why or why not?

After whole-class discussion, ask students to ponder the following question outside of class and bring their written response to the next lab session:

C. After considering these sources, what else would you like to know about how earning a bachelor's degree affects women's and men's salaries 20 years after they graduate?

3. Honing Honesty

This lesson engages students in self-examination about what they do and do not know about a specific issue or topic in order for them to identify what they need to know to conduct inquiry-driven, open-ended research.

Part 1 (30 mins): Ask students to review their responses to C in 2 above.

Next, ask them to draw a vertical line down the center of a sheet of paper, dividing it into two columns. At the top of the page on the left side, label the column "Do Know"; label the right side "Do Not Know." Students should list in the left column what they think they know about how earning a bachelor's degree affects women's and men's salaries 20 years after they graduate, and in the right column what they think they do not know.

Part 2 (30 mins): Ask students to review both columns and their responses to C in 2 above. Then, ask them to leave the room for 20 minutes and respond in writing, on the back side of the same sheet of paper, to the following prompt:

> What do you need to know about this issue? What will it take for you to discover what you need to know? How will you find the information you need?

When students return, ask them to sit in different places than they were sitting before they left the room—to gain a new perspective—exchange papers with their classmates, and read each other's "Know" and "Do Not Know" lists and prompt responses. Student should bring this work to the next lab session.

4. Engaging Energeia

This lesson refines research questions to guide a search for information. Students will likely find a variety of different kinds of sources, some more appropriate than others for a scholarly research paper. They will need to exhibit persistence and allow time for the process of information creation.

Part 1 (20 mins): Ask students to review their writing from Lessons 2 and 3 and then respond in writing to the questions below:

> What 2–3 questions related to this issue do you want to focus on exploring? You can include, combine, and change ideas you wrote about in the previous lessons as you focus and revise your questions.

Part 2 (40 mins): Students use their 2–3 focused, revised questions to do the following:

> What do you need to know to start exploring your questions? Review what you wrote for Lesson 3. *Then find two different sources_*that you can use to start investigating. Retrieve the sources if they are physically in the library, or download or print abstracts for articles.
>
> Write the full bibliographic information for the sources you find correctly according to the style assigned by your instructor. Bring the sources and/or their bibliographic information along with your 2–3 focused, revised questions to the next lab session.

5. Researching Through Inquiry

This lesson challenges students to think about the process of searching for information; by sharing search experiences and strategies with each other and the faculty, they will come to understand more about the strategic nature of searching.

Part 1 (20 mins): Ask students to skim one source they located in Lesson 4 and write 1–2 sentences briefly summarizing the source, explaining how it responds to their research question(s), and why it is useful.

Part 2 (40 mins): Ask a few students to name their sources, explain connections with their questions, how and where they found them (try to generate discussion about 2–3 different kinds of sources). Faculty should show the processes on screen or sketch on the board steps that students followed as they explain how they found the sources (for example, call up Google, ask for keywords students used to search, etc., and ask—is this how you did it?).

As part of these conversations and research process screenings, faculty review with students strategic search techniques for finding authoritative information to advance their research.

Ask students to bring their written responses to activities in Lessons 4 and 5 and sources to the next lab meeting.

6. Expanding Research Through Dialogue and Inquiry

This lesson illustrates the dialogic nature of inquiry as students contribute to each other's research. Although students may not yet speak the language of scholarly conversation in their disciplines, they are developing their own community of practice and by now have developed a conversation around the topic for the class research project.

Part 1 (35 mins): Pair students in teams of two. Ask them to exchange research questions from Lesson 4 and share sources they found and what they wrote about them in Lesson 5. After students read each other's work, ask them to respond in writing, individually, to A–C below:

A. What do you think your classmate needs to know to begin to answer her/his questions in addition to what he/she has already found?
B. Why do you think knowing that is important for pursuing your classmate's questions?
C. What question/s do you have about your classmate's question?

Give your written responses to your classmate.

Part 2 (25 mins): Ask students to read their classmate's responses to A–C and then respond to the following question in writing:

How does your classmate's thinking about your questions and source add to / enrich / change your original question/s? Bring this response and your sources with you to the next lab meeting.

7. Examining Scholarship, Creating Information

This lesson focuses on examining information from sources in light of specific exigencies—in this case, students' own research questions—through

Source	Whose ideas?	For what audience?	Is there a review process involved? If not, should there be?	What is omitted? What else are you wondering?	What is the value of the source?

Figure 9.1 The process of information creation. (Source: Vella, L., & Holles, C. [2014]. Collegiate research: More than Google. Unpublished lesson plan, Center for Academic Services and Advising, Colorado School of Mines.)

conversation in the creation of new information. It continues dialogue about sources, practices flexibility, strengthens the inquiry-information connection, and broadens students' search perspectives by asking them to find a source for their classmate.

Part 1 (40 mins): Faculty introduce "The Process of Information Creation" chart (see Figure 9.1) and ask students to do the following in pairs:

> Exchange your research questions, information about sources you found, and how your classmate's thinking changes your thinking from Lesson 6. After reading this work, use the chart to evaluate one of your sources.

When students finish completing a chart on one of their sources, they complete a second chart on one of their classmate's sources. Return the completed chart to her/him.

Part 2 (20 mins): Ask students to apply processes the librarian suggested in 5, find another source for their classmate applicable to one of her/his questions, and note the complete bibliographic information. Students should also note the source's connection with their classmate's question.

Students should bring their completed charts to the next lab session.

8. Revisiting Ethos, Rhetoric, and Invention

This lesson practices metacognitive thinking and reflection about what students have learned through the lesson sequence, to consider how their

rhetorical authority and, in turn, their ethos (about an issue, subject, or topic) has changed.

Part 1 (25 mins): Faculty share completed charts and summaries on screen, document viewer, or smartboard; then discuss, suggest additional avenues for or refinements of research or other questions the students' completed chart results and summaries suggest.

Part 2 (35 mins): Ask students to write for 10 minutes about what they think the words rhetoric and ethos mean (without consulting any sources). Faculty then lead a quick discussion about these terms' meanings and ask students to respond to the following questions:

> How has the seven-step sequence helped hone your researcherly ethos? Did this approach build your rhetorical authority on the issue, and strengthen your credibility and investigative technique? How have these steps, through processes of discussion, inquiry, and research, changed your original questions and thinking?

Ask students to write a page that reflects on their learning throughout the sequence. Possibilities include comparing their original and their revised questions, sources they and their classmates found, summaries, rubrics, and bibliographic information. Students may finish this outside of class but should turn the work in to faculty, perhaps as part of a research paper proposal. Faculty can, in subsequent classes, ask students to apply the same sequence, a modified sequence, or selected sequence steps in focusing research topics and centering papers on questions.

CONCLUSION

In addition to developing students' research skills through content and activities in the lab hour, it is crucial that faculty involved from the writing program and library perform as equal partners teaching the sequence. By working together as fellow scholars, practitioners, and authorities in their respective fields, they model the researcherly ethos that we hope to cultivate in students. Librarians have typically not operated in a full teaching role at many academic institutions. Yet, if our endeavor is to succeed, librarians must participate fully—at least in the one-credit lab portion of the course, if not more—as co-teachers: planning lessons and session activities, fully engaging in the sessions, grading and providing feedback to student work. While it is true that librarians represent a specific discipline, they must not be treated as guest lecturers or technicians who train students in rote tasks (such as how to look up books in the library catalog) any more than compositionists should be treated as students' editors or grammarians, for this diminishes librarians and writing specialists as teachers and trivializes the disciplines of both library and information science and rhetoric and composition.

Therefore, we argue that any course that requires students to engage in significant written research should structurally reflect that requirement through a research and writing intensive course designation. Courses designated as research and writing intensive should be offered with the addition of a weekly, one-credit-hour, researched writing lab. While we provide an 8-week lesson sequence for use in the first half of a 16-week semester to prepare students for individual research and writing in the semester's second half, that additional weekly hour could alternate between meetings in the library or campus writing center, continuing to engage students and faculty with social epistemic praxis. Finally, we argue that faculty should encourage students to consider extending their research outside the scope of the class and present their findings to public audiences. Opportunities for continued scholarly dialectic (Berlin, 2003a) might take the form of interdisciplinary campus or regional undergraduate research conferences or submission of students' work to undergraduate research publication venues.

Ultimately, writing and library faculty must convince administrators and campus constituents of their disciplinary expertise and value, of the importance of allowing the necessary time, space, and compensation to effectively impart to students the essentials of these most crucial disciplines. The typical 3-credit-hour composition course simply does not allow time or space to develop either the skills or the ethos that students need to become confident writers and users of information, to develop a researcherly ethos. Writing and information literacy must cease to be invisible competencies, taken for granted and expected to be acquired through osmosis. Rather, they should have focal places in the curriculum so that students may acquire facility in these crucial knowledge areas that underlie competency in all other disciplines.

NOTES

1. Aristotle includes energeia in his three-part figure of speech taxonomy to denote activity, dynamism, energy, and vigor of oral or written rhetoric. See Jeanne Fahnestock (2008).
2. This lesson sequence is adapted from original lessons designed by the authors as well as Katie Loehrlein (2016), Instruction and Outreach Librarian at the University of Southern Indiana.

REFERENCES

Association of College and Research Libraries. (2016). *Framework for information literacy for higher education*. Retrieved from http://www.ala.org/acrl/standards/ilframework

Berlin, J. A. (1987). *Rhetoric and reality: Writing instruction in American colleges, 1900–1985*. Southern Illinois University Press.

Berlin, J. (2003b). Rhetoric and ideology in the writing class. In V. Villanueva (Ed.), *Cross talk in comp theory: A reader* (pp. 717–738). Urbana: National Council of Teachers of English.

Berlin, J. A. (2003a). Contemporary composition: The major pedagogical theories. In V. Villanueva (Ed.), *Cross-talk in comp theory: A reader* (pp. 255–270). Urbana: National Council of Teachers of English.

Booth, C., Lowe, M. S., Tagge, N., & Stone, S. M. (2015). Degrees of impact: Analyzing the effects of progressive librarian course collaborations on student performance. *College & Research Libraries, 76*(5), 623–651. https://doi.org/10.5860/crl.76.5.623

Butler, J. (1993). *Bodies that matter: On the discursive limits of "sex."* New York: Routledge.

Connors, R. (1997). *Composition-rhetoric: Backgrounds, theory, and pedagogy.* University of Pittsburgh Press.

Council of Writing Program Administrators, National Council of Teachers of English, & National Writing Project. (2011). *Framework for success in postsecondary writing.* Retrieved from http://wpacouncil.org/framework

Downs, D. ,& Wardle, E. (2007). Teaching about writing, righting misconceptions: (Re)envisioning "First Year Composition" as "Introduction to Writing Studies." *College Composition and Communication, 58*(4), 552–584.

Elmborg, J. K. (2003). Information literacy and writing across the curriculum: Sharing the vision. *Reference Services Review, 31*(1), 68–80.

Enos, T. (1996). *Gender roles and faculty lives in rhetoric and composition.* Carbondale: Southern Illinois University Press.

Enos, T. (2003). Gender and publishing scholarship in rhetoric and composition. In G. E. Kirsch, F. S. Maor, L. Massey, L. Nickson-Massey, & M. P. Sheridan-Rabideau (Eds.), *Feminism and composition: A critical sourcebook* (pp. 558–572). Boston: Bedford/St. Martin's.

Enos, T. (2009). Mentoring—and (WO)mentoring—in composition studies. In *Renewing rhetoric's relationship to composition: Essays in honor of Theresa Jarnagin Enos* (pp. 159–167). Routledge Taylor & Francis Group. https://doi.org/10.4324/9780203869222

Fahnestock, J. (2008). Aristotle and theories of figuration. In A. G. Gross & A. E. Walzer (Eds.), *Rereading Aristotle's* Rhetoric (pp. 166–184). Carbondale: Southern Illinois University Press.

Freire, P. (2000). *Pedagogy of the oppressed.* New York: Continuum.

Gibson, C., & Jacobson, T. (2014). *Framework for information literacy for higher education, draft 1, part 1.* Association of College and Research Libraries. Retrieved from http://acrl.ala.org/ilstandards/wp-content/uploads/2014/02/Framework-for-IL-for-HE-Draft-1-Part-1.pdf

Gregory, M. W. (2001). Curriculum, pedagogy, and teacherly ethos. *Pedagogy, 1*(1), 69–89.

Hartwell, P. (2003). Grammar, grammars, and the teaching of grammar. In V. Villanueva (Ed.), *Cross-talk in comp theory: A reader* (pp. 205–233). Urbana: National Council of Teachers of English.

Loehrlein, K. (2016). Searching as strategic exploration: Approaching problems like a professional. Unpublished lesson plan, David L. Rice Library, University of Southern Indiana.

Miller, S. (1991a). The feminization of composition. In R. H. Bullock, J. Trimbur, & C. I. Schuster (Eds.), *The politics of writing instruction: Postsecondary* (pp. 39–53). Portsmouth, NH: Boynton/Cook.

Miller, S. (1991b). *Textual carnivals: The politics of composition.* Carbondale: Southern Illinois University Press.

Murray, D. M. (2003). Teach writing as a process not product. In V. Villanueva (Ed.), *Cross-talk in comp theory: A reader* (2nd ed., pp. 3–6). Urbana: National Council of Teachers of English.

Oakleaf, M., Hoover, S., Woodard, B. S., Corbin, J., Hensley, R., Wakimoto, D. K., . . . Iannuzzi, P. A. (2012). Notes from the field: 10 short lessons on one-shot instruction. *Communications in Information Literacy, 6*(1), 5. Retrieved from http://www.comminfolit.org/index.php?journal=cil&page=article&op=view&path%5B%5D=v6i1p5

Schell, E. E. (1992). The feminization of composition: Questioning the metaphors that bind women teachers. *Composition Studies, 20*(1), 55–61.

Schell, E. E. (1998). *Gypsy academics and mother-teachers: Gender, contingent labor, and writing instruction*. Portsmouth, NH: Boynton/Cook.

Vella, L., & Holles, C. (2014). Collegiate research: More than Google. Unpublished lesson plan, Center for Academic Services and Advising, Colorado School of Mines.

PART III

Pedagogies and Practices

CHAPTER 10

IN, INTO, AMONG, BETWEEN

Information Literacy Skills in Transition

Crystal Bickford
Megan Palmer

The seemingly endless options for composition studies outcomes, and what form those outcomes should take, have been present for decades. Additionally, the concept of information literacy (IL) is no stranger to being the focus of debate as schools have addressed and/or integrated the practice quite differently from one another. In some cases, IL instruction remains an isolated activity within the confines of the library's responsibility; other times, librarians are invited into the classroom as guests. Arguably, the best models provide a collaborative approach where writing faculty and librarians work together, equally, to create curricula targeted to students' abilities to recognize and integrate quality sources appropriately into their writing.

Building these relationships is tedious, slow, and confusing; both parties work to carve out class time, debating the use of the *Framework* offered by the Association for College and Research Libraries (ACRL). Artman, Frisicaro-Pawlowski, and Monge (2010) argue,

> even as institutions are beginning to embrace direct information literacy instruction as part of the twenty-first century college curriculum, sustained attention to students' use of information resources has not yet become a central curricular component of first-year composition, where information and research instruction is so often relegated to a one-shot library session. (p. 94)

The "why" for IL curriculum is clear; the "how to" of integrating it into writing classes, however, is not—especially since the ACRL's 2000 guidelines were replaced by a broader *Framework* (ACRL *Annual Report 2015–2016*) that opens the interpretation of outcomes and best practices further.

BRIEF HISTORY OF "INFORMATION LITERACY"

The term "information literacy" has been worked and reworked for several decades, most often by university libraries seeking to support programs within their institutions. Understanding the evolution of the term, as well as the concepts surrounding it, provides a valuable context to the current situation of how libraries and writing programs currently build their partnerships.

Paul Zurkowski (1974), former president of the Information Industry Association, is credited with coining the phrase "information literacy" when he discussed the increasing amount of public information and described information-literate individuals as those who have "learned techniques and skills for utilizing the wide range of information tools as well as primary sources in molding information solutions to their problems" (p. 6), referring to private-sector resources, emerging information banks, the publishing industry, and so on. Additionally, he claimed that only "one-sixth of the U.S. Population [was] information literate" (p. 27), thus prompting him to write a proposal to the National Commission on Libraries and Information Science (Corrall, 2008, p. 26) in an effort to standardize IL specifications.

By the mid-1980s, the term "information literacy" was being applied to individual schools. For instance, Auraria Library, a library in Colorado serving several branches of higher education ranging from a local community college to a university, committed to a definition that stated, "Information literacy is the ability to effectively access and evaluate information for a given need" (Breivik, 1985, p. 723) and subsequently included a set of characteristics that encouraged the ability to utilize skills to obtain information that included "persistence," "attention to detail," and "caution [in] accepting printed word and single sources" (p. 723) while acknowledging the time required for developing and maintaining successful IL.

As other schools pondered their guidelines, the National Forum on Information Literacy was founded by representatives from business, government, and educational sectors charged with developing "a consensus on a definition of the term information literacy and nam[e] outcome measures for the concept" (Doyle, 1992, p. 2). Their final definition read, "*information literacy is the ability to access, evaluate, and use information from a variety of sources*" (original emphasis) (p. 2) along with a list of "attributes of an information literate person" (using the aforementioned Zurkowski term), each of which could be used as part of "potential rubrics for a checklist of skills comprising the process" (p. 2).

In 2000, the Association for College and Research Libraries (ACRL) and the American Library Association (ALA) released a list of competency standards in hopes of unifying the outcomes of IL across the country in their report, *Information Literacy Competency Standards for Higher Education.* The report's opening statement reads, "Information literacy is a set of abilities requiring individuals to recognize when information is needed and have the ability to locate, evaluate, and use effectively the needed information" (ALA & ACRL, 2000, p. 2).

The document addresses IL in the context of technology, higher education, pedagogy, and the suggested use of the standards in that the competencies allow "faculty, librarians and others [to] pinpoint specific indicators that identify a student as information literate" (p. 5); however, they also emphasize the fact that institutions should "first review [their] mission and educational goals to determine how information literacy would improve learning and enhance the institution's effectiveness. To facilitate acceptance of the concept, faculty and staff development is also crucial" (p. 6).

Johnston and Webber (2003) adjusted their definition to include the statement that IL should include a "critical awareness of the importance of wise and ethical use of information in society" (p. 336) while acknowledging that other definitions emphasize broader "cultural, social and economic developments associated with the information society" (p. 336). These more encompassing definitions of IL relate, certainly, to Zurkowski's original (and broader) view of IL from some thirty years earlier.

Still other institutions addressed IL in technological terms, especially in the early 2000s, thus addressing the increasing multimodality of digital literacy and consequently placing higher demands on already taxed IL programs (Brown & Slafter van Tryon, 2010; Fahser-Herro & Steinkuehler, 2009–2010). As with other disparities in IL, technology is another facet of debate where "a teacher looking to the literature for guidance will find that specific recommendations for considering the differences between new literacy needs and traditional approaches are lacking" (Brown & Slafter van Tryon, 2010, p. 235).

The lack of uniformity in established outcomes mirrored the diverse locations where IL ultimately "lived" in any given institution, including but not limited to being housed only within the school's library, integrated into cross-disciplinary writing programs, covered in first-year transition/seminar programs, and/or addressed in first-year composition

IL TIMELINE

- **1974:** Paul Zurkowski discusses the "information literate" individual and coins the phrase "information literacy" (Zurkowski, 1974)
- **1987:** Presidential Committee on Information Literacy formed ("Presidential Committee on Information Literacy: Final Report," 1989)
- **1988:** *Real World Intelligence (2)* written by Herbert E. Meyer (applied to managing business with access to too much information) ("Presidential Committee on Information Literacy: Final Report," 1989)
- **1989:** Presidential Committee on Information Literacy publishes report regarding the importance of IL (Brose, 2002)
- **1991:** World Wide Web is available to the public (Bryant, 2011)
- **1992:** National Forum on Information Literacy founded (*The Prague Declaration*, 2003)
- **1998:** First credit-bearing information literacy class (University of Strathclyde) appears in the research (Mayer & Bowles-Terry, 2013)
- **1999:** Society of College, National and University Libraries (SCONUL) publishes "The Seven Pillars of Information Literacy" ("Seven Pillars of Information Literacy," 2017)
- **2000:** Association for College and Research Libraries (ACRL) standards implemented (ACRL *Annual Report 2015–2016*)
- **2003:** National Forum on Information Literacy and National Commission on Libraries and Information sponsors an international conference on IL (*The Prague Declaration*, 2003)
- **2006:** The first national Summit on Information Literacy is held (Crawford, 2013).
- **2009:** California establishes a Digital Literacy Leadership Council (Executive Order S-06-09, 2009)
- **2009:** President Barack Obama designates October 2009 as National Information Literacy Awareness Month ("Presidential Proclamation National Information Literacy Awareness Month," 2009)
- **2016:** ACRL standards rescinded (ACRL *Annual Report 2015–2016*)
- **2017:** ACRL frameworks implemented (ACRL *Annual Report 2015–2016*)

courses. In the past forty years, IL remains a fluid entity in higher education.

IL MEETS COMPOSITION STUDIES

The days of *The Periodical Guide to Literature*, card catalogs, and journal stacks where students photocopied articles or checked out microfiche are gone. But, nostalgia be what it may, also gone is the rather streamlined ability for students to access and review information and have confidence in its credibility. The digital natives in today's classroom now have endless possibilities for information retrieval, but that benefit carries an overwhelming amount of information to process and evaluate. Even prior to the age of technology and the Internet, Zurkowski (1974) recognized the ability to become overwhelmed with the sheer amount of information. When combined with a current generation often lacking in sustained concentration and reading abilities, IL is an overwhelming task for undergraduates (Behrens, 1994; Brown & Slafter van Tryon, 2010; Doyle, 1992).

Despite the overall agreement regarding the need to incorporate more IL engagement into the curriculum, many factors have hindered the process. One argument places blame on institutions that hold a double standard for teachers and librarians, stating that librarians are not teachers and to think of them in that role is "simply illogical" (Asher, 2003, p. 52). Artman, Frisicaro-Pawlowski, and Monge (2010) pointed out that it was the students who were slow to adjust their "habits as information seekers" (p. 93), slowing down successful classroom integration. In sum, both sides of the desk have been held accountable.

Norgaard (2003), on the other hand, places blame on the libraries who offer only "the quick field trip, the scavenger hunt, the generic stand-alone tutorial" (p. 124), as well as the composition instructors who failed to "adequately theorize the role of libraries and information literacy in its own rhetorical self-understanding and pedagogical practice" (p. 124). Others argue that as composition instruction transitioned from product to process, thus losing the "skills and drills" philosophy of teaching grammar, "similar instruction on the use and citation of sources has yet to be welcomed" (Harris, 2005, p. 5). And yet another position hypothesizes that librarians have failed to "articulate the contributions that [their] theoretical tradition can make to rhetoric and composition and, by extension, learning in general" (Bowles-Terry, Davis, & Holliday, 2010, p. 225).

Gullikson's (2006) multi-university study sums up the validity of all of these arguments; their findings indicate that faculty using ACRL standards specifically agree on their importance; however, there is "little agreement on when students would acquire them" (p. 583), and thus, ultimately, how. Additionally, there was little agreement "on the academic level at which IL outcomes are expected by faculty" (p. 591). Other instructors merely question time. How does a content area teacher decide what to sacrifice or cut from a syllabus in order to add IL in its place (Junisbai, Lowe, & Tagge, 2016; Kitchens & Barker, 2016)?

Ultimately, it is important to note that the progress of IL parallels the progress of composition classrooms during these same decades; writing instruction was moving away from product to process and writing labs were transitioning into writing centers. Writing outcomes lacked standardization as well and were undergoing their own metamorphosis. Jacobs and Jacobs (2009) aptly note that "like effective writing, effective research does not happen in just one sitting but involves iterative processes such as revision, reworking, rethinking, and above all, reflection" (p. 72). Without innovative IL programming to match the progression of composition theory and practice, the integration of the two stagnated, regardless of the observation that both are process-driven.

Highlighted Programs

The past two decades outline a wide variety of approaches of integrating IL with composition and writing, and a variety of factors are found to be at the root of building these relationships. A general consensus exists regarding the need for IL and for IL programming; in fact, one study including over 5,000 faculty representing multiple disciplines from four-year colleges and universities across the United States recorded that 50% strongly agreed that their "undergraduate students have poor skills related to locating and evaluating scholarly information" (Housewright, Schonfeld, & Wulfson, 2013, p. 53).

Institutional availability of dedicated staff, funding for training, general education outcomes, writing program standards, and institutional assessment criteria can all represent how and why partnerships are or are

APPROACHES TO IL

- **One-Shot/Workshop:** Libraries offer topic-specific workshops independent of the classroom
- **Embedded:** IL librarians and faculty work together to decide curriculum and write course objectives and/or outcomes together; library instruction is offered as part of a course
- **Credit-Bearing:** Institutions require credit-bearing courses as part of General Education and/or program requirements

not formed. That being said, there is some interesting programming happening across the country.

Although it paints a somewhat broad picture of IL programming, the majority of current IL programs tend to fall into one of three categories: (1) one-shot/workshops, (2) embedded approaches, or (3) credit-bearing/stand-alone courses. The one-shot/workshop approach has librarians offering individual workshops on specific IL skills (i.e., database searches, plagiarism, documentation, etc.), and students attend outside of class or as part of a class fieldtrip. The embedded approach works to tailor these workshops for a specific course, thus customizing and making the workshops a part of the course. The credit-bearing/stand-alone course requires that students take a class (of varying credit assignment) dedicated solely to IL practices.

One-Shot/Workshop Approach

Interestingly, many of the models described forthcoming are built on the "one-shot" model (Artman et al., 2010; Jacobs & Jacobs, 2009; Kitchens & Barker, 2016), where workshop approaches run the risk of "provid[ing] just enough basic skill training for the student to find the 3–5 sources required to write their composition paper" (p. 94). With the increased demands of IL proficiency, however, many schools strive to make even workshop models more prevalent, integrative, and meaningful—for both student and classroom teacher. One of the essential elements of workshopping success is that, rather than allow IL professionals to conduct workshops in isolation, or "farm out," as described by Artman, Frisicaro-Pawlowski, and Monge (2010), creating workshops that integrate the expertise and knowledge of *both* the instructor and the IL professional is critical. Writing and IL are integrative skills; neither can be taught in isolation from each other.

Embedded Curricula

One way in which IL is being brought to undergraduate students is by bringing it directly to the classrooms in which these skills will be applied. Most often, students attend librarian-designed, course-related workshops that have been tailored to a specific course.

At Hostos Community College of the City University of New York, students working in groups are required to research a specific course-specific theme for which they individually maintain research logs, but collaboratively write a final narrative after attending a workshop on searching techniques, plagiarism concerns, and how to then apply that research (Henderson, Nunez-Rodriguez, & Casari, 2011).

Southern New Hampshire University (SNHU) follows a similar model where reference librarians are assigned to each college within the university. These dedicated librarians design workshops to support course objectives. For instance, in the sophomore-level writing course, a research writing course, the librarians often maintain notes on student projects and either hold class in a library classroom and/or visit classes throughout the entire semester. Topics of these workshops range from searching for sources, to appropriate documentation styles, plagiarism concerns, seeking quality information, writing sessions, and so on; however, each is tailored to the course theme and students' research topics.

Embedded Information Literacy

Where integrated workshops can act as a bridge between the classroom and the library, other universities have built their programs so that there is no need for a "bridge" at all; the library becomes as much a part of the curriculum and the environment as the classroom itself. As such, information literacy is embedded into the classroom, curriculum creation, and the university culture.

Utah State University's first- and second-year writing courses maintain an IL-centered program. Holliday and Fagerheim (2006) explain that "the curriculum is divided into four lessons. Two lessons take place in the English classroom and last for 30–35 minutes, and two take place in the library and last for approximately 50 minutes" (p. 179). With this model, there is a more even split between in-class and in-library instruction. Students are not merely exposed to IL as a means of meeting the class's requirements, but rather are able to experience IL in a way that is applicable and meaningful for the lifelong learner.

Information Literacy Across the Curriculum

Another form of embedded IL is built on the foundations established by Writing Across Curriculum (WAC) models. Nuemann University developed a "task force" dedicated to developing and implementing successful IL standards and practices. Comprised of faculty spanning disciplines, including "two from Arts and Sciences with one from science and the other from humanities, one from Business, one from Nursing, one from Adult Programs, one from Education, along with [an] individual from Information Technology, the Director of the Library, and the Reference Librarian" (Corso, Weiss, & McGregor, 2010, p. 11), this team developed "IL Institutional Goals" (p. 14) that correlated with the ACRL standards while also meeting the needs of the university and the individual students.

The task force implemented what they called a developmental model, where IL is introduced alongside the skills associated with students' major programs of study. This necessitated the revision of "basic entry-level courses for each major or minor program to incorporate expected IL standards," as well as the revision of "middle- and upper-level courses . . . to enhance and to extend IL concepts, building on the prior knowledge, skills, and values of the students" (p. 16). By embedding IL into these major-specific courses, this curricular and holistic model emphasizes students' current learning and future career-oriented goals.

Echoed at Arizona State University (ASU), IL skills and standards are built into core classes and are major specific. Corso (2010) writes, "Through integration of IL with the writing genres and styles of technical communication, students are gaining an understanding of the importance of finding, evaluating, and using information that is relevant within the context of their profession" (p. 216). This goal, alongside the university's collaborative approach between ASU's writing program and library, has enabled students to effectively develop IL skills in discipline and career specific ways.

A Flexible Approach

As seen with other embedded models, the librarian plays a key and functional role in the overall dissemination of IL. The following embedded IL model, which will be referred to as the "Flexible Approach," empowers faculty members to play an equal partnership when it comes to incorporating active IL skills into their courses (Junisbai et al., 2016).

Noticing a desire for IL, but a lack of IL incorporation, the library at Piltzer College created a three-tiered model of IL and librarian integration for all first-year seminar (FYS) courses. Faculty may select from "minimal, intermediate, and substantial collaboration," depending on the individual faculty member's preference and comfort level (Junisbai et al., p. 606). Each level allows the faculty member and the librarian to tailor the IL needs to the course as follows:

- Level 1 (or "Minimal Collaboration") includes "Brief mention of IL in syllabus; Minimal librarian input into research; assignment(s) design; One-shot library instruction; Course-specific online research guide; Students may complete online research tutorial and quiz" (p. 606).
- Level 2 (or Intermediate Collaboration) includes "IL directly integrated into syllabus and course, but not graded assignment; Modest librarian input into assignment(s) design; 1–2 instruction sessions; Course-specific online research guide; Students may complete online tutorial and quiz" (p. 606).
- Level 3 (or Substantial Collaboration) increases the partnership where "IL [is] directly integrated into syllabus, course, and graded assignment(s); Significant librarian input into assignment(s) design; 2+ instruction sessions/class visits; Course-specific online research guide; Students complete online tutorial and quiz" (p. 606).

This tiered strategy, or flexible approach, has allowed several benefits. Junisbai, Lowe, and Tagge report that

> faculty are now actively drawing upon the library's IL rubric and student learning outcomes to help them assess students' written work in a time- and energy-conscious manner. Faculty also turn to librarians as they seek to adapt best practices in the teaching of undergraduate research. (p. 609)

Most importantly, the authors indicate that faculty engage in the strategies that are most meaningful to them and their classroom designs.

Digital Initiatives

One of the more innovative approaches represented in the literature is the use of three-dimensional virtual worlds, as implemented by the University of Central Missouri. With the implementation of Second Life, an online role-playing environment of great popularity in the early 2000s, into the standard writing courses and expectations, students were required to perform a variety of tasks from leading virtual reference consultations to building a virtual branch location of the university library (Davis & Smith, 2009). Although the authors admit that the practice introduced a variety of challenges, this level of embedded instruction, especially via digital platforms, continues to hold a great deal of possibility, especially with the growing popularity of virtual reality (VR).

Credit-Bearing Information Literacy

Embedded information literacy models demonstrate that writing composition courses and IL have the potential to go hand-in-hand under the right curriculum and collaboration; however, some institutions have created stand-alone courses and IL curriculum that are required education for all first-year students, much like traditional first-year writing seminars (Deitering, 2008; Johnston & Webber, 2003; Loo & Chung, 2006).

Universities have achieved and implemented credit-based information literacy courses at a variety of intensity levels. Below is a small sample of descriptions gathered from schools' websites describing their courses:

Excelsior College

All students must complete "the minimum of a one-semester hour course or examination in information literacy with a grade of C or better to satisfy this requirement" ("Information Literacy Requirement: Statement of Policy," 2017a).

Weber University

All students must complete "a four-part Computer and Information Literacy (CIL) requirement to receive a bachelor's degree from WSU. It is suggested that CIL classes be taken within the first year of study. . . . A score of 73% is required to pass Computer and Information Literacy courses and exams" ("Computer and Information Literacy [CIL]," 2017).

University at Albany; State University of New York

All students must select from a list of "[a] pproved courses [that] introduce students to various ways in which information is organized and structured and to the process of finding, using, producing, and distributing information in a variety of media formats, including traditional print as well as computer databases" ("Information Literacy Courses," 2017).

Delta State University

All students are required to complete *Fundamentals of Information Literacy* (LIB 101), "an introduction to the principles, concepts, and practices of information literacy, including the critical thinking skills necessary to identify, evaluate, and use diverse information sources effectively" ("LIB101 Fundamentals of Information Literacy," 2017).

University of Baltimore

All students are required to complete *Introduction to Information Literacy* (INFO110), which "teaches students the fundamentals of information literacy. Students will determine their research needs, develop a search strategy to select appropriate sources, access those sources, critically evaluate the material found for relevance and credibility, and synthesize that material into original work" ("Information Literacy," 2017).

Ottawa University

All students are required to complete *Research Techniques and Technology* (LAS113525), which "focuses on the fundamental elements of information literacy and the concepts and skills involved with locating, evaluating, and using information from a variety of print and electronic sources in an effective and ethical manner" ("Information Literacy Requirement," 2017b).

COMMON ELEMENTS OF THE BEST PRACTICES

In examining the most successful practices in IL, common key factors stand out among the programs. The first is the emphasis—and success—of library/classroom collaboration. The programs mentioned, particularly the most holistic and integrated ones (i.e., Utah State University, Neumann University), all mention the importance of this partnership. IL cannot occur in a vacuum; therefore faculty spanning the classroom and the library are necessary.

Another key aspect that manifests in the more successful programs is collaboration on the creation of outcomes and programs themselves, ultimately manifesting in critical faculty buy in. What many of these programs have in common is how they were formed, in that they gave autonomy to multidisciplinary groups of faculty members charged with implementing and tracking the success of the standards (Davis & Smith, 2009; Holliday & Fagerheim, 2006; Junisbai et al., 2016). As D'Angelo and Maid verify, "Programs succeed when they are led by dynamic personalities with vision" (2004, p. 213).

Ultimately, there is no one-size-fits-all methodology. Each program employs different structures, goals, and levels of integration. In this, however, each program has in common its own focus on its own university. Building on available frameworks, each university must understand the needs of its student population and the capabilities of its faculty (Deitering, 2008; Henderson et al., 2011; Junisbai et al., 2016). Each university that has built any level of curriculum around IL has demonstrated an assessment of what that university, that environment, and that student population requires.

COMPETENCY STANDARDS AND FRAMEWORKS

Before concluding, the shift from ACRL's *Competency Standards* to a *Framework* is worth noting, especially due to the recent transition in January 2016 ("Framework for Information Literacy for Higher Education," 1996–2017). Part of the justification of the organization's change emphasizes the interconnectedness of student, faculty, and librarian:

> [T]he rapidly changing higher education environment, along with the dynamic and often uncertain information ecosystem in which all of us work and live, require new attention to be focused on foundational ideas about that ecosystem. Students have a greater role and responsibility in creating new knowledge, in understanding the contours and the changing dynamics of the world of information, and in using information, data, and scholarship ethically. Teaching faculty have a greater responsibility in designing curricula and assignments that foster enhanced engagement with the core ideas about information and scholarship within their disciplines. Librarians have a greater responsibility in identifying core ideas within their own knowledge domain that can extend learning for students, in creating a new cohesive curriculum for information literacy, and in collaborating more extensively with faculty.

Last, as readers of this text ponder strategies and initiatives for their own institutions, perhaps it is best to also share the current definition provided by ACRL. The *Framework* states:

Because this *Framework* envisions information literacy as extending the arc of learning throughout students' academic careers and as converging with other academic and social learning goals, an expanded definition of information literacy is offered here to emphasizes dynamism, flexibility, individual growth, and community learning:

> Information literacy is the set of integrated abilities encompassing the reflective discovery of information, the understanding of how information is produced and valued, and the use of information in creating new knowledge and participating ethically in communities of learning. ("Framework for Information Literacy for Higher Education," 1996–2017)

In other words, the new *Framework* allows for more fluidity, while encouraging and supporting not only the initiatives outlined in this chapter, but the myriad of programs other schools are implementing. While not writing or composition specific, the *Framework* strengthens interdisciplinary conversations, partnerships, and pliability of programs, coursework, and curriculum development across any given campus.

CONCLUSION

The authors hope that this chapter outlines the plethora of opportunities that lie ahead in IL and writing studies, which will continue to change as schools reconsider their positions in light of the new *Framework*. The authors also acknowledge important topics that are not covered. For instance, how information literacy links to independent learning and social responsibility are untapped subjects in this chapter in addition to commentary about when information literacy education should begin, how it may or may not be addressed in secondary education, and how students transition from secondary to postsecondary information-seeking activities. Another area for exploration is the application of IL to students after graduation and its relationship to careers and citizenship.

But the goal, we hope, has been achieved in the reassurance that there is no single "cure-all" in the efforts of librarians and writing faculty. Taking the time to examine personnel, current courses, general education requirements, resources, campus space, desired outcomes for IL and writing, and student profiles are just a few of the factors schools should take into consideration during their discussions.

REFERENCES

ACRL *Annual Report 2015–2016*. (n.d.). Retrieved August 9, 2017, from http://crln.acrl.org/index.php/crlnews/article/view/9594/10975

ALA & ACRL. (2000). Information literacy competency standards for higher education. Retrieved from http://www.ala.org/acrl/ilcomstan.html

Artman, M., Frisicaro-Pawlowski, E., & Monge, R. (2010). Not just one shot: Extending the dialogue about information literacy in composition classes. *Composition Studies, 38*(2), 93–109.

Asher, C. (2003). Separate but equal: Librarians, academics and information literacy. *Australian Academic & Research Libraries, 34*(1), 52–55.

Behrens, S. J. (1994). A conceptual analysis and historical overview of information literacy. *College and Research Libraries, 55*(4), 309–322.

Bowles-Terry, M., Davis, E., & Holliday, W. (2010). "Writing information literacy" revisited: Application of theory to practice in the classroom. *References & User Services Quarterly, 49*(3), 115–230.

Breivik, P. S. (1985). Putting libraries back in the information society. *American Libraries*, p. 723.

Brose, F. K. (2002). Information competency and community college librarians: California moves toward a graduation requirement. *Community & Junior College Libraries, 11*(1), 37–44.

Brown, A., & Slafter van Tryon, P. J. (2010). Twenty-first century literacy: A matter of scale from micro to mega. *Clearing House, 83*, 235–238.

Bryant, Martin. (2011). 20 years ago today, the World Wide Web opened to the public. Retrieved from https://thenextweb.com/insider/2011/08/06/20-years-ago-today-the-world-wide-web-opened-to-the-public/#.tnw_11C3jjEO

Corrall, S. (2008). Information literacy strategy development in higher education: An exploratory study. *International Journal of Information Management, 28*, 26–37.

Corso, G., Weiss, S., & McGregor, T. (2010). Information literacy: A story of collaboration between the writing program coordinator and colleagues 2003–2010. National Conference of the Council of Writing Program Administrators, Philadelphia, PA, July 16, 2010.

Computer and Information Literacy. (2017). Retrieved from http://www.weber.edu/cil

Crawford, J. (2013). Relevant policy documents both from within and beyond the LIS profession. In J. Crawford & C. Irving (Eds.), *Information literacy and lifelong learning: Policy issues, the workplace, health, and public libraries* (pp. 35–58). Oxford, UK: Chandos Publishing.

D'Angelo, B., & Maid, B. (2004). Moving beyond definitions: Implementing information literacy across the curriculum. *Journal of Academic Librarianship, 30*(3), 212–217.

Davis, M. G., & Smith, C. E. (2009). Virtually embedded: Library instruction within second life. *Journal of Library and Information Services in Distance Learning, 3*(4), 120–137.

Deitering, A.M. (2008). Step by step through the scholarly conversation: A collaborative library/writing faculty project to embed information literacy and promote critical thinking in first year composition at Oregon State University. *College and Undergraduate Libraries, 15*(1/2), 57–79.

Doyle, C. S. (1992). Outcome measures for information literacy within the National Education Goals of 1990. Final report to National Forum on Information Literacy. Summary of Findings. *Viewpoints*, pp. 2–16.

Executive Order S-06-09. (2009). Retrieved from https://www.gov.ca.gov/news.php?id=12393

Fahser-Herro, D., & Steinkuehler, C. (2009–2010). Web 2.0 literacy and secondary teacher education. *Journal of Computing in Teacher Education, 26*(2), 55–62.

Framework for Information Literacy for Higher Education. (1996–2017). Retrieved from http://www.ala.org/acrl/standards/ilframework#introduction

Gullikson, S. (2006). Faculty perceptions of ACRL's information literacy competency standards for higher education. *Journal of Academic Librarianship, 32*(6), 583–592.

Harris, B. R. (2005). Credit where credit is due: Considering ethics, *ethos*, and process in library instruction on attribution. *Education Libraries, 28*(1), 4–11.

Henderson, F., Nunez-Rodriguez, N., & Casari, W. (2011). Enhancing research skills and information literacy in community college science students. *American Biology Teacher, 73*(5), 270–275.

Holliday, W., & Fagerheim, B. A. (2006). Integrating information literacy with a sequenced English composition curriculum. *Library Faculty & Staff Publications*, 169–184.

Housewright, R., Schonfeld, R., & Wulfson, K. (2013). Ithaka S+R US faculty survey 2012. *ITHAKA*. Retrieved from http://www.sr.ithaka.org/publications/us-faculty-survey-2012/

Information Literacy. (2017). Retrieved from http://langsdale.ubalt.edu/about-us/information-literacy/

Information Literacy Courses. (2017). Retrieved from http://www.albany.edu/generaleducation/information-literacy.php

Information Literacy Requirement. (2017a). Retrieved from https://info.excelsior.edu/student-policies/information-literacy-requirement/

Information Literacy Requirement. (2017b). Retrieved from http://ottawa.smartcatalogiq.com/en/2015-2016/Catalog/Graduation/Adult-Campuses-and-Online/Graduation-Requirements-The-College/Information-Literacy-Requirement

Jacobs, H. L. M., & Jacobs, D. (2009). Transforming the one-shot library session into pedagogical collaboration: Information literacy and the English composition class. *Reference & User Services Quarterly, 49*(1), 72–82.

Johnston, B., & Webber, S. (2003). Information literacy in higher education: A review and case study. *Studies in Higher Education, 28*(3), 335–352.

Junisbai, B., Lowe, M. S., & Tagge, N. (2016). A pragmatic and flexible approach to information literacy: Findings from a three-year study of faculty-librarian collaboration. *Journal of Academic Librarianship, 42*, 604–611.

Kitchens, R. K., & Barker, M. E. (2016). Synthesizing pedagogies and engaging students: Creating blended eLearning strategies for library research and writing instruction. *Reference Librarian, 57*(4), 323–335.

Lib101 Fundamentals of Information Literacy. (2017). Retrieved from http://www.deltastate.edu/academics/libraries/lib-101-fundamentals-of-information-literacy/

Loo, A., & Chung, C. W. (2006). A model for information literacy course development: A liberal arts perspective. *Library Review, 55*(4), 249–258.

Mayer, J., & Bowles-Terry, M. (2013). Engagement and assessment in a credit-bearing information literacy course. *Reference Services Review, 41*(1), 62–79.

Norgaard, R. (2003). Writing information literacy: Contributions to a concept. *Reference & User Services Quarterly, 43*(2), 124–130.

Prague Declaration. (2003). *The Prague Declaration: Towards an Information Literate Society.* Retrieved from http://www.unesco.org/fileadmin/MULTIMEDIA/HQ/CI/CI/pdf/PragueDeclaration.pdf

Presidential Committee on Information Literacy: Final Report. (1989). Retrieved from http://www.ala.org/acrl/publications/whitepapers/presidential

Presidential Proclamation National Information Literacy Awareness Month. (2009). Retrieved from https://obamawhitehouse.archives.gov/the-press-office/presidential-proclamation-national-information-literacy-awareness-month

Seven Pillars of Information Literacy. (2017). Retrieved from https://www.sconul.ac.uk/page/seven-pillars-of-information-literacy

Zurkowski, P. G. (1974). The information service environment relationships and priorities. (Related Paper No. 5, Ref. NCLiS-NPLIS-5). Washington, D.C.: National Commission on Libraries and Information Science. Retrieved from http://eric.ed.gov/PDFS/ED100391.pdf

CHAPTER 11

READING TO WRITE

Using Disciplinary Expertise and Source Reading With the ACRL Framework to Enhance the Conceptual Depth of Writing Students

William Badke

INTRODUCTION

Writing instructors regularly require students to do close reading of a variety of types of published material, the goal being to familiarize the student with the ways in which published writers express themselves. A strong movement within writing studies has been "disciplinary literacy" instruction that "emphasizes the unique tools that the experts in a discipline use to engage in the work of that discipline" (Shanahan & Shanahan, 2012, p. 8). When combined with close reading, emphasis on disciplinary distinctions can serve as a powerful means to enable students to grasp how scholars write, thus informing their own writing. Despite the fact that much of writing instruction today is generic, thus teaching general skills outside of disciplines (Russell, 1993; Shanahan & Shanahan, 2008; Smagorinsky, 2015), the number of advocates for a disciplinary emphasis in writing instruction is growing in recognition of the fact that disciplinary differences are crucial to higher education writing.

The idea that librarians might be instrumental in helping students to understand the disciplines within which they research and write is not a new one (Farrell & Badke, 2015; Luke & Kapitzke, 1999; Simmons, 2005). Nor is there anything unique about teaching students in higher education to understand the nature of disciplines in order to write like members of those disciplines write. While the ACRL *Framework for Information Literacy in Higher Education* (ACRL, 2015) can inform efforts of librarians to impart disciplinary understanding, it must be recognized that ACRL's is not the only relevant framework. In fact, the field of writing studies itself is blessed with a significant number of frameworks, each of which address disciplinary literacy instruction in some way or other. Our task, therefore, will be to determine how the ACRL *Framework* within a reading to write context can uniquely guide students into the disciplines within which they must write.

Writing instructors and librarians often operate in isolation from one another (except for short library instruction sessions in writing courses), but there is good reason to believe that the ACRL *Framework* could enhance the existing goals of writing instructors, specifically addressing a key challenge in the teaching of writing—enculturation, the task of leading students to become insiders within the variety of knowledge systems that inform their writing. Students generally lack understanding of what scholarship (or disciplinary discourse) is, how it functions, how to write within it, and how to evaluate one's own writing and the writing of others through disciplinary eyes. Thus they express themselves artificially, not at all like scholars in their disciplines. The *Framework* offers an opportunity to guide these students to learn to write like insiders.

APPROACHES TO UNDERSTANDING DISCIPLINES

If there ever was a notion that disciplines comprise merely specialized bodies of knowledge, that view has been strongly disabused by scholars in the field of disciplinary studies. In the midst of the abundant discussion about the nature of disciplines in writing studies, two approaches predominate: seeing disciplines as displayed through discourse patterns of written work and seeing disciplines as social constructions. These, however, are not mutually exclusive (Rainey, 2016), since both discourse patterns and social constructions obviously do operate within disciplines. If we wish a metaphor for the difference, the discourse pattern approach would be archaeology (study of written artifacts) and the social construction approach would be anthropology (study of the culture that produces the artifacts).

The discourse pattern view essentially asserts that writers in various disciplines have their own writing conventions, patterns of evidence and argumentation, terminology, and so on. A discipline is revealed through the distinctive ways discourse has been practiced in it (so Draper & Siebert, 2010; Greenleaf & Schoenbach, 2004; Habib, Haan, & Mallett, 2015; Schoenbach, Greenleaf, & Murphy, 2012; Spires, Kerkhoff, Graham, & Lee, 2014). Draper and Siebert argue, for example, that no matter what cultural forces may have produced texts within disciplines, "it is simply the case that texts must be read and written differently depending on the discipline in which they are being used or created" (p. 32). In essence, the student is left with texts, so studying the discourse of those texts reveals what is distinctive about the discipline that created them.

Those who see disciplines as social constructions do consider the texts of disciplines but argue that those texts do not reveal the nature of disciplines without due consideration of the cultures out of which the texts emerged. Lave and Wenger (1991; compare Choi, 2006) coined the expression that disciplines are essentially "communities of practice," meaning that ideas come out of a social setting that gives them their form. In turn, ideas shape and reshape communities. Moje (2008) identified three central features of this socially constructed view of disciplines: discourses and practices, identities and identifications, and knowledge (p. 100). This is a much more dynamic view of disciplines, which sees them as evolving through the interactions of their practitioners. Thus methods and forms of discourse, while relatively stable, are subject to change over time. Linton, Madigan, and Johnson (1994) argue, "Disciplinary styles are not just frames or shells into which content can be cast, but habits of thought and communication grounded in the objectives, values, and 'world view' of each discipline. To ignore these realities in a general composition course seems irresponsible" (p. 65). Other expressions in use regarding this approach see disciplines as "active ways of knowing" (Carter, 2006, p. 387) or "social action" (Miller, 1984, 2015), thus emphasizing the dynamism of disciplinary work.

An objection to this approach comes from those who argue for a critical or constructivist view of the disciplines. Some from this camp argue that it is the reader who constructs the meaning of texts, not the discipline that defines meaning (Flower, 1990; Haas & Flower, 1988; Horning, 2007). Others encourage students to move beyond disciplinary restrictions (Bartholomae, 1986; Schroeder, 2001), while still others even encourage active critique of disciplinary conventions (Moje, 2007). Russell (1993) argues, however, that it is impossible for students to contribute to and transform disciplines until they have participated in them. Wingate (2012) argues: "It is difficult to see, however, how students would be able to challenge practices before they have fully understood them" (p. 28).

While critical and constructivist activities are no doubt valuable, the approach of this chapter will be to find means to lead students into disciplinary cultures, out of which distinctive forms of writing emerge. It may seem simpler to teach students the discourse conventions of disciplines, but a deeper

LEGITIMATE PERIPHERAL PARTICIPATION

"Learning viewed as situated activity has as its central defining characteristic a process that we call *legitimate peripheral participation*. By this we mean to draw attention to the point that learners inevitably participate in communities of practitioners and that the mastery of knowledge and skill requires newcomers to move toward full participation in the sociocultural practices of a community."

—Lave & Wenger, 1991

understanding of disciplinary dynamic functioning, and an opportunity to enter more fully into various disciplinary environments, comes best through an understanding of disciplinary culture and practice.

WRITING STUDIES FRAMEWORKS AND DISCIPLINARY UNDERSTANDING

The field of writing studies has put forward a number of frameworks and standards documents that relate in part to disciplinary understanding. It is now fairly common, though not universal, to base such frameworks on Meyer and Land's (2003, 2005) "threshold concepts" research, which views key insights as crucial doorways into new understanding.

The most prominent writing studies document in this regard is *Framework for Success in Postsecondary Writing* (2012) issued by the Council of Writing Program Administrators and two other national bodies. While putting quite a lot of emphasis on disciplinary understanding and writing, it is essentially a standards-based guide rather than the sort of framework that emphasizes threshold concepts (Hansen, 2012; McComiskey, 2012). Its main emphasis with regard to disciplines is that students need to gain knowledge of writing conventions, including those of various genres.

Other frameworks and framework-like statements have emerged over the past few decades. Lea and Street (1998) developed an "Academic Literacies Framework" related to practices involved in reading and writing within disciplines, viewed as academic communities. The Reading Apprenticeship Framework (Greenleaf & Schoenbach, 2004; Greenleaf et al., 2010; Schoenbach, Greenleaf, & Murphy, 2012) involves a metacognitive process in which someone knowledgeable in a discipline walks alongside a student using guided questions that reveal the processes by which a disciplinary text was created. The READI Framework of Knowledge Informing Literary Reading (Goldman et al., 2016; Lee & Goldman, 2015) draws on both the knowledge and the methods disciplinary scholars enlist in writing texts.

The most significant set of threshold concepts for writing studies is that of Adler-Kassner and Wardle, *Naming What We Know* (*NWWK*) (2015), which bases its work on the Meyer and Land approach. Through 37 threshold concepts, *NWWK* details what instructors of writing know about the understandings their students must have. Of particular significance are the emphases that students need to write as disciplinarians do and that they need to learn how to communicate with disciplinarians as disciplinarians communicate. Student writing is thus enculturated in disciplinary thinking. Johnson and McCracken (2016) point out that *NWWK* shows several strong correspondences with the ACRL *Framework for Information Literacy in Higher Education.* For example, the ACRL concept Scholarship as Conversation has the similar statements in *NWWK* that "Writing Is a Social and Rhetorical Activity" and that "Texts Get Their Meaning From Other Texts."

Clearly scholars of writing education have thought deeply about the nature of disciplinarity, including the best practices to be sought in teaching students how to read, and thus to write, in disciplines. It is our contention that we need to move beyond studying artifacts and find a means to introduce students to disciplinary cultures. The ACRL *Framework* offers a further way to do that effectively.

SITUATED INFORMATION LITERACY

"Information literacy instruction in higher education, if it is to meet the needs of an information age that demands skilled handlers of information, must therefore move beyond its current status as generic, short-term, and remedial and embrace a more comprehensive understanding of IL's situated place within the socio-cultural practices of the disciplines. IL must locate itself at the foundation of disciplinary education and be a crucial element of the curriculum throughout a student's educational program."

—Farrell & Badke, 2015

THE UNIQUE CONTRIBUTION OF THE ACRL *FRAMEWORK*

Moje (2007) argued: "We need a more carefully detailed archaeology of the disciplinary practices, one that mines both the cognitive processes and the cultural practices that mediate those processes." Existing frameworks in writing studies are useful guides for doing that archaeology, but they are less focused on studying living disciplinary cultures (anthropology) than studying artifacts (archaeology). The ACRL *Framework* offers an opportunity to do anthropology. While *NWWK* (Adler-Kassner & Wardle, 2015) says a lot about disciplinary cultures, it focuses on how those cultures produce written work. The ACRL *Framework* inhabits disciplinary cultures in a more direct way. Jacobsen and Gibson (2015) emphasize the uniquely anthropological emphasis in the ACRL *Framework* as they state: "The Framework affords a broader, integrated set of 'big ideas' about research, scholarship, and information." This the world of anthropology rather than mere archaeology.

This is not to say that the ACRL *Framework* is unique. Most of its principles are reflected in the various writing frameworks, particularly that of *NWWK.* The distinctiveness of the ACRL *Framework* may well lie more in emphasis than in content, since it tends to stand back from the written product itself to consider issues like scholarly discourse, authority, inquiry, development of information resources, and so on. We will show that the ACRL *Framework* uniquely leads its instructors to the cultures out of which disciplinary writers write rather than simply to the artifacts that are to be interpreted.

AN ACRL *FRAMEWORK* APPROACH TO READING FOR WRITING IN THE DISCIPLINES

Our approach seeks to enlist the culture of disciplines to enable students to read disciplinary writing anthropologically, that is, in a way that sees and understands the underlying society of disciplinarians as they do their work. Most students come to a new discipline as visitors and thus tend to be alienated from disciplines (like foreigners in a new land). More seriously, they tend not to understand the values, thinking processes and methods unique to each discipline.

Librarians, as they interact with disciplinary faculty as well as professors in writing courses, have a unique opportunity to guide anthropological understanding that can open disciplines to students so that they can become part of disciplinary culture, something Lea and Street (1998) referred to as "academic socialization." They can do this by enlisting disciplinary faculty to open up about their culture and their work. A potential drawback, however, is that disciplinary faculty can have difficulty explaining the requirements of disciplinary writing to their students (Lea & Street, 1998; Middendorf & Pace, 2004). This is likely because their disciplinary work is intuitive and thus difficult to describe in words. But what if disciplinarians were asked actually to talk about themselves, about their own culture, through a set of guiding questions?

We are suggesting that librarians go directly to authors of such works and have them explain the cultures out of which they write. The ACRL *Framework* can be a very helpful document for this opportunity, because it opens doors to move more deeply into disciplinary cultures than what is found in merely reading texts. In essence, if a librarian informed by the ACRL *Framework* were to talk a disciplinary scholar through questions intended to reveal disciplinary culture and then have that scholar provide a close reading of a disciplinary work, students could find a doorway into the discipline and a much deeper sense of what it means to write from within a disciplinary culture.

We need to establish a few foundational concepts at this point. First, disciplines are cultures, communities of practice. As such, they may be characterized as having an epistemology (foundational knowledge base established by specifically disciplinary criteria), a metanarrative (a cultural understanding of who the community is, including its beliefs and aspirations), and a method (Farrell & Badke, 2015). Second, the ACRL *Framework* is essentially a set of concepts to help describe how disciplines function and do their work. This is specified in the *Framework*'s introduction: "At the heart of this Framework are conceptual understandings that organize many other concepts and ideas about information, research, and scholarship into a coherent whole" (ACRL, 2015).

If we think about the means by which immigrants to a society are enculturated, we find that it is best done through a combination of cultural explanation and actual lived experience within the culture where the newcomer can observe it in practice. If the goal of disciplinary educators is to have students engage in "legitimate peripheral participation" (Lave & Wenger, 1991) or "enter that community and its culture" (Brown, Collins, & Duguid, 1989, p. 33) in order to "think like historians and physicists" (Flower, 1990, p. 5), they need to enlist tools that enable cultural invitation.

AN ACRL *FRAMEWORK* APPROACH IN PRACTICE

How would the use of ACRL *Framework* as an enculturation tool work? It would need to include willing disciplinary faculty who could, either as guests in writing courses or as professors in their own courses, provide two crucial services: to elucidate their disciplinary cultures though a process of ACRL *Framework*–guided interviews; and to provide close readings that reveal their disciplinary culture (anthropology) through its artifacts.

Steps to Be Taken

An approach to enabling students to find their way into disciplines could look like this:

1. Librarians approach writing instructors and key disciplinary faculty with the essential problem that students do not write like disciplinarians.
2. Librarians then establish a process that enables disciplinary faculty to articulate their cultures in such a way that dominant cultural and discourse values are revealed. This can best be done through a series of questions, first answered in writing by the disciplinarian, then reviewed in concert with the librarian, and finally presented live by the disciplinarian in the classroom.
3. Having used a question and answer session live in the classroom to establish a set of disciplinary elements that reveal disciplinary culture, the faculty member would then walk students through a close reading of a self-written paper, showing how those values were articulated.
4. Students would follow up with an analysis of the same paper, revealing their understanding of the disciplinary culture it reveals. Further writing in the discipline would be assigned.

Of importance to this process, from the ACRL *Framework*, are five of its threshold concepts: Authority Is Constructed and Contextual, Information Creation as a Process, Research as Inquiry, Scholarship as Conversation, and Searching as Strategic Exploration. Each reflects an aspect of the scholarly cultures found in various disciplines.

The Questions

The first task would be to create a question set to show how each ACRL *Framework* concept connects with an aspect of disciplinary scholarship (see Box 11.1). It would be helpful for disciplinary participants to provide students with a one- or two-page summary of the essential values and methods of their disciplines, based on the questions they have answered.

The Close Reading

The second part of the disciplinary exercise would involve the disciplinarian walking students through a representative example of disciplinary writing, preferably a work written by the disciplinarian leading this activity. The close reading would illustrate disciplinary thinking, values, and methods. The questions in Box 11.2 could serve as a guide.

BOX 11.1

GUIDED QUESTIONS FOR DISCIPLINARY EXPERTS, BASED ON THE ACRL FRAMEWORK

Authority Is Constructed and Contextual: With regard to authority, the very heart of any discipline is trust in the information base and the voices that speak authoritatively to the discipline's core beliefs. Disciplinarians guard both their ability to speak with authority and the expertise criteria used to validate authority.

1. How did the knowledge base in your discipline come into being?
2. What criteria do you use to test the validity of research in it and thus its authority?
3. How does the discipline determine which voices within it have authority and which do not? How important, for example, is the number of citations a piece of writing has received?
4. How does your discipline respond to challenges to the authority of its knowledge base and key voices? These might include the work of dissenters or outliers who do not fit well within the discipline's mainstream.

Information Creation as a Process: The manner in which information is created speaks strongly to its depth and quality.

1. How do you go about choosing a goal for research?
2. How do you go about researching and writing your paper? What steps do you take? In what ways do they vary?
3. How do you choose the journal or publisher to which you plan to submit your work?
4. How has peer review worked in your experience? Can you highlight some of the joys and sorrows of having your work peer reviewed?
5. How long does the writing process generally take for a research paper? How long does it take from submission to publication?
6. Have you tried alternative forms of publication (blogs, columns, etc.)? If so, how is that kind of publication different?

Research as Inquiry: Disciplinary research shapes its patterns of inquiry in specific ways.

1. Can you describe the nature of inquiry in your discipline, including tools, methods, evidence, and so on?
2. What are the goals of inquiry in your discipline, that is, what are you trying to accomplish?
3. To what extent are your methods flexible or open to change?
4. How does the discipline respond to scholars within it who suggest new methods of inquiry or reject old ones? How do you measure the validity of suggested method revisions?

Scholarship as Conversation: All scholarly work within a discipline is essentially a social activity bound up in discourse around points of view, evidence, and the contributions of the discipline's scholars. This conversation helps explain the culture of the discipline.

1. Describe the pattern of interaction with your fellow scholars over issues. Is it confrontational, collaborative, or would you use some other term to describe it?
2. Can you explain your scholarly culture, the academic values you all share that enable your conversation to function well?
3. What does legitimate conversation look like in your discipline? What kinds of conversations would you view as illegitimate or detrimental to advancing your discipline?

Searching as Strategic Exploration: The patterns of activity in identifying relevant resources for research help to explain how a discipline does its work.

1. What common tools do you use in identifying relevant sources for your writing (e.g., citation-chaining, databases, use of personal contacts, perusing key journals on a regular basis)?
2. Can you give an example of a time you struggled to identify relevant resources, and how you resolved that struggle?
3. How do you organize your resources in order to reveal patterns of thought within them?

BOX 11.2
QUESTIONS FOR CLOSE READING OF A DISCIPLINARY TEXT

1. What was the motivation in writing this paper?
2. How did the author formulate the main question/thesis? How does the way it is expressed describe the values your discipline operates by?
3. What can we learn about your discipline from the way the data is presented, how it was developed, and what evidential value it has?
4. How does the author interact with other scholars? What does this say about the nature of discussion that is carried out in the discipline?
5. What does the paper reveal about the nature of good evidence? What is the difference between legitimate and illegitimate evidence?
6. How do the conclusions make the case?

Once these exercises have been completed in class, disciplinary faculty can develop a rubric that sets requirements for the crucial elements that must be found in writing within the discipline under study. That rubric would then form the basis for creating and evaluating an assigned student research paper in the discipline.

CONCLUSION

Our basic premise is that disciplines are socially constructed so that student understanding of them is best done anthropologically through interaction with real disciplinarians and then in a secondary way archaeologically through the study of disciplinary writing. "Reading" a discipline requires entering into the active disciplinary environment, studying not just how it functions but why it functions in the ways it does. We thus define "source reading" as something more than scanning lines on a text. Rather, students learn to read disciplines through active interaction with the disciplines' sources: the scholars themselves. The ACRL *Framework for Information Literacy in Higher Education* forms an able description of key understandings required for disciplinary scholarship and thus can enable disciplinarians to articulate what it means to function within their disciplines.

Whether or not this will produce better disciplinary writing has yet to be seen. What it will certainly do is to move students from the outside looking in (thus struggling to create pale or faulty imitations of disciplinary discourse) to the inside where they can begin thinking as disciplinarians do, based on a much deeper understanding of disciplinary culture. That is surely the basis for more informed writing.

REFERENCES

ACRL (2015) *Framework for information literacy for higher education*. Retrieved from http://www.ala.org/acrl/sites/ala.org.acrl/files/content/issues/infolit/Framework_ILHE.pdf

Adler-Kassner, L., & Wardle, E. (2015). *Naming what we know: Threshold concepts of writing studies*. Boulder, CO: Utah State University Press.

Bartholomae, D. (1986). Inventing the university. *Journal of Basic Writing, 5*(1), 4–23.

Brown, J. S., Collins, A., & Duguid, P. (1989). Situated cognition and the culture of learning. *Educational Researcher, 18(*10), 32–42.

Carter, S. (2006). Redefining literacy as a social practice. *Journal of Basic Writing, 25*(2), 94–125.

Choi, Mina. (2006). Communities of practice: An alternative learning model for knowledge creation. *British Journal of Educational Technology, 37*(1), 143–146. https://doi.org/10.1111/j.1467-8535.2005.00486.x

Draper, R. J., & Siebert, D. (2010). Rethinking texts, literacies, and literacy across the curriculum. In R. J. Draper, P. Broomhead, A. P. Jensen, J. D. Nokes, & D. Siebert (Eds.), *(Re) imagining content-area literacy instruction* (pp. 20–39). New York: Teachers College Press.

Farrell, R., & Badke, W. (2015). Situating information literacy in the disciplines: A practical and systematic approach for academic librarians. *Reference Services Review, 43*(2), 319–340.

Flower, L. (1990). *Reading-to-write: Exploring a cognitive and social process.* New York: Oxford University Press.

Framework for Success in Postsecondary Writing. (2012). *College English, 74*(6), 525–533; also available at http://wpacouncil.org/files/framework-for-success-postsecondary-writing.pdf

Goldman, S. R., Britt, M. A., Brown, W., Cribb, G., George, M., Greenleaf, C., & . . . Shanahan, C. (2016). Disciplinary literacies and learning to read for understanding: A conceptual framework for disciplinary literacy. *Educational Psychologist, 51*(2), 1–28. https://doi.org/10.1080/00461520.2016.1168741

Greenleaf, C., & Schoenbach, R. (2004). Building capacity for the responsive teaching of reading in the academic disciplines: Strategic inquiry designs for middle and high school teachers' professional development. In D. S. Strickland & M. L. Kamil (Eds.), *Improving reading achievement through professional development* (pp. 97–127). Norwood, MA: Christopher-Gordon.

Greenleaf, C. L., Litman, C., Hanson, T. L., Rosen, R., Boscardin, C. K., Herman, J., & Schneider, S. A. (2010). Integrating literacy and science in biology: Teaching and learning impacts of Reading Apprenticeship Professional Development. *American Educational Research Journal, 20,* 648–717. https://doi.org/10.3102/0002831210384839

Haas, C., & Flower, L. (1988). Rhetorical reading strategies and the construction of meaning. *College Composition and Communication, 39*(2), 167–183. https://doi.org/10.2307/358026

Habib, A. S., Haan, J., & Mallett, K. (2015). The development of disciplinary expertise: An EAP and RGS-informed approach to the teaching and learning of genre at George Mason University. *Composition Forum, 31.* Retrieved from http://files.eric.ed.gov/fulltext/EJ1061558.pdf

Hansen, K. (2012). The "Framework for Success in Postsecondary Writing": Better than the competition, still not all we need. *College English, 74*(6), 540–543.

Horning, A. S. (2007). Reading across the curriculum as the key to student success. *Across the Disciplines, 4.* Retrieved from http://wac.colostate.edu/atd/articles/horning2007.cfm

Jacobson, T. E., & Gibson, C. (2015). First thoughts on implementing the Framework for Information Literacy. *Communications in Information Literacy, 9*(2), 102–110.

Johnson, B., & McCracken, I. M. (2016). Reading for integration, identifying complementary threshold concepts: The ACRL Framework in conversation with *Naming what we know: Threshold concepts of writing studies. Communications in Information Literacy, 10*(2). Retrieved from http://www.comminfolit.org/index.php?journal=cil&page=article&op=view&path%5B%5D=v10i2p178&path%5B%5D=242

Lave, J., & Wenger, E. (1991). *Situated learning: Legitimate peripheral participation.* Cambridge, UK: Cambridge University Press.

Lea, M. K., & Street, B. V. (1998). Student writing in higher education: An academic literacies approach. *Studies in Higher Education, 23*(2), 157–172.

Lee, C. D., & Goldman, S. R. (2015). Assessing literary reasoning: Text and task complexities. *Theory into Practice, 54*(3), 213–227. https://doi.org/10.1080/00405841.2015.1044369

Linton, P., Madigan, R., & Johnson, S. (1994). Introducing students to disciplinary genres: The role of the general composition course language. *Language and Learning Across the Disciplines, 1*(2), 63–78.

Luke, A., & Kapitzke, C. (1999). Literacies and libraries: Archives and cybraries. *Curriculum Studies, 7*(3), 467–491.

McComiskey, B. (2012). Bridging the divide: The (puzzling) "Framework" and the transition from K–12 to college writing instruction. *College English, 74*(6), 537–540.

Meyer, E., & Land, R. (2003). Threshold concepts and troublesome knowledge 1—Linkages to ways of thinking and practising. In C. Rust (Ed.), *Improving student learning—Theory and practice ten years on* (pp. 412–424). Oxford: Oxford Centre for Staff and Learning Development.

Meyer, J., & Land, R. (2005). Threshold concepts and troublesome knowledge (2): Epistemological considerations and a conceptual framework for teaching and learning. *Higher Education, 49*(3), 373–388.

Middendorf, J., & Pace, D. (2004). Decoding the disciplines: A model for helping students learn disciplinary ways of thinking. *New Directions for Teaching and Learning, 98*, 1–12.

Miller, C. R. (1984). Genre as social action. *Quarterly Journal of Speech, 70*(2), 151–167.

Miller, C. R. (2015). Genre as social action (1984), revisited 30 years later (2014). *Letras & Letras, 31*(3), 56–72.

Moje, E. (2007). Developing socially just subject-matter instruction: A review of the literature on disciplinary literacy teaching. *Review of Research in Education, 31*, 1–44.

Moje, E. B. (2008). Foregrounding the disciplines in secondary literacy teaching and learning: A call for change. *Journal of Adolescent & Adult Literacy, 52*(2), 96–107. https://doi.org/10.1598/JAAL.52.2.1

Rainey, E. C. (2016). Disciplinary literacy in English language arts: Exploring the social and problem–based nature of literary reading and reasoning. *Reading Research Quarterly, 52*(1), 53–71. https://doi.org/10.1002/rrq.154

Russell, D. (1993). Vygotsky, Dewey, and externalism: Beyond the student/discipline dichotomy. *Journal of Advanced Composition, 13*(1), 173–197.

Schoenbach, R., Greenleaf, C., & Murphy, L. (2012). The Reading Apprenticeship Framework. In *Reading for understanding: A guide to improving reading in middle and high school classrooms* (2nd ed., pp. 17–53). San Francisco: Jossey-Bass.

Schroeder, C. L. (2001). *Reinventing the university: Literacies and legitimacy in the postmodern academy.* Logan, UT: Utah State University Press.

Shanahan, T., & Shanahan, C. (2008). Teaching disciplinary literacy to adolescents: Rethinking content-area literacy. *Harvard Educational Review, 78*(1), 40–59.

Shanahan, T., & Shanahan, C. (2012). What is disciplinary literacy and why does it matter? *Topics in Language Disorders, 32*(1), 7–18.

Simmons, M. H. (2005). Librarians as disciplinary discourse mediators: Using genre theory to move toward critical information literacy. *portal: Libraries and the Academy, 5*(3), 297–311.

Smagorinsky, P. (2015). Disciplinary literacy in English language arts. *Journal of Adolescent & Adult Literacy, 59*(2), 141–146.

Spires, H. A., Kerkhoff, S. N., Graham, A., & Lee, J. (2014). Relating inquiry to disciplinary literacy: A pedagogical approach. *Raleigh: Friday Institute of Educational Innovation, North Carolina State University.* Retrieved from http://www.literacytakesflight.com/uploads/7/8/9/3/7893595/relating_inquiry.pdf

Wingate, U. (2012). Using academic literacies and genre-based models for academic writing instruction: A "literacy" journey. *Journal of English for Academic Purposes, 11*(1), 26–37.

CHAPTER 12

CROSSING THE BRIDGE

Writing and Research Bridge Programming for an Intensive English Program

Matthew R. Kaeiser
April D. Mann
Ava M. Brillat

INTRODUCTION

In 2015–2016, the University of Miami (UM) developed an Assessment in Action (AiA) project that can serve as a case study for how libraries can use their position as a university-wide resource to partner with other entities to attempt to address institutional gaps that often feel insurmountable. AiA is a 3-year IMLS-funded program in partnership with the Association for Institutional Research (AIR) and the Association of Public and Land-Grant Universities (APLU). In this case study, UM Libraries in partnership with the Writing Center and the Intensive English Program focused on strengthening the support international students were receiving to prepare them for their university-level writing and research requirements. By focusing on international students, the UM Richter Library and the Writing Center can develop the information literacy and writing skills of a population in need of specialized support.

BRIDGE PROGRAMMING AND INTERNATIONAL STUDENTS

The population of international students enrolled at colleges and universities in the United States has been steadily increasing. More and more institutions are depending on international student enrollment to keep their programs healthy, promote diversity, and create international exchange programs. According to the Open Doors Report (Institute of International Education, 2016), the number of international students in the United States exceeded one million students in 2016, which was an increase of 7% from the previous year and an all-time high. Programs and services that help international students make the transition into life at an American university have also been on the rise. According to the Commission on English Language Program Accreditation (CEA), the main accrediting body for English language programs at colleges and universities, the number of accredited English Language Programs has also grown substantially since the Accreditation Act of 2013 (CEA, n.d.), tripling its accrediting body. The act requires that all programs approved by the U.S. government's Student and Exchange Visitor Program (SEVP) be certified by CEA. They currently accredit around 300 institutions. In terms of economic impact, the National Association of Foreign Student Advisors (2016) estimates that the overall influence of international students on the U.S. economy is $32.8 billion annually. Clearly, international students are an attractive market for many institutions and a growing population on American campuses, but they also bring with them many unique challenges.

CHALLENGES TO BRIDGE PROGRAMMING

Assuring that international students entering American college or university programs have the English language skills they need to succeed has been one of these unique challenges. The standard language test for international student university admission has long been the Test of English as a Foreign Language (TOEFL) developed by Educational Testing Services (ETS). According to ETS (2011), the original TOEFL was launched in 1964 and since then has gone through some major transformations based on advances in English language teaching and theory. ETS reports that the earliest version of the TOEFL was paper-based and created by a collaborative effort of more than 30 public and private organizations concerned with the English competence of nonnative speakers preparing for academic studies. They report that the original 1964 test was reflective of the best of current theory and technology for the era but that it was lacking in certain critical areas, namely speaking and writing, which, they stress, were hard to assess at that time due to the lack of techniques for doing so on the massive scale needed. Of critical concern was what Carroll (1961) termed "integrative skills," which involve combining different elements of language for real-world communication. ETS reports that it was well aware of these weaknesses and, in the 1970s, they rolled out the second generation of the TOEFL, which was comprised of a "suite" of tests, including the Test of Spoken English (TSE) and the Test of Written English (TWE).

It was during this second stage of development that technological and theoretical advances enabled ETS to move toward what Brown (2003) reports was a major improvement in the implementation of more communicative language testing supported by a broad range of theories (Bachman & Palmer, 1996; Canale & Swain, 1980; Carroll, 1961; Hymes, 1972). Since that time, the TOEFL has gone through two additional transformations from the Computer-Based TOEFL (CBT) to the current Internet-based test or iBT. The modern TOEFL is able to contextualize test content much better than ever before, and it can more efficiently allow test administrators to pull out and evaluate both written and spoken samples. Unlike its earlier versions, it is not as tied to grammatical recognition and traditional multiple-choice formats, better integrating real-world examples. Instructors in academically focused intensive English programs have, for the most part, applauded these changes, which they feel are more in alignment with the real world of academic studies. They feel that there has long been too much focus on just passing the TOEFL rather than developing the practical skills needed in the classroom. However, for all of its improvements, the TOEFL remains a less-than-perfect measure, and ETS guidelines clearly lay out that the test has limitations.

Like the TOEFL, academic prep programs for nonnative speakers have also evolved. The most common model for college and university intensive English programs (IEPs) has typically been what Jochum (2011) calls the Traditional Program Model. In this model, students get sheltered intensive instruction from ESL experts in specific skills such as listening, speaking, and writing before entering mainstream classes. Placement is based on exam results that determine which level in the program best suits the needs of the students. Naturally, most university-based programs have an academic focus, and the content of both the placement exam and the course curricula are designed to reflect this focus.

A major theoretical underpinning for modern IEP curricula comes from the work of Cummins on what he calls Basics Interpersonal Communication Skills (BICS) and Cognitive Academic Language Proficiency (CALP) (Cummins, 1996). The crux of the theory is that there is a divide between what ESL students need to know in order to communicate daily versus the level of language needed for academic communication in English. Illuminating this divide is the work of Ilona Leki (2007). Leki completed a longitudinal study that followed the challenges of a small group of university-level ESL students as they branched away from their IEP work into regular classes. She discusses the limitations and challenges of the ESL writing courses they took, stating, "Those early writing courses simply could never have anticipated the varied writing the students would be required to do later in college. Yet the expectation on the part of the institution, the faculty, and the students was that 1st-year writing courses would prepare students for writing later in college" (p. 251). It seems evident that many institutions have underestimated student needs and how long it takes their programs to meet those needs.

Leki emphasizes that many of the traditional writing genres taught in ESL classes provide a firm foundation for academic writing. Unfortunately, that basic framework does not always match the real-world assignments that students are given. A big part of this issue is the fact that to reach the level of CALP that is needed for high-level academic work, students often need far more time than the typical IEP program allows, needing what Cummins terms "scaffolding." Scaffolding involves providing students as much support as they need in order to create a manageable challenge that will help them to build their CALP. Scaffolding is sometimes the only way to get ESL students moving toward measurable goals without overwhelming them. In Cummins's model, the scaffolding is only temporary and must be delicately balanced so that there is never too much or too little challenge. It is very much in alignment with Sanford's widely accepted theory of challenge and support (Sanford, 1962).

Providing effective scaffolding is not the only issue. As students transition out of the IEP and into majors and other programs, IEPs and university departments need to coordinate more to ensure that IEP students are prepared for the challenges that lie ahead. IEP instructors and curriculum designers sometimes make assumptions about what is happening in university classrooms that don't match the facts. The reality is that students can successfully complete an IEP curriculum and obtain the required TOEFL score for admission while still facing gaps in their CALP, technology skills, and cultural knowledge. Many students, in fact, bypass IEP work altogether by submitting all of the required test scores and paperwork. A major frustration for many IEP faculty members is that graduates of their programs often make major advancements that are not recognized, or IEPs are blamed for the weaknesses of students who have never passed through their gates. Once IEP students are thrown into the fire of regular coursework, they are often overwhelmed by the challenges of the new hurdles in front of them. It then becomes easy to lose track of their gains. Unfortunately, many of these students turn to academic dishonesty out of frustration or out of fear that their language deficiencies will lead them to failure.

In order to remedy the above situation, various tools and strategies have been developed to help students through the arduous journey toward CALP. Among these models is the support services model. The University of Miami Library (UML) Learning & Research Services Department is an example of a service that fits this model. It consists of subject liaison librarians who work closely with students, faculty, and staff to provide research support and instruction based on the *Framework for Information Literacy*. The UM Writing Center is another support service that offers one-on-one writing assistance for all types of writing. The Writing Center is staffed by graduate students in English and by the English Composition faculty. The staff works with traditional university students and students from UM's IEP, which follows the Traditional Program Model mentioned earlier. Yet despite these current resources, international students entering the University of Miami still often seem and feel underprepared.

BRIDGE PROGRAMMING AND INFORMATION LITERACY

Librarians and writing instructors are natural partners in developing information literacy, critical thinking, and writing skills. As such, librarians and writing instructors are potential resources for supporting international students. A simple comparison of the Council of Writing Program Administrators' (WPA) *Framework for Success in Postsecondary Writing* with the ACRL *Framework for Information Literacy for Higher Education* reveals a number of similarities that form the foundation for collaboration in addressing these issues. Both the ACRL and WPA frameworks focus on the core concepts behind thoughtful and engaging research and writing, respectively. For example, the ACRL frames Research as Inquiry and Scholarship as Conversation embody the spirit of the WPA's descriptions of Habits of Mind, in particular, that of Curiosity and Openness. Curiosity and Research as Inquiry are both centered on inquiry as a process by which writers and researchers develop relevant questions within their disciplines. Both frameworks employ language such as "habits of mind" in the case of the WPA and "knowledge practices" in the case of the ACRL framework in an attempt to reveal the critical thought processes driving behavior. Because of the conceptual overlap between the two frameworks, it is natural to link writing and research skills together through the lens of critical thinking skills.

BRIDGE PROGRAMMING AT THE UNIVERSITY OF MIAMI

At UM, many have long recognized that the two-semester, first-year writing sequence is not fully meeting the needs of some of the students, especially those who are simultaneously learning English and academic writing. As mentioned earlier, the great divide between BICS and CALP takes time to conquer and presents many challenges. A primary concern is that students be provided the assistance that they require so that they are not tempted to hire ghostwriters or plagiarize. There have been numerous proposals designed to remedy, or at least improve, the situation. All proposals aimed at first-year students have failed to secure institutional support, and, more recently, those aimed at incoming graduate students have found limited departmental, rather than university-wide, support.

FIRST-YEAR STUDENTS

UM faculty members from both the IEP and the Writing Program have attempted to create special programs and exchanges designed to meet the needs of the incoming international first-year students. These efforts have involved various strategies for transitioning IEP students into the first-semester composition classes. For example, first-year composition instructors have taught for a semester in the IEP in order to gain experience working with developing IEP students' writing skills. IEP and first-year composition instructors have also met and discussed the expectations of first-year composition courses to further cement understanding between the two departments.

In the Writing Program, faculty members have also attempted to create programs designed for international students. Katharine Komis, a senior lecturer with the Writing Program, has twice led semester-long Teaching Circles designed to lay the groundwork for an increase in institutional support for struggling international students. In 2010, and again in 2013, Professor Komis worked with fellow faculty members to draft extensively researched proposals designed to persuade administrators that the current two-semester sequence was not meeting the needs of the students, and that alternatives could be constructed that could do a much better job. In her Teaching Circle's 2013 report, Komis and colleagues noted that "as the academic quality of incoming freshmen [at the University of Miami] has grown overall, the gap has widened for academically underprepared students."[1]

The 2013 report suggested that the Writing Program adopt a "Stretch" format, modeled after a similar program being used at California State University Northridge (CSUN, n.d.). International students would have the equivalent course experience of the University of Miami's first-year composition course workload, but it would be stretched out over two semesters through two credit-bearing classes. As a result, the students would have the time they needed to adapt to the work of the academic curriculum, allowing them to learn how to write academic English prose while providing extra support and focus on the benefits of iterative writing and revision.

Komis and colleagues noted that the program would require more resources than the current method, which offers no special placement for international students, but her research suggested that the benefits in terms of retention and student success would far outweigh the costs. Despite the support of the colleagues in the Writing Program, Komis was never able to get any kind of institutional support for her initiatives. It was even difficult to tell where the lack of support originated. It was unclear who would or would not forward the initiatives to the next administrative level and whether or not those forwarding had indicated their support for the ideas. Thus, there have been ideas put forth from several entities on campus, but it has been very difficult to get enough administrative support to make these programs happen.

GRADUATE STUDENTS

Although university administrators have been inconsistent in addressing the challenge of providing additional support to those international undergraduates who are unprepared for academic English, they seem to be more willing to provide support at the graduate level. In 2012, the Writing Center was first contacted by representatives from the School of Nursing and Health Studies (SONHS). They were finding that their incoming graduate students were unable to apply the conventions of standard academic English needed for the graduate-level coursework they were taking. The faculty identified the students' poor command of written English as one of the primary problems keeping them from succeeding in their individual programs.[2]

The SONHS had already developed a series of online modules designed to help incoming graduate students prepare for some of the more challenging coursework they would be facing. Topics in this "pre-immersion" module included perennially difficult topics such as Pathophysiology and Pharmacology. Instructional designers at SONHS wanted to add a writing component to the module to address these potential issues before the students began struggling in their coursework. The resulting modules covered some of the more basic writing issues, such as developing a thesis and using topic sentences. Importantly, a section of the module was dedicated to avoiding plagiarism through proper research and citation techniques. The modules also contained information about resources available to the students, including the Writing Center and the subject librarians. Although the modules were created with the understanding that they would not "inoculate" graduate students from the possibility of ever again producing poor writing, at the very least, professors could be absolutely sure that students had been instructed in U.S. standards of plagiarism and were familiar with the expectations of prosodic clarity and organization. Additionally, students would also be familiar with the various campus resources they could turn to for help.

Within a few years, the Masters of Public Health (MPH) at the Miller School of Medicine contacted the Writing Center with a similar problem. The SONHS modules provided the framework for the MPH, requiring minimal revision to create an appropriate resource. Nursing-based articles were swapped for public health–based articles, and the module was ready to go. It was immediately staffed and began running within a few months of the initial contact.

Specialized bridge programming has also been established within specific degree programs, such as the graduate bridge program coordinated by the University of Miami School of Law LL.M. program and the IEP. Students in the program must submit the required TOEFL or IELTS scores. Once they are accepted, students take an oral communication course as well as a reading and writing course. These two courses are coordinated with a companion course taught by a School of Law professor. All three courses are closely coordinated through their content and assignments to prepare students for the rigors of law school. The bridge classes consist of two skills-based 12-week courses that are run during the regular academic semesters. The ESL courses serve as a bridge for international students who are still struggling to build not only their CALP, but also their ability to adjust to campus culture, technology requirements, and the myriad of resources available to them such as the Writing Lab and the resource librarians. During the summer, there is a condensed 3-week intensive that is offered following the same basic model. However, in the summer courses, instruction is sheltered and designed to prepare students for the semester ahead in contrast to the 12-week courses, which are coordinated with a regular LL.M. course. Thus the graduate programs, which often have paying students and a different funding model, have been better able to develop and implement support programs addressing the needs of international students than the undergraduate programs.

One of the lessons from the successful implementation of the graduate modules is that program-based initiatives are easier to get off the ground and sustain than broader, cross-disciplinary, university-wide initiatives. Another lesson is that the more profitable programs in the university are more likely to fund programs aimed at ensuring their students' success than programs aimed at a more general population. Given these lessons, one response could be to target small-scale programs directly to the IEP students themselves, while they are still in that program. Recently, the Richter Library and the Writing Center teamed up with the IEP to try to pilot such a targeted support program through the Assessment in Action Program.

Bridge programming provides an opportunity for social and cultural mentoring in university culture. Although a search of library science literature will result in a small number of articles, librarians do describe and acknowledge the value of social capital in bridge programming (Schroeder, 2014). Bridge programs that contain a research component are essential to acclimating students to the expectations of the academic programs into which they are matriculating. Additionally, while students can theoretically receive mentoring and support from their peers regarding a variety of academic expectations, research is a skill that few students receive instruction in prior to attending college. In the case of the AiA project at UM, the majority of students in both the control and treatment groups lacked any instruction in research. Students were more likely to have had previous writing instruction rather than research instruction. As a result, there is a clear need for having a research component in bridge programming aimed at helping students understand and meet academic standards of research in their new university environments.

EXPLORATORY BRIDGE PROGRAMMING (AIA PROJECT)

During the 2015–2016 academic year, the UM Libraries applied to be part of a national action-learning assessment program called Assessment in Action (AiA). AiA is a 3-year IMLS-funded program in partnership with the Association for Institutional Research (AIR) and the Association of Public and Land-Grant Universities (APLU). The focus of the program was to support academic libraries in the design and implementation of action learning projects to increase cross-campus collaboration. The project for the UML AiA project centered on a collaboration between the UML Learning & Research Services Department, the Writing Center, and the IEP. UML Learning & Research Services consists of subject liaison librarians who work closely with students, faculty, and staff to provide research support and instruction based on the *Framework for Information Literacy*. The project focused on answering the following question: How might intentional collaboration between UML Learning & Research Services and the Writing Center help students in the IEP develop their research and writing skills?

UML Learning & Research Services collaborated with the Writing Center to develop a study of "control" classes in the fall semester of 2015. In the spring semester of 2016, UML Learning & Research Services and the Writing Center offered collocated, collaborative services to a "treatment" class during the regularly scheduled "lab" session, during which students would work on their homework while having access to a writing tutor and a liaison librarian. This pilot project contains elements necessary for successful bridge programming.

PROJECT TIMELINE

Fall 2015

Two control classes received instruction sessions with the English liaison librarian, which is part of their curriculum. Each class also completed a survey on the writing and research instruction they received prior to joining the IEP program. Bibliographies from the final papers were collected and analyzed for quality of sources.

Spring 2016

One treatment class received an instruction session with the English liaison librarian. The class completed the same survey as the control class on previous writing and research instruction. Unlike the control class, the treatment class had access to both a writing tutor and a research librarian during their regularly scheduled "lab" sessions, during which they would typically work on homework consisting of completing their final research paper. The treatment class received two such sessions. After any interaction with a writing tutor or a research librarian, students would fill out a postsurvey on their comfort levels after working with a writing tutor or research librarian. Additionally, students were interviewed to get their impressions of where the challenges in writing and research lie. Finally, bibliographies from final papers were collected and analyzed for quality of sources in order to be compared to the bibliographies of the control class.

FINDINGS

Comparing the bibliographies of the control and treatment classes showed little to no discernible difference between the two. One explanation for the lack of difference could be that all classes received an instruction session with the liaison librarian, during which students honed their search strategies and were introduced to scholarly databases to use in their research. Students from the control classes did report a higher level of comfort and self-perceived efficacy after working with either a writing tutor or a research librarian. Finally, interviews and survey data suggest that students are much more comfortable with writing and are more likely to have received previous writing instruction than research instruction. Students are more likely to be less comfortable with research. Comparing previous writing and research education revealed some interesting trends, especially across gender lines. Again, although the sample size was very small, male students were more likely than female students to have some sort of previous research experience.

Cross-training and communication between service partners can help spread understanding to the unique pedagogical approaches of each service partner to identify shared challenges. The collocation of writing and research consultation services is a natural fit. Students often talked about writing and research interchangeably during interviews. This can also help writing tutors and research librarians proactively refer students between services when necessary. The University of Miami has a department focused on institutional research, the office of Planning, Institutional Research, and Assessment (PIRA). UML already gathers a number of key statistics for PIRA. Liaising with PIRA can help reveal other areas of strategic reporting that may already be covered by the AiA project.

The University of Miami has a number of strategic documents that dovetail with the UML/Writing Center AiA project. The *Common Purpose, Values, and Behaviors* document outlines a number of directives that are emphasized by the culture change. One such value is "Excellence," which describes a number of attributes associated with efficacy, including performing tasks to the highest level of quality. The AiA project revealed a student's self-perceived efficacy is increased through interactions with writing tutors and research librarians, showing how the Writing Center and UML Learning & Research Services are working to support the culture transformation. By extension, the Learning Commons as a whole can also use the AiA assessment methods in order to more clearly communicate how they are serving the University of Miami strategically.

NOTES

1. Komis, K., Culver, K. C., Hickman, Z., Wheat, C., Panton, R. TC report fall 2013: Suggestions for ENG 105; 2013.
2. Another easily identifiable problem was that the students were often returning to academia after years working in the field. These students were used to writing notes on charts, not writing term papers for professors.

REFERENCES

Bachman, L. F., & Palmer, A. S. (1996). *Language testing in practice.* Oxford: Oxford University Press.

Brown, H. D. (2003). *Language assessment: Principles and classroom practices.* New York, NY: Pearson Longman ESL

California State University Northridge. (n.d.). *Stretch composition program.* Retrieved from http://www.csun.edu/undergraduate-studies/stretch-composition-program

Canale, M., & Swain M. (1980). Theoretical bases of communicative approaches to second language teaching and testing. *Applied Linguistics, 1,* 1–47.

Carroll, J. B. (1961). Fundamental considerations in testing for English proficiency of foreign students. In *Testing the English proficiency of foreign students* (pp. 31–40). Washington, DC: Center for Applied Linguistics.

Commission on English Language Program Accreditation. (n.d.). *About CEA.* Retrieved from http://cea-accredit.org/about-cea

Cummins, J. (1996). *Negotiating identities: Education for empowerment in a diverse society.* Ontario, CA: California Association for Bilingual Education

Educational Testing Services. (2011). *TOEFL iBT research insight: TOEFL program history, 1(6).* Retrieved from https://www.ets.org/s/toefl/pdf/toefl_ibt_insight_s1v6.pdf

Hymes, D. (1972). On communicative competence. In B. J. Pride & J. Holmes (Eds.), *Sociolinguistics.* Harmondsworth: Penguin.

Institute of International Education. (2016). *Open doors 2016.* Retrieved from https://www.iie.org/Research-and-Insights/Open-Doors/Open-Doors-2016-Media-Information

Jochum, C. (2011). ESL program models and court cases: An overview for administrators. *Academic Leadership (15337812), 9*(3), 1–8.

Leki, I. (2007). *Undergraduates in a second language: Challenges and complexities of academic literacy development.* New York, NY: Lawrence Erlbaum Associates.

National Association of Foreign Student Advisors. (2016). *The United States of America benefits from international students.* Retrieved from http://www.nafsa.org/Policy_and_Advocacy/Policy_Resources/Policy_Trends_and_Data/NAFSA_International_Student_Economic_Value_Tool/

Sanford, N. (1962). *The American college.* New York, NY: Wiley, 1962.

Schroeder, R. (2014). Transitioning students transforming higher education. *OLA Quarterly, 20*(1), 40–43.

CHAPTER 13

PROBLEM-BASED LEARNING AND INFORMATION LITERACY

Revising a Technical Writing Class

Kelly Diamond

INTRODUCTION AND BACKGROUND

Courses in technical writing are common offerings in colleges and universities as a means of preparing students for job-centered writing and research. West Virginia University (WVU) is no exception; English 305, Technical Writing, offered in the classroom and online, focuses on "writing in scientific and technical fields" and introduces "students to typical genres, workplace practices, document design, and conventions of writing for experts and non-experts" (West Virginia University, 2015–2016). While instructors of English 305 have a certain freedom in designing the course, the WVU department recommends that students in writing courses complete at least 25 pages of polished prose by the end of the class. Typically, students are asked to research and write about professions; create a document providing instructions; and, for the final assignment, propose a feasible solution to a real-life problem supported by outside research.

Professor Gregg Thumm, a colleague in WVU's Department of English, has taught English 305, Technical Writing, for ten years, teaching at least one online section every academic year. Like most English 305 instructors, his course requires students to complete the typical assignments listed above: a set of instructions, a mechanism description, and a proposal, supported by outside research with an annotated bibliography. Thumm also likes to have group work in his classes as this practice reflects current workplace environments. While these assignments and practices work for onsite students, he found that the student performance and engagement in the online sections were not at the same level as that of his onsite students. Particularly, online student performance on the final proposal assignment was notably weaker. While the onsite students enjoyed working together in their groups, online students resisted group work by not participating in a timely fashion with their group members. Additionally, Thumm noted that submitted proposals had an "assembly-line" feel to them: assignments were poorly researched and not well organized or clearly written. The proposal assignment also seemed to discourage, rather than promote, collaboration and engagement. Online students were also reluctant to use WVU Libraries' resources, despite the availability of an embedded librarian.

COURSE GOALS

Professor Thumm and I began working in the summer of 2014 to revise his online English 305 course. At the initial meeting, Thumm stated that he wanted the English 305 students to:

- Understand how assignments worked together and had practical application
- Collaborate effectively with classmates
- Become more information literate
- Use WVU Library resources
- Integrate sources into writing projects
- Use correct citations in the text

However, from an instructional design perspective, these course outcomes are weak as they are neither observable nor measurable: for example, an instructor can't measure "understanding" as this transformation takes place internally. However, an instructor can ask a student to demonstrate understanding through an assortment of assessments such as research papers, tests, quizzes, presentations, and so on. After consultation with

Thumm, we generated a new set of measurable outcomes.

According to our revised outcomes, students finishing the course would be able to:

- Demonstrate the effects of word choice, sentence structure, organization, and document design on the meaning and effectiveness of documents.
- Demonstrate rhetorical principles that shape technical writing to suit a range of readers in a variety of writing situations.
- Identify the needs of an audience and use that understanding to design documents.
- Use databases and other electronic sources to find information.
- Choose relevant sources to support an information need.
- Evaluate and modify a document to ensure its usability and persuasiveness for an audience.

We had measurable learning outcomes for the course, but how would we get the students to achieve them?

ADDIE AND BACKWARD DESIGN

The basis of most instructional design processes is ADDIE (Analyze, Design, Develop, Implement, and Evaluate). Designing instruction using the ADDIE system requires creators to analyze the instructional needs, or deficiencies, of the learners; design instruction to address these needs; develop an instructional strategy; implement the instructional strategy; and evaluate not only the learners' success but the success of the instruction (Gagné, Wager, Golas, & Keller, 2005, pp. 21–37).

For this project, I used a combination of the ADDIE system and backward design. In backward design, course developers first generate the learning outcomes for the course; then create assessments that will determine whether those learning outcomes were met; and lastly design instruction that gives students the knowledge and skills to achieve the outcomes (McTighe & Wiggins, 2005). Now that we had a set of measurable course outcomes, we needed a set of assessments along with appropriate instructional strategies to measure whether students had achieved these outcomes. Thumm and I decided that we wanted final assessments in the course to replicate workplace writing and research assignments as much as possible.

Technical writing in the classroom often does not replicate technical writing performed in the professional world: supervisors assign workplace writing tasks whose requirements may present research and writing challenges. Professional writing requires varied formats and complex research and analytical skills. Mabrito's (1997) survey of factory supervisors found that required workplace writing was not only "rhetorically diverse" but also written for a variety of audiences as well as purposes (p. 68). Professional writing consisted of not just memos, but "short reports and instructional documents" (Mabrito, 1997, p. 68). As supervisors were promoted, workplace writing became more challenging; assigned writing required "greater documentation and the ability to synthesize and summarize information from a variety of sources" (Mabrito, 1997, p. 68). Survey respondents noted that they had difficulties meeting the readers' needs and expectations, which they attributed to a "lack of specific triaging writing strategies" (Mabrito, 1997, p. 69).

To better replicate workplace writing and research tasks, we decided to create a final assessment in which students would be assigned a workplace-situated research scenario. This research scenario would require writing multiple and different documents in diverse formats for different audiences. Not only would assigned research scenarios remove the stress of choosing an appropriate topic, a cognitive task that appeared to impede student success in English 305, it would also more closely replicate authentic workplace writing.

PBL AND ASSIGNMENT DESIGN

As we worked on designing the final assignments, we decided to give students more open-ended direction for each assigned writing task. While the research scenarios would provide students with contextual details, the instructions for the assignments were intentionally left unrestricted. While we wanted to replicate the workplace writing experience, as described by Mabrito (1997), our design choice was also informed by problem-based learning, or PBL. While PBL was initially developed in the 1960s for medical education, its elements are readily applied to teaching technical writing to juniors and seniors who will be expected to perform problem-solving writing and research in their careers (Barrows, 1996). Barrows (1996) outlines six foundational principles of PBL:

- Learning Is Student-Centered
- Learning Occurs in Small Student Groups
- Teachers Are Facilitators or Guides
- Problems Form the Organizing Focus and Stimulus for Learning
- Problems Are a Vehicle for the Development of Clinical Problem-Solving Skills
- New Information Is Acquired Through Self-Directed Learning (Barrows, 1996, pp. 5–6)

While we did not require students to work in groups, based on Thumm's past experience with online group work, we wanted students to tackle and to solve the problems outlined in the research scenarios by implementing the foundational skills of the semester's first half, but also to work through research issues and writing issues on their own. Students were encouraged to contact the instructor and the librarian with questions while the instructor and librarian would occasionally facilitate more difficult problems. We believed that requiring students to focus on the research scenario's problems and related writing tasks would stimulate implementation of previous foundational skills; considering how to present these solutions and recommendations to diverse audiences would require students to exercise critical thinking skills regarding the needs of diverse audiences. However, these research/writing skills and tasks are complex; students needed a foundation of skills and knowledge practices to be successful.

SCAFFOLDING THE ASSIGNMENTS

To give students the skills and knowledge that they would need to effectively complete the final assessment, we designed a series of scaffolded assignments leading up to the assigned research scenarios. During the first half of the semester, assignments focused on foundational and basic skills, which would be used for the major assignment for the class, the research scenarios.[1]

Module 1: Ethics of Writing/ Concision and Clarity

Students were given an article from the *Charleston Gazette* (West Virginia) reporting a link between taking Lexapro and a reduced risk for depression among stroke patients (Smith, 2015).[2] Students were then asked to (1) find the original peer-reviewed study using information found in the newspaper article; (2) complete a brief log outlining their search strategies and providing the citation for the original study; (3) compare and reflect on the differences between the newspaper article and peer-reviewed article; (4) read letters and blog posts on ethical violations present in the original study; (5) rewrite the newspaper article so that the information was accurate but written at an appropriate level for a newspaper audience; and (6) write a brief memo reflecting on their editing decisions and choices. Online instructional support consisted of the course LibGuide; a video tutorial on using Summon, our discovery system at the time; and a PowToon video, *What's the Deal With Peer-Review?* (Diamond, 2015c)

Foundational skills and knowledge for this module included an introduction to the WVU Libraries' resources, learning how peer review works in academic publishing, considering the audience's information needs, and writing different documents for those needs. This module asked students to consider how to present information accurately and ethically while also considering the needs of different audiences as well as editing documents for an audience. The assignment also required students to use WVU Library resources to find information to support and inform their writing decisions.

Module 2: Professional Analysis Memo

Students researched their potential career and produced a report for an audience who did not know anything about this profession and wanted to learn more. Students first consulted the *Bureau of Labor Statistics Occupational Handbook* website to research entry-level professional positions to determine training or education required; the scope and type of work required; the salary range; and the current hiring market. Using WVU Library resources and others, students then researched relevant professional associations and conferences, professional trade journals and peer-reviewed journals, and finally, the best professional social media resources. Next. they prepared a professional report synthesizing this information. For online instructional support, students viewed a Powtoon video, *What's the Deal With Trade Journals?* (Diamond, 2014); a Captivate video, *Using ABI/Inform to Find Trade and Peer-Reviewed Journals*; and an embedded *ABI/Inform* demonstration video from ProQuest as well as links to the *BLS Occupational Handbook*.

This module focused on having students practice using a proprietary database; learning the purpose of trade journals and the type of information found within; and synthesizing information for a specific audience in a report.

Module 3: Infographic

Using the information from their professional analysis report, students next created an infographic for high school seniors or first-year college students trying to decide upon a major. Students also drafted a reflective memo explaining what information they chose to highlight and why and their design decisions such as color choices, font choice, layout, and so forth. Foundational skills focused on identifying an audience's needs and choosing appropriate rhetorical devices as well as effectively communicating with visuals. The online instructional support included a resources page with recommended software for creating infographics plus a link to the Life Hacker article, "How to Create Stunning Infographics in 30 Minutes or Less" (Seda, n.d.).

FINAL ASSESSMENT: RESEARCH SCENARIO

Research Scenario Assignments

This module spanned the latter half of the semester and included multiple assignments revolving around assigned research scenarios based on the following areas of study: business, communication, agriculture and forestry, psychology, education, engineering, and public health. The most common majors for students taking English 305 include the hard sciences (biology, chemistry, and physics), mathematics, engineering, and agriculture/forestry.

Each research scenario asked the students to complete the following:

- Part A: Annotated Bibliography
- Part B: Background Report based on their research
- Part C: Final Report with recommendations to a supervisor
- Part D: Visual presentation of their report to an outside group

The six research scenarios were assigned to students based on their majors. While the scenarios are different, each scenario presented the students with a problem at their workplace that their supervisor assigned them to research and solve. Students had to prepare a background report for their boss; a recommendation document for how to proceed to solve or ameliorate the problem; and a presentation to stakeholders outside of the workplace. This assignment replicates workplace writing and research in that the task is assigned and different documents are prepared for different audiences.

As the culminating module, students were assessed on mastery of the course outcomes, particularly demonstrating a control of various rhetorical and presentation strategies and formats informed by the documents' various purposes and audiences. Students were also assessed on their abilities to find, to select, to evaluate, and to synthesize appropriate information for the varying research and audiences needs of each document.

These concluding assignments also required students to draw upon the foundational skills from previous assignments: searching WVU Library databases and other relevant sources of information; effectively synthesizing this information; understanding and implementing appropriate rhetorical and format conventions of different workplace writing genres; as well as reflecting on multiple audiences' needs regarding not only the information provided but its presentation as well.

The Annotated Bibliography assignment, while a standard assignment in research writing classes, was designed to encourage students to begin their research as well as to allow the course librarian ample time to provide feedback before students progressed too far into the assignment. Unlike the usual annotated bibliography assignment, we did not require or specify specific genre or publication types. Our only requirements were that students find 10 sources that were "current, relevant, authoritative, accurate, and [had] an academic or *informative* purpose" [emphasis added]. We wanted students to think critically about the authority of their sources—not all of the research scenarios required peer-reviewed sources for effective research—as well as the needs of the audience/s specified in the research scenario. This decision was informed by the Association of College and Research Libraries' (ACRL) *Framework for Information Literacy for Higher Education* frame Authority Is Constructed and Contextual (ACRL, 2016). We wanted students to reflect on their audiences' information needs and to critically think about what sources were authoritative for their research scenarios.

To help students successfully complete this assignment, we provided a PowToon video, *What's the Deal with Annotated Bibliographies?* (Diamond, 2015b); an embedded YouTube video, *Research Therapy: What's an Annotated Bibliography?*; a Captivate video, *APA Citations*, which outlined the purpose of citations; and links to vendor database demonstration videos, such as EbscoHost and ProQuest. The course librarian graded the submitted Annotated Bibliographies and sent the graded, commented copies to Thumm, who assigned final grades based on her comments.

The Background Report required students to write a factual and objective report detailing background information related to their scenario. Instructions for this assignment simply state that "[y]our report should refrain from making any judgments or evaluations about the scenario." The specific directions for the Recommendation Report and Visual Presentation were based on the particular research scenario but generally were minimal, instructing students that "[y]our report to your supervisor needs to be detailed, organized, and have cited sources. For your presentation, consider your audience and what information you'll need to include and exclude and how to present it effectively." Thumm and I believed that students would produce more thoughtful work if they were given open-ended instructions, as is common in workplace writing (Mabrito, 1997) and as part of our PBL-based and ACRL *Framework* assignment philosophy.

EVALUATING THE COURSE

We performed a citation analysis of the annotated bibliographies and final reports from fall 2014 and spring 2015. For each research assignment, students were not given specific requirements for sources to be used, but were instructed to use their best judgment in regard to the sources needed. The sources in the Annotated Bibliographies as well as the sources found in the Background Reports' Works Cited pages were counted as well as categorized based on source and publication types. We found that students primarily cited trade journals, peer-reviewed journals, popular articles from library databases, and government websites for these two assignments (see Figures 13.1 through 13.4).

In addition to the quantitative data, we also wanted to know how students perceived instructional elements, of course. We surveyed the students using the survey function in LibGuides, asking the following questions:

1. Which instructional videos did you find useful?
2. Which instructional videos did you find least useful?
3. Please comment on the instructional videos' usefulness.
4. Please comment on the librarian's helpfulness.

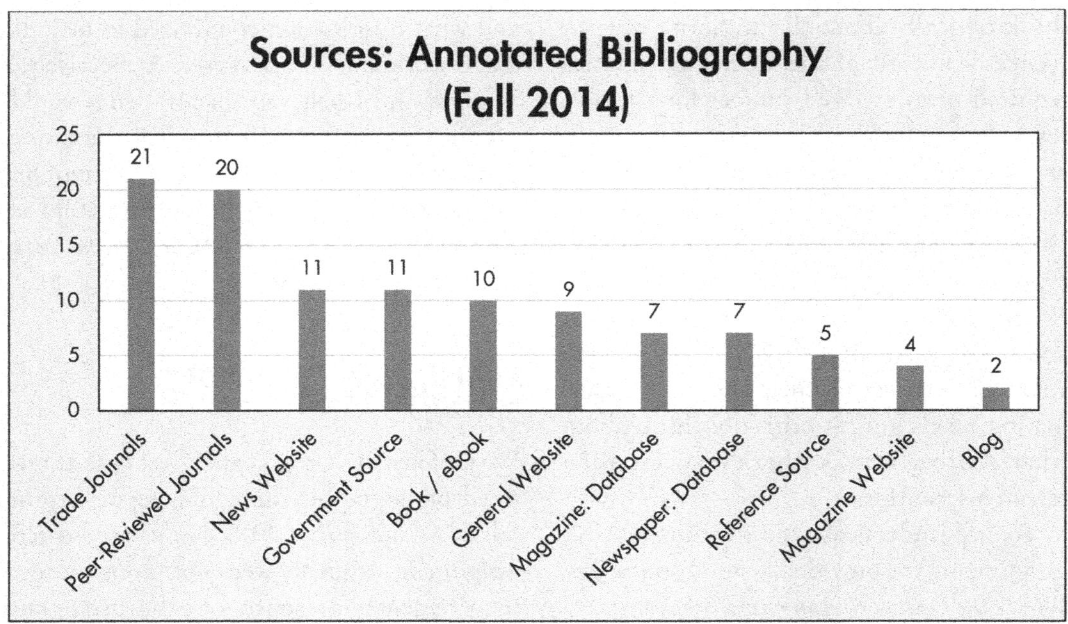

Figure 13.1 Citation analysis of works cited pages: Graph 1.

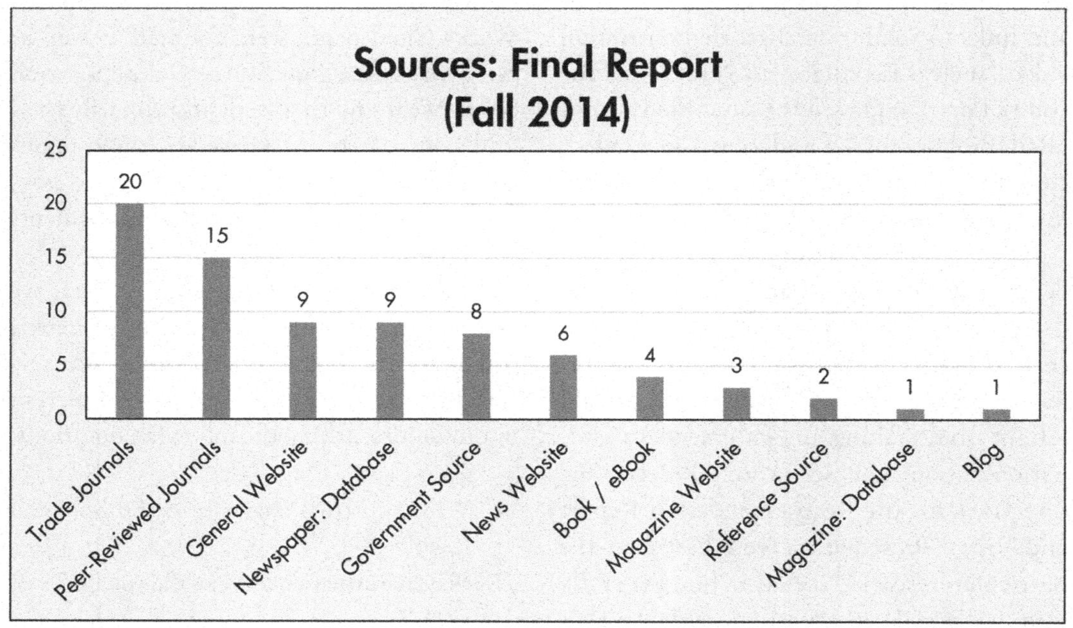

Figure 13.2 Citation analysis of works cited pages: Graph 2.

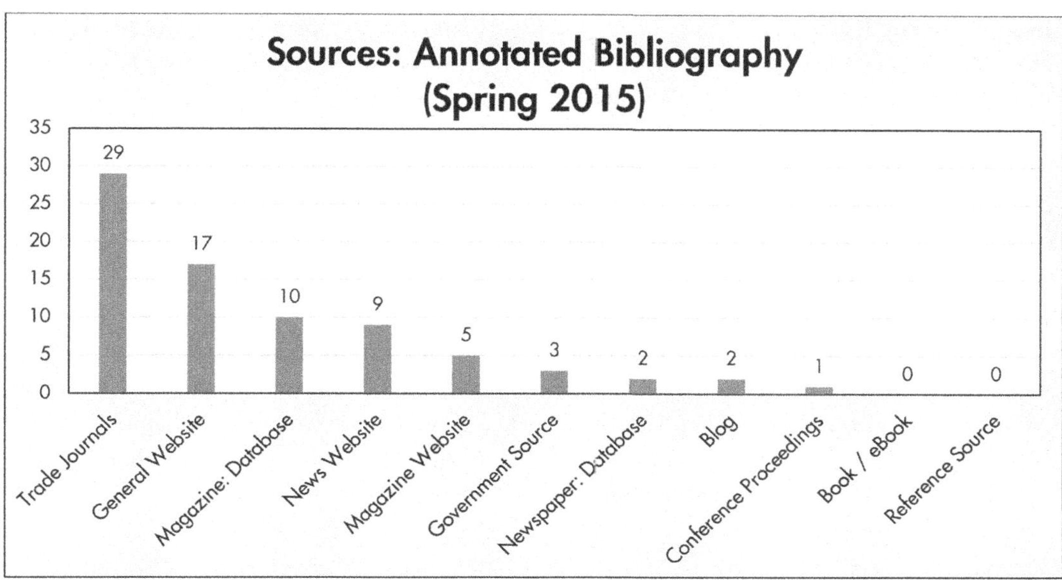

Figure 13.3 Citation analysis of works cited pages: Graph 3.

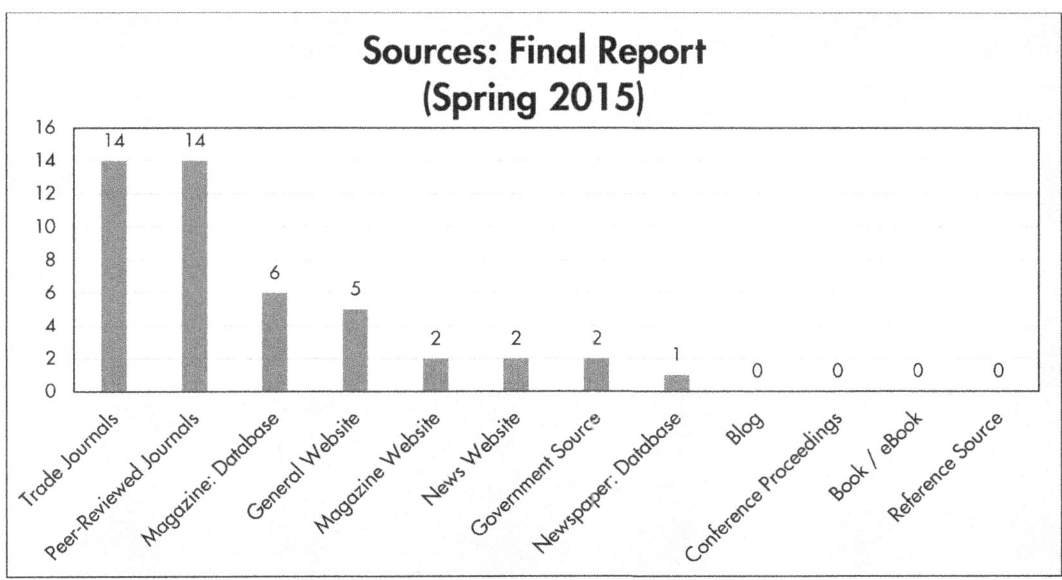

Figure 13.4 Citation analysis of works cited pages: Graph 4.

Student Survey Results

From the fall 2014 and spring 2015 semesters, we received 41 responses to the Student Survey.

Which instructional videos did you find useful? [*n* = 41]

- *What's the Deal With Trade Journals?* 67%
- *What's the Deal With Annotated Bibliographies?* 55%
- *Database Demonstration: How to Search ABI/Inform* 45%
- Embedded links within weekly modules (to usa.gov, for example) 36%
- English 305 Technical Writing Research Guide 36%
- *What's the Deal With Peer-Reviewed Journals* 27%

Which instructional videos did you find least useful? [*n* = 41]

- *What's the Deal With Peer-Reviewed Journals?* 45%
- *What's the Deal With Annotated Bibliographies?* 18%
- Embedded links within weekly modules (to usa.gov, for example) 1%
- *What's the Deal With Trade Journals?* 1%
- *Database Demonstration: How to Search ABI/Inform* 1%
- English 305 Technical Writing Research Guide 1%

Please comment on the instructional videos' usefulness.

- These links simply made the work a bit less tedious and did a good job of supplementing other readings assigned.
- Annotated Bibliographies is [*sic*] the only item that has not been fully covered in any previous classes that I have taken, therefore; the information pertaining [*sic*] Annotated Bibliographies were [*sic*] the most helpful to me.
- I now understand how to search for trade and peer review journals which is why I think this resource was most helpful. Also, the infographic links were tremendously helpful.
- I didn't know what a trade journal was or how to find them, so the database demonstration told me exactly where to find them.
- I thought the websites were helpful because it gave me visual examples that I could keep referring back too [*sic*].
- Used the link to the APA basics sheet as a reference for my annotated bib, [*sic*] Very helpful for quick structure reference.

Please comment on the librarian's helpfulness.

- Mrs. [*sic*] Diamond seemed to [be] involved with the class once the research portion came around. She seemed helpful and sent out multiple emails telling students to contact whenever they needed help or if they ever had questions.
- I never asked for help directly but she seemed ready to help if I ever had a question.
- I only emailed her once to ask a question, but she responded in a timely manner and was helpful.
- Did not need him/her!
- I didn't talk to the librarian at all.
- I did not use her during the course.
- N/A. She was readily available but I never needed her assistance.

COMMENTS ON SURVEY RESULTS

We believed that students' unfamiliarity with trade journals and using *ABI/Inform* led them to rank those videos highly. We also found that students appreciated the refresher on annotated bibliographies, particularly as this video outlines why instructors assign them and their usefulness for students, instead of focusing on the mechanics of the annotated bibliography's creation. The peer-reviewed journals video was ranked last, probably due to students' familiarity with these journals for past research assignments as most students were juniors or seniors. While few students contacted me, the course librarian, most seemed to appreciate my visibility in the course, my e-mails, and my posts on the discussion board.

SUMMARY/REFLECTION

The course outcomes that we started with included the following:

- Demonstrate rhetorical principles that shape technical writing to suit a range of readers in a variety of writing situations.
- Identify the needs of an audience and use that understanding to design documents.
- Use databases and other electronic sources to find information.
- Choose relevant sources to support an information need.
- Evaluate and modify a document to ensure its usability and persuasiveness for an audience.

Students' performance on the assignments succeeded in achieving these course outcomes. By researching a solution to workplace problem and creating various documents for diverse audiences, students needed to show a command of rhetorical principles, understand the needs of different audiences, choose appropriate sources, and incorporate them effectively, considering the documents' and audiences' needs. Professor Thumm was pleased with improved student performance in the class and found the new assignments reenergized the course, student engagement, and his involvement. He continued to use these assignments until he retired in the spring of 2017.

Part of our success was not only the incorporation of PBL principles into course design but also the incorporation of elements of the ACRL *Framework* into the course design. PBL works well, especially conjoined with the *Framework*, in that both encourage students to move away from following step-by-step directions for assignments and quantifiable assignment directions (page length, number of sources used or cited, etc.) and instead focus on problem solving through critical thinking and self-directed learning with minimal facilitation from instructors. While not explicitly stated in the lesson objectives, the frame Authority Is Constructed and Contextual's knowledge practices and dispositions—"learners recognize that authoritative content may be packaged formally or informally and may include sources of all media types. . . . Learners motivate themselves to find authoritative sources, recognizing that authority may be conferred or manifested in unexpected ways"—encouraged us to let our students explore and use resources without explicit directions from us about what types they "should" be using and how many they needed to fulfill an assignment's requirements (ACRL, 2016).

By directing students to focus on the needs of assigned documents instead of artificial source type and number requirements, we found that they chose appropriate sources for their research scenarios: students examining 3-D printers for office purchase consulted technology blogs and trade magazines;

students who were given a medical issue to research relied heavily on PubMed and the CDC's website. Requiring students to focus and to engage with solving the problem meant their attention shifted from finding sources to check off a list of assignment requirements to critically engaging with the research scenario's problem as well as reflecting on the differing needs of multiple audiences. Workplace writing inverts the standard classroom assignment paradigm: instead of choosing a topic and fulfilling specific assignment requirements, workers are assigned topics, or tasks, with little to no directions. While a college technical writing course cannot entirely replicate the experience of workplace research and writing, a well-designed course can give students the tools to tackle the writing job at hand.

NOTES

1. Complete text of all the research scenarios, assignment directions with rubrics, and links to online supporting materials can be found at the English 305 LibGuide at http://libguides.wvu.edu/english305_thumm
2. This assignment was adapted from an assignment developed by Paul Smith.

REFERENCES

Association of College and Research Libraries (ACRL). (2016). Authority is constructed and contextual. *ACRL Framework for Information Literacy in Higher Education*. Retrieved from http://www.ala.org/acrl/standards/ilframework#authority

Barrows, H. S. (1996). Problem-based learning in medicine and beyond: A brief overview. In L. Wilkerson & W. H. Gijselaers (Eds.), *New directions for teaching and learning* (pp. 3–11). San Francisco: Jossey-Bass.

Diamond, K. (2014, October 8). *What's the deal with trade journals?* [Video]. Retrieved from https://www.powtoon.com/online-presentation/c9EcUz69Lh1/whats-the-deal-with-trade-journals/

Diamond, K. (2015a, June 2). *EbscoHost and subject databases.* [Video]. Retrieved from https://www.powtoon.com/online-presentation/bSHxeJkbho9/ebscohost-and-subject-databases/#/

Diamond, K. (2015b, June 2). *What's the deal with annotated bibliographies?* [Video]. Retrieved from https://www.powtoon.com/online-presentation/eg268tMvc5c/whats-the-deal-with-annotated-bibliographies/#/

Diamond, K. (2015c, June 2). *What's the deal with peer review?* [Video]. Retrieved from https://www.powtoon.com/online-presentation/deFWSk3b7eG/whats-the-deal-with-peer-review/#/

Gagné, R. M., Wager, W. W., Golas, K. C., & Keller, J. M. (2005). *Principles of instructional design* (5th ed.). Belmont, CA: Wadsworth.

Mabrito, M. (1997). Writing on the front line: A study of workplace writing. *Business Communication Quarterly, 60*(3), 58–70.

McTighe, J., & Wiggins, G. (2005). *Understanding by design*. Alexandria, VA: Association for Supervision and Curriculum Development.

Seda, L. (n.d.). How to create stunning infographics in 30 minutes or less. Retrieved from http://www.lifehack.org/articles/work/how-to-create-stunning-infographics-in-30-minutes.html

Smith, P. (2015, May 11). JAMA-Leo controversy. [Research guide]. Retrieved from http://library.lmunet.edu/Jamaleo

West Virginia University. (2015–2016). ENGL 305: Technical writing. *Undergraduate catalog*. Retrieved from http://catalog.wvu.edu/search/?edition=2015-16&P=engl.+305/

CHAPTER 14

TEACHING THE LITERATURE REVIEW

Leveraging the ACRL Framework to Integrate Information Literacy Into Graduate Writing Education

Linda Macri

Kelsey Corlett-Rivera

INTRODUCTION

When our current Graduate School Writing Center–Research Commons partnership was still new, in fall 2014, we offered a surprisingly popular "How to Write a Literature Review" session. We began with the writing portion of the workshop and focused on four touchstones: the Burkean parlor as a metaphor for the situation of academic research, the idea that a literature review begins with a research question, understanding a literature review as a specific rhetorical situation, and stasis theory as a tool for organization and synthesis. The approach resonated with students and librarians, who noted that this rhetorical, learner-centered approach to instruction was more effective with graduate students. In hindsight, we recognize that we were anticipating the resonance and relevance that the ACRL *Framework*, with its focus on metaliteracy, offers.

The fields of writing studies and library and information studies share many aims and approaches; one of these shared approaches is a concentration on undergraduate students and their information literacy (Monroe-Gulick & Petr, 2012; Switzer & Perdue, 2011). Unlike the ongoing debate at the undergraduate level, particularly in first-year composition, about whether the research paper is dead, the dissertation and the master's thesis are alive and well, and, indeed, the need for graduate students to write for publication is stronger than ever. But the two situations are necessarily interconnected; if, as Claire McGuinness (2006) reminds us, there's "a tacit assumption among faculty that [undergraduate] students would somehow absorb and develop the requisite knowledge and skills" (p. 577) to write papers, and, as compositionist Wendy Hayden and librarian Stephanie Margolin (Margolin & Hayden, 2015) note, that "the remembered experience of some faculty . . . [is that] it just somehow happens" (p. 605) is true for undergraduates, it is all the more true at the graduate level. Doug Brent (2017), in his investigation of how students at the end of their undergraduate careers understand the process of finding and writing with sources, concludes that faculty "could do well to let their masks slip from time to time and let students in on what it's like to be not just a teacher but also a researcher" (p. 21). Graduate students, in their apprentice roles, need to see what is behind the mask even more; rarely can graduate students expect a writing course in their programs, and often they are lucky to be given access to a more advanced student's work as a comparison or model, let alone see the process of research and writing done by their professors and advisers.

At the graduate level, the writing classroom is not the usual site for developing information literacy.[1] Instead, the challenge for both writing and information literacy instruction is to find authentic contexts in which graduate students are writing and researching. One oft-targeted graduate research output is the literature review, which Hannah Rempel characterizes as "a significant grounding element for students' research" (2010, p. 532). Rosemary Green and Mary Bowser (2006) also note the literature review as both a challenge for graduate students and an area where research and writing support can greatly benefit the students (pp. 186–187). David Boote and Penny Beile (2005), writing about the centrality of the literature review for the field of education, position the role of the genre in a manner echoed by similar articles in other fields:[2] "Acquiring the skills and knowledge required to be education scholars should be the focal, integrative activity of pre-dissertation doctoral education. Preparing students to analyze and synthesize research in a field of specialization is crucial to understanding educational ideas. Such preparation is prerequisite to choosing a productive dissertation topic and appropriating fruitful methods of data collection and analysis" (p. 3). Boote and Beile address the challenges graduate students face in writing an effective literature review with a thoughtful approach and a sense of how the component fits into not only other genres of academic writing but also the whole effort of becoming a scholar; others, in contrast, offer a list of tips or steps, a kind of linearity that rarely meets the experience of students in the actual writing of a literature review.

In this chapter, we share the approach that shapes our graduate student programming, one that emphasizes that writing and information literacy are inseparable for graduate students. In particular, we discuss our "How to Write a Literature Review" workshop, a session we presume to be a familiar offering at many graduate degree–granting institutions. We explore the ways that the flexibility of the ACRL *Framework*, with its rhetorical and metacognitive approach to information literacy, has provided our library-writing partnership a pedagogy particularly suited to graduate students because it emphasizes the ways that research and writing do and must work in synergy.

BACKGROUND

The University of Maryland, College Park (UMD) is the state's flagship university, home to more than 37,000 students, nearly one-third of whom are graduate students (University of Maryland Graduate School, n.d.). Of those, about 40% are doctoral students and one-third are international students. Our graduate student population likely faces challenges similar to those confronted by graduate students at other large research universities.

Until the Graduate School Writing Center was created in 2013 in response to graduate student requests, there was no institution-wide writing support for graduate students; they were not permitted to access services at the existing undergraduate Writing Center. Most information literacy support for graduate students was provided through subject specialist librarians, who presented at grad student orientations in their departments and offered one-shot instruction sessions in graduate classes, frequently followed by one-on-one consultations. This approach provided many students, especially those pursuing a doctorate, with strong subject-specific information literacy skills. However, not all students knew about or took advantage of their subject specialist librarian, and those who did often had other more general information literacy–related needs that went unmet, such as how to manage their research processes and organize and incorporate sources into their writing. Often, faculty were unaware of all the services the libraries offered graduate students and so did not recommend us as a resource.

In late 2012, Kelsey, who later directed graduate and faculty library services as the first head of the Research Commons, assembled a team of librarians to address the lack of awareness of library resources. The group planned and executed an inaugural workshop in early 2013, an open house called the Info Expo, structured as a half-day mini conference featuring presentations on topics of interest to graduate students and faculty members (Measuring Scholarly Impact, Tips for Submitting ILL Requests, Citation Managers, etc.). While some sessions saw high attendance, overall the event was a great deal of work with limited impact. Only a few graduate students attended; the primary audience was faculty members.

The then-director of the newly formed Graduate Student Writing Center worked with several librarians in spring 2013 to offer new graduate student workshops, Research and Writing Boot Camps, in specific disciplines. Engineering workshops were well attended, but others, such as Business, saw lower interest. The library group who planned the initial Info Expo shifted focus, becoming the Graduate Student Outreach Team, and reached out to the Graduate School Writing Center to develop more general Humanities, Social Sciences, and Science workshops in the fall of 2013. We learned that students attended whatever session best fit their schedule regardless of discipline and again saw lower turnout than expected. This first iteration of Research and Writing Boot Camps stuck with traditional information literacy concepts:

- Grad student–specific library services (e.g., document delivery, borrowing, etc.)
- Plagiarism (deemed especially important for international students)
- Research overview (e.g., library website, WorldCat Local, online database directory)
- Citation management tools

The presentation during these workshops was linear: research was covered in the morning, and participants were tasked with finding an article to use in the afternoon writing session, which the librarians did not participate in or attend. Each part was two hours, with a one-hour break for lunch during which participants were free to leave.

After offering these boot camps with reasonable attendance numbers (average of 19 at each workshop) for three semesters, the library and Graduate School Writing Center organizers put together an additional, more focused workshop, "How to Write a Literature Review." One 2-hour workshop was scheduled, with limited advertising and advance notice. Registration numbers quickly exceeded our expectations and room capacity. We added two sessions; overall, 119 students attended. We offered the "boot camp" one more time and continued to offer multiple literature review workshops each semester; their popularity has stayed consistent, averaging 45 attendees each. (See Figure 14.1.)

While focusing on finding, accessing, organizing, and using information to write effective literature reviews, the Libraries Graduate Student Outreach team, by then a part of the Research Commons led by Kelsey, collaborated with Linda to emphasize the interconnected nature of the research and writing process. The success of these literature review workshops highlights key strategies to reach graduate students, such as the integration of research and writing instruction in an authentic context, and denotes the shift to the more fluid ACRL *Framework* from the more linear ACRL *Standards*. In 2014, the *Framework* had not yet been filed, but the purpose and context-focused approach that Linda developed as a rhetorician made good sense to the librarians, and was further justified when the *Framework* was adopted in 2016.

ACRL *Standards*

The *Information Literacy Competency Standards for Higher Education* were developed by the Association of College and Research Libraries in 2000 to "provide a framework for assessing the information literate individual"

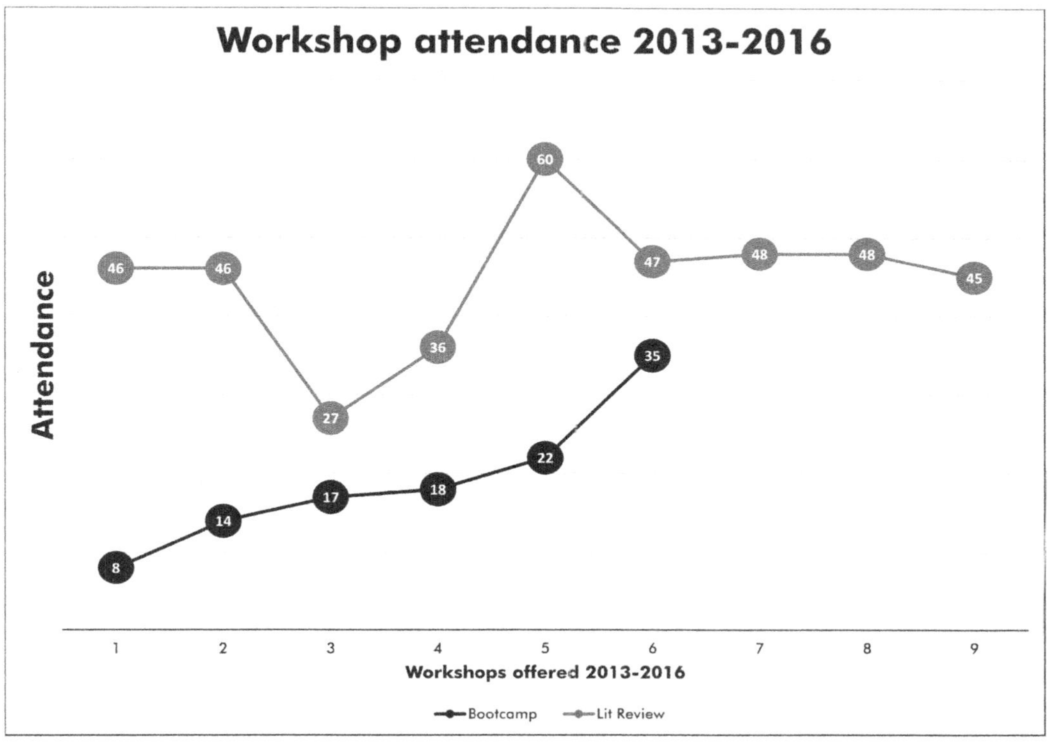

Figure 14.1 Workshop attendance chart.

(Association of College and Research Libraries [ACRL], 2000, p. 5). Five standards were accompanied by 22 performance indicators designed to measure students' progress to becoming information literate. While the *Standards* allow for students to return to an earlier part of the process and repeat their steps if needed, they are designed to be followed in order—first locating, then evaluating, and finally using the information (ACRL, 2000). The *Standards* were rescinded in 2016, having been replaced by the *Framework for Information Literacy for Higher Education* (ACRL, 2016).

While a great deal of literature has been published exploring the ACRL *Standards* in relation to undergraduate information literacy, the authors have chosen to focus on a few studies that investigate the use of the *Standards* in supporting graduate students and research/writing interventions.

Amalia Monroe-Gulick and Julie Petr (2012) interviewed 15 incoming graduate students in the social sciences to assess their understanding of the research process, then evaluated those interviews for mastery of the ACRL *Standards* (p. 316). In analyzing the interviews, they recognized that the *Standards* were less applicable to graduate students, who overall met more of the information literacy competencies than expected. They concluded that graduate students need broader support in navigating the research process, rather than skill-based instruction in specific tasks (p. 331).

Anne Switzer and Sherry Perdue (2011) concurred, citing graduate students' lack of ability to effectively evaluate and synthesize sources at the expert level necessary for a dissertation. They describe the outcomes of a course based on the ACRL *Standards* to "address the information literacy and writing needs of graduate education writers at Oakland University" (p. 7). While they proceed through each *Standard*, their primary goal is increasing support for doctoral students by enabling graduate students to produce a high-quality literature review, in hopes of reducing the percentage of doctoral students who never complete the dissertation.

ACRL *Framework*

The ACRL *Framework for Information Literacy for Higher Education* consists of six nonsequential frames "based on a cluster of interconnected core concepts, with flexible options for implementation, rather than on a set of standards or learning outcomes, or any prescriptive enumeration of skills" (ACRL, 2016, p. 2). Several authors have explored the major differences between developing information literacy instruction based on the *Framework* in comparison to the *Standards*, including Brittany Brannon and Nancy Foasberg.

Brannon (2017) explains that the *Standards* converted information into a mere object, which allowed librarians to "develop mechanistic approaches to information literacy, laying out abstracted, sequential steps that all students could learn in order to become information literate" (p. 125). That mechanistic approach was especially problematic for graduate students, who are expected to not only find and synthesize existing research, but also participate in the process by identifying and filling knowledge gaps. While the traditional definition of information literacy did recognize information use, it has rarely, if ever, been a focus in library instruction sessions, as evidenced by a question asked of librarian Robert Miller after he helped a student find a source: "But what do you want me to do with it?" (Friedman & Miller, 2016, p. 198). The *Framework*, and its focus on the purpose for carrying out research, has opened the door for a more rhetorical approach to information literacy that can be incorporated into authentic contexts for graduate students; we have found this extremely effective in our literature review workshops for graduate students.

Foasberg (2015) also recognizes the "commodification" of information by the *Standards*, in which "the information seeker acquires a commodity, rather than (for instance) participating in a conversation" (p. 704). She contends that information literacy should be more active, allowing students to interact with the information rather than just extracting and recording it (pp. 707–708). A positivist philosophy underlies the *Standards*, whereas the *Framework* takes a constructivist approach, in which information is a social phenomenon and very dependent on context. The shift away from a mechanical, skills-based approach tracks with the changes in how writing is being taught as well (p. 707), and "the Framework better recognizes the complexities of information and information behavior, and explicitly makes space for students as participants in the process of knowledge production" (p. 703).

The *Framework*'s acknowledgment of the importance of context and community in interacting with information better serves graduate students in particular, because of their need to "comprehend the community and genre within which they write" (Foasberg, 2015, p. 709). Some onus is placed on the students to think rhetorically about their sources (p. 710), that is, "to develop, in their own creation processes, an understanding that their choices impact the purposes for which the information product will be used and the message it conveys" (ACRL, 2016, p. 5).

REFLECTIONS

In our workshop, we find that three of the frames—Scholarship as Conversation, Research as Inquiry, and Searching as Strategic Exploration—shape the outcomes we aim for in our brief introduction to writing from sources at the graduate level.

Scholarship as Conversation

> Research in scholarly and professional fields is a discursive practice in which ideas are formulated, debated, and weighed against one another over extended periods of time. (ACRL, 2016)

> "Imagine that you enter a parlor. You come late. When you arrive, others have long preceded you, and they are engaged in a heated discussion, a discussion too heated for them to pause and tell you exactly what it is about. In fact, the discussion had already begun long before any of them got there, so that no one present is qualified to retrace for you all the steps that had gone before. You listen for a while, until you decide that you have caught the tenor of the argument; then you put in your oar. Someone answers; you answer him; another comes to your defense; another aligns himself against you, to either the embarrassment or gratification of your opponent, depending upon the quality of your ally's assistance. However, the discussion is interminable. The hour grows late, you must depart. And you do depart, with the discussion still vigorously in progress."
>
> —Burke, 1974, pp. 110–111

Our sessions are broadly aimed at our graduate student population, which means students who attend are not only from a wide range of disciplines, but they are also at various stages of their degrees. For both the novice and the dissertating student, the reminder that in entering graduate school they have entered a Burkean parlor—where the conversation has been going on for years and no one will offer a full recap, yet where they must nevertheless get a sense of the debate before joining in—resonates and offers a shared context across their many fields. Burke's sense of the unending conversation brings a rhetorical focus to graduate level study; while the frame Scholarship as Conversation applies across levels, graduate students, who have taken on the mantle of researcher, are keenly aware of their role in the conversation and of the challenge that conversation poses. As the Burkean reference suggests, we repeatedly use the frame of Scholarship as Conversation to understand scholarship as a rhetorical move, one which requires graduate students to consider whom they speak to in a literature review, why their audiences engage in discourse to begin with, how they might address their audience (or audiences) more effectively—in other words, elements of the rhetorical situation. Scholarship as Conversation also suggests an ethos they adopt, particularly in their role as apprentice scholars, since it underscores the need for engagement rather than more overt polemics. The Research Commons librarians also focus on strategies such as citation-chaining and saved search alerts during their portion of the workshop, which situate a particular source within the literature and make the discussions that take place between different pieces of scholarship more apparent.

The Burkean parlor metaphor could also be interpreted through the lens of the Authority Is Constructed and Contextual frame, since the need to be familiar with the conversation represents the need for authority—what writing teachers would refer to as *ethos*—while responding to the tenor of the conversation speaks to recognizing the context, or the rhetorical situation. An essential element of being conversant in a field, of course, is understanding the issues and debates, an understanding that encompasses more than searching and finding texts. After introducing the idea of joining the conversation, we focus several minutes of the workshop on reading practices. The suggestion that graduate students need instruction in reading might be met with incredulity from faculty who are only just accepting that graduate writing instruction is not remedial, yet what brings graduate students, apprentices in their various disciplines, to seek support from our Graduate School Writing Center in connection with their literature reviews very often stems from challenges they face in connecting the form and content of what they read to what they write. And, indeed, the primary complaint of academics across disciplines about the failures of literature reviews by graduate students is the lack of synthesis the student creates (Boote & Beile, 2005). Such synthesis comes from effectively reading and making sense of sources students identify for their literature reviews, so before we address searching for articles, we offer guidance on reading and taking reading notes, focusing on two practices, glossing and writing rhetorical précis, as methods for thorough understanding and laying the groundwork for summarizing and synthesizing later in a literature review.

Research as Inquiry

> Experts see inquiry as a process that focuses on problems or questions in a discipline or between disciplines that are open or unresolved. (ACRL, 2016)

After introducing the idea of graduate study as entering a conversation, we focus more specifically on the literature review. We ask where a literature review begins—and warn that they might find the answer to be a trick. The answer, of course, is that a literature review begins with a research question, as any research endeavor does. A credible researcher becomes a scholar in the field in order to pursue answers to the questions of that field.

Linda introduces the rhetorical concept of stasis theory as a method for understanding and categorizing what is at issue in any situation or dispute. With origins in classical rhetoric, stasis theory is a tool for recognizing, articulating, and ordering questions in a dispute and identifying what actually is disputed; stasis refers to the idea of "slowing down" or being at a standstill, with the idea being that when a question is in stasis, it is debated—until there is agreement, there can be no movement on an issue. Like other rhetorical tools, it can be used for both invention and analysis. After a brief introduction to the categories of stasis theory, we discuss their applicability in different disciplines. What disciplines, for instance, focus most inquiry in conjecture, in whether things exist or do not exist? Are questions of existence hotly debated—that is, are they common research questions—in your field? Recognizing the

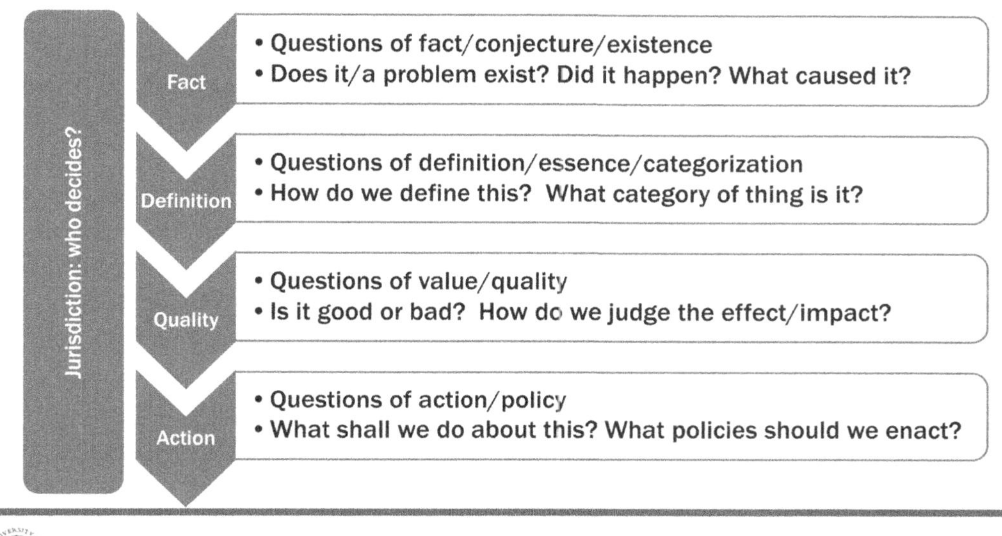

Figure 14.2 Organizing with stasis theory.

kinds of questions that different fields ask—students answer that education, for instance, often engages all the questions but that certain journals are more interested in the "action" (application) question than others—helps students articulate their understanding of their fields and the epistemologies of different disciplines. (See Figure 14.2.)

Once students have a general sense of what stasis theory offers in terms of understanding the research questions that motivate and animate their particular disciplines, we use examples of abstracts and introductions from published literature reviews to examine how these questions actually appear in published work in different disciplines. We also consider how anticipating the questions at issue in a topic offers a way to search for what they need and to help organize what they find in their sources.

Searching as Strategic Exploration

> The act of searching often begins with a question that directs the act of finding needed information. Encompassing inquiry, discovery, and serendipity, searching identifies both possible relevant sources as well as the means to access those sources. (ACRL, 2016)

A broad research question launches a literature review, and graduate students, unlike undergraduate students, generally know whether the questions they pose are good questions to pursue for their fields. "[T]he means to access those sources" not only refers to finding the text of the sources, but also reading and comprehending them. Stasis theory provides a way to "access" sources in terms of understanding where they fit into different kinds of questions in a field and, ultimately, how they fit into the student's research question.

At the end of the workshop, Research Commons librarians present a number of strategies within a recommended workflow, to provide real-life examples of exploring sources as envisioned in this frame. Librarians lead with a brief overview of grad-specific library services, as awareness on such a large campus is usually low, but do assume a more advanced level of information literacy skills; little time, for example, is spent on formulating search terms or evaluating sources. Instead, librarians work through finding and accessing relevant sources in Google Scholar, which provides the broad coverage necessary when faced with a large, multidisciplinary audience. After discussing strategies for ensuring a thorough literature search, such as cited reference searching, the instructor shows how to save relevant source to Zotero, entering notes that would be generated when processing the sources, as described in the writing portion. We close with a demo showing how Zotero can insert citations and create a bibliography when writing, allowing graduate students to leave with both a solid grounding in what it means to be a scholar in a discipline and interact with that scholarship as well as practical experience in how to implement these ideas and how they benefit.

We decided to begin with the "writing" portion of these sessions in part because it allowed us to put the rhetorical concepts (Burkean parlor, stasis theory, rhetorical situation) before the "search" steps. That ordering is an element of what we want to underscore by offering these sessions jointly. Foregrounding a rhetorical approach allows us to emphasize the theoretical underpinnings of the *Framework* and its focus on metaliteracy as a new way to understand information literacy. Unlike undergraduate students, graduate students actively work in their disciplines, rarely need to be told which journals to consult, and appreciate the necessity of research to their writing process. What they do need is support bringing considerable sources together. Overall, the complementarity of the ACRL *Framework* and a rhetorical approach to invention has provided an effective way to engage and address the wide-ranging information literacy needs of a large and interdisciplinary group of graduate students. As we have negotiated the best approach to reaching our graduate students and their need to produce and not only consume knowledge, a writing studies–librarian partnership informed by and anchored in the rhetorical approaches offered by the ACRL *Framework* has yielded successful cross-disciplinary initiatives.

CONCLUSION

We believe the ACRL *Framework* has helped us communicate one of the most essential learning outcomes of the two-hour "How to Write a Literature Review" workshop: the understanding that the workshop is not an inoculation against all future challenges posed by writing with sources but, instead, an introduction. We aim to alert students to the resources available through both the Graduate School Writing Center and the library and provide tools to address the process of writing with sources. The *Framework*, with its emphasis on inquiry, context, and process, offers new ways for us to help graduate students move from finding information to analyzing and synthesizing information in the context of their own understanding. It has also provided a stronger grounding for more collaboration between our groups, and the Graduate School Writing Center and the Research Commons have continued to work together to offer new programming such as academic integrity workshops targeting international graduate students and a speed-geeking event that enables graduate students to better communicate with a non-expert audience about their research.

One question posed by this volume is whether the ACRL *Framework* can be adopted by Writing Studies and where the boundary between the roles of librarians and writing instructors lies. Our experience has been that the synergy of the *Framework* and a rhetorical approach to writing instruction is both desirable and relevant, particularly for graduate students. Its theory yields a practice that helps graduate students recognize that the boundary between finding and using sources is necessarily blurred in their work and that the distinction between what librarians and writing instructors can offer in terms of support is not a line in the sand but rather a continuum of inquiry and approaches.

NOTES

1. In the introduction to the recently published *Supporting Graduate Student Writers: Research, Curriculum, and Program Design*, Steve Simpson (Simpson, Caplan, Cox, & Philips, 2016) catalogues the ways that support for graduate communications has grown in recent years, and in a later chapter, "The State of Graduate Communication Support: Results of an International Survey," Nigel Caplan and Michelle Cox note that 70.5% of 139 U.S. respondents to their survey noted that their institution offers a for-credit writing course, and 36.7% responded that they offer a noncredit writing class (p. 27). However, these numbers don't tell the entire story; Caplan and Cox later note that "in many cases, if a writing course is offered, it is only open for ESL and/or international students, although some universities offer these classes to all" (p. 32). Simpson's introduction provides the context for this when he notes that "while composition studies has just recently joined the conversation on graduate writing, second language writing studies and other fields within applied linguistics and English language learning have researched graduate communication support for decades" (p. 3).
2. Jeffrey Knopf (2006) begins the broadly titled "Doing a Literature Review," a brief article aimed at political science students, with the broad recognition that "students entering a graduate program often encounter a new type of assignment that differs from papers they had to write high school or as college undergraduates: the literature review" (p. 127), presuming that students have had little to no training in writing, particular research writing. For the field of computational biology, Marco Pautasso (2013) offers "Ten Simple Rules for Writing a Literature Review," built on the exigence that "it is likely that most scientist have not thought in detail about how to approach and carry out a literature review" (p. 1). Similar guidance is available for the field of information systems (Webster & Watson, 2002), psychology (Baumeister & Leary, 1997), nursing (Cronin, Ryan, & Coughlan, 2008), and criminal justice (Denney & Tewksbury, 2013), to name just a few.

REFERENCES

Association of College and Research Libraries. (2000). *Information literacy competency standards for higher education* (Text). Chicago, IL. Retrieved from http://www.ala.org/acrl/standards/informationliteracycompetency

Association of College and Research Libraries. (2016). *Framework for information literacy for higher education* (Text). Chicago, IL. Retrieved from http://www.ala.org/acrl/standards/ilframework

Baumeister, R. F., & Leary, M. R. (1997). Writing narrative literature reviews. *Review of General Psychology, 1*(3), 311. https://doi.org/1089-2680/97/S3.00

Boote, D. N., & Beile, P. (2005). Scholars before researchers: On the centrality of the dissertation literature review in research preparation. *Educational Researcher, 34*(6), 3–15.

Brannon, B. (2017). The service implications of a rhetorical approach to information literacy. *Public Services Quarterly, 13*(2), 124–133. https://doi.org/10.1080/15228959.2017.1301843

Brent, D. (2017). Senior students' perceptions of entering a research community. *Written Communication, 34*(3), 333–355. https://doi.org/10.1177/0741088317710925

Burke, K. (1974). *The philosophy of literary form: Studies in symbolic action* (3rd ed.). Berkeley: University of California Press.

Cronin, P., Ryan, F., & Coughlan, M. (2008). Undertaking a literature review: A step-by-step approach. *British Journal of Nursing, 17*(1), 38–43. https://doi.org/10.12968/bjon.2008.17.1.28059

Denney, A. S., & Tewksbury, R. (2013). How to write a literature review. *Journal of Criminal Justice Education, 24*(2), 218–234. https://doi.org/10.1080/10511253.2012.730617

Foasberg, N. M. (2015). From standards to frameworks for IL: How the ACRL framework addresses critiques of the standards. *Portal: Libraries and the Academy, 15*(4), 699–717.

Friedman, S., & Miller, R. (2016). Launching students towards source-based writing: An introduction for librarians. *College & Research Libraries News, 77*(4), 198–201.

Green, R., & Bowser, M. (2006). Observations from the field: Sharing a literature review rubric. *Journal of Library Administration, 45*(1/2), 185–202. https://doi.org/10.1300/J111v45n01_10

Knopf, J. W. (2006). Doing a literature review. *PS: Political Science & Politics, 39*(1), 127–132. https://doi.org/10.1017/S1049096506060264

Margolin, S., & Hayden, W. (2015). Beyond mechanics: Reframing the pedagogy and development of information literacy teaching tools. *Journal of Academic Librarianship, 41*(5), 602–612. https://doi.org/10.1016/j.acalib.2015.07.001

McGuinness, C. (2006). What faculty think—Exploring the barriers to information literacy development in undergraduate education. *Journal of Academic Librarianship, 32*(6), 573–582. https://doi.org/10.1016/j.acalib.2006.06.002

Monroe-Gulick, A., & Petr, J. (2012). Incoming graduate students in the social sciences: How much do they really know about library research? *Portal: Libraries and the Academy, 12*(3), 315–335. https://doi.org/10.1353/pla.2012.0032

Pautasso, M. (2013). Ten simple rules for writing a literature review. *PLOS Computational Biology, 9*(7), e1003149. https://doi.org/10.1371/journal.pcbi.1003149

Rempel, H. G. (2010). A longitudinal assessment of graduate student research behavior and the impact of attending a library literature review workshop. *College & Research Libraries, 71*(6), 532–547. https://doi.org/10.5860/crl-79

Simpson, S., Caplan, N. A., Cox, M., & Philips, T. (2016). *Supporting graduate student writers:*

Research, curriculum, and program design. Ann Arbor: University of Michigan Press.

Switzer, A., & Perdue, S. W. (2011). Dissertation 101: A research and writing intervention for education graduate students. *Education Libraries*, *34*(1), 4–14.

University of Maryland Graduate School. (n.d.). Students | The University of Maryland Graduate School. Retrieved July 25, 2017, from https://gradschool.umd.edu/admissions/choose-maryland/facts-and-figures/students

Webster, J., & Watson, R. T. (2002). Analyzing the past to prepare for the future: writing a literature review. *MIS Quarterly*, *26*(2), xiii–xxiii.

CHAPTER 15

LIBRARIAN INTERVENTION

Where Support Meets Need

Kathleen F. Kempa

Who helps students when they begin their senior research? Who guides a junior or senior's choice of research question? Who knows each student's passion and skills? Their professors provide that help to students. Well, then, why would upper-division professors ask a librarian to visit their class when their juniors and seniors begin a major research project?

The answer depends on the professor's goal for the course. Will his class begin the research process? During one class period, a librarian can open students' eyes to resources and research within their discipline. Does the teacher want his students to have an awareness of current research within their discipline? Librarians are aware of current electronic tools for keeping updated with recently published research. Will the class produce research reports? Students can save hours of manual documentation and citation with not much more than an hour's introduction to citation management tools. Upper-level classes delve into the discipline's discourse and current research. Students need guidance as they begin working with unfamiliar databases. Librarians work closely with professors to be sure that critical understandings about information as well as specific researching skills are imparted during the class. In junior- and senior-level classes librarians teach efficient use of specific database tools and skills required for searching discipline-related resources.

Librarians using the Association of College and Research Libraries' *Framework for Information Literacy for Higher Education* expose students to the nature of information, how it is created, organized, evaluated, and used (Association of College and Research Libraries Board, 2015). Student expertise will require an understanding of why the way information is produced affects the resulting information. Students need to appreciate that their desired information use, their personal context, will determine where to look for information. New researchers must learn to pay attention to earlier research producers and learn how to participate in sharing their own research. Being able to contribute to expanding the discipline's knowledge matters to them. Librarians guide students to understand the unique organization of information within a discipline's databases. They help learners appreciate why each discipline finds its organizational method particularly useful. While professors almost intuitively understand the criteria used in evaluating information in their discipline, beginning researchers do not. Librarians, whose researching focus is on reliable information, can guide students to question data trustworthiness and author credibility. Recognizing that context matters in information production and in its use and reuse is another important understanding that budding researchers must acquire.

INFORMATION ENVIRONMENT

Historically, information has been treated as a commodity. Like a commodity, there could be assumed scarcities. Data had to be stored and retrieved. It could be locked away from some and made available to others. In those days, research was considered intrinsically true and unbiased. Using this mindset, students learned to be careful consumers of the commodity, information. Librarians taught core competencies in general knowledge discovery, retrieval, and citation. Students learned how to use the intellectual "material" they found. Schools tested and assessed students' acquisition of instruction.

With the explosion of freely available, unedited, dynamically changing news, opinions, and research results, scholars and librarians confronted knowledge's unique attributes. They recognized the fact that ideas are very unlike commodities. Information, if it ever was, is certainly no longer a scarce, contained, static, singular commodity. Nor is it ever really owned. It isn't lessened by being shared, edited, reused, and repurposed.

Knowledge is critical to today's economy. Because it is at the core of growth and productivity, it is imperative that every student have an understanding of the nature of information and an appreciation for the conventions and power of its use and misuse. While this is true of intellectual understandings in general, it is even more apparent within disciplines. Each scholarly field has its own vocabulary and conventions for sharing its research and discoveries. Sciences and humanities establish their own pace and acceptable timelines. Students who know only how to search using Google, general databases, and Web-based information sources will be unable to progress in their scholarly field. They will remain outside the vital, ongoing discourses.

Academics and researchers have acquired their discipline's understanding of information and its characteristics gradually over the course of years as that information has grown. Students need to comprehend and work with concepts and resources whose vocabularies they are struggling to learn. Reaching a knowledge of the theoretical underpinnings of information, particularly those within disciplines, has been compared to crossing over a threshold. Students need help to approach and then cross these intellectual thresholds (J. H. F. Meyer & Land, 2006, p. 24).

What this means for writing professors and librarians is that while librarians may visit a writing class during a student's freshman year, they cannot share much more than an introduction to one or two general concepts about the nature of information. Freshmen often have research skills that might be compared to subsistence-level life skills. Librarians who visit freshman writing and composition classes attempt to lure those freshmen to more sophisticated general databases and knowledge resources by exposing them to research learning experiences. After the librarian introduction, writing teachers and professors guide students along the learning continuum to new intellectual thresholds; they provide their students with skills, practice, and experiences to help bring the students to an awareness of concepts about and qualities of information in their chosen discipline. Librarians should revisit the students in their sophomore, junior, and senior years to help with the very complex challenge of guiding students to learn subject-specific researching techniques. As students begin to grasp new knowledge, they may stumble over concepts that are counterintuitive. They might find some ideas threatening to their earlier research practice and their previously held suppositions about the nature of information in general (J. Meyer, Land, & Baillie, 2010, pp. ix–x). The librarian, as an unbiased outsider, understands some of these difficulties. Should the professor request it, librarians can contribute to assessment measures by helping students demonstrate their grasp of difficult concepts.

GETTING OVER "RIGHT ANSWER" SYNDROME

One of the concepts students struggle with, when they begin researching or looking for information for their papers, is the idea that every research topic has a correct answer that simply needs to be found. In fact, there are several assumptions about knowledge, which were identified by Brenda Dervin and briefly described in a chapter titled "Generation Z: Information Facts and Fictions." She concisely describes "right answer" syndrome as: objective facts contain the only knowledge that has value; data can be used and understood outside of context; relevant facts are available for every need; there is an objective solution for every problem; when and where information was produced is irrelevant when considering future use (Cole, Napier, & Marcum, 2015, p. 112).

As long as students are content with their assumptions about information and research, particularly the myth that there is an answer for every question, they will not cross the mental threshold to a different and expanded understanding. This is particularly distressing as students attempt to grow in their discipline. Within the librarian's *Framework for Information Literacy for Higher Education* (ACRL, 2015) is the concept Research as Inquiry, which can help students at least begin to glimpse the possibility that what they know as research may be, at best, insufficient.

"In the *Framework*, research is less about finding answers and more about asking questions" (Drabinski, 2016, p. 383). In order to help students understand research as questioning, Colleen Burgess suggests, "I would model the dispositions of this frame by expecting more of my students: by coaching them to push past the first or easiest answer, by asking questions to help them develop their own research questions, and by encouraging them to seek multiple perspectives in their research beyond what might align with their thesis or hypothesis" (Burgess, 2015, p. 5).

Many librarians are not discipline specialists, but they can help students in any discipline understand research as a questioning process. Kevin Klipfel (2015), in his article "Developing a Research Question," suggests modeling the procedure of finding a personally interesting question within a mandated topic. He introduces an exercise involving what a student knows and cares about. Moving students' understanding of legitimate research away from dry impersonal facts to questions touching their daily lives can help broaden students' understanding of research. Students can begin adapting the information they have. They can use knowledge-seeking processes to find solutions to new situations and problems (pp. 52–53).

We assume that upper-level students are already accustomed to searching for simple answers using Google protocols and practices. Librarians use the *Framework* to help students move their understanding of information away from single, definitive answers and solutions to the more complex open possibilities required by research.

Searching as Strategic Exploration is another of the frames that can help students understand what research is. This frame opens the door for students to the unique resources favored by active scholars. Students learn that where they look for information impacts the kind of information that they will find. "Failed searches" are often the most productive teaching/learning moments for fledgling researchers. In one-on-one instruction, librarians suggest a variety of words and phrases so that the student becomes aware of alternate aspects of the topic. Librarians guide students into their discipline's databases and demonstrate some of the resource tools available. If students are working with their own laptops, they can set bookmarks and save links to resources. Students can install time-saving apps. If they are working on public computers, students can e-mail their search results or save their research to cloud storage. While individual personal assistance at the time of need produces the most effective learning, it is not always possible to provide one-on-one instruction for every student.

When librarians visit class groups, they can guide group activities, dividing the class into smaller independent working groups all searching for similar information. After a period of searching, each group reports on where they searched, what terms they used, and what results they found. At the conclusion of that activity, the librarian introduces another resource. The class has an opportunity to explore the new resource. Class members keep a written record of their process of searching along with a list of the usable results they retrieved. The written record can be used as a formative assessment.

A similar type of search can illustrate the advantage of exploring multiple resources. Students can search a group of keywords or phrases related to a research question, which they will use to discover the diverse results that occur in different resources and databases. Students could search YouTube, Facebook, and Twitter and use a variety of search engines, such as Google, Yahoo, or Dogpile. They should also try several scholarly databases. Along with the research, students will discuss why there might be different results from similar searches and why researchers would want to discover multiple results from their research. Students could journal the results of their searches. Student journals can provide information for a formative assessment.

TAKING A STAND ON FAKE NEWS

Outrage over "fake news" seems to crop up periodically. In today's environment of abundant, unedited, dynamic information growth, it is inevitable that there will be misinformation. It can occur when correct information is misunderstood, miscommunicated, or misused. It can also happen when information is incorrect, incorrect in context, or outdated. Understanding information correctly is the responsibility of both the sender and the receiver. The inability to identify erroneous information is widespread.

The Stony Brook University School of Journalism was appalled at the results of a student population survey that showed overwhelming evidence that students were unable to discern fake news from real news. They established a semester-long course to help university students gain the ability to discern real news (Klurfeld & Schneider, 2014). The ability to identify fake or questionable information falls most heavily upon experts in disciplines. Students, who will be the experts of the future, need more than simple guidelines about specific sources or types of information to avoid.

The *Framework* has provided multiple frames to help students begin to confront the inaccurate and misleading information they encounter in their researching and daily information accumulation. Authority Is Constructed and Contextual is both the strongest and most faceted statement about information that the ACRL proposed. The statement can be used to focus on the authority or expertise of the speaker/writer. Because college students may conflate the term authority with power, librarians and professors often use the term "credibility" when introducing the idea that respected experts tend to produce information that can be trusted. Juniors and seniors are aware of some discipline experts. Using that knowledge, students can appreciate "authority" as an earned or constructed quality that confers credibility within their field. Librarians help students assess information validity based on trustworthy producers or authors. They guide the students' focus to information accuracy, then allow students to recognize the value of using credibly produced sources. When students are able to determine the credibility of an information author or producer, they can better determine fake or real news/information. The challenge to professors and information literacy teachers becomes that of awakening students to qualities that confer authority.

Librarians, using the *Framework* electronic mailing list message, share their experiences in leading students to critically assess expert credibility by asking students to explore journalists' reaction to experts who speak outside their area of expertise. Mark Meola (2017) provides two examples of press criticism of experts in one field expressing their opinions in disciplines in which they are not authorities, or as in the second example, speaking beyond their acknowledged expertise:

1. "Top Hedge Fund Manager: Global Warming Isn't a Danger" (Gandel, 2015)
2. "Ben Carson's Gray Matter" (Bruni, 2017)

After Meola's students read each article, he leads a discussion regarding the credibility of the statements of experts and persons in authority. Meola's discussions center around the question of whether the authority of speakers is as credible when they speak outside their area of expertise.

In the same electronic mailing list message, Ethan Pullman's (2017) approach is to help students to assess what characteristics or accomplishments determine who is an authority and who is credible. Pullman's emphasis is on helping students recognize expertise and authority beyond that which is conferred by academic credentials. Here are the videos he uses to get the project started:

1. *The Success of Nonviolent Civil Resistance* (TEDx Talks, 2013, p. n.p.)
2. *Dr. King: Nonviolence Is the Most Powerful Weapon* (msremmu, 2008)

"Students are asked to identify the main argument, the conclusions reached, any gaps, and to discuss which they view as more authoritative (appropriate to use for their paper) and why" (Pullman, 2017). Pullman says that the students generally have no difficulty with the first part of the assignment. However, students struggle to extend their definition of authority and credibility beyond academic credentials to include the expertise of lived experience.

"The *Framework* is explicit about the socially constructed nature of authority, arguing that information literacy includes the ability to 'acknowledge biases that privilege some sources of authority over others, especially in terms of others' worldviews, gender, sexual orientation, and cultural orientations'" (Drabinski, 2017, p. 87). Drabinski encourages librarians to expose students to the social aspects of establishing authority and suggests an open-ended discussion, with no right or wrong conclusions. "For example, a scholarly journal article about Pokémon carries one kind of authority in a certain discourse community, while the fan discussions in the online encyclopedia Bulbapaedia have authority in fan cultures" (Drabinski, 2017, p. 87). Rather than conducting a discussion on real or fake news, Drabinski encourages a vigorous discussion about fake news to help spark curiosity and critical thinking. She claims that the *Framework* inspires a discussion "that seeks to produce a future of critical engagement rather than compliance with an external learning outcomes document" (Drabinski, 2017, p. 88).

Critical thinking and engagement are the goals of classes and assignments that lead students beyond simple determinations of the accuracy of specific information. Critical thinking demands a consideration of why and how certain research was produced and published. Librarians teach the Authority Is Constructed and Contextual frame with an additional emphasis on the context of the user's needs, as well as the writer's intent, in determining the appropriateness and authority of the message. The information literacy (IL) instructor could provide multiple scenarios requiring research on a particular topic. Students would find one resource for each scenario and explain why that particular resource was appropriate in the described situation. In upper-level classes, for example, in nursing education, students could be confronted by a need to produce a report about a particular illness for a class paper. In the next scenario students would explain the illness to a recently diagnosed patient. In a third scenario, the students could provide research for a pharmaceutical conference. That activity could be followed by a discussion about why each presentation, although not fake, was not appropriate, complete, or adequate in alternative scenarios. As nursing students provide different resources and answers to the same question, they could also discuss currency of information, differences of practice, and cultural preferences to stimulate more engagement.

CAN WE TALK?

What professors and librarians teaching IL are trying to accomplish for their upper-level students is to help them become fluent in the current discourse of the discipline. The *Framework* acknowledges discipline dialogue in the frame Scholarship as Conversation. While it is fun to introduce freshmen to the concept that research and publishing and academic conferences are focused around conversation, freshmen and sophomores don't have enough knowledge of a field of study to join the discussion. They are usually mentally standing off on the sidelines trying to understand what is being said.

By the time students become juniors, seniors, and graduates, they are aware of the research being done in their field. They have contributed to discussions in their classes and have produced writing within their study. They may have engaged in discipline-related conversations outside the classroom. These burgeoning scholars are ready to see where their interests and contributions fit in the discourse of the field. Upper-level students are ready to be introduced to ". . . the social nature of disciplinary discourses and practices, librarians can emphasize to students that disciplinary ways of communicating are not static but rather are fluid and changing and very much sites of contested power" (Simmons, 2005, p. 302). The librarian can introduce citation styles and journal publication specifications. Students will understand citations as an acknowledgment of who else is speaking in the conversation.

Just as in conversations, students recognize that they can disagree with, question, and add to what others have said. Today students can converse with established authors through social media and e-mail. Students can collaborate on a writing assignment, initiate a wiki, Google Doc, or blog. In a study done by Mimi Li and Wei Zhu (2017), collaborative writing done by equally contributing second language students produced the best examples of writing (p. 39). In a blog set up by Rodesiler

(2017), student teachers incorporated a blog to expand their professional growth. The professor provided his own blog as mentor writing that the students could critique (p. 350). These authoring opportunities extend the conversation metaphor and allow students to experience scholarly conversation and move toward an understanding of Scholarship as Conversation. The conversation metaphor is appealing because conversation is engaging. Conversation, whether verbal or written, is powerful because its primary goal is the expansion of knowledge and information, as was pointed out by Benjamin Harris (2008): "Disciplines and disciplinary discourse communities are also sites of value creation and dissemination" (pp. 430–431).

A PENNY FOR YOUR THOUGHTS

Students live in a world of free information where bloggers and website producers grab, republish, and repurpose information without reference to authorship or context or accuracy. The understandings within the concept Information Has Value contradict what students know of the Internet world. Students have already interacted with value when paying for commodities or service. Knowledge and research, unlike commodities and service, often have worth beyond their initial expression and use. A librarian can bring up value discussions in nearly any class.

Suppressed information has a value component that may spark social justice considerations. Journalism and communication students can explore questions of value in withholding information in full or in part. They can discuss the monetary aspects of producing and disseminating partial truths or untruths. Even an examination and discussion of their own research practices of exploring only those resources that agree with their premise become excellent opportunities for students to experience the concept Information Has Value.

Plagiarism can enter this librarian/student discussion, in terms of one scholar usurping or diluting an author's income or reputation by failing to acknowledge and credit the originator. There are many examples of prominent people whose names, positions, and works have been discredited by their earlier plagiarism, resulting in financial loss to the guilty person and unsuspecting collaborators, publishers, and businesses. Librarians can provide research activities where students can be guided to find deliberate plagiarism and its results.

Students can confront questions that impact their personal values. "Classes that deal with values, either explicitly or in general, are ideal situations for exploring the impact of information, research sources, and outside communications on value systems. Research methodology courses, where students might receive instruction on dealing with authors, arguments, and information that may stand in opposition to their own beliefs is another possible location" (Harris, 2008, p. 434).

CONCLUSION

Librarians have long been curators of information. Part of that responsibility includes ensuring that the information can be retrieved and understood. Librarians do not claim the breadth or depth of the subject knowledge held by professors. However, librarians play a valuable role in assisting professors and students by teaching advanced researching skills and foundational concepts about information, its production, and its use.

REFERENCES

Association of College and Research Libraries Board. (2015, February 2). *Framework for information literacy for higher education*. American Library Association. Retrieved from http://www.ala.org/acrl/standards/ilframework

Bruni, F. (2017, March 8). Ben Carson's gray matter. *The New York Times*. Retrieved from https://www.nytimes.com/2017/03/08/opinion/ben-carsons-gray-matter.html

Burgess, C. (2015). Teaching students, not standards: The new ACRL information literacy framework and threshold crossings for instructors. *Partnership: The Canadian Journal of Library & Information Practice & Research, 10*(1), 1–6.

Cole, A., Napier, T., & Marcum, B. (2015). Generation Z: Information facts and fictions. In T. A. Swanson & H. Jagman (Eds.), *Not just where to click: Teaching students how to think about information* (pp. 107–137). Chicago, Il: Association of College and Research Libraries.

Drabinski, E. (2016). Turning inward. *College & Research Libraries News*, 383–384.

Drabinski, E. (2017). A kairos of the critical: Teaching critically in a time of compliance. *Communications in Information Literacy, 11*(1), 76–94.

Gandel, S. (2015, March 11). Top hedge fund manager: Global warming isn't a danger. Retrieved from http://fortune.com/2015/03/11/climate-change-cliff-asness/

Harris, B. R. (2008). Values: The invisible "ante" in information literacy learning? *Reference Services Review, 36*(4), 424–437. https://doi.org/10.1108/00907320810920388

Klipfel, K. M. (2015). Developing a research question: Topic selection. In P. Bravender, H. McClure, & G. Schaub (Eds.), *Teaching information literacy threshold concepts: Lesson plans for librarians* (pp. 50–54). Chicago: Association of College and Research Libraries.

Klurfeld, J., & Schneider, H. (2014). *News literacy: Teaching the internet generation to make reliable information choices* (p. 25). Washington, DC: Brookings. Retrieved from https://www.brookings.edu/wp-content/uploads/2016/06/Klurfeld-SchneiderNews-Literacyupdated-7814.pdf

Li, M., & Zhu W. (2017). Good or bad collaborative wiki writing: Exploring links between group interactions and writing products. *Journal of Second Language Writing, 35*, 38–53. https://doi.org/10.1016/j.jslw.2017.01.003

Meola, M. (2017, March 13). Re: Authority from one area does not necessarily transfer to another area [Electronic mailing list message]. Retrieved July 11, 2017, from http://lists.ala.org/sympa/arc/acrlframe/2017-03/msg00020.html

Meyer, J. H. F., & Land, R. (Eds.). (2006). *Overcoming barriers to student understanding: Threshold concepts and troublesome knowledge*. New York: Routledge.

Meyer, J., Land, R., & Baillie, C. (2010). *Threshold concepts and transformational learning*. Rotterdam and Boston: Sense Publishers.

msremmu. (2008). *Dr. King: Nonviolence is the most powerful weapon*. Retrieved from https://www.youtube.com/watch?v=74XJJ3Tq5ew

Pullman, E. (2017, March 13). Re: Authority from one area does not necessarily transfer to another area [Electronic mailing list message]. Retrieved July 11, 2017, from http://lists.ala.org/sympa/arc/acrlframe/2017-03/msg00017.html

Rodesiler, L. (2017). Sustained blogging about teaching: Instructional methods that support online participation as professional development. *TechTrends: Linking Research & Practice to Improve Learning, 61*(4), 349–354. https://doi.org/10.1007/s11528-017-0164-6

Simmons, M. H. (2005). Librarians as disciplinary discourse mediators: Using genre theory to move toward critical information literacy. *Portal : Libraries and the Academy, 5*(3), 297–311.

TEDx Talks. (2013). *The success of nonviolent civil resistance: Erica Chenoweth at TEDxBoulder.* Retrieved from https://www.youtube.com/watch?v=YJSehRlU34w

CHAPTER 16

NO MORE FIRST-YEAR WRITING

Suggestions From the LILAC Project

Jeanne Law Bohannon
Janice R. Walker

According to an article in the *Washington Post*, the term "fake news" has now lost any meaning (Borchers, 2017). While it once referred to obviously made-up stories, such as "Pizzagate," the term is now bandied about to suggest that any news with which one disagrees is "fake." In conjunction with research into and testing of students' skills in information literacy, defined as the ability to locate, evaluate, and use information from outside sources, it seems obvious that what we do now to teach essential information literacy skills to our students takes on paramount importance. What we know, however, is that even though teachers and librarians have tried a wide variety of ways to teach these skills, students continue to fare poorly in assessments of those skills. The problem is not a lack of instruction or a lack of instructional materials dealing with information literacy, of course. Instead, we argue that we need to reconsider how, when, and where we provide students with this instruction. Understanding students' existing information literacy skills, particularly as they seek information in online spaces, and adapting pedagogy to improve teaching and learning of these skills can improve student writing across disciplines by helping students better incorporate more credible sources from which they create a foundation of research that demonstrates an improved ability to quote, paraphrase, and summarize research without patchwriting from their online sources.

According to Andrew Asher, principal researcher for the Ethnographic Research in Illinois Academic Libraries (ERIAL) Project, "Students do not have adequate information literacy skills when they come to college . . . [a]nd they're not getting adequate training as they're going through the curriculum" (quoted in Kolowich, 2010). Recognizing this need, most first-year writing classes routinely assign students to write a "research paper," with instructors sometimes partnering with librarians to teach research skills, sometimes working with librarians to design the assignment, sometimes working with an "embedded" librarian, or, often, offering only a "one-shot" library instruction session. Many of our institutions and their libraries are already stretched to the limit, of course, so having the time and the personnel to provide additional instruction is not always feasible. Nonetheless, some colleges and universities require an additional course beyond or in conjunction with first-year writing course(s), one that often teaches study skills as well as providing an introduction to the library and to research skills, recognizing that relying on a single course to teach essential information literacy skills is not enough. But, according to information being gathered by the Learning Information Literacy Across the Curriculum (LILAC) Project, an ongoing, multi-institutional study of student information-seeking behaviors, we are still falling short of achieving the outcomes recommended by both the Association of College and Research Libraries' (ACRL) *Framework for Information Literacy for Higher Education* and the WPA *Framework for Success in Postsecondary Writing*.

In the first edition of the *Purdue Information Literacy Handbook*, researchers with the LILAC Project described a case study conducted with 50 multilingual first-year writers that sought to measure information literacy through both quantitative and qualitative means (2018). All told, LILAC researchers have collected data from 412 participants, both undergraduate and graduate students, including those included in the aforementioned case study, from both research and comprehensive universities. What we present here are preliminary conclusions and pedagogical recommendations on how to address what we have measured as gaps in students' information literacy skills. We seek to initiate solutions and not focus simply on deficits. Our conclusions are based on research conducted in recent years across the field of information literacy and writing studies. We focus our recommendations based on information-seeking in online spaces, as these spaces have reshaped what Donald J. Leu, Lisa Zawilinski, Elena Fozani, and Nicole Timbrell (2015) call "the nature of literacy education" (p. 344).

BACKGROUND

Our empirical study employs a mixed methods design, which is a new approach in describing and evaluating students' digital information-seeking behaviors. LILAC is the first empirical project of its kind to utilize both a survey of perceived information-seeking behaviors and research aloud protocols (RAPs) to collect actual behavioral data from students.

Mixed Methods—Surveys and RAPs

To begin each research session, participants first complete a 5- to 10-minute survey about their prior instruction and perceptions of information literacy skills. The survey also captures demographics and psychographics from participants. After tabulating this information to gain an overview, we then compare survey data with associated RAP videos, which participants complete in the last 15 minutes of the session.

Students' on-screen information-seeking processes are observed and recorded using Camtasia Studio software to capture their screen activity and voice narrative (RAPs) while they conduct research on a given topic. The purpose of this protocol is to observe actual information-seeking behaviors and strategies to determine where pedagogical intervention might be needed. Such a protocol allows for determining the independent and dependent nature of information behaviors and strategies. For example, the information behavior of "power browsing" (spending less than 10 seconds on a Web page) may be identified by timing the movement between pages on the screen as well as vocalizations that indicate rapid decisions on information available on-screen.

From the data collected and analyzed through a qualitative coding template of participant behaviors and quantitative survey data, results reveal how students perform secondary research and how they feel about doing it; further, the results suggest what we, as instructors, can do to increase their growth in this area as they move through academic programs at their universities.

REVIEW OF RELATED LITERATURE

In addition to the work of Lilian W. Mina, Jeanne Bohannon, and Jinrong Li (2018), Bohannon, Arnett, and Greer (2017) have also described recent scholarship in the field in their work with technical communications student participants at a research-comprehensive university in the ProComm (IEEE) Conference Proceedings. Mina and Janice R. Walker (2016) have also discussed findings from the LILAC Project specifically from a population of international students in a U.S. university, identifying the information literacy skills of this growing population, as well as pointing to "the possible role(s) that writing instructors and librarians play in helping to evaluate, understand, and achieve the literacies articulated in the ACRL and WPA Frameworks" for international students (p. 64). Outside of LILAC scholars, researchers from the fields of education and library science have also provided context for what needs to be done to help students improve their information literacy skills.

Gaps in Information Literacy

Writing in the *CARReader* in 2013, Elena Forzani and Cheryl Maykel discuss problems with students' source evaluation skills when searching for online content (p. 23). Els Kuiper and Monique Volman (2008) also concluded that students in secondary school environments are not adept at searching online for academic sources. In their study, the researchers concluded that students do not possess the competency to locate reliable information online. While their study focused on high school students, we can draw parallels from their work because the overwhelming majority of first-year writers studied by the LILAC project are just a year or two out of high school when they enter the university.

Indeed, the International Reading Association places significant emphasis on online information literacy as paramount to 21st-century learning. Its position statement begins,

> The Internet and other forms of information and communication technologies (ICTs) are redefining the nature of reading, writing, and communication. These ICTs will continue to change in the years ahead, requiring continuously new literacies to successfully exploit their potentials. (2009)

Although the statement itself is almost a decade old, we can draw a needs assessment from it, as both instructors and librarians seek to provide students with relevant strategies for successful source-searching and source-evaluation practices in online spaces.

Educational scholars Leu et al. (2015) remind us that, although many "digital natives" (Prensky, 2001) do possess proficiency in literacies such as social media, texting, and gaming, "this does not necessarily mean that they are skilled in the effective use of online information, perhaps the most important aspect of the Internet" (p. 344). Their study also touches on the material reality that first-year writing instructors and librarians operate in now: the need to provide students with best practices for writing and research that embrace the digital.

Literature That Supports the Need for LILAC Research

We know that the practice of critically reading online in search of reliable source information is changing almost every day as new technologies emerge. Search engines are no longer "new tech." Google itself is 18 years old; Yahoo has been around for more than two decades. While many multimodal sources are more a decade old (YouTube = 12 years; TEDTalks = 15 years), new forms of source information are constantly emerging. Social platforms (Twitter, SnapChat, Facebook, Instagram), wikis, and video streaming websites are evolving as they incorporate public, searchable information. Scholars are just now uncovering how students operate across these digital platforms, specifically how they seek out and evaluate information to produce academic writing. Julie Coiro and Jill Castek (2010) found that seeking out information online usually involves some sort of problem-solving assignment. Leu et al. (2015) put it in context: "[I]n short, online reading comprehension is online research" (p. 346). These scholars also argue for the importance of keyword entry and source evaluation as necessary literacy skills, because without those skills, search engines cannot deliver the credible information student researchers need, and students cannot determine if that information is indeed credible as well as useful. LILAC protocols have measured both of these skills and found that students do indeed have deficits. We now need to use those findings to help our students gain these necessary skills so that they may continue to grow into informed writers during and after their university experiences. LILAC researchers believe that digital information literacy skills are essential for students' success in academic writing in various disciplines.

KEY QUANTITATIVE FINDINGS THAT INFORMED RECOMMENDATIONS

LILAC is a multi-institutional, mixed methods study. Over the past four years, LILAC researchers across Georgia Southern University, Lamar University, University of Miami–Ohio, Kennesaw State University, and University of Auburn–Montgomery have collected data from 412 participants in 30-minute sessions that included both surveys (quantitative research) and observed behavior (qualitative research) components. First, students completed surveys that asked them their demographic information as well as their attitudes toward their personal experiences with information literacies. This quantitative and attitudinal data helps shed light on what students *say* they know and do when seeking information for academic writing in online spaces.

Demographics

The average age of participants is 21, with an equal percentage of self-identified males and females. More than 80% of participants report English as their first language; they range in academic level as follows: Freshman 39%; Sophomore 16%; Junior 26%; Senior 17%. Their majors run the gamut from the arts to STEM. When asked where they received their bibliographic research instruction, 30% reported English courses, while only 10% got their instruction from the library. This number is particularly interesting to us, as our preliminary recommendations include partnerships between librarians and instructors of English—the *who* part of the equation. Of the instruction they reported, students received it via lecture 37% of the time, via hands-on work 28% of the time, and via online tutorials 13% of the time. This data shows us *how* we can most effectively deliver research instruction.

More than 88% of the 412 participants surveyed reported that they had "been required to include information from library and/or online research in a paper or project" (Q12). This data further points to the emerging trend of requiring students to produce work that contains sources evaluated, obtained, and sourced online. When asked what they had been taught, the majority listed keyword, author/title searches, citation practices, and plagiarism avoidance in that order. When asked where they do most of their online research, participants reported home (69%) and school library (27%) as their most often chosen places to work. And, not surprisingly,

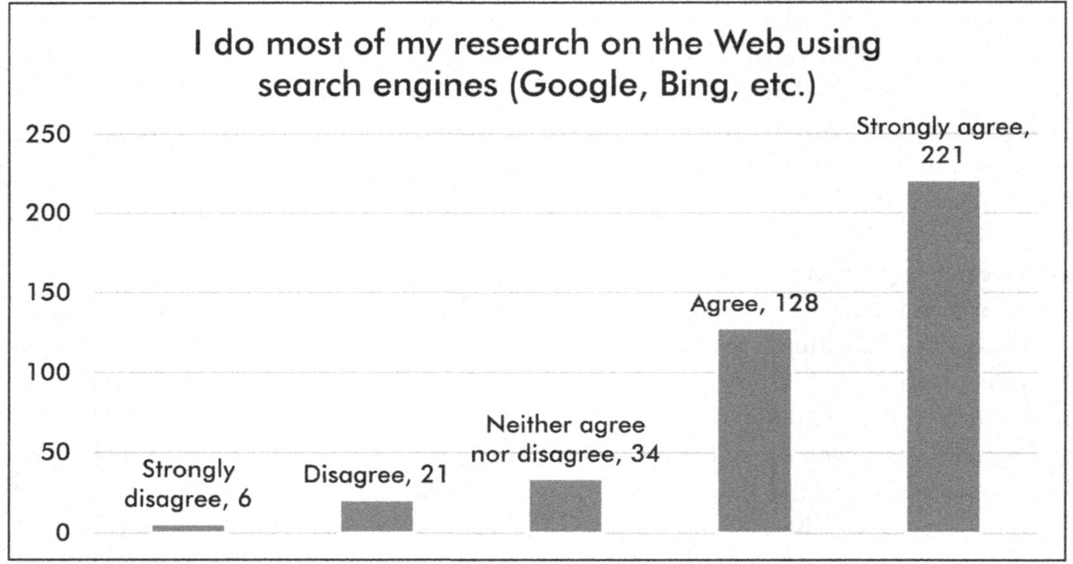

Figure 16.1 Where students do their research.

as Figure 16.1 shows, most participants performed their online bibliographic research using search engines such as Google, Yahoo, or Bing. The key "Strongly Agree" number represents more than half of all respondents. In addition, this data point shows us where students are not doing their online bibliographic research and can inform how we teach them about library databases.

Attitudes Toward Information Literacies

With more than 400 participants, we were able to draw a few significant conclusions regarding attitudes toward information literacies. For example, when asked if they knew how to evaluate information found on the Web, only 8% (n = 33) of participants reported yes. However, those same participants answered (14%; n = 30) that they feel strongly about their ability to evaluate the reliability of online information sources. Participants either did not understand the questions or they did not equate evaluating information and evaluating the reliability of that information. The latter percentage was roughly similar when participants were asked if they felt confident locating scholarly information on the Web. What we can conclude from this data is that students can locate the information, and they think they can evaluate it; however, they also think they need more help in doing so. Since participants also reported that they conduct most of their bibliographic research in Web spaces, not in library databases, we know that our pedagogical recommendation must include efforts to meet students in the online spaces in which they operate when searching for reliable information.

KEY QUALITATIVE FINDINGS THAT INFORM RECOMMENDATIONS

Now we want to look at the second part of LILAC's mixed methods protocol. To examine students' actual experiences with information-seeking behaviors compared to what they report that they do, the LILAC Project collects and analyzes screen-captured data containing a video record of screen activity and students' voice narrative while conducting bibliographic research on a topic. LILAC researchers collect this qualitative data in addition to survey data that aims to dig deeper into students' experiences with their information literacy. Although we have not coded nearly as many RAP sessions as we have survey results, we can still assert preliminary trends based on the 38% of the collected videos we analyzed.

One interesting finding of this study is that many participants privileged multimodal sources such as videos, images, and podcasts. For example, Mina, Bohannon, and Li's (2018) chapter in the first edition of the *Purdue Information Literacy Handbook* describes how "many participants showed appreciation of multimodal digital sources while diligently seeking those sources to use in their FYW writing assignments" (p. 263). Pedagogical recommendations should act as the springboard for both librarians and instructors in terms of helping students navigate digital spaces and multimodal sources. In one specific RAP video, for example (21023), the participant articulated the validity of multimodal sources, in this case TEDTalk videos, and actively sought out this source for an academic paper. Other participants performed similar multimodal searches, seeking out videos and podcasts to use as sources for their academic writing (21025, 21032, 14054). We may view these RAP sessions as a lesson in how students seek out multimodal sources, both informal and formal, to locate credible information for bibliographic research. These findings indicate that students search for multimodal sources and consider those sources relevant inclusions for their research projects and end products.

RECOMMENDATIONS

Integrated Information Literacy Instruction (Partnerships Between Library and FYW)

According to the chapter LILAC researchers published in the first edition of the *Purdue Information Literacy Handbook*, we understand that to prepare students more effectively for the opportunities and challenges in their navigation of academic writing mediated by information technologies, researchers and practitioners have moved from simple bibliographic instruction or one-shot library instruction (Spievak & Hayes-Bohannan, 2013) to a more networked approach, where information literacy skills are integrated into writing curricula (Bohannon, 2015; Pinto, Cordón, & Díaz, 2010; Purdy, 2010). This approach is especially relevant in the first-year writing (FYW) classroom, a primary gateway for most university students to academic writing and research. These classrooms are usually the environment where most college students are introduced to information literacy as they prepare to write research papers.

One example of potential opportunities to improve instruction—and, hence, student learning—in information literacy skills might be how we introduce students to the concept of peer-reviewed scholarship. The LILAC Project generally shows that students do not really know what "peer reviewed" means or why it is important. Part of this misunderstanding might be because these same terms are often used in the classroom to describe student review of each other's work, without connecting students' peer reviews with those of scholars. Moreover, many of the peer-reviewed sources that students locate, either on the Web or through our library databases, are not written at a level that most first-year students can understand. Thus, as the Citation Project has clearly shown, students end up "quote mining" these works, often from the first page or two of a "scholarly" source, with most of their citations coming from a single source, as often as not a website, news article, or other source that students can more readily apprehend (Jamieson, 2013; Jamieson & Howard, 2013). By encouraging or even requiring students to limit library searches to scholarly, peer-reviewed journal articles, then, we may actually be working against providing students with the opportunity to learn to evaluate sources on their own. Furthermore, much important peer-reviewed scholarship is published in anthologies or edited collections, such as this one. Unfortunately, time after time, we hear students opine in their RAP sessions that they don't want books, so they may bypass these collections, even though a book may contain an important chapter (or chapters) on their topic. How can we help students understand the ins and outs of scholarly publishing to help them better determine how and where to look for information?

Inclusion of Multimodal Source Instruction

Gunther Kress (2003) noted almost 15 years ago that student writers were changing, both in how and what they researched and wrote for academic and personal purposes. He argued that students were moving more and more into online spaces and that teachers could not afford to ignore how to reach students in those spaces. Flash-forward to 2017. The technologies may have changed and continue to do so, but teachers of writing still make that argument. Andrea Lunsford calls it a revolution of literacy that we haven't seen in millennia (quoted in LaForce, 2009). The Conference on College Composition and Communication (CCCC) produced a position statement on what multimodal and its associated synonyms mean to learning and meaningful text production. Part of the statement reads:

> Creating images, sounds, designs, videos, and other extra-alphanumeric texts is an aesthetic, self-originated, self-sponsored activity for many writers. Digital technologies have increasing capacity for individuals to adapt the tools for their own information and communication purposes. Students have the capability to apply literacy skills to real world problems and knowledge-building. They are able to exercise creativity, work for social justice, and pursue personal passions. (2004)

LILAC researchers have found that student writers in 2017 are not only seeking out and giving credibility to multimodal sources, they are often specifically articulating their searches as multimodal. In several RAP sessions, students named "multimodal sources" as preferred to print sources. What this data tells us is that our information literacy instruction must not only address multimodal sources in terms of search and evaluation, it must also take on multimodality as a medium through which we reach students with information literacy content. Furthermore, we need to do more when explaining how to cite multimodal sources, both those that belong in a list of References or Works Cited, as well as those that more appropriately belong in a List of Images or image credit line. Delivering this content through videos, podcast episodes, gamification (such as Kahoot), and interactive digital activities (drag and drop, e-flashcards) will allow students to network with other students and their instructors and interface with content in inventive ways.

We also note in many of the RAP sessions that students are looking for quick answers to their questions. They will usually skim through sources quickly, perhaps grabbing a quote or two, or looking at subheadings to locate sections they might read without having to read an entire article or website. They often are also looking for visual information (charts, graphs, etc.) to include in their projects, without having to synthesize textual information themselves.

Often, too, we steer students away from Google to find academic sources. Instead, perhaps we should be meeting them where they are; Google, and especially Google Scholar, can help students locate sources, but, as the RAPs show, students are often frustrated when they click on the link to find that they may need to subscribe (and pay a fee) to access the source. Students are often surprised to learn during the debriefing session after the RAP session that they can take the information on the source they located through Google Scholar, go to the library database, and perhaps have access to the source for free. And even fewer students remember being taught that, even if their library does not have the source they are looking for, it may be available for free through interlibrary loan.

In terms of encouraging students to interact with content housed in a university's library, we encourage librarians and instructors to work together to develop digital handouts that demonstrate different search processes on library sites including keyword searches, database use, catalog searches, and what we call "relevance to topic" searches. Our findings also point to possibilities for intervention beyond the classroom and the library. For example, following a just-in-time approach, we see opportunities for providing information at the point of need, perhaps through an app or browser add-on, developed in concert with teachers and librarians, that can follow students' research, perhaps learning what students need, asking questions, and offering advice (e.g., "You might also consider searching for X through your library database" or "Don't forget to check to see if this is available through interlibrary loan" or "Would you like more information on evaluating the information you are finding? Information on the CRAAP test at http://www.csuchico.edu/lins/handouts/eval_websites.pdf can help!"). Some members of the LILAC Project are considering seeking grant funding to further explore technological options, using artificial intelligence agents perhaps, to ensure that important instruction in information literacy skills can move along with students throughout their tenure at our institutions.

Helping students avoid plagiarism and quote-mining through instructional practices that help students understand how and why (and when) scholars decide to cite the work of others also needs greater attention in the classroom. Too often, the RAP sessions indicate students seek the number of sources of different types they are required to include, rather than learning to determine for themselves when and how they might need to substantiate their assertions and opinions with those of "experts" or scholars in the field, including being able to recognize what constitutes an "expert" and how the scholarly, peer-review process works.

As the title of this chapter indicates, we would also like to suggest that perhaps including information literacy instruction in the first-year writing class might not be the most effective means of teaching either information literacy *or* first-year writing. Instead, it might be worth considering turning our first-year writing classes on their heads, perhaps teaching first-year information literacy in its stead; that is, beginning the first-year writing class by helping students first determine when they need information, what kind of information they need (and why), where to look for that type of information, and how to evaluate what they find. With these goals foregrounded, students can, perhaps, better understand how and why to synthesize the information and use it in their own projects, whether the projects are traditional text-based projects or multimodal projects.

CONCLUSION

Over more than four years, the Learning Information Literacy Across the Curriculum (LILAC) Project has collected 412 mixed methods data that show a clear trend toward how students learn and process information literacies in online spaces. In this chapter, we have offered preliminary recommendations based on several data points; these recommendations may help instructors and librarians approach information literacy instruction in ways that meet students in their comfort zones and increase how students use information literacy as a tool in their academic writing.

The RAPs further indicate that, for the most part, students are listening to us and they are trying to master these skills. However, they are often confused, especially as information they learn in one class might need to be unlearned in another. For example, many students have reported being taught (often in high school classes) that .orgs are always credible but that *Wikipedia* (a .org) is to be avoided. They do not seem to have been taught that encyclopedias of any ilk are not considered "scholarly" sources, even though they may be useful sources for background information or to determine what the issues might be within a given subject. Often, students are afraid to cite *Wikipedia* even when they do use it, appropriately or not. It would be nice if evaluating a source was as easy as looking at the domain type (.org, .com, .gov, .net, etc.), but of course it's not that easy. Students (and others) need to evaluate all information to determine its usefulness and relevance, its authority, and its credibility. A tweet might be a very credible source—or not—as many of us learned during the last presidential election when conspiracy theories such as Pizzagate were promulgated through retweets and reposts in online spaces by one of the candidates.

Where we go from here must include partnerships between library and teaching faculty; productive iterations of collaboration also include more LILAC research with diverse groups of student participants at institutions of higher learning throughout the country. As part of the LILAC Project, we are posting RAP videos to a publicly accessible YouTube channel, to be used for purposes of teaching, research, or scholarship. We also are making all of our IRB applications, instructions for partners and subjects, and other materials available online so that other researchers may join us as official LILAC partners or may pursue their own spin-off research, following our protocols or amending the protocol for their own institution. Given the collaborative, multi-institutional nature of the LILAC project, we invite instructors and librarians to network with us as we continue to collect and analyze this important data. Check out the LILAC Project, and some of our presentations, publications, and collaboration opportunities on our website at http://lilac-group.blogspot.com/, or by following us on Twitter: @LILACProject, or e-mail the authors for additional information.

REFERENCES

Bohannon, J. L. (2015). Not a stitch out of place: Assessing students' attitudes towards multimodal composition. *Bellaterra Journal of Teaching & Learning Language & Literature, 8*(2), 33–47.

Bohannon, J. L., Arnett, J., & Greer, E. (2017). "Learning Information Literacy Across the Curriculum (LILAC) and its impacts on student digital literacies and learning across the humanities." *2017 IEEE International Professional Communication Conference (ProComm)*, Madison, WI, pp. 1–8.

Borchers, C. (2017, February 9). "Fake news" has now lost all meaning. *The Washington Post*. Retrieved from https://www.washingtonpost.com/news/the-fix/wp/2017/02/09/fake-news-has-now-lost-all-meaning/?utm_term=.56773f9b517b

Coiro, J., & Castek, J. (2010). Assessment frameworks for teaching and learning English language arts in a digital age. In D. Lapp & D. Fisher (Eds.), *Handbook of research on teaching the English language arts* (3rd ed., pp. 314–321), New York: Routledge.

Conference on College Composition and Communication. (2004). CCCC position statement on teaching, learning, and assessing writing in digital environments. Retrieved from http://www.ncte.org/cccc/resources/positions/digitalenvironments

Forzani, E., & Maykel, C. (2013). Evaluation of Connecticut students' abilities to critically evaluate online information. *CARReader, 10*, 23–27.

International Reading Association. (2009). *New literacies and 21st-century technologies: A position statement by the International Reading Association*. Newark: IRA.

Jamieson, S. (2013, December 11). Reading and engaging sources: What students' use of sources reveals about advanced reading skills. *Across the Disciplines, 10*(4). Retrieved from http://wac.colostate.edu/atd/reading/jamieson.cfm

Jamieson, S., & Howard, R. M. (2013). Sentence-mining: Uncovering the amount of reading and reading comprehension in college writers' researched writing. In R. McClure & J. P. Purdy (Eds.), *The new digital scholar: Exploring and enriching the research and writing practices of NextGen students* (pp. 111–133). Medford, NJ: Information Today.

Kolowich, S. (2010, September 29). Searching for better research habits. *Inside Higher Ed*. Retrieved from https://www.insidehighered.com/news/2010/09/29/search

Kress, G. (2003). *Literacy in the new media age*. London: Routledge.

Kuiper, E., & Volman, M. (2008). The web as a source of information for students in K–12 education. In J. Coiro, M. Knobel, C. Lankshear, & D. Leu (Eds.), *Handbook of research on new literacies* (pp. 241–266). Mahwah, NJ: Erlbaum.

LaForce, Thessaly. (2009, September 1). A new literacy? *The New Yorker*. Retrieved from: http://www.newyorker.com/books/page-turner/a-new-literacy

Leu, D., Zawilinski L., Fozani, E., & Timbrell, N. (2015). Best practices in teaching the new literacies of online research and comprehension. In L. B. Gambrell & L. M. Morrow (Eds.) *Best practices in literacy instruction* (pp. 343–364). New York, NY: Guilford Press.

Mina, L., Bohannon, J., & Li, J. (2018). Google, Baidu, the library, and ACRL framework:

Assessing information-seeking behaviors of first-year multilingual writers through research-aloud protocols. In G. Veach (Ed.), *Teaching information literacy and writing studies: Vol. 1. First-year composition courses.*West Lafayette, IN: Purdue University Press.

Mina, L. W., & Walker, J. R. (2016). International students as future scholars: Information literacy skills, self-assessment, and needs. In R. McClure & J. P. Purdy (Eds.), *The future scholar: Researching and teaching the frameworks for writing and information literacy* (pp. 63–88). Medford, NJ: Information Today.

Pinto, M., Cordón, A. J., & Díaz, G. R. (2010). Thirty years of information literacy (1977–2007): A terminological, conceptual and statistical analysis. *Journal of Librarianship and Information Science, 42*(1), 3–19.

Prensky, M. (2001). Digital natives, digital immigrants. *On the Horizon, 9*(5), 1–6.

Purdy, J. P. (2010). The changing space of research: Web 2.0 and the integration of research and writing environments. *Computers and Composition, 27*(1), 48–58.

Spievak, E. R., & Hayes-Bohannan, P. (2013). Just enough of a good thing: Indications of long-term efficacy in one-shot library instruction. *Journal of Academic Librarianship, 39*, 488–499.

PART IV

Writing and Information Literacy in Multiple Contexts

CHAPTER 17

NOT JUST RESEARCH PARTNERS

Librarians' Perceptions of Their Roles in Writing Instruction

Matthew Bodie

The *Framework for Information Literacy for Higher Education* may have caused a stir in the library and information science field when it replaced, in 2016, the *Information Literacy Competency Standards for Higher Education* (Jackman & Weiner, 2016; New Jersey Library Association, 2014), but the *Framework*'s contributions strengthen the connection between research and writing studies, moving us more closely toward the composite concept, argued by Norgaard (2003), of "writing information literacy," a "literacy more situated, more process-oriented, and more relevant to a broad range of rhetorical and intellectual endeavors" (p. 129).

Considering the adoption of this theoretical and implicit unity between research and writing studies, the microstudy, here, not only aims to work toward a solution to an institutional exigency of providing a greater level of out-of-classroom writing instruction to a larger number of students, but it also tests how close one group of librarians feels to the writing process, to the "creating new knowledge" portion of the definition of information literacy found in the *Framework* (Association of College and Research Libraries, 2015, para. 6).

INSTITUTIONAL HISTORY

To provide a brief history, this microstudy focused on Writing Studios found within the libraries at St. Petersburg College (SPC), a multicampus, four-year institution in Pinellas County, Florida. Starting in 2011, SPC began making significant changes to its organizational culture under the leadership of a new college president. The goal of these changes aimed to advance student retention that would move SPC further toward meeting the then relatively new completion agenda of the Obama administration (Obama, 2009). One of the college's new initiatives led to the establishment of the Learning Resources department, pulling tutoring centers, formerly managed autonomously at each site, alongside the already centralized library system and placing them all under the administration of one executive director. What is more, in keeping with the "library-as-place" trend in higher education (Freeman, 2005), SPC campuses underwent significant renovations to integrate and connect tutoring services, and in particularly writing tutorial services, within libraries.

In spring 2012, the first Writing Studios opened at SPC's two largest campuses in Clearwater and St. Petersburg. These Writing Studios combined writing-and-research assistance, across the curriculum, all in one place. With the same model eventually expanding to all learning sites within the college, writing tutorial services registered 32,140 student visits in 2015, a more than 165% increase in visits from the first year the Writing Studios opened in 2012 (St. Petersburg College, personal communication, February 28, 2016). Because of this high volume of traffic, coupled with the institution's commitment to a first-come-first-served policy, one of the pitfalls of the Writing Studios became that students experienced long wait times, but the situation proved even more curious when deeply examining usage statistics. That is, statistics show that, although both spend the same amount of time in the same space, librarians assisted three times fewer students in a year than writing specialists. For example, in 2015, 9,275 visits were registered for research, and 32,140 visits were registered for writing tutorial services (St. Petersburg College, personal communication, February 28,

2016). Based on those statistics, and the fact that personnel budgets grow minimally each year, this microstudy aimed to determine how the college might leverage the knowledge of librarians to help with writing instruction in SPC's Writing Studios. Therefore, the microstudy's two major research questions were as follows: At what levels are librarians already participating in writing instruction, and are librarians willing to participate in greater ways in the writing process?

Literature Review

The literature review sought to discover a historical foundation concerning librarians' work with writing instruction. Its results showed that the theme of collaboration transcended others when making connections between writing instruction and librarianship, showing most notably that academic librarians build strong partnerships with writing instructors and writing center personnel. For example, Todorinova (2010) reported that 26% of 268 libraries surveyed collaborate with writing centers. Moreover, through the curriculum and concept of information literacy, Norgaard (2003), as mentioned in the introduction of this chapter, argued that a partnership between librarians and other academic fields should be based on "genuine intellectual engagement." What is more, Elmborg and Hook's (2005) collection noted numerous ways libraries and writing centers collaborate, ranging from space planning to archival collections. Even more so, in looking at past and current trends within the profession, Virgil (2013) emphasized collaboration as key to "expand[ing] the role of librarian" (p. 125).

Although the literature review provided meaningful examples of librarians working in collaboration with writing center personnel and writing instructors, it produced only a small number of examples of librarians working individually toward providing students with writing instruction. On the more theoretical side, Reid argued that the writing and research processes are "intricately linked," and writing center personnel and reference librarians use strategies that "resemble" one another (as cited in Elmborg & Hook, 2005, p. 80). On the practical side, Shields (2014) not only reported librarians' collaborative efforts with faculty teaching first-year composition through work in creating content connecting Writing Program Administration outcomes[1] with the Association of College and Research Libraries standards,[2] but she also found ways to focus on the rhetorical elements of writing instruction: inquiry and invention. Likewise, Bronshteyn and Baladad (2006) reported pedagogical activities outside of the typical wheelhouse of librarians by describing how they taught students to paraphrase and integrate sources into their research projects. Overall, secondary research regarding librarians performing writing instruction bore out only a short list of results, meaning space for primary research in this area proved ample.

METHODS

Procedure

Because the college in this study has multiple campuses, a survey seemed the most efficient way to reach the participant-librarians and to garner the greatest feedback. As such, I created a 36-question anonymous survey, and I sent a link to it in a personalized e-mail to the 25 active librarians throughout the college, giving participants two weeks to respond to the survey.

Instrument

This microstudy used a mixed-methods approach: one part quantitative and another part qualitative with a case study methodology undergirding its design. Because of its approach, the 36 questions in the survey were both objective, forming greater opportunity for quantitative analysis, and open-ended, allowing for greater rhetorical interpretation associated with qualitative analysis. To be more specific, the survey itself contained 15 questions about the participant's Willingness to perform a certain aspect of writing. Respondents were given four options: Very Willing, Willing, I will if no other help is available, or Not Willing (see Figure 17.1).

Then, the next 15 questions were grouped as Frequency tasks, asking participants how frequently they perform certain aspects of writing. The choices were as follows: Daily, Weekly, Every Couple of Weeks, Monthly, Less Than Monthly, and Never (see Figure 17.2).

Three more questions followed about professional status, asking participants the number of years they have been a librarian, their current role with the institution, and number of hours they spend offering public or instructional services each week. The final three questions were open ended, asking participants to consider the aspects of writing with which they have the most and least comfort as well as their level of training with regard to writing instruction.

***1.** How willing are you to work with students on brainstorming (e.g., listing, clustering, mind mapping) a writing project?

- ○ Very willing
- ○ Willing
- ○ I will if no other help is available
- ○ Not willing

Figure 17.1 Sample survey question concerning willingness to perform an activity. This question addresses how willing respondents are to work with students on brainstorming activities.

***1.** How frequently do you work with students on brainstorming (e.g., listing, clustering, mind mapping) a writing project?

- ○ Daily
- ○ Weekly
- ○ Every couple of weeks
- ○ Monthly
- ○ Less than monthly
- ○ Never

Figure 17.2 Sample survey question concerning frequency of activity. This question addresses how frequently respondents work with students on brainstorming activities.

Coding

Creswell (2013) defined themes within research as "broad units of information that consist of several codes aggregated to form a common idea" (p. 186). Along similar lines, I invented a rubric (see Figure 17.3) for the survey questions to help create themes based on the survey responses. The themes were not original but are Cicero's Five Canons of Rhetoric found in his *De Oratore,* written in 55 BCE: Invention, Arrangement, Style, Memory, and Delivery. I selected these divisions of discourse—which I will refer to as themes from here on—because, although ancient, they are still well regarded for their holistic and rhetorical approach to understanding the tenets of writing.

Conversely, while the themes attached to each of the questions may be Cicero's, the categorizations in Questions 1–30, which each asked about a particular aspect of writing, were rooted in research and conversation with fellow practitioners.[3] As such, each of the 15 aspects of writing that the survey addressed appeared within a theme. Each theme had three questions attached to it, making for an even distribution of the survey's content in the Willingness and Frequency categories. Overall, this rubric allowed for creating thematic families in the coding process and added to the ease of bundling questions together for more meaningful results.

In addition to creating a rubric for the first 30 survey questions, the choices given to the participants in Questions 1–30 needed a scoring method in order to make meaning out of their individual results. For instance, in the category of Willingness, each of those questions contained four categorical variables, and in the category of Frequency, each of those questions contained six categorical variables. Thus, such questions arose as "Which variables should be counted? And for how much?"

Stemming from the chi-square test used in statistics, made for measuring categorical variables like these, I borrowed the idea of accepting and rejecting. This binary form of scoring established a baseline for how each question choice counted as being willing or unwilling, frequent or infrequent. As a result, I concluded that in questions related to Willingness, only the top two question choices—Very Willing and Willing—would count as acceptable, and in the questions related to Frequency, the top four—Daily, Monthly, Every Couple of Weeks, and Monthly—would count as acceptable. A visual of this scoring process can be seen in Figure 17.4. The accepted choices appear in light gray, and the rejected choices appear in dark gray.

#s	Invention	#s	Arrangement	#s	Style	#s	Memory	#s	Delivery
1,16	Brainstorming	3,18	Outlining	7,22	Vocabulary	11,26	Paraphrase	6,21	Contextualization
2,17	Thesis Building	5,20	Flow/Coherence	8,23	Spelling	12,27	Source Integration	13,28	Visuals
4,19	Arguments/ Evidence	10,25	Genre/Mode	9,24	Punctuation	15,30	Attribution	14,29	Presentation

Figure 17.3 Categorization of survey questions by theme. For coding purposes, each question on the survey was categorized by a rhetorical theme with a total of three questions per each theme.

Willingness	Frequency
Very willing	Daily
Willing	Weekly
I will if no other help is available	Every couple of weeks
Not willing	Monthly
	Less than monthly
	Never

Figure 17.4 Illustration showing which survey options were deemed as positive (light gray) and which as negative (dark gray) for scoring purposes.

Participants

After a two-week timeframe, the results of the survey showed that 80% of the participants invited to participate in the study—20 out of 25 librarians—responded in full to the survey. Based on the results, the makeup of the participants consisted of eight full-time librarians, five library administrators, and seven part-time librarians. Additional information about the participants found in the survey's professional status questions showed that one participant had been a librarian for 1–2 years; three participants had been librarians for 6–10 years; seven participants had been librarians for 11–15 years; three participants had been librarians for 16–19 years; and six had been librarians for 20 or more years.

RESULTS

General Results

The general results of the survey were that in all 15 aspects of writing articulated in the first 30 questions of the survey, the participants demonstrated a higher level of Willingness than they did Frequency to perform instruction. For instance, only four responses yielded Not Willing as a choice for questions in the Willingness category, but 27 responses yielded Never as a choice for questions in the Frequency category. In general, participants showed the highest level of willingness to perform instruction in aspects of attribution, and they showed the lowest level of willingness to instruct in the aspects of flow or coherence. Almost similarly, participants showed the highest level of frequency in instruction in aspects of attribution, and they showed the lowest level of frequency in instruction in the aspects of flow or coherence as well as in punctuation. They were tied. Also, another general finding was that most said they had no formal training in writing instruction, but they had training in research, mostly through their master's degrees in library science.

Specific Results

In keeping with the coding established in this study, I relay the results of each of the first 30 questions of the survey on Willingness and Frequency, here, by the thematic families of Invention, Arrangement, Style, Memory, and Delivery. For reference, the entire survey can be found at http://web.spcollege.edu/survey/24735.

In Invention (see Figure 17.5), the three aspects of writing coded in this theme were brainstorming, thesis building, and argument-and-evidence building. Eighty percent (n = 16) responded to Question 1 that they were very willing or willing to instruct students in brainstorming, and 55% (n = 12) responded to Question 16 that they performed instruction in brainstorming either monthly or more frequently. Seventy percent (n = 14) responded to Question 2 that they were very willing or willing to instruct students in thesis-building, and 45% (n = 9) responded to Question 17 that they performed instruction in thesis-building either monthly or more frequently. Ninety-five percent (n = 19) responded to Question 4 that they were very willing or willing to instruct students in argument-and-evidence building, and 75% percent (n = 15) responded to Question 19 that they performed instruction in argument-and-evidence building either monthly or more frequently.

In Arrangement (see Figure 17.6), the three aspects of writing coded in this theme were outlining, flow and coherence, and genre and mode. Eighty percent (n = 16) responded to Question 3 that they were very willing or willing to instruct students in outlining, and 40% (n = 8) responded to Question 18 that they performed instruction in outlining either monthly or more frequently. Forty percent (n = 8) responded to Question 5 that they were very willing or willing to instruct students in flow or coherence, and 35%

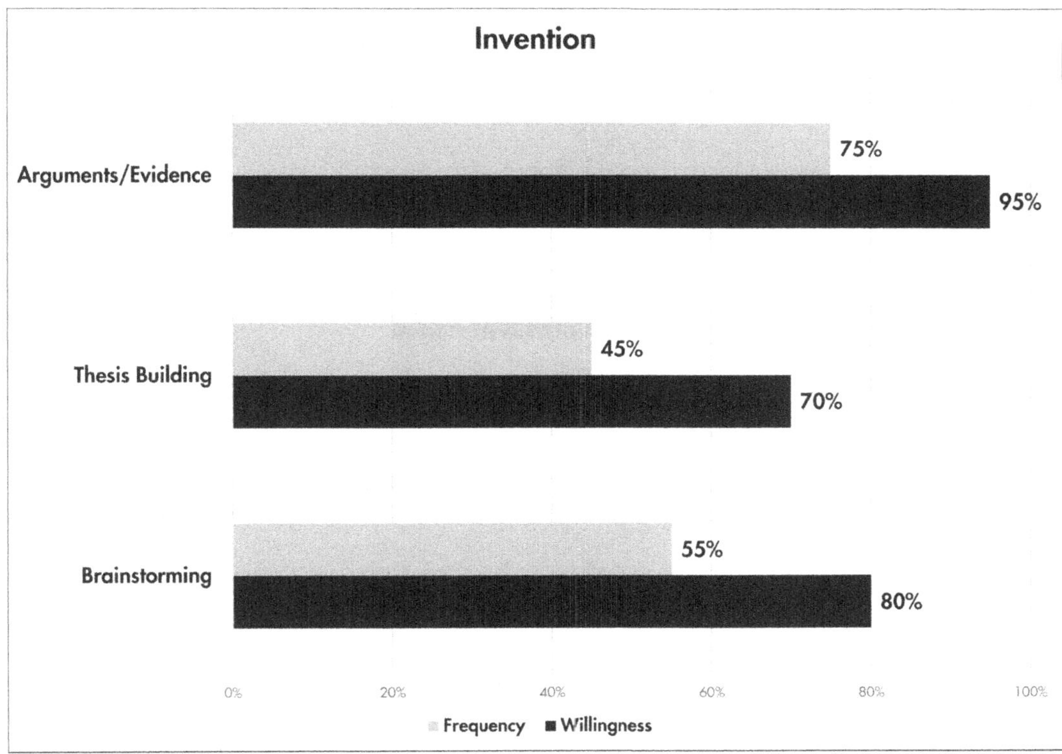

Figure 17.5 Chart indicating percentages of frequency (shown in gray) vs. percentages of willingness (shown in black) for the theme of Invention. Arguments/Evidence (argument-and-evidence building) has the least difference between the two measurements in this theme and has the second highest willingness factor in the survey.

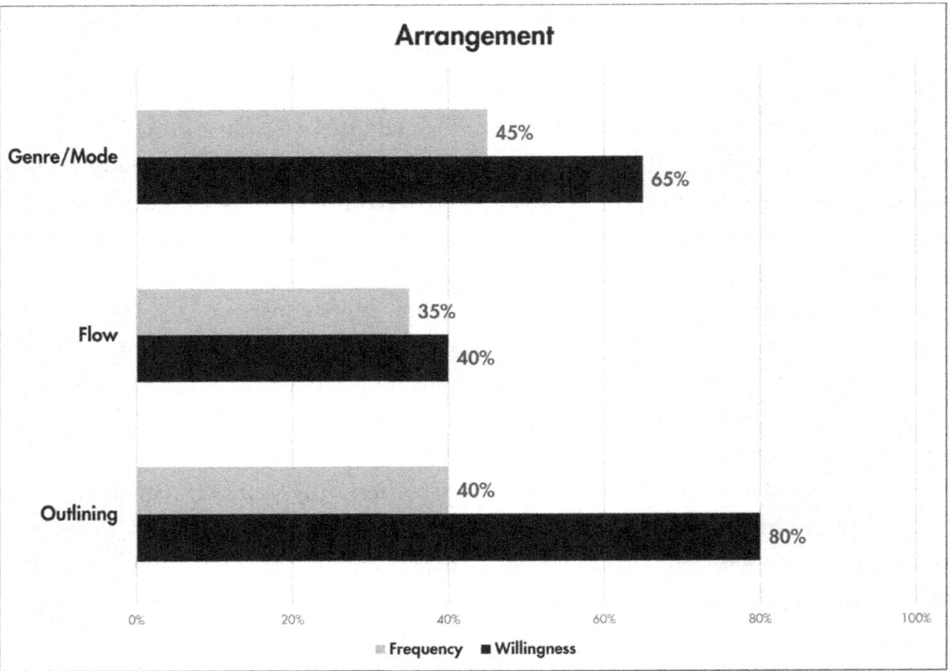

Figure 17.6 Chart indicating percentages of frequency (shown in gray) vs. percentages of willingness (shown in black) for the theme of Arrangement. Outlining's 40% spread is the largest of any in the survey, and the frequency of instructing in Flow ties with Punctuation for the lowest in the survey.

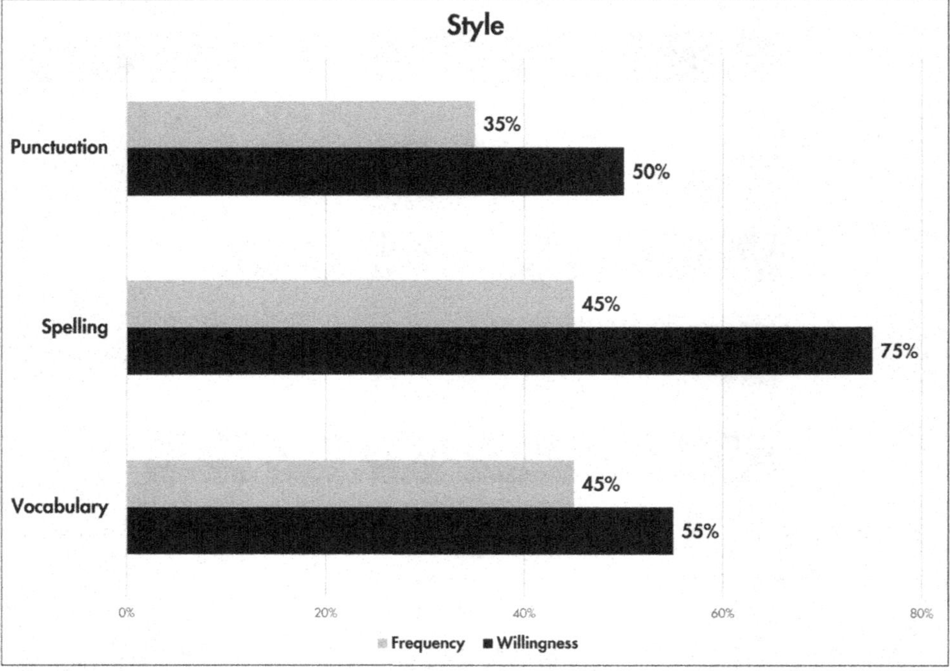

Figure 17.7 Chart indicating percentages of frequency (shown in gray) vs. percentages of willingness (shown in black) for the theme of Style. The survey showed that the frequency of instructing in Punctuation ties for the lowest in the survey with Flow (see Figure 17.5).

(n = 7) responded to Question 20 that they performed instruction in flow or coherence either monthly or more frequently. Sixty-five percent (n = 14) responded to Question 10 that they were very willing or willing to instruct students in genre or mode, and 45% (n = 9) responded to Question 25 that they performed instruction in genre or mode either monthly or more frequently.

In Style (see Figure 17.7), the three aspects of writing coded in this theme were vocabulary, spelling, and punctuation. Fifty-five percent (n = 11) responded to Question 7 that they were very willing or willing to instruct students in vocabulary, and 45% (n = 9) responded to Question 22 that they performed instruction in vocabulary building either monthly or more frequently. Seventy-five percent (n = 15) responded to Question 8 that they were very willing or willing to instruct students in spelling, and 45% (n = 9) responded to Question 23 that they performed instruction in spelling either monthly or more frequently. Fifty percent (n = 10) responded to Question 9 that they were very willing or willing to instruct students in punctuation, and 35% (n = 7) responded to Question 24 that they performed instruction in punctuation either monthly or more frequently.

In Memory (see Figure 17.8), the three aspects of writing coded in this theme were paraphrasing, source integration, and attribution. Ninety percent (n = 18) responded to Question 11 that they were very willing or

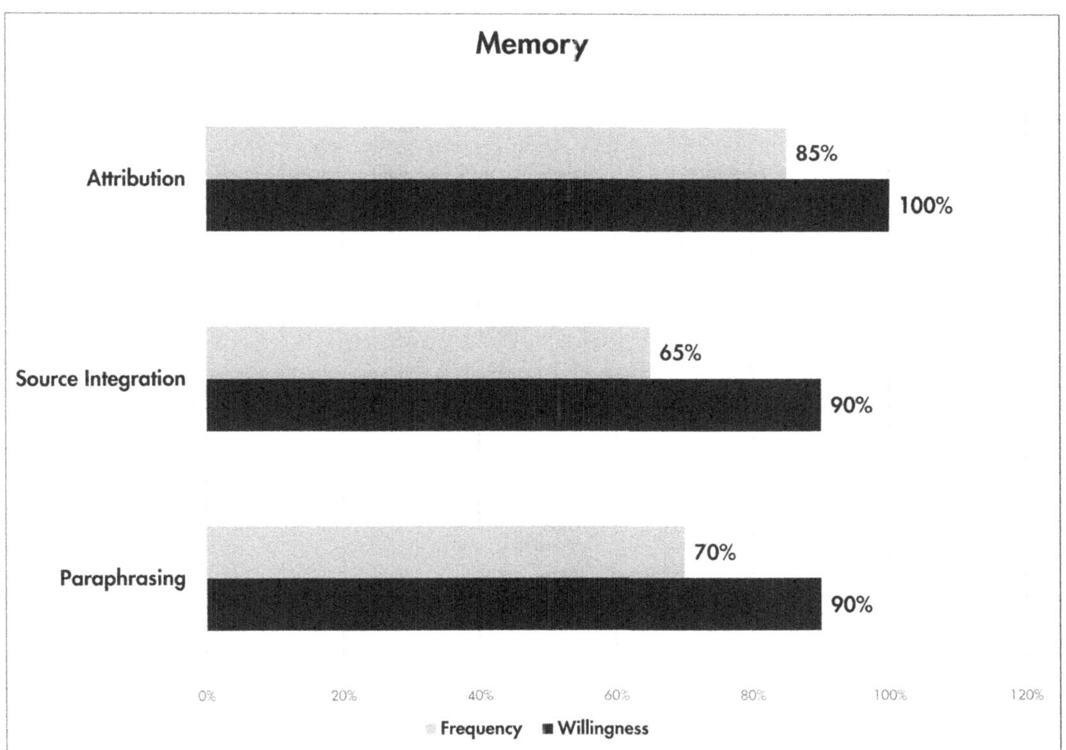

Figure 17.8 Chart indicating percentages of frequency (shown in gray) vs. percentages of willingness (shown in black) for the theme of Memory. The survey results featuring a 100% willingness for Attribution and a 90% willingness for both Source Integration and Paraphrasing showed the comfort that the respondents have in helping students work with sources.

willing to instruct students in paraphrasing, and 70% (n = 14) responded to Question 26 that they instructed students in paraphrasing either monthly or more frequently. Ninety percent (n = 18) responded to Question 12 that they were willing or very willing to instruct students in source integration, and 65% (n = 13) responded to Question 27 that they instructed students in source integration either monthly or more frequently. One hundred percent (n = 20) responded to Question 15 that they were willing or very willing to instruct students in attribution, and 85% (n = 17) responded to Question 30 that they instructed students in attribution either monthly or more frequently.

In Delivery (see Figure 17.9), the three aspects of writing coded in this theme were context (i.e., audience, focus, purpose), visuals (i.e., suggesting and using visual aids), and presentation (i.e., formatting and style guides). Fifty percent (n = 10) responded to Question 6 that they were very willing or willing to instruct students in contextualizing their writing to their specific project, and 40% (n = 8) responded to Question 21 that they instructed students in contextualizing their writing to their specific project either monthly or more frequently. Eighty-five percent (n = 17) responded to Question 13 that they were very willing or willing to instruct students in finding and using visuals for their writing projects, and 60% (n = 12) responded to Question 28 that they instructed students in using visuals for their

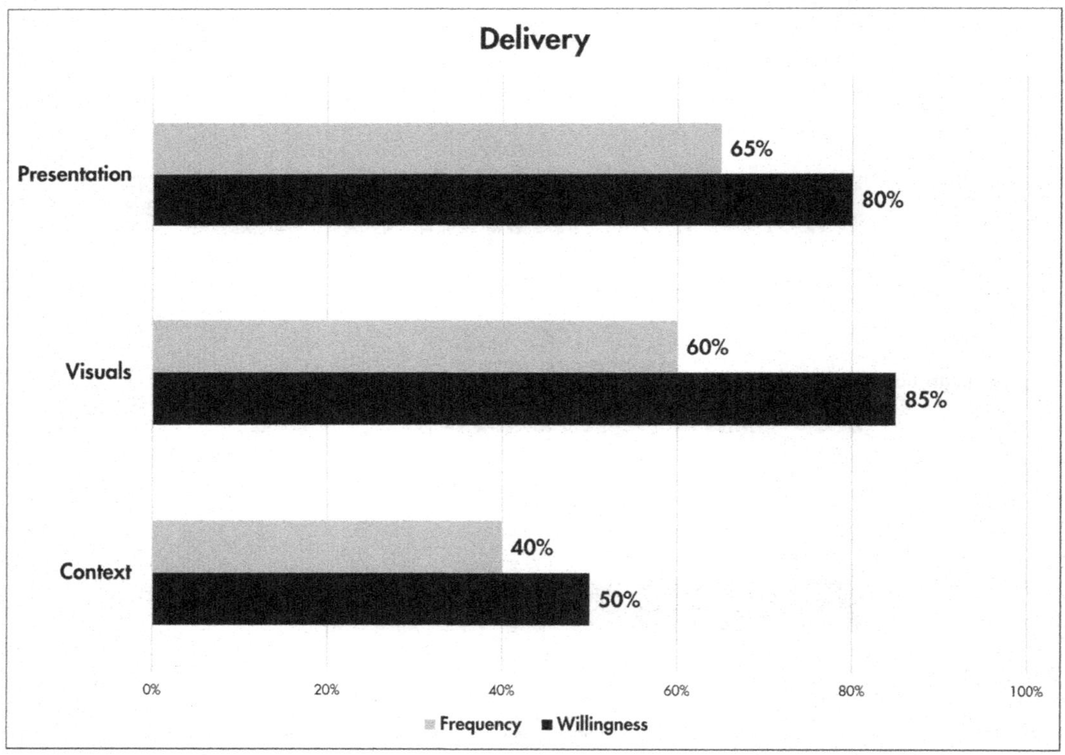

Figure 17.9 Chart indicating percentages of frequency (shown in gray) vs. percentages of willingness (shown in black) for the theme of Delivery. Context comes close to Punctuation (see Figure 17.6), ranking as the survey's second lowest aspect in which respondents are willing to instruct.

writing projects either monthly or more frequently. Eighty percent ($n = 16$) responded to Question 14 that they were very willing or willing to instruct students in the presentation of their writing project, and 60% ($n = 12$) responded to Question 29 that they instructed students in the presentation of their writing project either monthly or more frequently.

Limitations of the Study

Conducted within a short timeframe, this microstudy, while full of potential, would have benefited from greater analysis of the part of the survey that articulated the professional status—including role, hours worked, and years in the profession requested by Questions 34–36—of the participants. I did spend a good amount of time using analysis tools, attempting to see connections between professional status and the responses that the participants made in the survey, but no clear patterns seemed to emerge.

While a great deal has been said about the quantitative portion of the study, little, here, speaks to the qualitative, open-ended portion of the survey. With most of the efforts spent on coding, categorizing, and quantifying the objective portion of the survey, written responses did not receive the same level of treatment as the objective ones. A number of the open-ended responses were telling, and they could certainly be coded for thematic presentation in a larger study.

DISCUSSION OF RESULTS

Patterns and Anomalies

To give meaning to quantified results, one of the most useful approaches is to look for patterns and anomalies. In doing so, a few patterns emerged that helped to provide meaningful interpretation to the major research questions of this study and specifically to the question about what levels librarians were at in currently providing writing instruction. I highlight these patterns below through the five themes.

Theme of Invention

In considering the theme of Invention, the willingness factor was second highest, across all three aspects of writing, among the five themes (Memory is the highest). Of particular note was instruction related to arguments and evidence with its 95% willingness factor, the second highest in the entire survey, and its frequency factor at a strong 75%. To speak directly to argument-and-evidence building, the affinity for librarians to perform this aspect of writing—and to follow through with doing so—takes into consideration the nature of librarians' work. To elaborate, librarians, by leading students to gather and evaluate sources for their research projects, essentially teach them to build stronger forms of evidence and to examine a wide array of arguments to support their thesis. Moreover, the wider theme, here, of librarians teaching Invention—not only in argument-and-evidence building but also in brainstorming and thesis-building—has a strong correlation with the word's etymological roots. The word *invention* comes from the Latin root *invenire*, meaning "to find" (Invention, 2015), and based on those roots, it is not far-fetched to compare the work of librarians, as finders and discoverers, to this history of Invention and, likewise, to their current instruction that helps students "find" ways to develop and support their theses.

Theme of Arrangement

While the first two themes focus on the aspects of writing where librarians exhibited the most willingness and frequency, the results from those questions categorized as Arrangement lead us to examine aspects of writing where librarians show some of the least willingness and frequency of task. Looking at outlining, the interesting part about the results in this aspect of writing is that librarians are 80% willing to help students with arranging content, but only 40% responded that they regularly perform this task. This 40% spread is the largest of any in Questions 1–30, and perhaps it is because students are not outlining as much today but are, instead, using more contemporary organization tools, such as concept-mapping or mind-mapping.

Looking more deeply at the results in Arrangement, we also find the aspect of writing in the survey with the lowest score in Willingness and Frequency: flow and coherence. This result (40% willingness; 35% frequency) was not wholly surprising, as helping students hang their writing together, so to speak, requires serious drilling down into the details. The aversion librarians may have toward working with coherence is best summed up in a response made in the open-ended portion of the survey, in Question 32, where participants were asked to disclose the aspects of writing that made them the most uncomfortable. One respondent writes, "I feel most uncomfortable instructing students in areas of writing that are subjective or that I don't have a background in." Certainly, coherence is one of those areas where subjectivity weighs heavily, and without a strong background in writing, most librarians probably do not feel they have the skills to wade through the organization and transitions of student writing.

The final aspect of writing within Arrangement encompasses questions about genre and mode. A midrange 65% responded that they were willing to help instruct with genre and mode, and a low 45% said they do so frequently. To interpret these results leads me to the types of assignments that students taking general requirement courses—the greater proportion of those who come to the Writing Studios—are asked to complete. Most assignments are prescriptive about genre and mode. For instance, college composition courses often ask students to write comparison or descriptive essays, so students may not actually require as much help with genre or mode as students taking upper-level undergraduate courses where instructors give less prescription.

Theme of Style

Within Style, I would particularly like to address the aspect of punctuation. The survey showed that the frequency of instructing in punctuation ties for the lowest in the survey with flow and coherence (35%). This finding was not unanticipated. In fact, of all aspects of writing, this was the one I expected to have the lowest results. The aversion to punctuation, and its more frequently applied term *grammar*, is shared not only by librarians but by many. For example, with no coaching, most students who talk about problems with their writing will put grammar at the top of their list. The extent of current traditionalism and its focus on grammar (Bibb, 2012) has left a lasting specter that looms over the expectations students have about writing, and for the librarians who responded to this survey, that specter is just as large, as demonstrated in Question 32. The word *grammar* or *punctuation* appears in eight different responses about the aspect of writing with which participants were least comfortable. One response in particularly stands out: "Don't put me on the team for Name that Grammar Term. That was my initial challenge when working with tutors and Composition instructors. It was intimidating." Clearly, the fear of comma splices and run-on sentences is difficult to subdue.

Theme of Memory

While a tendency exists to consider Memory within discourse as the use of pneumonic devices or other memory aids, Hook reminds readers that Memory is actually "the treasury of things invented," linking memory with Invention (as cited in Elmborg & Hook, 2005, p. 22). Considering the results of the survey, where themes of Invention and Memory generated some of the highest scores, this reminder from Hook aptly applies. The survey results featuring a 100% willingness for attribution and a 90% willingness for both source integration and paraphrasing showed the comfort that librarians have in helping students work with sources. While these findings were unsurprising, thinking about how librarians can connect Invention with Memory in writing instruction offers implications worth exploring in applied settings.

Theme of Delivery

With digital writing, Delivery may have changed greatly since ancient oratory, and the survey addresses those changes with questions about visuals and formatting, but the results most worthy to discuss here coincide more with traditional rhetoric: contextualization. Application of contextualization was defined for participants as instructing students in finding focus, audience, and purpose or situating their writing for the occasion. Only half of the participants said they were willing to engage in this process, and only 40% said they frequently do. To compare, contextualization ranks right up there with punctuation in the willingness factor, the second lowest in the entire survey, and this seems anomalous since one of the first questions librarians often ask students is what assignment they are working on. In fact, one of the responses to Question 32 described uncertainty about "how to help students when I can't see the assignment and/ or [a] syllabus," and in Question 31, which asks respondents what aspects of writing they are most comfortable with, another respondent writes, "I often read the assignment with the student." This entry-level question librarians ask students about their assignments sets the tone for contextualization, and even more so, their work with finding and narrowing down topics—or "pre-thesis work," as one respondent describes it—adds to helping students find context in their writing. Perhaps the word in the question that alarmed the participants the most is the word "audience." Considering how amorphous audience often is in college-level writing (Bartholomae, 1985), reservations to teaching such a concept are justifiable, but looking at the larger picture, the idea of teaching context could open up a much greater conversation than space for here about rhetorical concepts—in particularly *kairos*[4]—and its absence in writing instruction.

Recommendations for the Future

In looking back at the initial research question about how librarians might participate in writing instruction in greater ways, how information literacy and writing might intertwine to form Norgaard's "writing information literacy," here are some recommendations from this study that may help impact the future of the Writing Studios at SPC, and perhaps by extension, other colleges and universities: In general, it seems reasonable to leverage each librarian's strengths. Let them focus on the aspects of writing that they seem most willing to work with, including those three items in Memory, such as paraphrasing, source integration, and attribution, as well as with argument-and-evidence building. In addition to leveraging their current strengths, writing instruction outside the classroom can also benefit from librarians' willingness. Finding willing partners in librarians and training them—maybe by different aspects of writing, instead of writing as a whole—would be a good model. Since, as the literature demonstrates, librarians are so collaborative, possibly they can be included as part of ongoing workshops that focus on particular aspects of writing, such as paragraphing, proofreading, or grammar. As they start to collaborate, they may be willing to take over more of writing instruction outside the classroom, making them more than just research partners but writing partners as well.

NOTES

1. For more on Writing Program Administration standards, visit http://wpacouncil.org/positions/outcomes.html
2. This refers to the now rescinded standards for information literacy. See this link for more information: http://www.ala.org/Template.cfm?Section=Home&template=/ContentManagement/ContentDisplay.cfm&ContentID=33553
3. Here, I would like to address the 15 aspects of writing and their categorization. Invention includes aspects related to the content of writing. Arrangement includes the organization of the content. Style includes the particulars of sentence-level writing. Memory does not reflect Cicero's original use of the word, which was related to rote memorization; instead, it accounts for the memory, or historical archive, through the use and implementation of sources within writing. Delivery also does not share the original meaning because it was related to oratory, not writing. Still, it retains some of its original meaning by usage of contextualization, which considers focus, audience, and purpose for the occasion; visuals, which refers to using, creating, identifying, or finding visuals to accompany writing, similar to how orators use visual aids in their delivery; and presentation, which refers to the formatting and style guidelines. As a word of note, the column with the number sign (i.e., #) refers to the question numbers that address each aspect of writing.
4. If unfamiliar with the concept of *kairos*, see Thompson, R. (2000). Kairos revisited: An interview with James Kinneavy. *Rhetoric Review, 19*(1/2), 73–88. Retrieved from http://www.jstor.org/stable/466055

REFERENCES

Association of College and Research Libraries. (2015). *Framework for information literacy for higher education.* Chicago, IL: Association of College and Research Libraries.

Bartholomae, D. (1985). Inventing the university. In M. Rose (Ed.), *When a writer can't write: Studies in writer's block and other composing-process problems* (pp. 134–165). New York, NY: Guilford.

Bibb, B. (2012). Bringing balance to the table: Comprehensive writing instruction in the tutoring session. *Writing Center Journal, 32*(1), 92–104.

Bronshteyn, K., & Baladad, R. (2006). Librarians as writing instructors: Using paraphrasing exercises to teach beginning information literacy students. *Journal of Academic Librarianship, 32*(5), 533–536. https://doi.org/10.1016/j.acalib.2006.05.010

Cicero, M. T. (1942). *Cicero: De oratore* (E. W. Sutton & H. Rackham, Trans.). Cambridge, MA: Harvard University Press.

Creswell, J. W. (2013). *Qualitative inquiry and research design: Choosing among five traditions.* Thousand Oaks, CA: Sage.

Elmborg, J. K., & Hook, S. (2005). *Centers for learning: Writing centers and libraries in collaboration.* Chicago: Association of College and Research Libraries.

Freeman, G. (2005). The library as place: Changes in learning patterns, collections, technology, and use. In *Library as place: Rethinking roles, rethinking space* (Chapter 1). Retrieved from http://www.clir.org/wp-content/uploads/sites/6/pub129.pdf

Invention. (2015). *Silva rhetoricae.* Retrieved from http://rhetoric.byu.edu/Canons/Invention.htm

Jackman, L. W., & Weiner, S. A. (2016). The rescinding of the ACRL 2000 information literacy competency standards for higher education . . . really?? *Libraries Faculty and Staff Scholarship and Research.* https://doi.org/10.1080/10691316.2016.1217811

New Jersey Library Association. (2014). Open letter regarding the framework for information literacy for higher education. Retrieved from http://cus.njla.org/node/593

Norgaard, R. (2003). Writing information literacy: Contributions to a concept. *Reference & User Services Quarterly, 43*(2), 124–130.

Obama, B. (2009, July 14). Remarks by the president on the American graduation initiative. Retrieved from https://obamawhitehouse.archives.gov/the-press-office/remarks-president-american-graduation-initiative-warren-mi

Shields, K. (2014). Research partners, teaching partners: A collaboration between FYC faculty and librarians to study students' research and writing habits. *Internet Reference Services Quarterly, 19*(3/4), 207–218. https://doi.org/10.1080/10875301.2014.983286

Todorinova, L. (2010). *Writing center and library collaboration: A telephone survey of academic libraries.* Retrieved from http://scholarcommons.usf.edu/tlas_pub/56

Virgil, C. L. (2013). *An analysis of the academic library and the changing role of the academic librarian in higher education: 1975–2012* (Doctoral dissertation). Retrieved from ProQuest Dissertations & Theses Global. (UMI No. 3601227)

CHAPTER 18

HOW TO TALK ABOUT COPYRIGHT SO KIDS WILL LISTEN, AND HOW TO LISTEN ABOUT COPYRIGHT SO KIDS WILL TALK

An Assignment at the Intersection of Multimodal Writing and Intellectual Property

Laura Giovanelli

Molly Keener

In 2011, Beyoncé's *Countdown* video was "instantly praised for its iconic pop-cultural references" (Tarsis, 2011, para. 1), paying homage to Diana Ross, Brigitte Bardot, Andy Warhol, and Audrey Hepburn, among others. Identifying those influences is not difficult, as the choreography, costuming, and music evoke impressions for the audience: one MTV writer caught references from the 1980s dance movie *Flashdance* to the 1957 musical *Funny Face* (Thomas, 2011). Inspiration crossed into infringement, however, when the Belgian choreographer Anne Teresa De Keersmaeker claimed that Beyoncé stole choreography from De Keersmaeker's *Rosas danst Rosas* and *Achterland* (Haye, 2011). When we broadly open the contemporary definition of writing to all composing, Beyoncé and students learning to write in college have more in common than at first glance. Indeed, as a contemporary text born of a remix, reuse, and rewriting culture, *Countdown* represents the complex questions and learning opportunities that many college writing teachers wish to stoke in their students: what is original writing and composing? Where does inspiration end and plagiarism begin? And how do writers ethically use the composing of others—text, video, music, and even choreography—to create their own work?

To better prepare and engage students for the writing they will do during and after their undergraduate years, there is movement for college writing instructors to design "multimodal" assignments, or assignments that ask learners to write in multiple modes. Such assignments, which include multimedia projects using video, audio, image, and text in combination to communicate in a digital environment, acknowledge the broadening definition and possibilities of writing, particularly digital writing, and literacy as "multiliteracies" (New London Group, 1996, p. 60) and ways of making meaning through "linguistic, aural, visual, gestural, and spatial means" (Ball & Charlton, 2015, p. 42). Best practices in writing instruction aim for adaptability in writing across technologies and platforms, including digital, and for understanding intellectual property (Council of Writing Program Administrators, *Outcomes Statement for First-Year Composition*, 2014); indeed, one of the biggest changes of writing instruction in recent years has been the shift toward writing as composing in various genres and modes, and recognizing "the plurality of situations writers face today and remain open to the inevitability of continuing changes in media, genres, and writing acts to come" (Dryer et al., 2014). The proliferation of social media and lower cost and learning thresholds also create a growing interest in teaching students writing with an emphasis on composing digital genres, such as videos. While some writing theorists point out that all writing is inherently multimodal, an emphasis on writing in multiple modes via digital media implies literacy today means more than text-based knowledge. This pushes library instruction, too, to move beyond what is traditionally associated with writing classes (database searching, citation workshops, etc.) to address ethical use of diverse composing elements like audio clips, videos, songs, images and photographs, and traditional text-based writing from sources like academic journal articles or popular publications.

Teaching multimodal assignments is not just a concern of writing instruction. Even if few engage directly with theories of multimodal pedagogy, a recent survey of college faculty across disciplines, for instance, found instructors assign a broad variety of writing genres that ask students to compose using multimedia: videos, websites, and technical writing for specialized fields; public writing; reflective writing, for example blogs, logs, and journals; creative writing; computer programs; and formal academic writing (Reid, Snead, Pettiway, & Simoneaux, 2016). Well-designed pedagogy recognizes multimodal writing's potential to foster student agency and ownership as increasingly participatory citizens where literacy means composing in a range of print and digital media, genres, and modes, where students are consumers *and* ethical creators.

With these writing opportunities come all of digital media's challenges and affordances, including responsible teaching concepts of intellectual property, fair use, and copyright. Many librarians offer unique knowledge and training in how copyright functions. In collaboration with writing instructors, their collective expertise and experience can add to learning outcomes that demystify arcane laws into writing projects with relevance for real-world audiences and exigency. As a writing instructor and a librarian at a private liberal arts college, we share values of teaching responsible and respectful use of intellectual property, whether it be correct citation use for an academic audience and purpose or adapting those attributions for a more popular audience and exigence. Just as we expect students to correctly cite a paraphrase or quotation from an academic journal article for a scholarly audience, we must shift to expecting similar responsible reuse and remixing of video and audio when assigning multimodal digital projects.

This bridge between academic and public writing echoes the complex writing genres college students may later encounter in their working and public lives. Moreover, as instructors who wish to empower novice writers, hands-on learning about copyright grounded in popular culture, for example the Marvin Gaye–infringing "Blurred Lines" song by Robin Thicke (Bravender, 2015), demonstrates that copyright law and citation ethics matter beyond academe. And it empowers students to create as well as consume digital writing: acknowledging that creation is an ongoing conversation where all writing—and more broadly, composition—inevitably has roots in previous human expression. Such projects reflect the forms of writing students usually consume daily, and create avenues to discuss responsible intellectual engagement and digital literacy beyond college.

Debating inspiration versus infringement in the choreography in Beyoncé's *Countdown* video is a particularly useful exercise. Choreography is a work eligible for copyright protection, although it must be "fixed" through notation to describe movements or through video recording; few choreographers attempt to actually register their choreography copyright with the U.S. Copyright Office (Gardner, 2011). While this accusation did not result in a lawsuit between De Keersmaeker and Beyoncé/Sony (her label), the *Countdown* controversy provides a template for discussing copyright, fair use, and plagiarism with real-life visuals generally of interest to students.

Framed by broader cultural discussion about creativity, originality, and ownership, and situated against specific learning objectives, librarian-facilitated intellectual property conversations in writing classrooms open opportunities for timely collaboration and interdisciplinary instruction. Helping students understand that copyright and fair use are applicable in environs beyond academe is challenging. Certainly, most are familiar with the "All rights reserved" disclaimers on broadcasts of major sporting events, and with the Federal Bureau of Investigation warnings at the start of DVDs, but such dire warnings only offer theoretical connections to copyright's role in daily life. Bringing conversations about intellectual property into the classroom, around a focused project, elevates student awareness around copyright, fair use, accessibility, and legal differences between music, sound, and video in the public space versus those in the public domain. Many students mistakenly believe that if media is available online, for free, then it is open for reuse, not realizing that public domain has a legal definition that is not merely that a work is made available to the public (Smith, 2014). Making this distinction leads into conversations about Creative Commons licenses, and how to find free, licensed-for-reuse digital media online. These conversations also create space to discuss the differences between copyright infringement (criminal violation) and plagiarism (ethical violation), and why proper citation protects against the latter, but not the former.

FRAMEWORK FOR SUCCESSFUL MULTIMODAL ASSIGNMENT DESIGN

Successful multimodal writing assignment design has much in common with strong assignment design of any writing project, and the learning goals remain the same: to teach writing as an active, adaptable, self-aware practice of rhetorically based strategies for distinct audiences and purposes. The goal of multimodal projects is not to produce perfect sound or audio projects; rather, for apprenticeship writers, the aim is to learn by doing "with the goal of thinking about what humans can accomplish when they use different modalities" through open-ended projects "that prompt writers to think in new ways" (Hess, 2007, p. 29).

Mickey Hess (2007) points to three best practices writing instructors should keep in mind as they design multimodal assignments: theory; structure and choice; and circulation. Through theory, Hess suggests faculty consider composition theory in designing their assignments: what are their existing pedagogical goals, and how can multimodal assignments specifically help them and students reconsider what they know about writing and composing? Through an assignment that accommodates both structure and choice, students have direction and guidance, but also agency to make choices. A multimodal assignment paired with metacognitive writing—reflection—on these choices helps students process why they are making writing choices. Circulation, or how students' multimodal writing will be seen, read, and heard, for example published on a website and shared with friends and family, may expand students' notion of an authentic audience. Within this framework, students' understanding of intellectual property takes on additional weight; students must choose what kinds of sources to use based on their audience and purpose, and then incorporate evidence and sources (theory) within the constraints and opportunities of a multimodal project's structure and choice. At the moment of publication, or circulation of their multimodal project, their writing will have to demonstrate responsible use of outside materials.

A SAMPLE MULTIMODAL ASSIGNMENT IN A WRITING CLASS

Our collaborative multimodal writing assignment builds on a previous, individual project where writing students are asked to write a traditional, text-based academic autoethnography focusing on a social group they identify with and belong to. Autoethnographic writing is often written by social scientists, such as anthropologists, interested in connections between their own identity and the larger society. This critical self-narrative "places the self within a social context" (Reed-Danahay, 1997, p. 9), "connecting the personal to the cultural" (Ellis & Bochner, 2000, p. 739). After reading, drafting, and revising autoethnographies as solo authors, students turn their attention to adapting these pieces of scholarly writing for a broader, popular audience using a different medium, digital video. This genre is digital autoethnography; it represents an emerging genre wherein an established genre of scholarly social sciences writing is adapted by writers for broader audiences via multimedia.

Team Digital Autoethnography Adaptation for a Popular Audience and Related Reflection Paper

Rhetorical Purpose

To adapt a scholarly piece of writing (namely, a team member's Project 3, their traditional autoethnography). To synthesize, build on, and contribute to a *popular conversation* about a social group/identity to which a team member belongs and a larger conversation about human behavior, perceptions, and attitudes, particularly related to questions of home and identity. And all of this in a new medium: video.

Audience

Video: Popular, broad, and generally college-aged—your class colleagues interested in social sciences questions about identity.

Paper: Other scholars interested in processes and rhetorical decisions and specifically Prof. Giovanelli.

Length

Video: 5 to 7 minutes.

Paper: 4+ pages, or at least 1,000 words.

Documentation/Citation

Video: Documentary style (end and/or in-text credits; we'll talk about this in class). Include an APA-style References citing your video's sources emailed to Prof. G due the same day and time as your video.

Papers: If you cite something in your reflection papers, use MLA or APA style, whatever you think might be more appropriate given your audience and purpose.

Our Learning Objectives

- **To practice composing/writing, revising, and working** as a team.
- **To practice adapting writing, namely** a scholarly piece of writing for a popular audience and media.
- **To practice acknowledging Fair Use and copyright** as composing constraints and possibilities.
- **To (more) practice critical thinking, analysis, and active reading.**
- **To (more) practice using textual evidence** (more than just text now: visual, verbal, and audio).
- **To practice (more) crafting an organized argument** for a popular audience and purpose with a beginning, middle, and end.
- **To practice (more) writing and research as process** through free writing, drafting, responding to other writers' drafts, processing constructive yet critical feedback, and revision.

Strong writers are flexible and adaptive. That often means communicating with a wide range of audiences. Today, many scholars and writers communicate their academic work to the larger public through social media, articles, interviews, podcasts, and videos. Our idea of writing is expanding from just words on paper.

In this two-part group collaboration, you will be first composing a video that adapts a team member's autoethnography (Project 3) for a popular audience. This is also a chance for revision: use your group's collective intelligence and skills to consider how you can tweak or even majorly revise a member's Project 3 thesis, evidence, and organization. Indeed, as you'll have more rhetorical choices now (sound, images, etc.), take advantage of a larger composition palette. While you'll be adapting just one of your group's autoethnographies, you will all have a big stake in this project: think of yourself as a team, working to bring your group member's autoethnography to a broader, more popular audience.

The Genres: Digital Autoethnography and Reflection Paper

A recent trend among some researchers is to compose popular digital videos. Through this work, scholars attempt to appeal to a broader audience. This is still composition, and indeed, a newer kind of writing, but the authors have more rhetorical choices. More is not necessarily better, though, so keep your group's choices in mind. As usual, we'll be analyzing examples of this genre together.

For your reflection paper, you've actually been practicing this kind of writing all semester. By now, you're probably pretty familiar with what it means to reflect on your process and more importantly, the value of this metagenre of writing. This will just be a more formal version.

Video Higher Order Concerns: Research, Evidence, and Organization

As you're composing a video, you will have to think about visual and audio textual evidence as well as verbal (written) textual evidence. You may additionally use media such as music, narration, still images, and video. We will talk in class about finding copyright-free and limited use material as well as fair use with a librarian expert. You are also highly encouraged to shoot your own video footage; a simple digital camera (even a smartphone) and an editing program such as Windows Movie Maker or iMovie are about all the hardware and software tools you need for this video. See the video technical tip sheet on our website to help assuage your technology fears. We will also have a visit from the library digital media support staff. You'll have lots of guidance if you seek it out.

Just remember, while there are numerous rhetorical choices in this project, it is still a composition attempting to make an argument to a specific audience. Consider your rhetorical situation, and how you can clearly and convincingly convey your purpose. Your evidence in this project will come from your sources in Project 3, plus any additional (particularly visual ones) sources your group wishes to add to beef up your proof, including credible popular ones. As you will only be adapting one autoethnography, that project's sources and research idea should be quite strong. You should not choose the project that received the best grade; you will have to use your critical thinking skills to select an autoethnography that has a strong thesis, evidence, and organization that you can adapt, add to, or even—and this is highly encouraged—revise.

Your job here is to take one of your team's autoethnographies and adapt that project for a popular audience through video. You may accomplish this through video, music, pictures, or voice-over narration; however, it must be relevant and convincing evidence to make an argument and contribute to knowledge about human behavior in general and a social group in particular.

An adaptation of your synthesized sources will help provide background and context for your viewers, and indicate what gap you will be trying to fill in our knowledge conversation. Interviews and personal evidence will build your case about your group. Remember rhetorical appeals—what works with one kind of audience might not work with another. How will you adapt field-specific social sciences information for a broader audience in a fresh, open, and engaged way?

Consider, too, organization (this is where a storyboard, outline, or script will really, really help in your drafting). Just because your medium in this project is a video does not mean you shouldn't have a central claim and some kind of beginning, middle, and end. In fact, most documentary-style videos do—we'll examine this more. And, as usual, your thesis should go a step further than the obvious. Don't forget the "so what?" for your viewers.

Finally, in the video, cite your sources using a popular documentary style, such as in-text and end credits, paying heed to copyright (we'll talk more about this in class). You will also submit via an APA-style References page the day your video is due. We'll be talking about and working with another of our fabulous librarians to understand concepts called fair use and copyright, which will help guide your source decision making in this composition using more than just verbal text.

Video Lower Order Concerns

Though this project is for a popular audience, your tone should still be reasonable and objective given what you want to accomplish. It may be a little less formal considering your audience, but keep in mind that your audience will likely look for specific proof over emotion. You will be asking them to buy into your curiosity and believe your argument. It may also help to define technical or field-specific language for your broader audience.

Finally, don't overlook proofreading your video, checking for grammar and spelling as well as concerns unique to this composition situation, such as sound, timing, pacing, and text size. In order to be convincing, you need to be understood. And as always, a polished final draft will enhance your *ethos* with your audience.

Reflection Higher Order Concerns: Research, Evidence, and Organization

By now, you're probably pretty familiar with what it means to reflect on your writing process. As this will be a larger and more formal part of this project, however, you will want to be very careful to consider, as usual, our class's general features of strong and effective writing. Just because this writing is about your personal experience doesn't mean you don't need to be convincing and argue a point; your thesis, or central argument, here will likely be a distillation of your overall (team and individual) experience(s) adapting Project 3 to 4. As evidence consider any credible sources that seem relevant, including your video itself; evidence of personal growth/changes throughout the semester from your writing journals; Projects 1–3; your experience during Project 4; free writing from this unit; and/or any class readings or other credible (given your purpose and audience) sources you find on your own.

Consider, too, how you faced challenges, what you learned, and how you have yet to grow. A general structure might be: *what?*, *so what?*, and *what next?* Strong reflections recognize we're all imperfect individuals on a journey. How we handle failure often says more about us than how we handle success. You'll also be writing in/as a group (something you may be doing more of the rest of your life), and with more composers comes more choices about how to handle and integrate a reflection of your collective impression. We'll talk more about this in class if we have time, but a good reference for writing as a group can be found at the University of North Carolina at Chapel Hill's Writing Center website (writingcenter.unc.edu /handouts/group-writing).

Reflection Lower Order Concerns

Strive for a formal, reasonable, and objective tone; this a little more formal than your Writer's Memo. It may help to define technical or field-specific language. A polished final draft will enhance your ethos with your audience, including spelling and grammatical concerns. Since you're working in a group, you have a built-in opportunity to get as many eyes as possible on your final draft.

To begin their adaptation, students are grouped into production teams of three to four. They pool their autoethnographies and after skimming them, select one to adapt into a video for a popular audience. In their original, primarily text-based autoethnographies, students must tell the story of their group with evidence, turning what social scientists call a critical mirror on part of their identity as they make the familiar strange. In their videos, they must do this, too; however, adapting a traditional, text-based autoethnography into a video creates exigence to write in multiple modes not always afforded by alphabetic-based text, namely a traditional academic paper, allowing student writers to add video, audio, and images to the story of their group in addition to traditional primarily text-based evidence from social sciences scholarship from their original project. As an example, when a student writes a traditional, text-based autoethnography about her experiences as a female collegiate basketball player, she relies largely on communicating her argument with evidence from social sciences literature on female student-athletes and her own personal experiences as part of this group. She of course may supplement some of that argument with photographs, charts, drawings, diagrams, and other visuals, but she still very often depends on alphabetic text. In her digital autoethnography adaption, she could—and indeed, to make a successfully strong argument, she may need to—include some of the same evidence, but because of the broader affordances of video as a medium and expectations of the genre, she may now add video and audio interviews with teammates; photographs of researchers who have studied student athletes' experiences; footage of workouts, practices, and games; a snippet of a popular song that reflects her experience; and so on to establish and support an argument about what it is like to be a member of her group and why it matters in a larger social context.

Through low-stakes invention writing and before doing any video work, students craft an informal proposal—to critically consider why they selected a project to adapt and what specific rhetorical choices given their shift in audience and purpose in this adaptation of a piece of academic writing. This prewriting is supplemented by significant class time devoted to critically analyzing other videos, both broadly as a medium (nonfiction videos such as short documentaries) and then more specifically as a genre, the digital autoethnography. As novice writers, students often find models helpful to transfer their previous writing knowledge to novel situations; transfer is sometimes compounded without explicit connections and conversations to the course's previous, more traditional academic writing projects and larger learning objectives, concepts, and assignment sequence, such as awareness of audience and purpose. This discussion allows students to see how other writers made deliberate audio, visual, and organizational choices they, too, as writers in this new rhetorical situation face as they make their own composing choices.

Given that students are now writing in multiple modes, the palette of writing choices can be overwhelming. Do they use voiceover narration or text to guide their audience, or a combination? Do they shoot their own video or use existing footage, and how do they obtain that? Can they just download it from YouTube? What about music? How do they incorporate and adapt their argument and evidence to support it, particularly discipline-specific scholarly sources, given that they are now writing for a popular audience? And writing in multiple modes complicates ownership: who needs to be credited for a song or video, and how? How much can the student authors use, and why does that matter?

Inevitably, our conversation turns to copyright (see the above question about YouTube). A purposeful copyright workshop early in the project helps address these questions formally. Inviting the library's copyright expert to class for a guest lecture alleviates the burden of providing copyright education on the writing instructor, lends an air of authority to the subject, and creates another opportunity for librarian outreach to students. To frame the conversation, the librarian provides a brief overview of copyright basics—what does and does not get copyright protection, how a work is copyrighted, how long copyright lasts—before introducing fair use, the public domain, trademarks, and plagiarism to the discussion. Students are surprised to learn that they themselves are copyright owners countless times over, simply through near-daily creative acts, from snapping photos to writing papers to making art. While readily able to identify copyrighted works such as novels, students struggle to extrapolate that copyright for written works covers all types of texts, including their own. Mistaken assumptions that works must be published or registered to receive copyright protection persist, despite never being part of the copyright law during these students' lifetimes. Personalizing copyright in this manner underscores the ease with which copyright just happens, the proliferation of copyright, especially digitally. It also reframes the copyright conversation, shifting perspective from free to access equals free to use, to free to access but not (necessarily) free of copyright. We go on to talk about how fair use works, and how we all exercise fair use without explicitly labeling our use as fair, such as when using direct quotes and citations in writing (Smith, 2014), and how they can apply fair use to the incorporation of digital media in their videos. These points are emphasized by popular culture examples of instances of alleged copyright infringement, from choreography in music videos (*Countdown*), to sampling and remixing (Gaye/Thicke), to political speeches (ample examples abound). This further underscoring of the broad reach and complexity of copyright and fair use is key to making copyright accessible to students. Supplementing instruction with technical resources such as links to open-source audio and video collections gives students options (and structure and choice) for their own project, and potential agency in a remix and reuse culture.

To practice ethical IP use, students are required to cite sources in their video using a vernacular attribution method, credits and captions (see Figures 18.1 and 18.2: screenshots of sample student digital autoethnographies). They must also turn in an APA References sheet of all their external sources, including music, video clips, and images regardless of copyright, open license, or public domain status.

Because intellectual property use is often new to students, formative feedback gives them time and space for focused revision, particularly as we consider ethical use of others' works. It also emphasizes that multimodal writing, like all writing, is a process and a negotiation with an audience. To frame and focus the feedback, students first brainstorm on "higher order" writing concerns that include intellectual property use: for example, how is evidence attributed in this video? Is it convincing given our audience and purpose? Though the videos are in draft form, such formative feedback gives their creators a sense of where they should focus their revision efforts and reconsider presenting evidence for their intended viewers. Students do not just learn from feedback about their own video, but also gain ideas about what is working and what is not as they act as audience members watching other groups' draft videos. Collaboration in groups also facilitates informal peer response. Some students have generally commented that writing in groups acts as de facto built-in peer response, facilitating collaborative troubleshooting and problem solving while videos are still works in progress.

The project concludes with a class screening and discussion of the final drafts of videos and publishing on a class website (http://cloud.lib.wfu.edu/blog/we-wake-we-write) and via our YouTube channel, making students' multimodal writing public. At the same time, students submit a formal group reflection (see Figure 18.3: reflection assessment rubric) that asks them to reflect on the precise choices they made as writers and collaborators, and what they might consciously transfer to future writing projects wherein they frame their choices via understanding of audience and purpose. They also reflect on their teamwork and group problem-solving. Students typically recognize the benefit of transferring adaptability in communication and collaboration, including IP awareness—so-called soft skills or practices—well beyond college work.

Figure 18.1 Captions in a sample student digital autoethnography, an example of student writers adapting attribution for a broad, popular audience in a video.

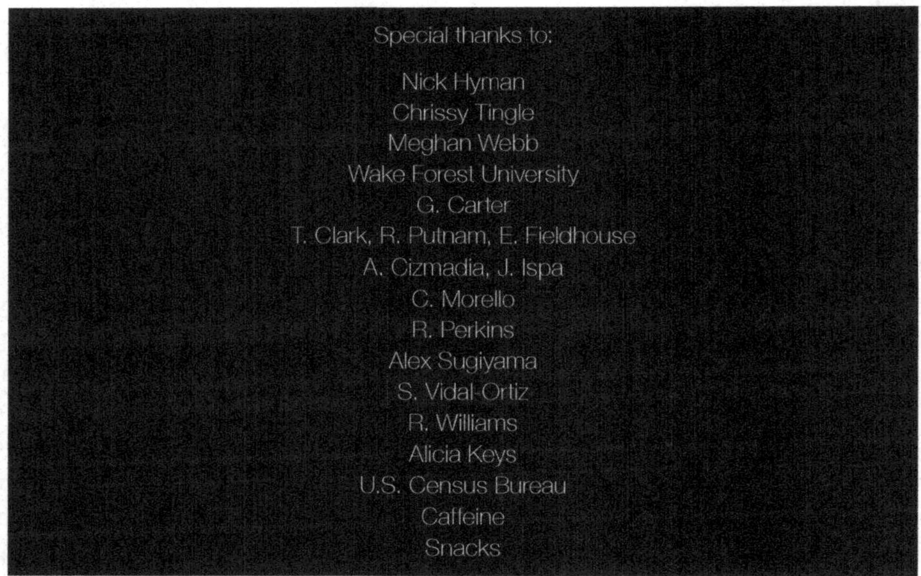

Figure 18.2 Credits at the end of sample student digital autoethnography, another example of student writers adapting attribution for a broad, popular audience in video composition.

TEAM REFLECTION PAPER OF A DIGITAL ADAPTION OF AN AUTOETHNOGRAPHY FOR A POPULAR AUDIENCE	Insufficient	Needs Major Revision	Needs Significant Revision	Needs Some Revision	Needs Little Revision
Rhetorical Purpose & Audience					
To critically and constructively reflect on the personal and team challenges and specific rhetorical decisions and process of adapting a scholarly work for a popular audience in a digital and primarily visual composition. **To look forward** on how you have yet to grow as a rhetorically aware communicator and what you will build on.					
Higher Order Concerns (the Bigger Things) *Use these questions to help you draft and revise.*					
Research & Evidence: Does our reflection introduce and set up our response/argument with a specific measured stance, or a main point, the "so what?" of your argument? Does our thesis go beyond the obvious, explaining the larger relevance of our argument and how our group experience possibly matters beyond our class?					
Research & Evidence: Does our reflection include personal and specific, concrete examples and detail as evidence as we adapted an essay to a video? Does it summarize our video? Is the point of view and other rhetorical considerations appropriate to a personal reflection? Does our reflection leave an impression on readers of our team's growth as flexible and adaptable writers and working in a group, and what needs more work?					
Organization: Is our reflection critical, linear, and cohesive ("What?," "So what?," "Now what?"), with a larger and insightful picture of our team's experiences and challenges as digital composers? Is the reader left with a thorough picture of our collective experience and future growth?					
Lower Order Concerns (the Smaller Things) *Keep asking these questions of your writing, too!*					
Language: Do we follow the grammar, mechanics, and usage of Standard Written English? And when and if our writing does not, did we "break the rules" in a deliberate and rhetorically aware way?					
Voice and Tone: Do we adopt a clear, fresh, and honest personal voice? Do we write with a curious, objective, open, and reasonable tone, adding to our *ethos* as curious writers engaged with a conversation?					
Final Touches: Does our reflection read as a polished and proofread work? Does it generally reflect our *ethos* as a group of critical, thoughtful, and reflective writers?					

Figure 18.3 Reflection assessment rubric. Here, students are asked to critically consider their collaborative writing efforts and rhetorical choices.

CHALLENGES

This project may be adapted for a range of writing classes, from upper-level courses focusing on academic writing to more general introductions to first-year writing. However, it is not a simple assignment. For our students, such a project comes toward the end of a semester-long conversation and assignment sequence designed to teach and practice writing concepts common in composition pedagogy: attention to audience, purpose, evidence, organization, argumentation, and so on. This multimodal project asks them to shift audiences as well as media. Many novice student writers, in other words, would likely not be as successful at navigating a new audience without a previous working and growing self-awareness about what it means to write with a specific audience and exigence in mind; one reason this project works well as a sequence is that students are adapting previous writing and research, not starting from scratch. However, together, this project pair and experiential learning may take up fully half of the semester.

Timelines have to be considered carefully, as students may be learning as they go, particularly if they have never made a video. This project's timeline includes frequent low-stakes invention and reflection writing, checking in with student production teams at various points of their project timeline with "proof of progress," for example a script or storyboard, peer response, a copyright workshop, and open class discussion in process as students stumble, problem solve, and reflect. While a project such as this one could of course be modified and scaled back, realistically, successful multimodal assignment design takes a great deal of scaffolding and steps toward the end writing product; such a project could be scaffolded out further as the focus of an entire semester and a cumulative assignment. The challenges are worth it. We have found students to be proud, engaged, and intrigued by composing in ways they never thought they would be doing in college writing seminars, putting a semester's worth of conversation about persuasion, evidence, organization, and rhetorical choices into hands-on practice in a novel and collaborative way.

While students share and consume digital media via social media and other outlets, these so-called digital natives are not necessarily innately agile at creating it in responsible ways, nor in understanding the rights protecting digital media. In college, students tend to be much more comfortable practicing responsible traditional academic citation than they are attributing sources and building credibility for a popular audience. One common pitfall in this project despite all our explicit conversations, activities, and workshopping is to cite sources in APA style in video, an attribution format that would likely confuse a popular audience; another is to not attribute sources at all. Such a misstep is frequently pointed out by students in workshopping, and is an example while in-process and learning as we go workshops help students see where their draft video is lacking or missing the mark. Using more of the source than is justifiable as a fair use, that is using more than is necessary, is also a common mistake. One crucial way to encourage ethical use of intellectual property is to tie the final project's learning goals and grade to rhetorically aware attribution of any outside sources, video, and music. This expectation echoes source attribution in more academic modes in which students are already enculturated (see "Team Digital Autoethnography Adaptation for a Popular Audience and Related Reflection Paper" earlier in this chapter and Figures 18.1, 18.2, 18.3, and 18.4: corresponding project

TEAM DIGITAL ADAPTATION OF AN AUTOETHNOGRAPHY FOR A POPULAR AUDIENCE ASSESSMENT RUBRIC	Insufficient	Needs Major Revision	Needs Significant Revision	Needs Some Revision	Needs Little Revision
Rhetorical Purpose & Audience					
To **adapt** a scholarly piece of writing (one of your group's Project 3s) for a popular audience. To **synthesize, build on, and contribute** to a *popular conversation* about a social group/identity to which a team member belongs and a larger conversation about human behavior, perceptions, and attitudes, particularly related to questions of home and identity. **And all of this in a new medium, video!**					
Higher Order Concerns (the Bigger Things) *Use these questions to help you draft and revise.*					
Research & Evidence: Do we introduce and set up our digital autoethnography with a main idea, or thesis? Does our thesis go beyond the obvious to explain the larger implications and relevance of our autoethnography, the "so what" and "who cares?" Do we convince viewers of this main idea's importance, relevance, and contribution to a larger conversation about in-groups and identity? Do we attempt to not just answer "what?" but reflect on "why?" and "so what?"					
Research & Evidence: Do we use specific textual evidence from at least six scholarly articles (shown including Allport), relevant personal evidence, and an interview through quotations, paraphrases, and summaries, demonstrating that you're working within a conversation and then building off it (these are listed in your APA References)? Are these sources from Project 3 revised and/or adapted for a popular audience? Do we use auxiliary credible sources and evidence if we feel our team's argument needs more support? Is our textual evidence supported by analysis and explanation? Are our summaries, paraphrases, and quotations accurate and used with care, supporting our claims about the research and how our argument will contribute to this conversation about groups, with minimal and targeted quoting, if any?					
Research & Evidence: Does our video **summarize** our group's selected autoethnography's sources to demonstrate our ethos to our popular audience? Do we adapt academic terminology and explain knowledge for a popular audience? Are our sources **synthesized** to show connections between sources and an evolution of knowledge? Does our digital autoethnography avoid simply listing sources without connecting them or indicating their relevance to each other?					Names:
Organization: Does our video's structure move from the general to the specific, setting up our digital autoethnography with a measured stance, or thesis, and moving onto group significance, literature review, and the gap? Does the middle narrative elaborate on our contribution to the gap and argument about one of our group member's in-groups with precise evidence? Does the conclusion return to our main idea, yet push it further, explaining our digital autoethnography's larger implications and relevance to a larger conversation about human behavior, attitudes, and perceptions?					
Research & Evidence: Do our rhetorical choices and textual evidence possibly include music, stills, video, and narrative that advance our claims and appeal to our popular audience, proving our argument visually as well as verbally to popular viewers? Is our digital autoethnography engaging and creative as well as informative?					

Figure 18.4 Digital autoethnography assessment rubric. (*Figure continued on next page.*)

TEAM DIGITAL ADAPTATION OF AN AUTOETHNOGRAPHY FOR A POPULAR AUDIENCE ASSESSMENT RUBRIC	Insufficient	Needs Major Revision	Needs Significant Revision	Needs Some Revision	Needs Little Revision
Research & Evidence: Do we use a documentary style (credits, narration, in-video text) to cite sources in the video's body and end credits, guiding viewers and also building our own credibility with a popular audience? Do we heed concepts of copyright and Fair Use, crediting and limiting use of all external work?					
Lower Order Concerns (the Smaller Things) *Keep asking these questions of your writing, too!*					
Language: Do we follow the grammar, mechanics, and usage of Standard Written English? And when and if our writing does not, did we "break the rules" in a deliberate and rhetorically aware way?					
Voice and Tone: Do we adopt a clear, fresh, and honest personal voice? Do we write with a curious, objective, open, and reasonable tone, adding to our ethos as curious writers engaged with a conversation?					
Final Touches: Does our digital autoethnography view as a polished and proofread work? Does it generally reflect our ethos as a group of video composers for a popular audience? Did all group members attend our video screening and Q&A?					

Figure 18.4 Continued.

guide and video assessment rubrics and screenshots of credits in student videos).

Finally, though this is not an assignment solely assessed on its technical expertise or success, some students struggle with shooting and editing an original video. Grouping students has helped with this challenge as they are able to divide work based on their interest and expertise, mimicking collaborative learning and working environments that students are likely to encounter in their academic, working, and public lives.

SUMMARY AND RECOMMENDATIONS

In written reflection and informal class discussion, our students generally report a broader and deeper understanding of copyright and intellectual property. Their questions in class discussion, particularly during direct library instruction with the library's copyright expert, and revision workshops reveal a growing awareness of not just ethical intellectual property use, but also its possibilities. They see that this kind of writing, like all writing, depends on intertextuality, reuse, and remix, but that additionally an attention to their videos' audience and purpose is key to their credibility. They are more likely to understand intellectual property as nuanced, rather than something they should not care about or as too complicated and therefore should completely avoid the use of others' materials. And they report more general growth as writers adapting to varied audience and purposes. While many students take advantage of intellectual property knowledge to enhance their own writing through use of popular songs, cultural references, videos, or images, some shy away from understandably perceived gray areas of copyright law by avoiding use of any copyrighted material, for example excluding copyrighted music when it may have been a strong rhetorical choice and in fact help to enhance their argument. Other students point to copyright discussions being specific parts of their collaboration and group process, for example, as they debate choices about what songs and videos to use and how much they can include under fair use. Additionally, not all students specifically comment on their intellectual property choices in their written reflection, possibly due to the open-ended nature of the reflection prompt. A future writing assignment that focuses specifically on the incorporation of others' works into their own as a learning outcome may include a reflection prompt that explicitly solicits intellectual property metacognition.

Our experience suggests an intellectual property–focused multimodal writing assignment like ours is a beginning, not an end; copyright conversations should be ongoing in a student's education. Similar to traditional library instruction in writing classrooms, conversations and projects about intellectual property have increased impact if they move beyond a one-shot experience; greater understanding and empowerment will come from continued experience and across disciplines, not just writing courses. Just as students gain confidence in their academic writing by working with more sources, they will gain confidence in using a broader spectrum of intellectual property as they write across modes and for varied audiences and purposes. For us as college instructors it is particularly important that our students feel ownership in their writing and content creation; indeed, conversations about originality and copyright are ones where we consider with our students possibility, creativity, innovation, and how to ethically and creatively build on what has come and situate multimodal writing in a larger and relevant conversation.

Given the growing interest and assigning of multimodal writing projects across disciplines and widespread use of multimedia, especially videos, to communicate outside of academe, it is clear that writing instructors and librarians would do well to reconsider if and how they are preparing students to write in multiple modes. Through this multimodal assignment collaboration as just one example, we propose a hands-on pedagogy of copyright fundamentals and ethical intellectual property use. We link learning outcomes of multimodal writing projects to assignment design grounded in composition theory with an emphasis on attention to audience and purpose, and scaffold the assignment on a careful timeline, including attention to intellectual property in process, in workshops, and in final drafts. This affords students rich opportunities for choice and agency within structure. And we propose circulation of such projects to make writing projects more public and, thus, accountable to viewers, readers, and listeners outside of the classroom and students more thoughtful, ethical consumers and creators of digital media in future classes and beyond.

REFERENCES

Ball, C. E., & Charlton, C. (2015). All writing is multimodal. In L. Adler-Kassner & E. A. Wardle (Eds.), *Naming what we know: Threshold concepts of writing studies* (pp. 42–43). Boulder, CO: Utah State University Press.

Bravender, P. (2015). Plagiarism v. copyright infringement. In P. Bravender, H. McClure, & G. Schaub (Eds.), *Teaching information literacy: Threshold concepts lesson plans for librarians* (pp. 157–162). Chicago, IL: Association of

College and Research Libraries, a division of the American Library Association.

Council of Writing Program Administrators. (2014). *Outcomes statement for first-year composition* (3.0). Retrieved from http://wpacouncil.org/positions/outcomes.html

Dryer, D., Bowden, D., Brunk-Chavez, B., Harrington, S., Halbritter, B., & Yancey, K. B. (2014). Revising FYC outcomes for a multimodal, digitally composed world: The WPA outcomes statement for first-year composition (version 3.0). *WPA: Writing Program Administration, 38*(1), 129–143.

Ellis, C., & Bochner, A. P. (2000). Autoethnography, personal narrative, reflexivity: Researcher as subject. In N. Denzin & Y. Lincoln (Eds.), *The handbook of qualitative research* (pp. 733–768). Thousand Oaks, CA: Sage.

Gardner, E. (2011, October 13). Why an allegation that Beyoncé plagiarized dance moves is truly unique (analysis). *The Hollywood Reporter*. Retrieved from http://www.hollywoodreporter.com/thr-esq/why-an-allegation-beyonc-plagiarized-248208

Haye, J. (2011, October 18). 10, 9, 8 . . . lawsuit? The blow up over Beyonce's "Countdown" choreography. [Web log post]. Retrieved from http://www.lawlawlandblog.com/2011/10/10_9_8lawsuit_the_blow_up_over.html

Hess, M. (2007). Composing multimodal assignments. In C. L. Selfe (Ed.), *Multimodal composition: Resources for teachers* (pp. 29–37). Cresskill, NJ: Hampton Press.

New London Group. (1996). A pedagogy of multiliteracies: Designing social futures. *Harvard Educational Review, 66*(1), 60–93.

Reed-Danahay, D. (1997). *Auto/ethnography: Rewriting the self and the social*. Oxford, UK: Berg.

Reid, G., Snead, R., Pettiway, K., & Simoneaux, B. (2016). Multimodal communication in the university: Surveying faculty across disciplines. *Across the Disciplines, 13*(1).

Smith, K. L. (2014). *Owning and using scholarship: An IP handbook for teachers and researchers*. Chicago, IL: Association of College and Research Libraries, a division of the American Library Association.

Tarsis, I. (2011, October 11). Copyright infringement in Beyoncé's "Countdown"? [Web log post]. Retrieved from https://itsartlaw.com/2011/10/11/copyright-infringement-in-beyonces-countdown/

Thomas, R. (2011, October 7). Beyoncé's "Countdown" video: A pop-culture cheat sheet. *MTV News*. Retrieved from http://www.mtv.com/news/1672170/beyonce-countdown-video-cheat-sheet

CHAPTER 19

INFORMATION LITERACY INSTRUCTION AND CITATION GENERATORS

The Provision of Citation and Plagiarism Instruction

Nathan Schwartz

College students struggle with plagiarism and citation styles while faculty are faced with the dilemma of imparting citation style knowledge and inspiring the next generation of expert information-seeking writers. Who best should guide and instruct students: faculty, academic librarians, and/or writing center staff? What place do citation generators and citation managers play in this process? How do faculty inspire students to join the community of scholarship in a chosen discipline and learn to love citations as a component of the fellowship in this community, rather than see citation as drudgery, bothersome busy work to avoid plagiarism, and enforced compliance with the university's policy of academic integrity? This author conducted two studies to explore these questions, titled Library Writing Instruction Survey (June 2016) and Library Webpage Study (May 2017). This chapter looks at the question of who is providing citation instruction and how they are providing it.

We have all seen the anxious look on students' faces as they desperately try to comprehend the scope of the professor's research assignment and what sources they should seek to fill the information need. At the core of the assignment is a disconnect between the expert researcher (faculty) and the student researcher. "Undergraduates typically have a hard time getting started on their research papers primarily because they do not know how to narrow either their reading or the topic" (Leckie, 1996, pp. 203–204). Composition faculty frequently ask students to select political or socially controversial topics. The faculty, having obtained a graduate degree and experienced many years of teaching, are expert researchers. There is a significant transition in information seeking and many years of experience that lead a person from undergraduate to full professor, including the study and research required to obtain a doctorate. Many years of searching databases, journals, and books helped to form habits of expert systematic investigation. When students seek to write on socially charged topics, they may have pre-formed opinions and convictions about the topics, which influence their information-seeking behavior. Undergraduates are often not fully psychologically developed to deal with alternative views. Leckie states that when faced with an alternative view, "they simply choose to ignore alternative views" (Leckie, 1996, p. 204). Expert researchers understand the value of alternative viewpoints and are open to processing this information. Faculty assign research paper writing as a tool to help students mature in their discipline.

CITATION, A COMMUNITY OF SCHOLARSHIP

Citation is "central to the social context of persuasion" (Mansourizadeh & Ahmad, 2011, p. 152). Citations substantiate and support the writer's assertions. The ACRL *Framework for Information Literacy* concept Information Has Value calls for researchers to "give credit to the original ideas of others through proper attribution and citation" (Association of College and Research Libraries [ACRL], 2015). Expert writers consider citations a "debt of ownership towards the texts and the authors we cite" (Robillard, 2006, p. 254). Students perceive citations as "bothersome busy-work" (Stevens, 2016, p. 713). Students often see citations as an afterthought. Rather than reading vast amounts of information on a full range of perspectives about the topic and then writing a paper, students sometimes just write the paper and then look for supporting citations. Expert researchers view citations as acknowledging a community of scholarship (Rose, 1989). Writing contributes to a body of knowledge, and scholars view citations as an honor to both cite and be cited. Writing and scholarship are part of the community of knowledge and a contribution to the discipline (Mansourizadeh & Ahmad, 2011). Without additional instruction, student writers often do not realize that "citation is a means of showing respect for your elders; the more novice the writer, the greater the need to establish one's authority by citing the writing of others" (Leverenz, 1998, p. 186). Many authors view citations as a means of acceptance into a scholarship field. New scholars are eager to be cited by others and view such behavior as acceptance by peers. Furthermore, "the ability to use a citation style properly marks one as a member of a particular discipline" (Leverenz, 1998, p. 187). "There is value in being cited by others in the field . . . as a form of exchange value in the academic marketplace" (Robillard, 2006, p. 260). How can expert researchers teach and inspire students to this greater realization of citation as an activity of the academic community?

Faculty are faced with the challenge of inspiring students to view citation and scholarship as a badge of honor and participation in a scholarly field. Shirley Rose considers citation a courtship of ideas and an act of love (Rose, 1989, p. 2). How can faculty inspire the students to see the research as more than just a compliance mechanism? What place does research hold within the course objectives and learning outcomes? Faculty, due to vast experience in researching and writing, have a disconnect from the college students struggling to find their place in the chosen field of study. Presenting students with a research assignment often overwhelms them. Faculty unfamiliar with the basics of writing instruction frequently assign the large topic with some basic details at the beginning of the semester and then provide little or no instruction until the project is due. Leckie talks about a "stratified course-integrated approach" (Leckie, 1996, p. 206), which others call scaffolding. In this approach, the large research project is divided into smaller chunks with clear expectations at each level, thus helping bridge the disconnect between the expert faculty researcher and the struggling student researcher. The question is, where should faculty place citation instruction in the scaffolding of the research assignment, and who should teach or guide students with the citation utilization in the research process?

THE GROUPS THAT TEACH CITATION

There are three groups of persons who may teach students how to conduct citation utilization in the research process: the teaching faculty, the writing center or support staff, or the academic librarians through direct instruction in the course, or at some later point when desperate students show up at the campus library. Repetition is a valuable technique for learning citation skills and when teaching citation development in the research process, so perhaps all three groups should cover citations. Faculty should clearly explain the research requirements and citation standards expected. Often plagiarism and citation are mentioned hand in hand, like a married couple. Academic integrity and the consequences of cheating should not be ambiguous. When citation instructors other than the course faculty, such as the writing center staff and librarians, come in contact with students, they also should remind students of the clear expectations for having appropriate citations in research papers and the university's policy on plagiarism and academic integrity.

Faculty, as expert researchers, are often "preoccupied with getting across the disciplinary content of their courses and simply not thinking about the skills-related issues that affect how students [research information not found in the required course readings]" (Leckie, 1996, p. 206). Faculty are expected to cover more discipline-related content than what may be possible, so when the research assignment is given, there may not be adequate time to fully cover citations, plagiarism, and expert information-seeking strategies. Breaking the assignment into various parts and separating segments to the writing center and/or academic librarians helps to provide repetition of skills and greater coverage of citing and plagiarism. In some cases faculty may call an academic librarian to come into the course and provide a bibliographic instruction session to explain discipline-specific research and information-seeking strategies. Faculty may feel preoccupied or overwhelmed with the content of the course, just as students may feel preoccupied and overwhelmed with the research assignment. South University found that "students needed the most help with searching tasks, citing resources, plagiarism, articulating an information need, understanding information formats, and interpreting sources" (Wilson, 2016, p. 8). "According to a Project Information Literacy report, 41 percent of undergraduates surveyed expressed difficulty in knowing how to cite sources" (Homol, 2014, p. 552).

LIBRARY WRITING INSTRUCTION SURVEY AND LIBRARY WEBPAGE STUDY

This citation and information-seeking knowledge skills gap with students led this researcher to question who teaches citations and plagiarism in colleges. The question prompted the Library Writing Instruction Survey, which was distributed through several e-mail lists in June 2016. The survey was sent to three e-mail lists: Association of Christian Librarians (ACL), Library and Information Technology Association List (lita-l), and Information Literacy discussion list (INFOLIT), and consisted of 13 questions about citation instruction. Because the survey involved human participants, Institutional Review Board approval was sought and obtained. A total of 229 participants began the survey and 176 respondents completed the survey. Here are the 13 questions from the Library Writing Instruction Survey:

Q1. Do you wish to participate in the research study?

Q2. How much time do you spend in citation instruction?

Q3. Who provides in person citation instruction in composition and writing classes? (select one or more)

Q4. Which citation styles do you usually cover during instruction? (select one or more)

Q5. How much time do you spend in citation tools/programs/websites instruction?

Q6. How much time do you spend on plagiarism instruction?

Q7. Do you instruct students about specific citation managers? (select one or more)

Q8. Do you instruct on citation generators such as? (select one or more)

Q9. Do your citation webpages discuss/explain plagiarism?
Q10. Do you have webpages about citation styles?
Q11. For which citation styles do you provide website instruction? (select one or more)
Q12. Do you have webpages about specific citation managers? (Select one or more)
Q13. Do you have webpages about citation generators such as: (Select one or more)

The last five questions in the survey ask about library webpages. While the survey results were interesting, they triggered more questions and made an evaluation of library webpages an obvious follow-up. The Library Webpage Study looked more closely at two groups of libraries. In May 2017, 240 library websites were examined. These libraries were part of either the Association of Research Libraries (124 members) or Council for Christian Colleges and Universities Libraries (116 members). Every library's website was checked by exploring the site and using Google site search to determine where information on citation, citation styles, and plagiarism might be found. For the purposes of this Library Webpage Study, only substantial information was counted. If a website mentioned the word "citation" and offered one sentence, that did not constitute substantial information. A full discussion and explanation of citing and citation styles that teaches the topic needed to be present. In order to count, the library would have to have some level of discussion, a few paragraphs, some citation examples, discussion about citation styles, and so on. Similarly, merely a sentence on plagiarism and academic integrity did not count as substantial information. Content and teaching information, not a link to OWL, was necessary. While the Purdue University Online Writing Lab (https://owl.english.purdue.edu/owl/) is a great resource for students, actual content concerning citations and plagiarism on the library or university website was required.

Who provides citation instruction (Table 19.1)? As previously stated, citation instruction may be provided by the teaching faculty, the writing center, or the academic librarians. The survey asked this with question number 3.

The survey indicated that 70% of the instructors teaching citation skills were librarians. However, this survey was primarily sent to librarians and not composition faculty, so the results may be skewed. The survey results show more responses than respondents, indicating many colleges are practicing repetition as the method of instruction with faculty, librarians, and/or writing center staff providing duplication of citation instruction. Students need to practice skills more than once,

TABLE 19.1 *Who provides in-person citation instruction in composition and writing classes?*

	No. of Responses	% of Respondents	% of Responses
Librarians	124	70.45	34.73
Writing Center Staff	83	47.16	23.25
English/Composition Faculty	146	82.95	40.90
N/A	4	2.27	1.12
	Total respondents 176		
	Total responses 357		

but how much citation content is really being taught? One indication would be the amount of time spent teaching the topic (Table 19.2).

This question of time spent on citation was actually the first question on the Library Writing Instruction Survey, after the IRB invitation to participate in the survey. Time spent on a topic is a strong indication of value placed on the information. It turned out that 81% of respondents spent at least 5 minutes on citation and 64% spent 10 minutes or more on citation. It was disappointing to see 15% of respondents spend fewer than 5 minutes on citation instruction, which is a topic integral to communicating within the community of academic scholarship.

Plagiarism, as a part of academic integrity, is increasingly more critical in today's college education process. Again, time was used as an indication of significance, and question 6 asked how much time is spent on plagiarism instruction (Table 19.3).

TABLE 19.2 *How much time do you spend on citation instruction?*

	No. of Responses	% of Responses
More than 30 minutes	68	38.64
15–30 minutes	24	13.64
15 minutes or more	92	52.27
10–15 minutes	21	11.93
10 minutes or more	113	64.20
5–10 minutes	31	17.61
5 minutes or more	144	81.82
Less than 5 minutes	27	15.34
N/A	5	2.84
	Total respondents 176	

TABLE 19.3 *How much time do you spend on plagiarism instruction?*

	No. of Responses	% of Responses
More than 30 minutes	41	23.30
15–30 minutes	30	17.05
15 minutes or more	71	40.34
10–15 minutes	24	13.64
10 minutes or more	95	53.98
5–10 minutes	31	17.61
Less than 5 minutes	43	24.43
N/A	7	3.98
	Total respondents 176	

The survey indicated 53% of respondents invested at least 10 minutes on the topic, while 24% thought it only worthy of 5 or fewer minutes of mention. Many colleges have students sign an academic honesty or integrity policy agreement. Students might find citing less onerous if they were introduced to citation as a form of acknowledgment and respect, as an author being honored by other researchers in a scholarly discipline by means of citation. It was rewarding to see that the survey showed 23% invested more than 30 minutes to inspire students to "give credit to the original ideas of others through proper attribution and citation" (Association of College and Research Libraries, 2015).

Many students may find library website instruction helpful. The Library Instruction Writing Survey asked if participants had webpage help on citations and plagiarism (Table 19.4).

The 67% response in the affirmative was positive; however, the question provided incomplete information and prompted the follow-up Library Webpage Study in May 2017 (Table 19.5).

TABLE 19.4 *Do your citation webpages discuss/explain plagiarism?*

	No. of Responses	% of Responses
Yes	115	67.25
No	56	32.75
	Total responses 171	

For the purposes of this Library Webpage Study, substantial information/training/demonstration on the topics needed to be present on the webpage. Comparing the data from the Library Instruction Writing Survey showing 67% of respondents claiming a webpage guide, to the Library Webpage Study, where only 41% address plagiarism and 50% address citation, presented two possible problems with the survey question. Either Library Writing Instruction Survey participants considered a mere mention as teaching on a topic, or the survey respondents were in libraries with citation and plagiarism guides. Overall, 31% of responding libraries had citation tutorials and 12% offered or had offered some type of citation workshop. Approximately 10% included only a chart of various Web-based citation tools like Zotero, Endnote, Refworks, and Mendeley.

CITATION STYLE AND CITATION TOOLS

One of the primary reasons students and faculty struggle with both teaching and using citations is the complexity of the various citation manuals and guides. Whether using APA, MLA, Chicago/Turabian, or any of a

TABLE 19.5 *Library Website Study, May 2017*

	Members	Plagiarism (%)	Citation Guide(s) (%)	Citation Tutorial(s) (%)	Workshops (%)	Chart (%)
ARL	124	45	61	17	18	10
CCCU	116	36	38	47	6	9
All Libraries	240	41	50	31	12	10

host of other manuals, there is the constant process of keeping them up-to-date. Often a faculty member may never have used the current edition of a manual of style. Students wrestle with following different styles depending on the course or discipline. Some courses allow students to select their preferred citation style, but others require a particular format, in some cases holding to an older edition because the faculty member feels more comfortable with that particular edition and style. The Library Writing Instruction Survey asked which citation styles are taught (Table 9.6).

Many schools teach and require APA, MLA, and Chicago/Turabian with 84% using one or more of these styles. This question allowed respondents to select multiple answers, therefore the results can be seen to have provided very high percentages, 75% of respondents offering both APA and MLA instruction. The next question asked which styles are taught on the library website (Table 9.7). It was not surprising to note that over 84% teach both APA and MLA and 94% teach APA. The Library Webpage Study did not examine which citation styles were present on websites.

TABLE 19.6 *Which citation styles do you usually cover during instruction?*

	No. of Respondents	% of Respondents	% of Responses
APA	135	76.70	37.29
MLA	132	75.00	36.46
Turabian	25	14.20	6.91
Chicago	42	23.86	11.60
Other	27	15.34	7.46
	Total respondents 176		
	Total responses 362		

TABLE 19.7 *For which citation styles do you provide website instruction?*

	No. of Responses	% of Respondents	% of Responses
NA	3	2.34	0.90
APA	121	94.53	36.12
MLA	108	84.38	32.24
Turabian	30	23.44	8.96
Chicago	52	40.63	15.52
Other	14	10.93	4.18
ACS, ASA, AMA	8	6.25	2.39
	Total respondents 128		
	Total responses 335		

With many librarians investing time teaching citation styles and providing library training materials on their websites, it is clear citation styles are taught. There are also other citation training tools available online. The number one resource for teaching any citation style is the current edition of the style manual. It takes time to build familiarity with a manual, and students should not expect instant understanding. Use of the citation manual is best taught through citation instruction by faculty, the writing center, or academic librarians. To aid in this understanding, many libraries provide webpage guides, tutorials, and examples to guide students. In addition to library guides, there are many websites and electronic citation tools.

CITATION GENERATORS AND CITATION MANAGERS

The citation tools should be grouped into two distinct categories. The more popular formats are the one-shot citation generators. Users type in the citation particulars such as title, author, journal, and so on and choose a citation style: APA, MLA, Chicago, and press a button. The citation generator creates the citation and users then copy the citation. Several popular generators are EasyBib, NoodleBib, BibMe, and Citation Machine. One form of citation generator is built into many research databases such as Ebsco's EDS, ProQuest, and others. These citation tools are the "cite as" database help buttons. The second citation tool category are the citation managers. Managers often harvest records from the database into a citation library. Citations can be grouped and shared. Many citation managers allow users to attach PDFs directly into the citation library. From the citation library, users can produce in-text citations, or full Works Cited lists, which are already alphabetized. Zotero, Endnote, and Refworks are a few of these citation managers. Citation mangers connect to programs like Microsoft Word to directly insert citations and bibliographies. Users need only populate the citation library with the correct information and the citation manager will update the paper in the requested citation style.

Many students already have at least some familiarity with these tools. "According to a 2012 EDUCAUSE study, the number of students using web-based citation/bibliography tools is five time greater than it was in 2010, with 80 percent of undergraduates surveyed indicating that they used these types of tools" (Homol, 2014, p. 552). Homol indicated, however, that many citation tools resulted in "1.5 errors per citation" (Homol, 2014, p. 553). The EDS (EBSCO Discovery Service) citation tool had one of the highest rates of errors, according to Homol. One of the more common errors was with the title. Many databases incorrectly make the title all capital letters, or capitalize every word in the title. APA requires only the first word and any word after punctuation to be capitalized. MLA requires every word except articles to be capitalized (Park, Mardis, & Ury, 2011, p. 44). In order to properly use citation tools "some knowledge of proper citation formats is necessary to use these programs effectively" (Kessler & Van Ullen, 2005, p. 310). The database tools "cite as" should be used as a teaching moment to highlight what is correct and what is incorrect in individual citations. These tools are a helpful avenue to explain citation formats and styles to students.

A study at the University of Delhi found 53% of the students learned about citation tools from the library website (Madhusudhan, 2016, p. 167). This was expressed in several questions on the Library Writing Instruction Survey (Tables 19.8 through 19.11): Do you teach students about citation generators and citation managers? Do you have instructional webpages on citation generators and citation managers?

It was noted that the Library Writing Instruction Survey questions about websites and citation tools showed the largest category of N/A with 53% not presenting citation generators on a website and 33% not presenting citation managers on the website. EasyBib was the most popular citation generator with 19% teaching about it and 16% declaring a website guide about EasyBib. Zotero was the most popular citation manager with 28% teaching about it and 27% having information on the library website. This again led to the Library Webpage Study to explore how many ARL and CCCU libraries taught about citation managers on the library website (Table 19.12).

TABLE 19.8 *Do you instruct on citation generators such as...?*

	No. of Responses	% of Respondents	% of Responses
EasyBib	48	27.27	19.20
NoodleBib	10	5.68	4.00
BibMe	15	8.52	6.00
Citefast	2	1.14	0.80
Citation Machine	15	8.52	6.00
Son of Citation Machine	17	9.66	6.80
"Cite As" (databases)	77	43.75	30.80
Other	66	37.50	26.40
	Total respondents 176		
	Total responses 250		

TABLE 19.9 *Do you instruct students about specific citation managers?*

	No. of Respondents	% of Respondents	% of Responses
Endnote	20	11.36	9.13
RefWorks	33	18.75	15.07
Zotero	51	28.98	23.29
Mendeley	14	7.95	6.39
Papers	3	1.70	1.37
Other	16	9.09	7.31
N/A	82	46.59	37.44
	Total respondents 176		
	Total responses 219		

TABLE 19.10 *Do you have webpages about citation generators such as...?*

	No. of Respondents	% Respondents	% Responses
NA	81	63.28	53.29
EasyBib	21	16.41	13.82
NoodleBib	5	3.91	3.29
BibMe	6	4.69	3.95
Citefast	0	0.00	0.00
Citation Machine	5	3.91	3.29
Son of Citation Machine	3	2.34	1.97
"Cite As" within online databases	11	8.59	7.24
Other	20	15.63	13.16
	Total respondents 128		
	Total responses 152		

TABLE 19.11 *Do you have webpages about specific citation managers?*

	No. of Respondents	% of Respondents	% of Responses
NA	52	40.63	33.77
Endnote	18	14.06	11.69
RefWorks	27	21.09	17.53
Zotero	35	27.34	22.73
Mendeley	9	7.03	5.84
Papers	0	0.00	0.00
Other	13	10.16	8.44
	Total respondents 128		
	Total responses 154		

TABLE 19.12 *Library Website Study, May 2017*

	Members	EndNote (%)	RefWorks (%)	Zotero (%)	Mendeley (%)
ARL	124	41	33	36	22
CCCU	116	5	8	10	1
All Libraries	240	24	21	24	12

The Library Website Study points out a difference between the ARL, which preferred EndNote ,and the CCCU libraries, which preferred Zotero. Zotero is a free alternative citation manager. EndNote can be pricy at around $200; however, there is the EndNote Web free alternative, though it is very limited.

Some educators may question the value of Web-based citation tools and citation managers due to concerns about errors. Still, proper understanding of the citation style will help students to avoid the errors. "Skipping directly to the citation managers may replace what might be a valuable part of the learning and research [process]" (Madhusudhan, 2016, p. 166). Citation instruction and the use of citation managers is critical to the learning process. Many databases lack the proper interface (Park et al., 2011, p. 45) to allow students to clearly recognize the source for proper citation attribution. Students may have trouble recognizing the proper format, book, article, or chapter of a book, and thus end up generating the wrong type of citation. Citation managers may likewise have trouble distinguishing format and generate incorrect citations. It is important not to develop an overreliance or overemphasis on citation managers, especially for undergraduates (Childress, 2011, p. 145). Students are "wrong to assume that the results [from the citation tool] will be error-free" (Mueller, 2009). For this reason Mueller points out that these tools produce a "teaching moment." The citation generators and citation managers are useful tools; if used properly, they can generate good citations, but they are not 100% accurate (Kessler & Van Ullen, 2005, p. 315). Students need citation training and guidance to understand how these tools can be applied.

CONCLUSION

Citation instruction should show correct examples (Mueller, 2009) in various citation styles. This demonstration can be done in a class presentation or on a library website. Many of the libraries that have resources counted by the Library Website Study used Springshare LibGuides as the primary tool to display citation styles and citation tools (Table 19.13).

The citation styles frequently included both APA and MLA in more than 75% of the libraries, according to the Library Writing Instruction Survey. These library guides showed many examples and often provided links to the style guide publishers and other premier websites dealing with citation style guides and tutorials. "Some librarians question whether students will ever learn to cite properly if they do not learn to do it manually first" (Kessler & Van Ullen, 2005, p. 311). Teaching citation skills, whether by faculty, writing center, or by academic librarians can be enhanced by citation guides on the library website, citation generators, and citation managers. In order to participate in the community of scholarship in their chosen discipline, students must learn to value the scholarship and ideas of others and demonstrate that respect with appropriate citations. Teaching citation styles, providing access to citation generators, citation managers, and online library citation guides all help to train the next generation of expert information-seeking writers.

TABLE 19.13 *Library Website Study, May 2017*

	Members	Plagiarism (%)	Citation Guide(s) (%)	Citation Tutorial(s) (%)	Workshops (%)	Chart (%)	EndNote (%)	RefWorks (%)	Zotero (%)	Mendeley (%)
ARL	124	45	61	17	18	10	41	33	36	22
CCCU	116	36	38	47	6	9	5	8	10	1
All Libraries	240	41	50	31	12	10	24	21	24	12

REFERENCES

Association of College and Research Libraries (ACRL). (2015). *Framework for information literacy for higher education* [Online]. Retrieved July 19, 2017, from http://www.ala.org/acrl/standards/ilframework

Childress, D. (2011). Citation tools in academic libraries: Best practices for reference and instruction. *Reference & User Services Quarterly, 51*(2), 143–152.

Homol, L. (2014). Web-based citation management tools: Comparing the accuracy of their electronic journal citations. *Journal of Academic Librarianship, 40*(6), 552–557. https://doi.org/10.1016/j.acalib.2014.09.011

Kessler, J., & Van Ullen, M. K. (2005). Citation generators: Generating bibliographies for the next generation. *Journal of Academic Librarianship, 31*(4), 310–316. https://doi.org/10.1016/j.acalib.2005.04.012

Leckie, G. J. (1996). Desperately seeking citations: Uncovering faculty assumptions about the undergraduate research process. *Journal of Academic Librarianship, 22*(3), 201–208. https://doi.org/10.1016/S0099-1333(96)90059-2

Leverenz, C. S. (1998). Citing cybersources: A challenge to disciplinary values. *Computers and Composition, 15*(2), 185–200. https://doi.org/10.1016/S8755-4615(98)90053-6

Madhusudhan, M. (2016). Use of online citation tools by students and research scholars of Department of Library and Information Science, University of Delhi. *DESIDOC Journal of Library and Information Technology, 36*(3), 164–172. https://doi.org/10.14429/djlit.36.3.9428

Mansourizadeh, K., & Ahmad, U. K. (2011). Citation practices among non-native expert and novice scientific writers. *Journal of English for Academic Purposes, 10*(3), 152–161. https://doi.org/10.1016/j.jeap.2011.03.004

Mueller, S. (2009). Database citation generators: Generating what, exactly? *Writing Lab Newsletter, 33*(6), 6.

Park, S., Mardis, L. A., & Ury, C. J. (2011). I've lost my identity oh, there it is . . . in a style manual: Teaching citation styles and academic honesty. *Reference Services Review, 39*(1), 42–57. https://doi.org/10.1108/00907321111108105

Robillard, A. E. (2006). "Young Scholars" affecting composition: A challenge to disciplinary citation practices. *College English, 68*(3), 253–270. https://doi.org/10.2307/25472151

Rose, S. (1989, March). *Citation rituals in academic cultures*. Presented at the Annual Meeting of the Conference of College Composition and Communications (40th, Seattle, WA, March 16–18, 1989). Retrieved from ERIC Database (ED309434).

Stevens, C. R. (2016). Citation generators, OWL, and the persistence of error-ridden references: An assessment for learning approach to citation errors. *Journal of Academic Librarianship, 42*(6), 712–718. https://doi.org/10.1016/j.acalib.2016.07.003

Wilson, D. (2016). Managing an information literacy needs assessment across multiple campuses. *Library Leadership and Management, 31*(1), 1–22.

CHAPTER 20

LEARNING IN THE MIDDLE

Writing Centers as Sponsors of Information Literacy Across the University

Katie McWain

INTRODUCTION

Uniquely positioned in the space between writing studies and information literacy studies, writing centers are a hub for cross-disciplinary and cross-program collaboration in higher education. Writing center professionals not only work one-to-one with student writers, but also partner with faculty and program staff to facilitate workshops and information sessions on topics ranging from crafting annotated bibliographies and publishing science manuscripts to applying for specialized scholarships and designing computer programming problem sets. In today's constantly shifting configuration of academic units on campus, writing center staff must move agilely between the roles of research facilitators and writing facilitators, offering an invaluable institutional perspective for sponsoring information literacy across the university.

Located as they are in this institutional boundary space, writing centers also provide opportunities for enacting and fostering the commitments outlined in the ACRL's *Framework for Information Literacy for Higher Education* (2015). Many of goals articulated in the *Framework* overlap with writing center pedagogy, including engaging inquiry as a process (p. 2), fostering metaliteracy (p. 2), and expanding the "one-shot" model of instruction (p. 10). Writing studies scholars such as Linda Adler-Kassner and Elizabeth Wardle (2015) have also echoed the *Framework*'s call to articulate and explore disciplinary threshold concepts in order to facilitate student transfer of knowledge, a key concern of writing center work. The ACRL's commitments are especially relevant in light of the writing center's increasing responsibility for cross-disciplinary outreach; like librarians, writing center staff may only have one class meeting or tutoring session to familiarize students with information literacy in their discipline.

Furthermore, as James Elmborg (2006) has noted, writing centers function as mediators between faculty and students, sponsoring "the daily transactions of academic commerce, a form of work that is undervalued or even unvalued by other academics" (p. 9). Such work tends to be nuanced, relational, and complex, such as translating unclear assignment guidelines for a confused writer or helping a professor craft a collaborative workshop that engages students while also requiring them to meet specific research and writing objectives. In these often invisible transactions, writing center staff must accommodate and advocate for student writers' needs while also addressing the complex informational, pedagogical, and rhetorical needs of faculty—a position requiring significant institutional flexibility and awareness.

While the *Framework* focuses primarily on students' development of information literacy, writing centers also sponsor cross-disciplinary information literacy among faculty and staff, a responsibility that is important yet often overlooked. For example, over the course of a semester, the same consultant might develop an undergraduate research workshop in collaboration with a STEM professor, work with faculty to scaffold required writing center visits for dissertating graduate students, or lead a résumé workshop alongside college advising staff—all interactions geared toward the development of information literacy. In order to negotiate this complex positionality as mediator among students, faculty, and academic programs, writing center professionals need flexible strategies for tapping into information literacy knowledge across disciplines and sponsoring student writers' access to and engagement with this knowledge.

COMMON CHALLENGES FOR WRITING CENTERS AS INFORMATION LITERACY SPONSORS

While cross-disciplinary and cross-program collaborations are fruitful opportunities for sponsoring the development of information literacy, writing center staff can face significant obstacles in conducting this work. Challenges often take the form of faculty and student misconceptions or lack of knowledge about the writing center's purpose, pedagogy, and policies.

Faculty and Students May Have a Limited Understanding of Writing Centers

Scholarship dating back to Stephen North's (1984) foundational missive "The Idea of a Writing Center" has outlined the prevalence of misguided faculty assumptions about writing centers, including faculty from English departments. These assumptions might include that the writing center is a remedial service; that it relieves instructors of the responsibility for teaching writing; that it serves as a "fix-it" shop where students can have their papers edited; that the tutor-student relationship poses a threat to academic integrity; or that a writing center consultation is designed to focus solely on grammar, syntax, and other sentence-level concerns, rather than on brainstorming, discussing ideas, facilitating substantive revision, or developing information literacy. Students may share these notions about the writing center, viewing it as a place where struggling writers go for help or a drop-off proofreading service. Outside of mistaken assumptions, many faculty members are simply unaware that the writing center exists as a resource not only for their students, but also for them—missing out on the wealth of collaborations they might pursue in working on their own writing, solving pedagogical problems, designing assignments, or helping students acquire a range of skills. Faculty may also be uninformed about the powerful role writing centers can play in facilitating information literacy across disciplines outside of English, from an introductory computer science course to a graduate program in plant health.

Faculty and Students May Have a Limited Understanding of Writing Studies, Writing Pedagogy, and the Writing Process

While most writing centers characterize their mission as assisting writers, rather than improving pieces of writing (North, 1984)—a focus on process and learning rather than producing perfect texts—this mission is not necessarily shared across university campuses. Not every discipline has a scholarly interest in pedagogy or the development of habits of mind such as those outlined in the ACRL's *Framework*, and faculty do not always have access to professional development in teaching writing or process pedagogy. Furthermore, students and faculty may have different priorities for writing and research tasks: while a student might visit the writing center with the goal of earning a higher score on an assignment, a faculty member may hope to receive papers that are error-free and therefore deemed easier to read. Conversely, many writing center staff members can recount stories of appointments where writers arrived hoping to have a paper polished, but instead spent the entire session learning how to use the university's library databases or tracing sources backward from a references page—noting afterward how helpful they found the experience. While this encounter might not reflect a visibly improved written product, it nevertheless contributes significantly to the development of information literacy skills. Unfortunately, such growth in learning might not be observable to the faculty member who receives the assignment submission after recommending the student visit the writing center, furthering misconceptions about the writing process and writing development: for example, that the ultimate goal of writing is a polished final text, that revision and proofreading are synonymous, or that a student needs to master basic sentence-level skills before engaging with more complex content and ideas.

Writing Center Staff May Feel Less Confident Offering Assistance to Writers in Other Disciplines or Programs

The challenges of working with writers in contexts outside of English and composition studies have been studied extensively in scholarship on writing across the curriculum (WAC) and writing in the disciplines (WID). Jean Kiedaisch and Sue Dinitz's (1993) research, for example, questions the effectiveness of a generalist writing tutor for consulting with discipline-specific assignments. As early as 1988, Susan M. Hubbuch inquired into the relationship between tutoring and subject matter, ultimately arguing that the best-qualified tutor "should be literate in the way that the ideal liberal arts education defines literacy"—being able to understand the conventions of a specific genre and field, approaching writing with a stance of logical inquiry, and cultivating intellectual skepticism (pp. 29–30). Although most consultants consider themselves generally competent writers with an interest and ability in helping other writers, research reveals that this confidence can break down in the face of unfamiliar genres, educational levels, or program needs. An undergraduate tutor who has never been published, for example, might feel intimidated by the task of assisting a writing center director with a workshop on targeting health science journals for publication in a graduate course. Even a seasoned graduate tutor or administrator might experience doubts about her ability to help a statistics student incorporate equations smoothly into a text or create a rhetorically effective linear regression table. In the same way, writers sometimes view their tutors as lacking expertise in subjects and contexts outside of English, expecting help with grammar and correctness rather than with skills such as evaluating journal articles in the hard sciences or determining the appropriate moves to make in a grant proposal. These assumptions can limit the ability of writing center staff, faculty, and students alike to draw on one another's prior knowledge and contexts in effectively collaborative ways.

Limitations on Time and Staff Resources Make Quality Collaborations Difficult to Scaffold

In the increasingly budget-strapped landscape of higher education, writing centers, libraries, and other academic programs are having to make difficult decisions about staffing, pay, hours, services, and the commitments they are ethically and logistically able to make. As a result, it may seem easier to create one generalized "Research Workshop" or "Citation Workshop" for writing center staff to deliver in a variety of contexts, rather than to collaborate extensively with faculty on creating multiple, unique information literacy resources tailored to particular needs. Encouraging writing center staff to focus on quality of collaborations over quantity is also difficult when directors feel pressured to produce evidence of their campus use value through engagement statistics and lists of services provided. Unfortunately, the most effective cross-disciplinary collaborations may not produce quantitative results that can be easily measured by an institutional research office or department budget allocations.

THEORETICAL FRAMEWORKS FOR INFORMATION LITERACY SPONSORSHIP

Research from writing center theory and information literacy studies offers useful lenses for reframing cross-disciplinary and cross-program collaborations in light of these challenges. Here are three significant theoretical takeaways for writing centers to consider implementing:

Shift From a Paradigm of Writing Versus Research to a Paradigm of Research-Writing

One of the foundational contributions of the recent collection *Rewired: Research-Writing Partnerships Within the Frameworks* (McClure, 2016), which focuses on productive connections between the ACRL's *Framework* (2015) and the Council of Writing Program Administrators' *WPA Outcomes Statement for First-Year Composition* (2014), is the idea of research-writing. As Randall McClure described it,

> Writing cannot escape research just as, in nearly all cases, researching leads to writing, whether the writing is a set of mental notes or a formal academic paper. To this end, we rewire the concept and use research-writing to highlight this partnership. (p. xii)

This notion of research-writing emphasizes the interdependence between writing studies and information literacy—between acquiring information and presenting information—and discourages focusing on one half of the skillset while ignoring the other. It is also a fundamental tenet of writing center work, the primary purpose of which is to assist writers at any stage of the process, from developing a research question to revising a conclusion. This interconnection between research process and writing process should feature more prominently in writing center staff development as well as in our cross-disciplinary outreach and communication.

Along the same lines, Susan Miller-Cochran (2016) noted the importance of working "to move beyond the binary and rethink how research-writing could be taught from a rhetorical perspective" (p. 298). Writing center professionals are by nature well versed in rhetoric and rhetorical theory, as well as in problematizing binaries, and can bring this theoretical stance to bear on our conversations with writers and faculty members alike. For example, if a professor constructs a potential collaboration as "I'm teaching the content and research, while you can teach the writing," the research-writing framework is a helpful theoretical tool for underscoring the rhetorical nature of all knowledge and information and can be a grounding commitment for our work with writers in disciplines across the university. Imagine, for example, a more productive response from a writing center administrator to the faculty member above:

> I'm really interested to learn more about the skills and knowledge you want students to develop through this assignment. The research in my field has found a strong connection among writing, understanding

content, and developing information literacy, and students use rhetorical knowledge in each area, so I'd love to work together on all of those elements with you.

Adopt the Stance of a Disciplinary Sociologist

While no writing center professional can be an expert—or even conversant—in every discipline, we can take an anthropological approach to interdisciplinarity that allows us to focus on threshold concepts and discourse conventions, and draw on existing metaliteracy. James K. Elmborg and Sheril Hook (2005) described this stance in their research on writing center-library partnerships:

> Librarians and writing teachers need to become more like anthropologists or sociologists in their study of academic disciplines. Although the advanced knowledge of the disciplines or specialties may be out of reach for these teachers, a sociologist's understanding of the cultures of these departments is not. (p. 13)

Acting as a disciplinary sociologist—or a program sociologist, or a sociologist of a particular course section—might involve the following steps for a writing center professional establishing a new partnership:

- Begin with an observational period. At the start of a collaboration, it's important to listen and pay attention to what faculty are already doing in a particular discipline or program. Acquire a sense of how they talk about their subject, how they talk to and about students, and the kinds of moves that characterize their discourse.
- Once you've established an initial connection, ask important questions about learning goals, practices, challenges, and expectations (see Table 20.1 for specific examples). Use the same terms the faculty member uses and make sure you understand them in context so that you can develop a shared language. Take field notes and annotate your findings to facilitate returning to them later.
- Think of yourself as a participant observer in disciplinary activities, rather than an interloper. When you visit a class or lead a workshop, ask other participants to share their customs and conventions with you. If their disciplinary community is most comfortable with lectures, see if you can incorporate aspects of this model into your collaboration. If they view objectivity or neutrality as a valuable stance, consider how you might inquire into this value in productive ways from a research-writing perspective.

A sociological approach encourages writing center representatives to gather information and participate in the activities of an outside discipline or program without simply appropriating or interceding in the established culture. It also allows them to develop cultural knowledge that will enrich future collaborations with writers, faculty, and staff across the university.

Practice a Multifaceted Theory of Conflicted Collaborations

Roberta D. Kjesrud and Mary A. Wislocki (2011) outlined a helpful and nuanced theoretical approach to writing center collaborations with administration, explaining that "A multifaceted theory of conflicted collaborations requires an enriched, layered praxis to help us achieve what is for most of us a daunting task: embracing administrative conflict both intellectually and emotionally" (p. 105). This theory of collaboration is also applicable to writing center interactions with cross-disciplinary and cross-program faculty and staff, as well as to information literacy sponsorship, which can benefit from the same thoughtful steps proposed by Kjesrud and Wislocki:

- Developing a rhetoric of inquiry
- Learning to reflect critically when emotions run high
- Balancing our advocacy with dialogue
- Considering the writing center community's role in professional development. (p. 91)

These recommendations build on the affective and interpersonal dynamics of collaboration, which are often undertheorized in academic contexts. They also draw writing center staff's attention to dispositions and habits of mind—similar to those advocated by the ACRL's *Framework* and WPA's *Outcomes* statement—rather than to a concrete product or success metric. This focus on inquiry, critical reflection, dialogue, and the role of the writing center through "enriched, layered praxis" might take many forms, some of which are outlined in the following section. Ultimately, the most important aspect of this theoretical framework is acknowledging and accounting for the intellectual and emotional work involved in cross-disciplinary and cross-program collaborations.

APPLICATION

Drawing on the theoretical frameworks outlined above, writing centers, librarians, faculty, and staff can implement key principles and actions in order to facilitate more effective cross-disciplinary information literacy sponsorship.

Design Collaborations Intentionally and Holistically

In the efficiency culture of higher education, collaboration is often by necessity designed to be quick, easy, and superficial. Approaching these partnerships with greater intentionality and with a holistic attention to development, design, and inquiry can facilitate the sponsorship of informational literacy skills in a more meaningful way. Table 20.1 provides a heuristic for three primary goals of successful writing center collaborations across the university, which writing center professionals, staff, faculty, and students might all draw upon in their work together.

Involve Multiple Stakeholders in Partnership Planning

While it is important for writing center directors and faculty members to work together at the beginning of a new collaboration, theirs are not the only perspectives that should be represented and considered in a cross-disciplinary or cross-program collaboration. Involving tutors, librarians, students from the course/program, and program staff members in the design and evaluation of a partnership will ensure it is more mutually beneficial for all parties. For example, faculty might ask students to write down questions they have about an assignment before a writing center class facilitation, or tutors might administer an exit survey to participants after a job application workshop to find out what was most and least useful. Similarly, a writing center director and librarian could work together to develop a research guide for a faculty member teaching an introductory law course that

TABLE 20.1 *Heuristic for Cross-Disciplinary and Cross-Program Collaborations Geared Toward Writing Center Sponsorship of Information Literacy*

Collaboration Goal	Generative Activities	Guiding Questions
Determining the goals and assets of the partnership	• Inventory meetings • Developing threshold concepts	• What drives the writing in your discipline? • What kinds of informational materials do you want your students to be literate in?[1] • What habits of mind would you like students to develop? • What is the specific context of your program/class/department?
Scaffolding partnership activities	• Backward design • Student piloting	• What are the smaller skills students will need to practice in order to reach the identified goal(s)? What types of knowledge will they need to access? • What challenges will students encounter? • What resources will help students navigate these challenges? • What knowledge or abilities can the writing center offer?
Assessing, documenting, and improving partnerships	• Partnership logs • Exit reflections	• How did students experience the partnership? • What were the key challenges of the partnership? Key assets? • What might future partnerships do differently? • How and where can partnership materials be stored or disseminated for future access?

[1]These first two questions came from a presentation at the 2017 Conference on College Composition and Communication. The session, entitled "Outcomes and Frameworks: Cultivating Information Literacy in Composition Classrooms," was facilitated by Margaret Atman, Erica Frisicaro-Pawlowski, Julie Slaby, and Robert Monge.

students in the class could then pilot for usability and accessibility.

Cultivate Faculty Metaliteracy

Rick Fisher and Kaisja Calkins (2016) conducted a study of faculty constructions of research-writing in syllabi from 67 sections of advanced communication courses at their institution. They concluded that writing and research professionals "need to help faculty identify the specific disciplinary skills and expectations of research-writing in their fields. Achieving the goal of metaliteracy for students requires a metaliteracy of faculty" (p. 36). However, faculty members' metaliteracy is often tacit and deeply ingrained. Seasoned professors may also lack practice in articulating what they know, especially to audiences outside of their disciplines. Writing center professionals can thus help unpack this metaliteracy by asking probing questions:

- What are the key priorities, commitments, and values for someone in your field?
- What are the common moves a writer in your discipline makes?
- What are the resources you turn to when you encounter research and writing challenges in your area?
- What are the primary genres in which you want students to feel comfortable writing?

What are the skills or habits of mind that might help them succeed in those genres?
- What is your own research and writing process like? What are the steps involved when you approach a new text or project?
- How did you learn how to research and write in your discipline as an undergraduate and graduate student? What was most helpful to you during this process of development, then and now?

Michael Carter's (2007) research on writing in the disciplines offers another useful lens for this work with professors, which he describes as "ways of doing":

> One way of helping faculty understand the integral role of writing in their various disciplines is to present disciplines as ways of doing, which links ways of knowing and writing in the disciplines. Ways of doing identified by faculty are used to describe broader general and disciplinary structures, metagenres, and metadisciplines. (p. 385)

This framework might lead to even simpler, more general inventory-taking questions to use as an opening strategy:

- How do people *do* things in your discipline?
- How do people *know* things in your discipline?
- How do people *write* things in your discipline?

Work to Make Institutional Discourse "Stick"

Facilitating cross-disciplinary and cross-program collaboration requires a significant amount of communication, from making initial contacts with names listed on department websites to sending e-mails hashing out the details of a workshop to exchanging a draft of an assignment or an agenda with a professor. Faculty members and staff across the university often operate within different discourse communities and use different terminology, norms, and conventions to exchange information. One strategy for helping writing center professionals cross these discourse boundaries is the idea of stickiness, proposed by Muriel Harris (2010) in the context of effective institutional rhetoric. Harris describes "stickiness" as follows:

> writing that is positive, appeals appropriately to our audiences, is highly memorable, and is concrete and specific. The goal of writing in sticky ways to our local constituencies is that they will understand and correctly remember who we are and what we contribute to the progress of student writing (pp. 48–49)

As an example, Harris offered the strategy of phrasing messages affirmatively (talking about what the writing center does or can do) rather than negatively (talking about what the writing center does not, cannot, or will not do) (p. 55). This is an especially important strategy in initial communications and inventory meetings with faculty who may assume the writing center will offer a one-time, generalized introduction on "how to write." Keeping our institutional discourse memorable, concrete, and specific—such as providing program directors with tangible examples of the activities we might co-facilitate—will help writing center professionals pave the way for more productive conversations.

Consider Cross-Training of Library Staff and Writing Center Staff

This strategy is derived from from Elmborg and Hook (2005), who explained its usefulness as follows:

> Writing tutors can refer students to librarians for information needs and librarians can refer students to writing centers for help with ideas, rhetoric, or presentation. Cross-training of tutors and librarians can help increase the likelihood that such referring will take place appropriately. (p. 11)

Writing center professionals and librarians are both fundamentally committed to fostering research-writing and can draw upon one another's knowledge and skill sets in service of this goal. For example, orientation for new writing center consultants might include a visit from a library staff member to share some of the information resources the library can provide not only to students, but also to faculty and tutors. Both student workers and full-time workers on the library staff can hear from writing center professionals about opportunities for collaboration, scaffolding the writing process, and the overlapping commitments and threshold concepts of each party. If writing centers and libraries view themselves as allies in the sponsorship of information literacy, they will be able to promote richer and more layered collaborations across the university. For example, while making writing center consultants and library staff available to students in the same physical space could be a useful move, a more authentic collaboration might involve a librarian and writing tutor visiting a sociology course together to facilitate a "Working with Sources in Sociology" workshop they created in consultation with the professor.

Consider Developing a Writing Fellows Program

In order to facilitate quality collaborations that are theoretically informed and enact "richly layered praxis," writing centers might consider implementing a writing fellows program. Within this model, undergraduate writing consultants who receive specialized training in peer tutoring and writing in the disciplines partner with faculty to work with student writers in a particular class. Writing fellows typically meet with the same students regularly and provide sustained feedback and assistance on their evolving projects. These collaborations are more embedded and intensive than one-shot tutoring because they often extend the same partnership throughout an entire semester and involve the contributions of multiple stakeholders (faculty, students, and tutors) to the same writing context. Writing fellows also facilitate the development of information literacy by foregrounding threshold concepts, metaliteracy, and disciplinary conventions over the course of tutors' work with students. As Jeanne Marie Rose and Laurie Grobman found, undergraduate writing fellows are "poised to apply their tutoring knowledge to address real-world institutional needs" (2010, p. 11), an essential aspect of meaningful collaboration.

Remember That Academic Literacy and Institutional Literacy Are Also Information Literacy

As research-writing professionals, writing center staff often find themselves introducing students to university programs, requirements, and resources in addition to working with concrete writing projects. For example, tutors might help students learn to navigate the online library catalog, draft an e-mail to a professor with questions about an assignment, or connect with career services if they have more specific questions about job application documents. Undergraduate writers must learn to negotiate a vast network of institutional policies and procedures as well as avail themselves of the support systems designed for them. While this may seem outside the purview of writing center work, institutional literacy is nevertheless also a form of information literacy, and cross-disciplinary and cross-program collaborations can help foster the development of this literacy by foregrounding the specific institutional knowledge and skills students might need or draw upon in order to succeed on a particular task.

SUMMARY

Today's writing centers serve as a hub for cross-disciplinary and cross-program sponsorship of information literacy in higher education. Writing center professionals not only work one-to-one with student writers in this capacity, but also partner with faculty and program staff in myriad configurations. Located in this institutional boundary space, writing centers also provide opportunities for enacting and fostering the commitments outlined in the ACRL's *Framework* (2015). Writing center staff must move agilely between the roles of research facilitators and writing facilitators, offering an invaluable institutional perspective on information literacy. In order to negotiate this complex positionality as mediator among students, faculty, and academic programs, writing center professionals need flexible strategies for tapping into information literacy knowledge across disciplines and sponsoring student writers' access to and engagement with this knowledge.

Writing centers encounter significant challenges in facilitating this kind of work, including potential misconceptions about writing centers, writing pedagogy, and the writing process. Writing center staff may feel less confident offering assistance in outside disciplines or programs, and limitations on time and staff resources make quality collaborations difficult to scaffold. Theoretical frameworks drawn from writing center scholarship and information literacy studies can provide a useful grounding for addressing the challenges of cross-institutional collaborations. These include shifting from a paradigm of writing versus research to a paradigm of research-writing, adopting the stance of a disciplinary sociologist, and practicing a multifaceted theory of conflicted collaborations. Writing center professionals can apply these frameworks by designing partnerships intentionally and holistically, incorporating tools such as collaboration heuristics, and involving multiple stakeholders in programming planning. They should also strive to cultivate metaliteracy among students, faculty, and staff and make their institutional discourse "stick." Centers might also consider implementing cross-training of library staff and writing center staff and developing a writing fellows program. Finally, writing centers can help stakeholders across the university to understand that academic literacy and institutional literacy are also forms of information literacy.

REFERENCES

Adler-Kassner, L., & Wardle, E. (Eds.). (2015). *Naming what we know: Threshold concepts of writing studies*. Boulder, CO: University Press of Colorado.

Association of College and Research Libraries. (2015). *Framework for information literacy for higher education.* Retrieved from http://www.ala.org/acrl/standards/ilframework

Carter, M. (2007). Ways of knowing, doing, and writing in the disciplines. *College Composition and Communication, 58*(3), 385–418.

Council of Writing Program Administrators. (2014). *WPA outcomes statement for first-year composition* (3.0). Retrieved from http://wpacouncil.org/positions/outcomes.html

Elmborg, J. (2006). Locating the center: Libraries, writing centers, and information literacy. *WLN: A Journal of Writing Center Theory, 30*(6), 7–11.

Elmborg, J. K., & Hook, S. (2005). *Centers for learning: Writing centers and libraries in collaboration*. Chicago, IL: Association of College and Research Libraries.

Fisher, R., & Calkins, K. (2016). Interpreting the *Frameworks*: Faculty constructions of research and the researching student. In R. McClure (Ed.), *Rewired: Research-writing partnerships within the* Frameworks (pp. 19–41). Chicago, IL: Association of College and Research Libraries.

Harris, M. (2010). Making our institutional discourse sticky: Suggestions for effective rhetoric. *Writing Center Journal, 30*(2), 47–71.

Hubbuch, S. M. (1988). A tutor needs to know the subject matter to help a student with a paper: ___agree ___disagree ___not sure. *Writing Center Journal, 8*(2), 23–30.

Kiedaisch, J., & Dinitz, S. (1993). "Look back and say "so what": The limitations of a generalist tutor. *Writing Center Journal, 14*(1), 63–74.

Kjesrud, R. D., & Wislocki, M. A. (2011). Learning and leading through conflicted collaborations. *Writing Center Journal, 31*(2), 89–116.

McClure, R. (Ed.). (2016). *Rewired: Research-writing partnerships within the* Frameworks. Chicago, IL: Association of College and Research Libraries.

Miller-Cochran, S. (2016). Afterword: Building meaningful, institution-specific partnerships. In R. McClure (Ed.), *Rewired: Research-writing partnerships within the* Frameworks (pp. 297–299). Chicago, IL: Association of College and Research Libraries.

North, S. (1984). The idea of a writing center. *College English, 46*(5), 433–446.

Rose, J. M., & Grobman, L. (2010). Scholarship reconsidered: Tutor-scholars as undergraduate researchers. *WLN: A Journal of Writing Center Theory, 34*(8), 10–13.

CHAPTER 21

A CONVERSATION

Academic and Workplace Information Skills

Barry Maid
Barbara J. D'Angelo

Scholars writing about information literacy (IL) and writing studies (WS) usually focus on academic writing. Given the number of partnerships and collaborations between librarians and first-year writing faculty, this is not surprising. Students need to learn how to use information effectively in an academic environment as they progress through their remaining college courses. However, a significant amount of research and writing that students do is applied. This is especially true for students in applied or professional degree programs. For the majority of both undergraduate and graduate students, the skills, including information skills, they learn in applied writing courses are the ones they will use most often in their future careers.

We argue that viewing both IL and writing within the framework of threshold concepts facilitates the teaching and learning of IL and writing and prepares individuals to understand the contextual nature of communicating in today's complex information environment (Maid & D'Angelo, 2017). As such, the emphasis on effective IL and writing becomes less focused on mechanical skills, whether they be the details of a specific database or grammar or citation practices, and more focused on the rhetorical practices of understanding audience and purpose and making the most effective decisions—including mechanical issues—within those constructs.

The ACRL *Framework for Information Literacy for Higher Education* (*Framework for IL*) is grounded in threshold concepts and metaliteracy. A collaborative project to identify threshold concepts for WS has identified Writing as a Rhetorical and Social Act as a threshold concept. For this chapter, we focus on the frame Scholarship as Conversation from the *Framework for IL* and Writing as a Rhetorical and Social Act from *Naming What We Know: Threshold Concepts of Writing Studies* (Adler-Kassner & Wardle, 2015) to explore and unpack how graduate students use information skills depending on whether they are writing an academic thesis or an applied project.

In traditional graduate study students are typically introduced to "academic conversations" and are expected to produce a culminating project—an academic thesis—where they take part in the professional scholarly conversation. However, students in applied professional programs often compose an applied project. The applied project forces students to engage in multiple professional conversations. They may be required to contextualize their work both within the academic scholarship of their area of study as well as within the workplace context. In our Master of Science (MS) in Technical Communication (TC) Program, students have the option to create an applied project consisting of a workplace deliverable that is targeted for a professional workplace audience. They also write a metacognitive statement articulating both the rationale for the project itself—why it is appropriate for the field and industry—as well as how and why they constructed the workplace deliverable. In that metacognitive statement, students need to take part in Scholarship as Conversation and Writing as a Rhetorical and Social Act. Students explain how they have obtained, processed, analyzed, and applied information to construct an appropriate workplace deliverable targeted to accomplish a particular task for a particular audience. Helping students learn how to engage in those conversations to shift discourses between academic and workplace audiences is challenging, but ultimately facilitates their ability to become information literate and successful communicators.

THE *FRAMEWORK FOR IL*: THRESHOLD CONCEPTS AND METALITERACY

Threshold concepts, for those not completely familiar with the idea, were proposed in the early 2000s by British researchers Jan Meyer and Ray Land as a way to better understand how people learn. Meyer and Land (2006) say:

> A threshold concept can be considered as akin to a portal, opening up a new and previously inaccessible way of thinking about something. It represents a transformed way of understanding, or interpreting, or viewing something without which the learner cannot progress. (p. 3)

Threshold concepts are characterized as transformative, irreversible, integrative, bounded, and troublesome. As such, individuals attempting to learn knowledge associated with threshold concepts may have difficulty and may show resistance since the new knowledge threatens their old way of thinking and being. Crossing the portal of a threshold concept, therefore, may result in a state of liminality—the in-between state in which the individual is learning and attempting to reconcile the old and new (and the loss of the old as they adopt the new) but has not yet been transformed.

The *Framework for IL* is grounded in threshold concepts as well as in metaliteracy. According to Trudi Jacobson and Thomas Mackey (Mackey & Jacobson, 2011), who defined the term:

> Metaliteracy promotes critical thinking and collaboration in a digital age, providing a comprehensive framework to effectively participate in social media and online communities. It is a unified construct that supports the acquisition, production, and sharing of knowledge in collaborative online communities. Metaliteracy challenges traditional skills-based approaches to information literacy by recognizing related literacy types and incorporating emerging technologies. (p. 62)

The underlying principle of metaliteracy is the recognition that students are, themselves, producers of information as well as consumers of it. Metacognition is also key as one of the metaliterate domains for learning—individuals' reflective understanding of how and why they learn and how to continue to learn.

There are six frames in the *Framework for IL*, each with associated dispositions and knowledge practices. They are:

- Authority Is Constructed and Contextual
- Information Creation as a Process
- Information Has Value
- Research as Inquiry
- Scholarship as Conversation
- Searching as Strategic Exploration

In many ways, these frames mirror the threshold concepts identified in a collaborative project of WS scholars led by Linda Adler-Kassner and Elizabeth Wardle . The five threshold concepts identified for WS by these scholars are:

- Writing Is a Social and Rhetorical Act
- Writing Speaks to Situations Through Recognizable Forms
- Writing Enacts and Creates Identities and Ideologies
- All Writers Have More to Learn
- Writing Is (Also Always) a Cognitive Activity

THE RHETORICAL AND SOCIAL ACT OF SCHOLARSHIP AS CONVERSATION

For this chapter, we focus mainly, though not exclusively, on the frame Scholarship as Conversation from the *Framework for IL* and Writing as a Rhetorical and Social Act (Adler-Kassner & Wardle, 2015) to explore and unpack how graduate students use information skills depending on whether they are writing an academic thesis or an applied project. When we shaped our MS in TC Program, we gave our students the option to write a traditional academic thesis or to create a workplace deliverable (not necessarily a text document) that is targeted for a professional workplace audience accompanied by a metacognitive statement. In other words, we ask them to engage in the type of metacognition that is a key principle underlying metaliteracy and threshold concepts. Our intent was that students who compose a thesis would enter into the academic conversation of the discipline as they prepare themselves to apply to doctoral programs (or other more academically inclined work). Part of that conversation would be an emerging fluency with the discourse of the field, research practices, and information practices. Students who choose the applied project, on the other hand, would demonstrate application of what they learned through their workplace deliverable and reflect upon how that application of learning showed their trajectory as emerging and growing professionals in the field. In both cases, we hope, students also recognize and acknowledge that their work (whether it be a thesis or workplace deliverable) is a contribution to the conversation. In the case of a thesis, it is a contribution to the scholarly research and discourse to contribute and share knowledge to advance the field. In the case of an applied project, the contribution is more specific to the workplace or, more broadly, the industry to facilitate improvement or solve problems.

In the metacognitive statement it is necessary, therefore, for students to take part in Scholarship as Conversation as well as Writing as a Rhetorical and Social Act. Indeed, Scholarship as Conversation is a rhetorical and social act since the requirements for the paper is that students reflect upon and articulate how their work is part of the conversation of their field. In addition, students must explain how they have obtained, processed, analyzed, and applied information to construct an appropriate workplace deliverable targeted to accomplish a particular task for a particular audience. In doing so, they articulate the rhetorical and social nature of their work.

THE BEST OF INTENTIONS

We believed all of that when we created the requirement. We still believe that. However, during the last academic year when we granted MS degrees to our first group of graduate students, we began to realize that while the workplace deliverable piece of their applied project demonstrated application of their learning, our students all had a difficult time articulating "what they did" and "what they knew" in their metacognitive statement.

Naturally, we were a bit confused with our results. On the one hand, we were pleased that our students consistently showed themselves capable of producing the kinds of deliverables they will be expected to produce in the workplace. On the other hand, they seemed hopelessly confused by the task of telling us what, how, and most importantly why they created the deliverable the way they did.

In retrospect, we shouldn't have been surprised. As Yancey, Robertson, and Taczak (2014) discovered in their research on teaching for transfer, students must learn a vocabulary or language in order to be able to engage in and articulate metacognition. For all kinds of reasons, asking our students to produce a metacognitive statement of their workplace deliverable was a much more difficult task than we had assumed. We should have known better. The easy answer to why our students demonstrated confusion with the metacognitive statement was that we were asking them to produce a genre they had little familiarity with. While both authors use metacognitive writing in their courses, we are now assuming students have very little practice with it in their other coursework. When composing the cover statement, then, our students responded in different, unique ways—though clearly confused. In many ways, students were quite capable of describing what they had done and explaining what they applied by picking and choosing concepts from courses they had taken. This is not surprising. As technical communication students, they were competent in the genre of "procedures" in which description predominates. But their statements tended to lack the kind of metacognition we were after. To ascribe their problems to an unfamiliarity with the genre—metacognition—would actually be similar to what we saw in those students who chose a traditional academic thesis. Anyone who has ever directed students in writing academic theses understands that one of the biggest problems students have is the fact that they've never written a thesis before (and it's compounded because it is unlikely they will ever write one again). Faculty who direct academic theses have developed pedagogical strategies to help their students navigate the thesis writing process. Was that what we needed here for our applied project students' metacognitive statement?

As adviser for the graduate program, the most common questions D'Angelo receives are about the applied project and metacognitive statement. Explanations and pointing to the program's Graduate Student Handbook, which includes instructions for both workplace deliverable and metacognitive statement, didn't provide students the concrete direction they wanted. And our students asked committee chairs if they could see previous examples of metacognitive statements. They thought by examining an established genre they could simply reproduce it—a common response. We couldn't accommodate their request because they were the first students through the program, so there were no previous statements to share. Another common question from students to committee chairs would be the "What are you looking for?" or "What do you want me to include?" type of queries. On the surface, these may seem like rhetorically smart questions—the desire to meet audience needs and expectations. But we suspect that unintentionally what students were really asking for was a list of concrete points to address in what we can now see is an outcomes-like mentality.

After thinking about it more, we feel the lack of examples and vagueness of instruction may have been a good thing. If we believe the second WS threshold concept, Writing Speaks to Situations Through Recognizable Forms, we understand that simply emulating a form is not sufficient. As Bill Hart-Davidson (2015) explains:

> Genres are constructions of groups, over time, usually with the implicit or explicit sanction of organizational or institutional power.
>
> This view of genre has several interesting implications most newcomers to the idea find challenging and fascinating. One is that no single text is a genre; it can only be an instance of that genre as it enters into contexts (activity systems) where it might be taken up as such an instance. (p. 40)

While we, as faculty, had had a conversation about the metacognitive statement and its role, students themselves had not been part of the conversation as we developed the applied project and the Student Handbook. So, part of what we were asking our first group of students to do was to enter the conversation to help create the genre of the metacognitive statement that would then be continually shaped by future students. The first group of students would identify and enter the conversation. Succeeding students would then contribute to and advance the conversation, a conversation that would continually evolve as students drew upon different workplace and industry contexts. However, while our students were no longer the novice writers we find in First-Year Writing, they still had not, understandably, attained the level of sophistication of experienced WS researchers. It is important at this point to remember, as Howard Tinberg (2015) reminds us:

> Metacognition is not cognition. Performance, however thoughtful, is not the same as awareness of how that performance came to be. (p. 75)

This is exactly what we've observed taking place. Our students are very capable of, to use Tinberg's term, performance. However, we haven't just asked them to apply what they learned; we've asked them to report on an awareness of the process of that performance. Therein lay the problem in our students' difficulty in responding to the metacognitive statement. In fact, in many ways our students' response is entirely understandable when we really think about how threshold concepts work.

THE MESSINESS OF LIMINALITY

Unlike an outcomes model, where students are assessed, often with a checklist, at demonstrating particular skills, using a threshold concepts perspective helps us understand that learning is messy and uneven—recursive and iterative—and about more than rote skills. When a student has actually moved through the portal of the threshold concept, there is no going back. The student's perception has been changed. However, reaching that point can take significant amounts of time—often not reached until long after the student has left our class or our program. What we usually observe is students in that liminal state of awareness where sometimes they can respond as though they have accepted the worldview of the threshold concept; however, they are as likely as not to move backwards to the more comfortable, older worldview. This may, perhaps, be especially true when students are in a stressful situation such as a culminating project in which their goal is to do whatever it takes to graduate. Metacognition may come later as they apply what they learn in the workplace and have the time and space to reflect upon what they are doing and why.

What we say, and what is reasonable to expect, is that students in a culminating project may be in a liminal state. Liminality occurs as individuals respond to the difficulty of grasping threshold concepts. Individuals may linger suspended between their old ways of thinking and new (Meyer & Land, 2006). While in this liminal state, students may attempt to show understanding through mimicry (hence the call for samples or examples) or their writing may appear unauthentic. In fact, they are demonstrating an attempt to grasp what may be troublesome knowledge—knowledge that they are grasping to understand in order to cross the portal and enter the conversation, one that is rhetorically and socially constructed and situated. What we see, then, in our applied projects is that the workplace deliverable demonstrates a capable application of concepts. But the metacognitive statements appear to be a combination of seeming unsophisticated or unauthentic, or possibly attempts at mimicry to comply with unfamiliar genre conventions. What this represents is the students struggling to cross a portal. They know how to apply knowledge; what they are struggling to learn and to articulate is the why of the application, how it fits into the bigger context of the disciplinary and workplace conversation of which it is a part, and how that conversation shapes them as a professional—both currently and in the future.

We expect our observations of why our students struggle with the metacognitive statement part of their final applied project will resonate with people trained in WS. It has long been axiomatic that inexperienced writers who appear competent in some writing contexts struggle when they begin to compose at a more sophisticated level. Similarly, in her research on lawyers' information search process, Kuhlthau (2006) found that novices tended to emphasize being "right" and finding the right answer while experts tended to emphasize adding value and contributing to a conversation and knowledge building (Kuhlthau, 2006). In addition, Yancey et al. (2014) have demonstrated that inexperienced writers who have appeared to have attained a certain level of written performance must necessarily also reach a level of metacognitive awareness in order to transfer that performance to different contexts.

METACOGNITION AS . . . ?

Is that ability to articulate the "why" of application, the broader context for it, and the disciplinary or workplace conversation important? That ability requires students and individuals to engage in metacognition, which as we've seen is foundational to threshold concepts and metaliteracy. Without metacognition, students may only be mimicking genre conventions and applying rote skills. To be able to go beyond—to transfer knowledge and to exhibit dispositions associated with learning—requires metacognition.

For years, one of the authors has frustrated his technical communication students by often asking for a "cover paper" (similar to the metacognitive statement for the applied project) as part of an assignment for traditional technical communication projects. When his students asked him why he was making them do that, his response was that he wanted to train them to not only be able to write known workplace genres for known situations but to be the writer who could also create a new genre for their workplace or when needed to transform an old genre to meet changing contexts. It was his way of explaining that metacognitive skills were vital, though from an extremely naïve perspective.

Meyer and Land's work on threshold concepts give us all a theoretical base and a better language to explore and discuss pedagogical strategies many instructors have used for some time. However, what seems to be key to us at this point is the understanding that no matter what we do, our students will most likely not pass through the liminal state while they are our students. As instructors, we understand that realization can be frightening, especially in an era of administrative mandates to assess student performance. However, we also think, at some level, it can be liberating and exciting. Understanding and accepting that our students will most likely not pass through the portal in our class or our program requires that we must necessarily engage them in the professional conversation. They must understand (at least at the liminal level) that metacognitive awareness of what it is they do is part of that conversation. It also potentially liberates students. If they understand that they are entering a conversation and that it will be a conversation that will continue and evolve throughout their careers, it may relieve some of the pressure they feel to demonstrate they have mastered a set of skills to complete a checklist. Of course, that would mean they would also need to understand and accept that it is okay to be in a liminal state. Messy learning is okay.

We also think it means that while we get more experience and more graduating MS students who may struggle with the metacognitive statement, we need to understand that struggle is natural and acceptable. Our students might have a clearer idea of what to do if they get more experience doing more metacognitive work in more of their classes; however, we can't expect them to really get it all. The reality is that individual students may not completely pass through the portal and have their worldview changed forever until two, five, or maybe 20 years beyond graduation. It will vary with the individual and his or her particular circumstances.

CONCLUSION

We understand that at some level, it is possible to read what we've said and see as a kind of harkening back to some of the pedagogies of the late 1960s and 1970s when some instructors were more interested in empowering students than assuring that students met certain course goals. We are not doing that. We understand that we still live in the "Age of Assessment." We also believe that assessment is an important tool not only for accountability bur for program development. Still, for some time we have been saying that understanding frameworks and threshold concepts forces us into a "postassessment environment." This is not to say that we abandon outcomes and assessment but that we accept them as only one piece of what we are doing. We understand it is tempting to create rubrics based on defined outcomes and grade our students in that way. In fact, that would be easy to do with the workplace deliverable part of our final project. We understand it would be a disaster if we tried to define outcomes for the metacognitive statement.

Assessment leads us to want to check off outcomes. Understanding threshold concepts forces us to accept that our students are accomplished and proficient but perhaps still liminal. We know that's what's happening as our students try to explain things to us in their metacognitive statement. As we continue we need to remember that in those statements our students are engaging us in a rhetorical and social fashion in order to participate in several professional conversations. That, in and of itself, is quite an accomplishment. It's scholarship as conversation. It's writing as a rhetorical and social act.

REFERENCES

Adler-Kassner, L., & Wardle, E. (Eds.). (2015). *Naming what we know: Threshold concepts of writing studies*. Logan, UT: Utah State Press.

Hart-Davidson, B. (2015). Genres are enacted by writers and readers. In L. Adler-Kassner & E. Wardle (Eds.), *Naming what we know: Threshold concepts of writing studies* (pp. 39–40). Logan, UT: Utah State Press.

Kuhlthau, C. C. (2006). *Seeking meaning. A process approach to library and information services*. Westport, CT: Libraries Unlimited.

Mackey, T. P., & Jacobson, T. E. (2011, January). Reframing information literacy as a metaliteracy. *College & Research Libraries*, 62–78.

Maid, B., & D'Angelo, B. (2017). Threshold concepts: Integrating and applying information literacy and writing instruction. In D'Angelo et al. (Eds.), *Information literacy: Research and collaboration across disciplines* (pp. 37–50). Boulder: University Press of Colorado.

Meyer, J. H. F., & Land, R. (2006). Threshold concepts and troublesome knowledge. In J. H. F. Meyer & R. Land (Eds.), *Overcoming barriers to student understanding: Threshold concepts and troublesome knowledge* (pp. 3–18). New York: Routledge.

Tinberg, H. (2015). Metacognition is not cognition. In L. Adler-Kassner & E. Wardle (Eds.), *Naming what we know: Threshold concepts of writing studies* (pp. 75–76). Logan, UT: Utah State Press.

Yancey, K., Robertson, L., & Taczak, K. (2014). *Writing across contexts: Transfer, composition, and sites of writing*. Logan, UT: Utah State Press.

CONTRIBUTORS

William Badke is Associate Librarian for Associated Canadian Theological Schools and information literacy at Trinity Western University, Langley, BC, Canada. His engagement with information literacy began in the 1980s with the realization that students, undergraduate and graduate, lacked the essential understanding and skills to do effective informational research. He is the author of *Research Strategies: Finding Your Way Through the Information Fog*, 6th edition (Bloomington, IN: iUniverse.com, 2017), as well as numerous volumes and academic articles in the field of information literacy. His column, InfoLit Land, has been a regular feature in the trade publication *Online Searcher* since 2007.

Crystal Bickford, PhD, is currently an Associate Professor of English at Southern New Hampshire University with over twenty years' experience as a writing center director and writing program administrator. Her recent endeavors include serving as a two-term president for the Learning Assistance Association of New England, the leader of the Educational Technology and Distance Learning Special Interest Group for the College Reading and Learning Association, and the adviser to the Academic Scholars Association, a university club designed to support students involved in undergraduate research opportunities.

Joseph Bizup is Associate Professor of English and Associate Dean for Undergraduate Academic Programs and Policies in the College of Arts & Sciences at Boston University. His scholarly interests include style, argumentation, and writing pedagogy. He has revised Joseph M. Williams's *Style: Lessons in Clarity and Grace* (11th and 12th editions), is a co-editor of *The Norton Reader* (13th and 14th editions), and is a co-author of *The Craft of Research* (4th edition). He has co-directed or directed writing programs at Yale University, Columbia University, and Boston University.

Matthew Bodie is Executive Director of Learning Resources and instructor of English,

Information and Technology Studies at St. Petersburg College. His research, teaching, and administration have sought to find intersections between writing instruction and information literacy education, particularly as achieved within libraries and writing centers. Matthew holds bachelor's and master's degrees with concentrations in Mass Communications, English, and Library and Information Science from University of South Florida. He is completing his doctorate in English with primary concentration in Rhetoric and Writing Studies at Old Dominion University.

Jeanne Law Bohannon is an Associate Professor of English and an early-career distinguished faculty member at Kennesaw State University, teaching undergraduate and graduate courses in rhetorical grammar, research methods, and digital rhetorics. Research interests include: performing linguistic recoveries of underrepresented populations; conducting empirical studies in information literacies; and cultivating democratic-engagement learning in college writing. She has published in *Bellaterra Journal*; *Peitho*; *Writing Networks for Social Justice;* and the WAC Clearinghouse *Research Exchange Index*. She also blogs for Andrea Lunsford's *Multimodal Mondays* series. She believes in cultivating collaborative, democratic learning spaces where students become empowered stakeholders in their own rhetorical growth through engagement in diverse communities. Twitter: @drbohannon_ksu.

Ava M. Brillat is the Subject Librarian for English, Theatre, and Classics at the University of Miami. She has experience and research interests in instruction, information literacy, and assessment. She has previously worked as an Instructional Design Librarian and has received training through the Association of College and Research Libraries (ACRL) Immersion program in both assessment and instruction.

Melissa Cherry works as a Web Services Librarian at Miami University where she applies her background in reference and instruction to website development. She has a strong scholarly interest in the intersections among research-based writing, writing centers, and technology. She earned her MLIS from Kent State University and has held positions in the university libraries at Columbus State Community College, Ohio Wesleyan University, and Denison University.

Kundai Chirindo, PhD, is Assistant Professor of Rhetoric and Media Studies as well as a faculty affiliate and steering committee member of the Ethnic Studies program at Lewis & Clark College in Portland, Oregon. He teaches classes in rhetorical theory and criticism. Kundai's research centers on discursive practices that contest, contribute to, and ultimately constitute ideas of Africa in American public life. He explores questions that relate rhetorical theory to spatiality, environmental communication, and war and peace studies. In 2016, Kundai received the Lorry Lokey Faculty Excellence Award at Lewis & Clark.

Kelsey Corlett-Rivera is the Head of the Research Commons and a librarian for the School of Languages, Literatures, and Cultures at the University of Maryland. After five years as a project manager in the Language Services industry, and later obtaining her master's in Library Science, in 2012 she returned to academia as a subject-specialist librarian. In 2014, she was promoted to Head of the newly formed Research Commons. In that role, she is responsible for the majority of the University Libraries' initiatives targeting faculty members, graduate students, and researchers on campus. This includes campus partnership building, program development, and space planning, along with coordination among internal library divisions providing services to this population.

Barbara J. D'Angelo is Clinical Associate Professor of Technical Communication at Arizona State University. She is co-editor of *Information Literacy: Research and Collaboration Across the Disciplines*. Her publications include several book chapters and articles on the use of outcomes for curriculum development and assessment and on information literacy. She has presented on topics related to information literacy, technical communication, assessment, and curriculum development at the Council of Writing Program Administrators, Conference on College Composition and Communication, the Association for Business Communication annual conferences, and the International Writing Across the Disciplines conference.

Kelly Diamond is the Head of the West Virginia University Libraries' Office of Curriculum and Instructional Support (OCIS). As Head of OCIS, Diamond leads the development, design, implementation, and assessment of instruction within the libraries and with collaborative partners. Additionally, she investigates solutions to information literacy instruction challenges across campus. Diamond's research interests include information literacy in the teaching of composition and rhetoric, hybrid learning, and online instruction. With Laura Brady and Nathalie Singh-Corcoran, she co-authored "A Collaborative Approach to Information Literacy: First-Year Composition, Writing Center, and Library Partnerships at West Virginia University," which was published in *Ecologies of Writing Programs: Program Profiles in Context*.

Mark Dibble is the Instruction and Public Services Librarian at Texas Lutheran University. He lives in Seguin, TX with his wife, Jennifer, kids, Clara and Colin, and dogs, Ben and Olive. When he is not spending time with family or thinking about library things, he enjoys running and playing racquetball with fellow TLU faculty.

Caroline Fuchs is Associate Dean and Learning Design Librarian at St. John's University. She holds an MLS (St. John's University), and both an MA in English and an MA in history (CUNY). She teaches in the Division of Library and Information Science, as well as an undergraduate course that explores New York history through comics and graphic novels. She is a Senior Fellow at the Vincentian Center for Church and Society, a CTL Teaching and Technology Fellow, and a Writing Across the Curriculum Fellow. She serves on the Board of Directors for the Association of College and Research Libraries.

Laura Giovanelli now teaches in the Writing Program at Wake Forest University but comes to teaching writing as a working writer, one who has delighted in new genres, mediums, and audiences. She was a journalist for nine years. In 2012, she complicated things by earning a master's of Fine Arts in Creative Writing (concentration in fiction) from N.C. State University. Her professional interests are just as varied: she cares about personal essays (with work published in the *Washington Post* and *Full Grown People*), science writing, creative nonfiction, historical fiction, and writing studies, and particularly how we acquire information literacy and compose nontraditional texts such as digital videos. She also serves as Wake Forest College's Assistant Dean for Learning Spaces.

Rhonda V. Gray is a Professor of English at Roxbury Community College (RCC) in Boston. She co-authored RCC's *Honors Faculty Handbook* (2015) featuring BEAM as the Honors Program's research writing framework. Rhonda has presented nationally on topics addressing pedagogy, black feminist thought, and African American history and culture. Her research interests were recently featured as an NEA Visiting Scholar at The Graduate Center in New York City where she studied "The Visual Culture of the American Civil War and Its Aftermath." Currently, Rhonda is working with local cultural institutions to employ a black feminist paradigm to foster a culture of inclusion in historically white spaces. Rhonda earned a BA in English Literature from Wellesley College and her MSEd from Simmons College.

Autumn Haag is Librarian/Archivist for Research and Collections at the University of Rochester. She was previously Librarian Archivist at Roxbury Community College (RCC) in Boston, Massachusetts, and Reference Archivist at the Massachusetts Archives. At the 2017 conference of the Association of College and Research Libraries (ACRL), she presented on the use of BEAM in RCC's Honors Program. Her research interests include undergraduate archives instruction in the classroom and open educational resources. She earned her BA from McGill University and her MiST from the University of Toronto.

Kay Halasek is Associate Professor of English and Director of the University Institute for Teaching and Learning (UITL) at The Ohio State University. Her research spans a variety of areas within rhetorical theory and the teaching of writing, including feminist historiography, theories of writing, collaborative learning, writing program administration, portfolio assessment, and basic writing. Her current projects include *Metaphors We Teach By: Reflections on Writing Pedagogy in the Age of Big Teaching* and a longitudinal study of student and expert responses to college writing assignments in massive open and online courses.

Joshua D. Hill has taught composition in Texas, Florida, and Pennsylvania, and is currently an Assistant Professor of Composition and Communication at Pennsylvania College of Technology. His master's is in English from Texas A&M, and his PhD in Rhetoric from Duquesne University's philosophy-based communication department. This disciplinary crossover gives him a foundation from which to pursue the questions of literacy, from the broad perspectives of historical trends and ideas to the specific, concrete issues of inculcating literate practices in classrooms. A writer and copyeditor himself, in both academia and business, he tries to practice what he preaches in the writing classroom.

Matthew R. Kaeiser has more than twenty years of experience teaching English as a second language, a lot of graduate credits in counseling, and certification as an Appreciative Adviser. Therefore, he has a real interest in cross-cultural issues. His teaching interests include utilizing active and accelerated learning strategies and using different techniques to help students enhance their memory. His travel experience includes nearly two years in Honduras and extensive travel and study experience throughout Central America, Mexico, and Japan. He composed the background music for a professionally produced CD that is used to help relax cancer patients undergoing chemotherapy.

Molly Keener had a serendipitous journey to becoming the Director of Digital Initiatives and Scholarly Communication at the Z. Smith Reynolds Library, Wake Forest University. When she landed her first library job as a student assistant at the University of North Carolina at Chapel Hill, her current job did not yet exist in the field. From addressing copyright questions to consulting on thesis preparation to strategizing faculty outreach to teaching students about fair use, she is daily engaging with multiple constituencies across campus. She loves what she does; the complexity and challenges that copyright present continue to excite her, even more than twelve years into this work.

Kathleen F. Kempa is the Reference and Access Services Librarian at Southeastern University's Steelman Library. Kathleen oversees the staff and activities for circulation, interlibrary loan, stack control, and computer lab. She specializes in bibliographic instruction for the Composition 1 and 2 students, but also provides research instruction in other disciplines. Her primary area of research over the past three years has been an exploration of the Association of College and Research Libraries' *Framework for Information Literacy.* She has presented on the *Framework* at conferences and written two articles on aspects of the *Frameworks.*

Randi Gray Kristensen is Assistant Professor of Writing, and former Director of Writing in the Disciplines, in the University Writing Program at the George Washington University. An immigrant from Jamaica, she has an MFA and PhD from Louisiana State University, and publishes fiction, poetry, and memoir on themes related to border crossings. She is co-editor, with Ryan Claycomb, of *Writing Against the Curriculum: Anti-Disciplinarity in the Writing and Cultural Studies Classroom* (Lexington Books, 2009). Her current projects are a novel about women sex tourists in the Caribbean, and a scholarly work on the limits of humanitarian discourses for Caribbean development.

Melanie Lee earned her PhD in English, Rhetoric and Composition and Graduate Certificate in Women's and Gender Studies from Ohio University. Her dissertation was the first hybrid manuscript of its kind at OU. An Assistant Professor of English at University of Southern Indiana, she studies the social construction of masculinized L/logos' affects on ideology, composition/rhetoric, pedagogy, and their systemic issues. Her graduate and undergraduate courses in professional writing, rhetoric and composition histories, pedagogy, theory, and gender studies examine relationships between gender, authority, image, and text. Recent publications include a *Pedagogy* piece titled "The Melancholy Odyssey of a Dissertation with Pictures."

Ken Liss is the Head of Liaison and Instruction Services at the Boston University Libraries, where he leads outreach and information literacy efforts with the College of Arts & Sciences Writing Program and across the disciplines. As a member of a Writing Program team that revised the program's curriculum in response to a new university-wide general education initiative, he worked to incorporate information literacy more systematically into the program's writing seminars. Prior to joining BU in 2014, he worked at Boston College, the Harvard Business School, and the Boston Public Library.

Barry Maid is Professor and Founding Head of the Technical Communication Program at Arizona State University. He was head of that program for ten years. He is the author of numerous articles and chapters primarily focusing on technology, independent writing programs, and program administration including assessment. He and Barbara D'Angelo have written multiple articles on information literacy and writing. Maid and D'Angelo, along with Sandra Jamieson and Janice Walker, have edited *Information Literacy: Research and Collaboration Across Disciplines*. In addition, he is a co-author, with Duane Roen and Greg Glau, of *The McGraw-Hill Guide: Writing for College, Writing for Life*.

Linda Macri is the Director of Academic and Professional Development at the Graduate School at the University of Maryland, and in that capacity she directs the Graduate School Writing Center. She earned a PhD in English from Maryland, and from 2005 to 2013, she served as the director of the Academic Writing Program in the English Department. Her interests are in academic literacies, composition studies and rhetorical theory, graphic novels and comic studies, and women's literature. She has taught a range of courses from English 101 to Writing for Non-Profits and American Comics.

April D. Mann is the Director of the Writing Center and a Senior Lecturer in the English Composition Program at the University of Miami. She also works as a consultant for grant writers at the University of Miami's Miller School of Medicine. In 2014, she was given a SEEDS Grant award to conduct workshops for doctors and scientists on how to write clear and concise scientific prose. She is currently involved in a project examining the rhetoric of grant proposals for the National Institutes of Health and the National Science Foundation.

Christine I. McClure has a Master of Arts in English and 18 years of teaching experience in higher education, and is pursuing a PhD in Texts and Technology with an area of specialization in Scientific and Technical Communication at the University of Central Florida. She is currently a full-time instructor at Embry-Riddle Aeronautical University in the Humanities and Communication Department teaching Themes in the Humanities, Studies in Literature, and Technical Report Writing, and her research interests include information behavior theory and social constructivism in hybrid and online courses.

Randall McClure has taught writing at several universities, including Miami University and Minnesota State University, Mankato. He researches in the areas of information behavior and academic writing, teaching and learning online, and academic policy. He has published articles in journals including *portal: Libraries and the Academy*, *Computers and Composition*, *Writing Spaces*, *WPA*, and the *Journal of Literacy and Technology*. He is co-editor with James P. Purdy of three collections on research-writing, most recently *The Future Scholar*. His latest collections include *Rewired: Research-Writing*

Partnerships Within the Frameworks from the ACRL and *Labored: The State(ment) and Future of Work in Composition*, co-edited with Dayna Goldstein and Michael Pemberton, from Parlor Press.

Katie McWain is Assistant Professor of English and Director of First-Year Composition at Texas Woman's University, where she works closely with the writing center and university libraries to design programming for undergraduate writers. She was previously an Assistant Director of the Writing Center at the University of Nebraska–Lincoln. She is a book series editor for the Writing Across the Curriculum Clearinghouse as well as a member of the editorial board for *WPA: Writing Program Administration,* and her work has been published in *Teaching English in the Two-Year College* and the *Michigan Journal of Community Service Learning.* Her research interests include writing across the curriculum, teacher development, cross-level writing partnerships, and composition theory and pedagogy.

Patricia Medved is a doctoral candidate at St. John's University where, in addition to teaching First-Year Writing and Writing for Business, she has completed coursework in composition theory, issues in writing studies, and literature. Her dissertation investigates research perceptions and practices of student writers. Patricia also teaches at Suffolk Community College and Nassau Community College. Before working as a college instructor, Patricia was a senior editor at Random House. She published practical nonfiction books in areas such as reference, personal fitness, parenting, and self-help. She has an MA in Professional Writing and Rhetoric from the University of Texas, El Paso.

Megan Palmer is a recent graduate of Southern New Hampshire University with a Bachelor's in English Language and Literature, and minors in education and communication. During her university career, Megan dedicated her time and student leadership to a club founded for undergraduate research, as well as the student-run newspaper, *The Penmen Press,* which distributes content both on campus in print and digitally online. Following graduation, Megan plans on furthering her education and research endeavors beyond New Hampshire, through the path of education access work, rhetoric and composition, and social justice. She is very excited for this next chapter (pun intended).

James P. Purdy is an Associate Professor of English and director of the University Writing Center at Duquesne University. In 2016, he received Duquesne's Presidential Award for Excellence in Teaching. In addition to publishing in numerous scholarly journals and edited volumes, he has co-edited four books, most recently *Making Space: Writing Instruction, Infrastructure, and Multiliteracies* with Dànielle DeVoss and *The Future Scholar: Researching and Teaching the Frameworks for Writing and Information Literacy* with Randall McClure. His *The New Digital Scholar* and *The Next Digital Scholar* collections with McClure won silver and bronze medals, respectively, at the Independent Publisher Book Awards.

Teresa Quezada is an Assistant Professor of Practice in the Rhetoric and Writing Studies program at U.T. El Paso, where she teaches first-year composition, undergraduate technical writing, and graduate professional writing courses. She directs the Technical and

Professional Writing graduate certificate program and is part of the founding faculty for the Bilingual Professional Writing undergraduate certificate program. Her research interests include political and bureaucratic rhetoric, online writing instruction, writing program administration, first-year writing instruction, and first-year experience and success.

Kate Rubick is Instruction Services Librarian at Lewis & Clark College in Portland, Oregon, where she leads Watzek Library efforts in information literacy instruction and regularly partners with faculty to teach students how to do research-based writing. Her work with the BEAM framework began in 2013, and she has written and presented on it, most recently at the 2017 conference of the Association of College and Research Libraries (ACRL).

Through both scholarship and teaching, **Phyllis Mentzell Ryder** investigates what it means to write for social change. Her current projects analyze how the rhetorics of whiteness are institutionalized in public and academic spaces. Her 2011 book, *Rhetorics for Community Action,* is a guide to studying and teaching public writing. Ryder also studies how to teach information literacy, including serendipity. Her work has been published in *Rhetoric Review, JAC, Reflections,* and *Community Literacy Journal,* among others. She serves as Director of GWU's Writing Center.

Nathan Schwartz has been serving both students and librarians for over twenty years. He creates websites, organizes electronic resources, and maintains various library systems to help others access information. Although he spends much of his time helping behind the scenes, one of his favorite librarian duties is providing bibliographic instructions to students with a one-shot library session in the classroom. It is in this role that he addresses some issues with helping prepare students to become accomplished researchers and join this community of scholarship.

Dolsy Smith is a Librarian at the George Washington University, where he provides research instruction and support across the disciplines, in addition to developing strategy for the library's collections. His essays on pedagogy and librarianship (co-authored with Cathy Eisenhower) appear in the edited collections *Writing Against the Curriculum: Anti-Disciplinarity in the Writing and Cultural Studies Classroom* (Lexington, 2009) and *Critical Library Instruction: Theories and Methods* (Library Juice Press, 2009). Also a published poet, Dolsy is currently writing a monograph that mixes poetry, personal narrative, and academic argument in a critical examination of white male privilege.

Lia Vella holds a PhD in English from the State University of NY at Buffalo and a Master of Library and Information Science from the University of Washington. Her recent research studies investigate information literacy acquisition in relation to cognitive development stages, and the effect of information literacy instruction on academic performance in STEM undergraduates. She has worked as a reference and instruction librarian in several academic settings; she currently develops and delivers training and outreach programs as part of the National Park Service's Library Information Management team.

Janice R. Walker is Professor of Writing and Linguistics and Chair of the university's Institutional Review Board (IRB) at Georgia Southern University. She has published journal articles, book chapters, and books about online research, documentation, intellectual property, and information literacy. She is founder and coordinator of the Graduate Research Network at the annual Computers and Writing Conference and co-coordinator for the Georgia Conference on Information Literacy hosted by Georgia Southern University. Her current research includes the LILAC Project (Learning Information Literacy Across the Curriculum), a study of students' online information-seeking behaviors.

INDEX